NOBEL PRIZE WINNERS

1992–1996 SUPPLEMENT

Biographical Dictionaries from
The H. W. Wilson Company

Greek and Latin Authors 800 B.C.–A.D. 1000
European Authors 1000–1900
British Authors Before 1800
British Authors of the Nineteenth Century
American Authors 1600–1900
Twentieth Century Authors
Twentieth Century Authors: First Supplement
World Authors 1900–1950
World Authors 1950–1970
World Authors 1970–1975
World Authors 1975–1980
World Authors 1980–1985
World Authors 1985–1990
World Authors 800 B.C.–Present (CD-ROM)
World Authors 1900–Present (CD-ROM)
World Authors 1950–Present (CD-ROM)
Spanish American Authors: The Twentieth Century

The Junior Book of Authors
More Junior Authors
Third Book of Junior Authors
Fourth Book of Junior Authors and Illustrators
Fifth Book of Junior Authors and Illustrators
Sixth Book of Junior Authors and Illustrators
Seventh Book of Junior Authors and Illustrators

Great Composers: 1300–1900
Composers Since 1900
Composers Since 1900: First Supplement
Musicians Since 1900
Popular American Composers
Popular American Composers: First Supplement

American Reformers
American Songwriters

World Artists 1950–1980
World Artists 1980–1990
World Film Directors

Current Biography 1983–Present (CD-ROM)
Current Biography 1940–Present (CD-ROM)

NOBEL PRIZE WINNERS
1992–1996 SUPPLEMENT

An H. W. Wilson Biographical Dictionary

Editor
Clifford Thompson

Managing Editor
Joseph Sora

Associate Editors
Edward Moran

Selma Yampolsky

Staff Writers
Christopher Mari

Janet Pech

THE H.W. WILSON COMPANY

NEW YORK   DUBLIN

1997

Nobel Prize Winners. Supplement, 1992–1996: an H. W. Wilson biographical dictionary / editor, Clifford Thompson.
   p.   cm.
   Includes bibliographical references.
   ISBN 0-8242-0906-0 (alk. paper)
   1. Nobel Prizes. 2. Biography—20th century—Dictionaries.
I. Thompson, Clifford.
AS911.N9N59   1992 Suppl.
001.4'4'0922—dc21   97-669
                                        CIP

CONTENTS

LIST OF NOBEL PRIZE WINNERS,
1992–1996

LIST OF NOBEL PRIZE WINNERS, 1992–1996

NOBEL PRIZE WINNERS
BY PRIZE CATEGORY AND YEAR, 1901–1996

Nobel Prize for Chemistry

1901	Jacobus van't Hoff
1902	Emil Fischer
1903	Svante Arrhenius
1904	William Ramsay
1905	Adolf von Baeyer
1906	Henri Moissan
1907	Eduard Buchner
1908	Ernest Rutherford
1909	Wilhelm Ostwald
1910	Otto Wallach
1911	Marie Curie
1912	Victor Grignard
	Paul Sabatier
1913	Alfred Werner
1914	Theodore W. Richards
1915	Richard Willstätter
1916	Not awarded
1917	Not awarded
1918	Fritz Haber
1919	Not awarded
1920	Walther Nernst
1921	Frederick Soddy
1922	Francis W. Aston
1923	Fritz Pregl
1924	Not awarded
1925	Richard Zsigmondy
1926	Teodor Svedberg
1927	Heinrich Wieland
1928	Adolf Windaus
1929	Hans von Euler-Chelpin
	Arthur Harden
1930	Hans Fischer
1931	Friedrich Bergius
	Carl Bosch
1932	Irving Langmuir
1933	Not awarded
1934	Harold C. Urey
1935	Frédéric Joliot
	Irène Joliot-Curie
1936	Peter Debye
1937	Walter N. Haworth
	Paul Karrer
1938	Richard Kuhn
1939	Adolf Butenandt
	Leopold Ružička
1940	Not awarded
1941	Not awarded
1942	Not awarded
1943	George de Hevesy
1944	Otto Hahn
1945	Artturi Virtanen
1946	John H. Northrop
	Wendell M. Stanley
	James B. Sumner
1947	Robert Robinson
1948	Arne Tiselius
1949	William F. Giauque
1950	Kurt Alder
	Otto Diels
1951	Edwin M. McMillan
	Glenn T. Seaborg
1952	Archer Martin
	Richard Synge
1953	Hermann Staudinger
1954	Linus C. Pauling
1955	Vincent du Vigneaud
1956	Cyril N. Hinshelwood
	Nikolay N. Semenov
1957	Alexander Todd
1958	Frederick Sanger
1959	Jaroslav Heyrovský
1960	Willard F. Libby
1961	Melvin Calvin
1962	John C. Kendrew
	Max Perutz
1963	Giulio Natta
	Karl Ziegler
1964	Dorothy C. Hodgkin
1965	R. B. Woodward
1966	Robert S. Mulliken
1967	Manfred Eigen
	Ronald Norrish
	George Porter

1968	Lars Onsager		1996	Robert F. Curl Jr.
1969	Derek Barton			Harold W. Kroto
	Odd Hassel			Richard E. Smalley
1970	Luis F. Leloir			
1971	Gerhard Herzberg			

Nobel Memorial Prize in Economic Sciences

1972	Christian Anfinsen
	Stanford Moore
	William H. Stein
1973	Ernst Fischer
	Geoffrey Wilkinson
1974	Paul J. Flory
1975	John W. Cornforth
	Vladimir Prelog
1976	William N. Lipscomb
1977	Ilya Prigogine
1978	Peter D. Mitchell
1979	Herbert C. Brown
	Georg Wittig
1980	Paul Berg
	Walter Gilbert
	Frederick Sanger
1981	Kenichi Fukui
	Roald Hoffmann
1982	Aaron Klug
1983	Henry Taube
1984	R. Bruce Merrifield
1985	Herbert A. Hauptman
	Jerome Karle
1986	Dudley R. Herschbach
	YuanT. Lee
	John C. Polanyi
1987	Donald J. Cram
	Jean-Marie Lehn
	Charles J. Pedersen
1988	Johann Deisenhofer
	Robert Huber
	Harmut Michel
1989	Sidney Altman
	Thomas R. Cech
1990	Elias James Corey
1991	Richard R. Ernst
1992	Rudolph A. Marcus
1993	Kary B. Mullis
	Michael Smith
1994	George A. Olah
1995	Paul Crutzen
	Mario J. Molina
	F. Sherwood Rowland

Nobel Memorial Prize in Economic Sciences

1969	Ragnar Frisch
	Jan Tinbergen
1970	Paul Samuelson
1971	Simon Kuznets
1972	Kenneth Arrow
	John Hicks
1973	Wassily Leontief
1974	Friedrich A. von Hayek
	Gunnar Myrdal
1975	Leonid Kantorovich
	Tjalling C. Koopmans
1976	Milton Friedman
1977	James Meade
	Bertil Ohlin
1978	Herbert Simon
1979	W. Arthur Lewis
	Theodore Schultz
1980	Lawrence Klein
1981	James Tobin
1982	George Stigler
1983	Gerard Debreu
1984	Richard Stone
1985	Franco Modigliani
1986	James M. Buchanan
1987	Robert M. Solow
1988	Maurice Allais
1989	Trygve Haavelmo
1990	Harry M. Markowitz
	Merton H. Miller
	William F. Sharpe
1991	Ronald H. Coase
1992	Gary S. Becker
1993	Robert W. Fogel
	Douglass C. North
1994	John C. Harsanyi
	John F. Nash
	Reinhard Selten
1995	Robert E. Lucas Jr.
1996	James A. Mirrlees
	William Vickrey

NOBEL PRIZE WINNERS BY PRIZE CATEGORY AND YEAR, 1901–1996

Nobel Prize for Literature

1901	René Sully-Prudhomme
1902	Theodor Mommsen
1903	Bjørnstjerne Bjørnson
1904	José Echegaray
	Frédéric Mistral
1905	Henryk Sienkiewicz
1906	Giosuè Carducci
1907	Rudyard Kipling
1908	Rudolf Eucken
1909	Selma Lagerlöf
1910	Paul Heyse
1911	Maurice Maeterlinck
1912	Gerhart Hauptmann
1913	Rabindranath Tagore
1914	Not awarded
1915	Romain Rolland
1916	Verner von Heidenstam
1917	Karl Gjellerup
	Henrik Pontoppidan
1918	Not awarded
1919	Carl Spitteler
1920	Knut Hamsun
1921	Anatole France
1922	Jacinto Benavente y Martinez
1923	William Butler Yeats
1924	Władysław Reymont
1925	George Bernard Shaw
1926	Grazia Deledda
1927	Henri Bergson
1928	Sigrid Undset
1929	Thomas Mann
1930	Sinclair Lewis
1931	Erik Karlfeldt
1932	John Galsworthy
1933	Ivan Bunin
1934	Luigi Pirandello
1935	Not awarded
1936	Eugene O'Neill
1937	Roger Martin du Gard
1938	Pearl S. Buck
1939	Frans Sillanpää
1940	Not awarded
1941	Not awarded
1942	Not awarded
1943	Not awarded
1944	Johannes Jensen
1945	Gabriela Mistral
1946	Hermann Hesse
1947	André Gide
1948	T. S. Eliot
1949	Wlliam Faulkner
1950	Bertrand Russell
1951	Pär Lagerkvist
1952	François Mauriac
1953	Winston Churchill
1954	Ernest Hemingway
1955	Halldór Laxness
1956	Juan Jiménez
1957	Albert Camus
1958	Boris Pasternak
1959	Salvatore Quasimodo
1960	Saint-John Perse
1961	Ivo Andrić
1962	John Steinbeck
1963	George Seferis
1964	Jean-Paul Sartre
1965	Mikhail Sholokhov
1966	S. Y. Agnon
	Nelly Sachs
1967	Miguel Asturias
1968	Yasunari Kawabata
1969	Samuel Beckett
1970	Aleksandr Solzhenitsyn
1971	Pablo Neruda
1972	Heinrich Böll
1973	Patrick White
1974	Eyvind Johnson
	Harry Martinson
1975	Eugenio Montale
1976	Saul Bellow
1977	Vicente Aleixandre
1978	Isaac Bashevis Singer
1979	Odysseus Elytis
1980	Czesław Miłosz
1981	Elias Canetti
1982	Gabriel García Márquez
1983	William Golding
1984	Jaroslav Seifert
1985	Claude Simon
1986	Wole Soyinka
1987	Joseph Brodsky
1988	Naguib Mahfouz
1989	Camilo José Cela
1990	Octavio Paz
1991	Nadine Gordimer

NOBEL PRIZE WINNERS BY PRIZE CATEGORY AND YEAR, 1901–1996

1992	Derek Walcott	1931	Jane Addams
1993	Toni Morrison		Nicholas Murray Butler
1994	Kenzaburo Oe	1932	Not awaded
1995	Seamus Heaney	1933	Norman Angell
1996	Wisława Szymborska	1934	Arthur Henderson

Nobel Prize for Peace

1901	Henri Dunant	1935	Carl von Ossietzky
	Frédéric Passy	1936	Carlos Saavedra Lamas
1902	Élie Ducommun	1937	Robert Cecil
	Albert Gobat	1938	Nansen International Office for Refugees
1903	William Cremer	1939	Not awarded
1904	Institute of International Law	1940	Not awarded
1905	Bertha von Suttner	1941	Not awarded
1906	Theodore Roosevelt	1942	Not awarded
1907	Ernesto Moneta	1943	Not awarded
	Louis Renault	1944	International Committee of the Red Cross
1908	Klas Arnoldson	1945	Cordell Hull
	Fredrik Bajer	1946	Emily Greene Balch
1909	Auguste Beernaert		John Mott
	Paul d'Estournelles de Constant	1947	American Friends Service Committee
1910	International Peace Bureau		Friends Service Council
1911	Tobias Asser	1948	Not awarded
	Alfred Fried	1949	John Boyd Orr
1912	Elihu Root	1950	Ralph Bunche
1913	Henri La Fontaine	1951	Léon Jouhaux
1914	Not awarded	1952	Albert Schweitzer
1915	Not awarded	1953	George C. Marshall
1916	Not awarded	1954	Office of the United Nations High Commissioner for Refugees
1917	International Committee of the Red Cross	1955	Not awarded
1918	Not awarded	1956	Not awarded
1919	Woodrow Wilson	1957	Lester Pearson
1920	Léon Bourgeois	1958	Georges Pire
1921	Karl Branting	1959	Philip Noel-Baker
	Christian Lange	1960	Albert Luthuli
1922	Fridtjof Nansen	1961	Dag Hammarskjöld
1923	Not awarded	1962	Linus C. Pauling
1924	Not awarded	1963	International Committee of the Red Cross
1925	J. Austen Chamberlain		League of Red Cross Societies
	Charles Dawes	1964	Martin Luther King Jr.
1926	Aristide Briand	1965	United Nations Children's Fund
	Gustav Stresemann	1966	Not awarded
1927	Ferdinand Buisson	1967	Not awarded
	Ludwig Quidde	1968	René Cassin
1928	Not awarded	1969	International Labour Organization
1929	Frank Kellogg	1970	Norman Borlaug
1930	Nathan Söderblom		

1971	Willy Brandt		1906	J. J. Thomson
1972	Not awarded		1907	Albert A. Michelson
1973	Henry Kissinger		1908	Gabriel Lippmann
	Le Duc Tho		1909	Ferdinand Braun
1974	Sean MacBride			Guglielmo Marconi
	Eisaku Sato		1910	Johannes van der Waals
1975	Andrei Sakharov		1911	Wilhelm Wien
1976	Mairead Corrigan		1912	Nils Dalén
	Betty Williams		1913	Heike Kamerlingh Onnes
1977	Amnesty International		1914	Max von Laue
1978	Menachem Begin		1915	W. H. Bragg
	Anwar Sadat			W. L. Bragg
1979	Mother Teresa		1916	Not awarded
1980	Adolfo Pérez Esquivel		1917	Charles G. Barkla
1981	Office of the United Nations High		1918	Max Planck
	Commissioner for Refugees		1919	Johannes Stark
1982	Alfonso García Robles		1920	Charles Guillaume
	Alva Myrdal		1921	Albert Einstein
1983	Lech Wałesa		1922	Niels Bohr
1984	DesmondTutu		1923	Robert A. Millikan
1985	International Physicians for the Pre-		1924	Manne Siegbahn
	vention of Nuclear War		1925	James Franck
1986	Elie Wiesel			Gustav Hertz
1987	Oscar Arias Sánchez		1926	Jean Perrin
1988	United Nations Peacekeeping Forces		1927	Arthur H. Compton
1989	Dalai Lama			C. T. R. Wilson
1990	Mikhail Sergeyevich Gorbachev		1928	Owen W. Richardson
1991	Aung San Suu Kyi		1929	Louis de Broglie
1992	Rigoberta Menchú		1930	Venkata Raman
1993	Nelson Mandela		1931	Not awarded
	F. W. de Klerk		1932	Werner Heisenberg
1994	Yasir Arafat		1933	P. A. M. Dirac
	Shimon Peres			Erwin Schrödinger
	Yitzhak Rabin		1934	Not awarded
1995	Joseph Rotblat		1935	James Chadwick
	The Pugwash Conferences on Science		1936	Carl D. Anderson
	and World Affairs			Victor F. Hess
1996	Carlos Felipe Ximenes Belo		1937	Clinton J. Davisson
	Jose Ramos-Horta			G. P. Thomson
			1938	Enrico Fermi

Nobel Prize for Physics

1901	Wilhelm Röntgen		1939	Ernest O. Lawrence
1902	Hendrik Lorentz		1940	Not awarded
	Pieter Zeeman		1941	Not awarded
1903	Henri Becquerel		1942	Not awarded
	Marie Curie		1943	Otto Stern
	Pierre Curie		1944	I. I. Rabi
1904	J. W. Strutt		1945	Wolfgang Pauli
1905	Philipp von Lenard		1946	P. W. Bridgman

1947	Edward Appleton	1974	Antony Hewish
1948	P. M. S. Blackett		Martin Ryle
1949	Hideki Yukawa	1975	Aage Bohr
1950	Cecil F. Powell		Ben R. Mottelson
1951	John Cockcroft		James Rainwater
	Ernest Walton	1976	Burton Richter
1952	Felix Bloch		Samuel C. C. Ting
	Edward M. Purcell	1977	Philip W. Anderson
1953	Frits Zernike		Nevill Mott
1954	Max Born		John H. Van Vleck
	Walther Bothe	1978	Pyotr Kapitza
1955	Polykarp Kusch		Arno A. Penzias
	Willis E. Lamb Jr.		Robert W. Wilson
1956	John Bardeen	1979	Sheldon L. Glashow
	Walter H. Brattain		Abdus Salam
	William Shockley		Steven Weinberg
1957	Tsung-Dao Lee	1980	James W. Cronin
	Chen Ning Yang		Val L. Fitch
1958	Pavel Cherenkov	1981	Nicolaas Bloembergen
	Ilya Frank		Arthur L. Schawlow
	Igor Tamm		Kai Siegbahn
1959	Owen Chamberlain	1982	Kenneth G. Wilson
	Emilio Segrè	1983	Subrahmanyan Chandrasekhar
1960	Donald A. Glaser		William A. Fowler
1961	Robert Hofstadter	1984	Simon van der Meer
	Rudolf L. Mössbauer		Carlo Rubbia
1962	Lev Landau	1985	Klaus von Klitzing
1963	J. Hans D. Jensen	1986	Gerd Binnig
	Maria Goeppert Mayer		Heinrich Rohrer
	Eugene P. Wigner		Ernest Ruska
1964	Nikolai Basov	1987	J. Georg Bednorz
	Aleksandr Prokhorov		K. Alex Müller
	Charles H. Townes	1988	Leon M. Lederman
1965	Richard P. Feynman		Melvin Schwartz
	Julian S. Schwinger		Jack Steinberger
	Sin-itiro Tomonaga	1989	Hans G. Dehmelt
1966	Alfred Kastler		Wolfgang Pauli
1967	Hans A. Bethe		Norman F. Ramsey
1968	Luis W. Alvarez	1990	Jerome I. Friedman
1969	Murray Gell-Mann		Henry W. Kendall
1970	Hannes Alfvén		Richard E. Taylor
	Louis Neel	1991	Pierre-Gilles de Gennes
1971	Dennis Gabor	1992	Georges Charpak
1972	John Bardeen	1993	Russell A. Hulse
	Leon N. Cooper		Joseph H. Taylor Jr.
	J. Robert Schrieffer	1994	Bertram N. Brockhouse
1973	Leo Esaki		Clifford G. Shull
	Ivar Giaever	1995	Martin L. Perl
	Brian D. Josephson		Frederick Reines

NOBEL PRIZE WINNERS BY PRIZE CATEGORY AND YEAR, 1901–1996

1996	David M. Lee	1936	Henry H. Dale
	Douglas D. Osheroff		Otto Loewi
	Robert C. Richardson	1937	Albert Szent-Györgyi
		1938	Corneille Heymans

Nobel Prize for Physiology or Medicine

		1939	Gerhard Domagk
1901	Emil von Behring	1940	Not awarded
1902	Ronald Ross	1941	Not awarded
1903	Niels Finsen	1942	Not awarded
1904	Ivan Pavlov	1943	Henrik Dam
1905	Robert Koch		Edward A. Doisy
1906	Camillo Golgi	1944	Joseph Erlanger
	Santiago Ramón y Cajal		Herbert S. Gasser
1907	Charles Laveran	1945	Ernst B. Chain
1908	Paul Ehrlich		Alexander Fleming
	Ilya Metchnikoff		Howard W. Florey
1909	Theodor Kocher	1946	Hermann J. Muller
1910	Albrecht Kossel	1947	Carl F. Cori
1911	Allvar Gullstrand		Gerty T. Cori
1912	Alexis Carrel		Bernardo Houssay
1913	Charles Richet	1948	Paul Müller
1914	Robert Bárány	1949	Walter R. Hess
1915	Not awarded		Egas Moniz
1916	Not awarded	1950	Philip S. Hench
1917	Not awarded		Edward C. Kendall
1918	Not awarded		Tadeus Reichstein
1919	Jules Bordet	1951	Max Theiler
1920	August Krogh	1952	Selman A. Waksman
1921	Not awarded	1953	Hans Krebs
1922	Archibald V. Hill		Fritz Lipmann
	Otto Meyerhof	1954	John F. Enders
1923	Frederick G. Banting		Frederick C. Robbins
	John J. R. MacLeod		Thomas H. Weller
1924	Willem Einthoven	1955	Hugo Theorell
1925	Not awarded	1956	André Cournand
1926	Johannes Fibiger		Werner Forssmann
1927	Julius Wagner von Jauregg		Dickinson W. Richards
1928	Charles Nicolle	1957	Daniel Bovet
1929	Christiaan Eijkman	1958	George W. Beadle
	Frederick Gowland Hopkins		Joshua Lederberg
1930	Karl Landsteiner		Edward L. Tatum
1931	Otto Warburg	1959	Arthur Kornberg
1932	Edgar D. Adrian		Severo Ochoa
	Charles S. Sherrington	1960	Macfarlane Burnet
1933	Thomas Hunt Morgan		P. B. Medawar
1934	George R. Minot	1961	Georg von Békésy
	William P. Murphy	1962	Francis Crick
	George H. Whipple		James D. Watson
1935	Hans Spemann		Maurice H. F. Wilkins

NOBEL PRIZE WINNERS BY PRIZE CATEGORY AND YEAR, 1901–1996

1963	John C. Eccles		Hamilton O. Smith
	Alan Hodgkin	1979	Allan Cormack
	Andrew Huxley		Godfrey Hounsfield
1964	Konrad Bloch	1980	Baruj Benacerraf
	Feodor Lynen		Jean Dausset
1965	François Jacob		George D. Snell
	André Lwoff	1981	David H. Hubel
	Jacques Monod		Roger W. Sperry
1966	Charles B. Huggins		Torsten Wiesel
	Peyton Rous	1982	Sune Bergström
1967	Ragnar Granit		Bengt Samuelsson
	H. Keffer Hartline		John R. Vane
	George Wald	1983	Barbara McClintock
1968	Robert W. Holley	1984	Niels K. Jerne
	Har Gorbind Khorana		Georges Köhler
	Marshall W. Nirenberg		César Milstein
1969	Max Delbrück	1985	Michael S. Brown
	Alfred Hershey		Joseph L. Goldstein
	Salvador Luria	1986	Stanley Cohen
1970	Julius Axelrod		Rita Levi-Montalcini
	Ulf von Euler	1987	Susumu Tonegawa
	Bernard Katz	1988	James Black
1971	Earl W. Sutherland Jr.		Gertrude B. Elion
1972	Gerald M. Edelman		George H. Hitchings Jr.
	Rodney R. Porter	1989	J. Michael Bishop
1973	Karl von Frisch		Harold E. Varmus
	Konrad Lorenz	1990	Joseph E. Murray
	Niko Tinbergen		E. Donnall Thomas
1974	Albert Claude	1991	Erwin Neher
	Christian de Duve		Bert Sakmann
	George E. Palade	1992	Edmond H. Fischer
1975	David Baltimore		Edwin G. Krebs
	Renato Dulbecco	1993	Richard J. Roberts
	Howard M. Temin		Phillip A. Sharp
1976	Baruch S. Blumberg	1994	Alfred G. Gilman
	D. Carleton Gajdusek		Martin Rodbell
1977	Roger Guillemin	1995	Edward B. Lewis
	Andrew V. Schalley		Christiane Nüsslein-Volhard
	Rosalyn S. Yalow		Eric F. Wieschaus
1978	Werner Arber	1996	Peter C. Doherty
	Daniel Nathans		Rolf M. Zinkernagel

NOBEL PRIZE WINNERS
BY COUNTRY OF RESIDENCE, 1901–1996

In this listing, the editors have attempted to reflect all recent geopolitical changes.

Argentina
Bernardo Houssay
Luis F. Leloir (Born in France)
César Milstein
Adolfo Pérez Esquivel
Carlos Saavedra Lamas

Australia
Macfarlane Burnet
John W. Cornforth
John C. Eccles
Jose Ramos-Horta (Born in East Timor)
Patrick White (Born in United Kingdom)

Austria
Robert Bárány
Alfred Fried
Karl von Frisch
Victor F. Hess
Richard Kuhn
Otto Loewi (Born in Germany)
Konrad Lorenz
Fritz Pregl
Erwin Schrödinger
Bertha von Suttner
Julius Wagner von Jauregg

Belgium
Auguste Beernaert
Jules Bordet
Christian de Duve (Born in United Kingdom)
Corneille Heymans
Henri La Fontaine
Maurice Maeterlinck
Georges Pire
Ilya Prigogine (Born in Russia)

Bosnia
Ivo Andrić

Canada
Frederick G. Banting
Bertram N. Brockhouse
Gerhard Herzberg (Born in Germany)
Lester Pearson
John C. Polanyi (Born in Germany)
Michael Smith (Born in United Kingdom)
Richard E. Taylor

Chile
Gabriela Mistral
Pablo Neruda

Colombia
Gabriel García Márquez

Costa Rica
Oscar Arias Sánchez

Czechoslovakia
Jaroslav Heyrovský
Jaroslav Seifert

Denmark
Fredrik Bajer
Aage Bohr
Niels Bohr
Henrik Dam
Johannes Fibiger
Niels Finsen
Karl Gjellerup
Johannes Jensen
August Krogh
Ben R. Mottelson (Born in United States)
Henrik Pontoppidan

East Timor (Now part of Indonesia)
Carlos Felipe Ximenes Belo

Egypt
Naguib Mahfouz
Anwar Sadat

NOBEL PRIZE WINNERS BY COUNTRY OF RESIDENCE, 1901–1996

Finland
Frans Sillanpää
Artturi Virtanen

France
Maurice Allais
Henri Becquerel
Henri Bergson
Léon Bourgeois
Aristide Briand
Louis de Broglie
Ferdinand Buisson
Albert Camus (Born in Algeria)
Alexis Carrel
René Cassin
Georges Charpak (Born in Poland)
Marie Curie (Born in Poland)
Pierre Curie
Jean Dausset
Paul d'Estournelles de Constant
Anatole France
Pierre-Gilles de Gennes
André Gide
Victor Grignard
François Jacob
Frédéric Joliot
Irène Joliot-Curie
Léon Jouhaux
Alfred Kastler
Charles Laveran
Jean-Marie Lehn
Gabriel Lippmann (Born in Luxembourg)
André Lwoff
Roger Martin du Gard
François Mauriac
Frédéric Mistral
Henri Moissan
Jacques Monod
Louis Néel
Charles Nicolle
Frédéric Passy
Jean Perrin
Saint-John Perse
Louis Renault
Charles Richet
Romain Rolland
Paul Sabatier
Jean-Paul Sartre

Claude Simon (Born in Madagascar)
René Sully-Prudhomme

Germany
Kurt Alder
Adolf von Baeyer
Emil von Behring
Friedrich Bergius
Gerd Binnig
Heinrich Böll
Max Born
Carl Bosch
Walther Bothe
Willy Brandt
Ferdinand Braun
Eduard Buchner
Adolf Butenandt
Johann Deisenhofer
Otto Diels
Gerhard Domagk
Paul Ehrlich
Manfred Eigen
Rudolf Eucken
Emil Fischer
Ernst Fischer
Hans Fischer
Werner Forssmann
James Franck
Fritz Haber
Otto Hahn
Gerhart Hauptmann
Werner Heisenberg
Gustav Hertz
Hermann Hesse
Paul Heyse
Robert Huber
J. Hans D. Jensen
Klaus von Klitzing
Robert Koch
Georges Köhler
Albrecht Kossel
Max von Laue
Philipp von Lenard (Born in Austria-Hungary)
Feodor Lynen
Thomas Mann
Otto Meyerhof
Harmut Michel
Theodor Mommsen (Born in Denmark)

Rudolf L. Mössbauer
Erwin Neher
Walther Nernst (Born in West Prussia)
Christiane Nüsslein-Volhard
Carol von Ossietzky
Wilhelm Ostwald (Born in Latvia)
Wolfgang Pauli
Max Planck
Ludwig Quidde
Wilhelm Röntgen
Ernst Ruska
Nelly Sachs
Bert Sakmann
Albert Schweitzer
Reinhard Selten
Hans Spemann
Johannes Stark
Hermann Staudinger
Gustav Stresemann
Otto Wallach
Otto Warburg
Heinrich Wieland
Wilhelm Wien (Born in East Prussia)
Richard Willstätter
Adolf Windaus
Georg Wittig
Karl Ziegler
Richard Zsigmondy

Greece
Odysseus Elytis
George Seferis (Born in Turkey)

Guatemala
Miguel Asturias
Rigoberta Menchú

Holland
Tobias Asser
Christiaan Eijkman
Willem Einthoven (Born in Dutch
 East Indies, now Indonesia)
Heike Kamerlingh Onnes
Hendrik Lorentz
Simon van der Meer
Jan Tinbergen
Jacobus van't Hoff
Johannes van der Waals
Pieter Zeeman

Frits Zernike

Iceland
Halldór Laxness

India
Venkata Raman
Rabindranath Tagore
Mother Teresa (Born in Ottoman Empire
 [now Macedonia])

Ireland
Samuel Beckett
Seamus Heaney (Born in Northern Ireland)
Sean MacBride (Born in France)
George Bernard Shaw
Ernest Walton
William Butler Yeats

Israel
S. Y. Agnon (Born in Austria-Hungary)
Menachem Begin (Born in Poland)
Shimon Peres (Born in Poland, now Belarus)
Yitzhak Rabin

Italy
Daniel Bovet (Born in Switzerland)
Giosuè Carducci
Grazia Deledda
Enrico Fermi
Camillo Golgi
Guglielmo Marconi
Ernesto Moneta
Eugenio Montale
Giulio Natta
Luigi Pirandello
Salvatore Quasimodo
Carlo Rubbia

Japan
Leo Esaki
Kenichi Fukui
Yasunari Kawabata
Kenzaburo Oe
Eisaku Sato
Sin-itiro Tomonaga
Susumu Tonegawa
Hideki Yukawa

NOBEL PRIZE WINNERS BY COUNTRY OF RESIDENCE, 1901–1996

Mexico
Alfonso Garcia Robles
Octavio Paz

Myanmar (formerly Burma)
Aung San Suu Kyi

Nigeria
Wole Soyinka

Northern Ireland
Mairead Corrigan
Betty Williams

Norway
Bjørnstjerne Bjørnson
Ragnar Frisch
Trygve Haavelmo
Knut Hamsun
Odd Hassel
Christian Lange
Fridtjof Nansen
Sigrid Undset (Born in Denmark)

Pakistan
Abdus Salam

Palestine
Yasir Arafat (Born in Egypt)

Poland
Władysław Reymont
Henryk Sienkiewicz
Wisława Szymborska
Lech Wałesa

Portugal
Egas Moniz

Russia
Nikolai Basov
Ivan Bunin
Pavel Cherenkov
Ilya Frank
Mikhail Sergeyevich Gorbachev
Leonid Kantorovich
Pyotr Kapitza
Lev Landau
Boris Pasternak
Ivan Pavlov
Aleksandr Prokhorov
Andrei Sakharov

Nikolay N. Semenov
Mikhail Sholokhov
Aleksandr Solzhenitsyn
Igor Tamm

South Africa
F. W. de Klerk
Nadine Gordimer
Albert Luthuli (Born in Rhodesia
  [now Zimbabwe])
Nelson Mandela
Max Theiler
Desmond Tutu

Spain
Vicente Aleixandre
Jacinto Benavente y Martinez
Camilo José Cela
José Echegaray
Juan Jiménez
Santiago Ramón y Cajal

Sweden
Hannes Alfvén
Klas Arnoldson
Svante Arrhenius
Sune Bergström
Karl Branting
Nils Dalén
Ulf von Euler
Hans von Euler-Chelpin (Born in Germany)
Ragnar Granit (Born in Finland)
Allvar Gullstrand
Dag Hammarskjöld
Verner von Heidenstam
George de Hevesy (Born in Austria-Hungary)
Eyvind Johnson
Erik Karlfeldt
Pär Lagerkvist
Selma Lagerlöf
Harry Martinson
Alva Myrdal
Gunnar Myrdal
Bertil Ohlin
Bengt Samuelsson
Kai Siegbahn
Manne Siegbahn
Nathan Söderblom
Teodor Svedberg

NOBEL PRIZE WINNERS BY COUNTRY OF RESIDENCE, 1901–1996

Hugo Theorell
Arne Tiselius
Torsten Wiesel

Switzerland
Werner Arber
J. Georg Bednorz (Born in Germany)
Élie Ducommun
Henri Dunant
Richard R. Ernst
Albert Gobat
Charles Guillaume
Walter R. Hess
Paul Karrer (Born in Russia)
Theodor Kocher
K. Alex Müller
Paul Müller
Wolfgang Pauli (Born in Austria)
Vladimir Prelog (Born in Bosnia)
Tadeus Reichstein (Born in Russia)
Heinrich Rohrer
Leopold Ružička (Born in Austria-Hungary)
Carl Spitteler
Alfred Werner
Rolf M. Zinkernagel

Tibet
Dalai Lama

Ukraine
Ilya Metchnikoff

United Kingdom
Edgar D. Adrian
Norman Angell
Edward Appleton
Francis W. Aston
Charles G. Barkla
Derek Barton
James Black
P. M. S. Blackett
John Boyd Orr
W. H. Bragg
W. L. Bragg (Born in Australia)
Elias Canetti (Born in Bulgaria)
Robert Cecil
James Chadwick
Ernst B. Chain (Born in Germany)

J. Austen Chamberlain
Winston Churchill
John Cockcroft
William Cremer
Francis Crick
Henry H. Dale
P. A. M. Dirac
Alexander Fleming
Howard W. Florey (Born in Australia)
Dennis Gabor (Born in Hungary)
John Galsworthy
William Golding
Arthur Harden
Walter N. Haworth
Friedrich A. von Hayek (Born in Austria)
Arthur Henderson
Antony Hewish
John Hicks
Archibald V. Hill
Cyril N. Hinshelwood
Alan Hodgkin
Dorothy C. Hodgkin (Born in Egypt)
Frederick Gowland Hopkins
Godfrey Hounsfield
Andrew Huxley
Niels K. Jerne
Brian D. Josephson
Bernard Katz (Born in Germany)
John C. Kendrew
Rudyard Kipling (Born in India)
Aaron Klug (Born in Lithuania)
Hans Krebs (Born in Germany)
Harold W. Kroto
W. Arthur Lewis
John J. R. MacLeod
Archer Martin
James Meade
P. B. Medawar (Born in Brazil)
James A. Mirrlees
Peter D. Mitchell
Nevill Mott
Philip Noel-Baker
Ronald Norrish
Max Perutz (Born in Austria)
George Porter
Rodney R. Porter
Cecil F. Powell
William Ramsay

Owen W. Richardson
Robert Robinson
Ronald Ross (Born in Nepal)
Joseph Rotblat (Born in Poland)
Bertrand Russell
Ernest Rutherford (Born in New Zealand)
Martin Ryle
Frederick Sanger
Charles S. Sherrington
Frederick Soddy
Richard Stone
J. W. Strutt
Richard Synge
G. P. Thomson
J. J. Thomson
Niko Tinbergen (Born in Holland)
Alexander Todd
John R. Vane
Maurice H. F. Wilkins (Born in New Zealand)
Geoffrey Wilkinson
C. T. R. Wilson

United States
Jane Addams
Sidney Altman (Born in Canada)
Luis W. Alvarez
Carl D. Anderson
Philip W. Anderson
Christian Anfinsen
Kenneth Arrow
Julius Axelrod
Emily Greene Balch
David Baltimore
John Bardeen
George W. Beadle
Gary S. Becker
Georg von Békésy (Born in Hungary)
Saul Bellow (Born in Canada)
Baruj Benacerraf (Born in Venezuela)
Paul Berg
Hans A. Bethe (Born in Germany)
J. Michael Bishop
Felix Bloch (Born in Switzerland)
Konrad Bloch (Born in Germany)
Nicolaas Bloembergen (Born in Holland)
Baruch S. Blumberg

Norman Borlaug
Walter H. Brattain (Born in China)
P. W. Bridgman
Joseph Brodsky (Born in Russia)
Herbert C. Brown (Born in United Kingdom)
Michael S. Brown
James M. Buchanan
Pearl S. Buck
Ralph Bunche
Nicholas Murray Butler
Melvin Calvin
Thomas R. Cech
Owen Chamberlain
Subrahmanyan Chandrasekhar (Born in India)
Albert Claude (Born in Belgium)
Ronald H. Coase (Born in United Kingdom)
Stanley Cohen
Arthur H. Compton
Leon N. Cooper
Elias James Corey
Carl F. Cori (Born in Austria-Hungary)
Gerty T. Cori (Born in Austria-Hungary)
Allan Cormack (Born in South Africa)
André Cournand (Born in France)
Donald J. Cram
James W. Cronin
Paul Crutzen (Born in the Netherlands)
Robert F. Curl Jr.
Clinton J. Davisson
Charles Dawes
Gerard Debreu (Born in France)
Peter Debye (Born in Holland)
Hans G. Dehmelt (Born in Germany)
Max Delbrück (Born in Germany)
Peter C. Doherty (Born in Australia)
Edward A. Doisy
Renato Dulbecco (Born in Italy)
Vincent du Vigneaud
Gerald M. Edelman
Albert Einstein (Born in Germany)
Gertrude B. Elion
T. S. Eliot
John F. Enders
Joseph Erlanger
William Faulkner
Richard P. Feynman
Edmond H. Fischer (Born in China)

Val F. Fitch
Paul J. Flory
Robert W. Fogel
William A. Fowler
Jerome I. Friedman
Milton Friedman
D. Carleton Gajdusek
Herbert S. Gasser
Murray Gell-Mann
Ivar Giaever (Born in Norway)
William F. Giauque (Born in Canada)
Walter Gilbert
Alfred G. Gilman
Donald A. Glaser
Sheldon L. Glashow
Joseph L. Goldstein
Roger Guillemin (Born in France)
John C. Harsanyi (Born in Hungary)
H. Keffer Hartline
Herbert A. Hauptman
Seamus Heaney (Born in Northern
  Ireland)
Ernest Hemingway
Philip S. Hench
Dudley R. Herschbach
Alfred Hershey
George H. Hitchings Jr.
Roald Hoffmann (Born in Poland)
Robert Hofstadter
Robert W. Holley
David H. Hubel (Born in Canada)
Charles B. Huggins (Born in Canada)
Cordell Hull
Russell A. Hulse
Jerome Karle
Frank Kellogg
Edward C. Kendall
Henry W. Kendall
Har Gorbind Khorana (Born in India)
Martin Luther King Jr.
Henry Kissinger (Born in Germany)
Lawrence Klein
Tjalling C. Koopmans (Born in Holland)
Arthur Kornberg
Edwin G. Krebs
Polykarp Kusch (Born in Germany)
Simon Kuznets (Born in Ukraine)
Willis E. Lamb Jr.

Karl Landsteiner (Born in Austria)
Irving Langmuir
Ernest O. Lawrence
Joshua Lederberg
Leon M. Lederman
David M. Lee
Tsung-Dao Lee (Born in China)
Yuan T. Lee (Born in Taiwan)
Wassily Leontief (Born in Russia)
Rita Levi-Montalcini (Born in Italy)
Edward B. Lewis
Sinclair Lewis
Willard F. Libby
Fritz Lipmann (Born in Germany)
William N. Lipscomb
Robert E. Lucas Jr.
Salvador Luria (Born in Italy)
Rudolph A. Marcus (Born in Canada)
Harry M. Markowitz
George C. Marshall
Maria Goeppert Mayer (Born in Germany)
Barbara McClintock
Edwin M. McMillan
R. Bruce Merrifield
Albert A. Michelson (Born in Germany)
Merton H. Miller
Robert A. Millikan
Czesław Miłosz (Born in Poland)
George R. Minot
Franco Modigliani (Born in Italy)
Mario J. Molina (Born in Mexico)
Stanford Moore
Thomas Hunt Morgan
Toni Morrison
John Mott
Hermann J. Muller
Robert S. Mulliken
Kary B. Mullis
William P. Murphy
Joseph E. Murray
John F. Nash
Daniel Nathans
Marshall W. Nirenberg
Douglass C. North
John H. Northrop
Severo Ochoa (Born in Spain)
George A. Olah (Born in Hungary)
Eugene O'Neill

NOBEL PRIZE WINNERS BY COUNTRY OF RESIDENCE, 1901–1996

Lars Onsager (Born in Norway)
Douglas D. Osheroff
George E. Palade (Born in Romania)
Linus C. Pauling
Charles J. Pedersen (Born in Korea)
Arno A. Penzias (Born in Germany)
Martin L. Perl
Edward M. Purcell
I. I. Rabi (Born in Austria-Hungary)
James Rainwater
Norman F. Ramsey
Frederick Reines
Dickinson W. Richards
Theodore W. Richards
Robert C. Richardson
Burton Richter
Frederick C. Robbins
Richard J. Roberts (Born in United
    Kingdom)
Martin Rodbell
Theodore Roosevelt
Elihu Root
Peyton Rous
F. Sherwood Rowland
Paul Samuelson
Andrew V. Schalley (Born in Poland)
Arthur L. Schawlow
J. Robert Schrieffer
Theodore Schultz
Melvin Schwartz
Julian S. Schwinger
Glenn T. Seaborg
Emilio Segrè (Born in Italy)
Phillip A. Sharp
William F. Sharpe
William Shockley (Born in United
    Kingdom)
Clifford G. Shull
Herbert Simon
Isaac Bashevis Singer (Born in Poland)
Richard E. Smalley
Hamilton O. Smith

George D. Snell
Robert M. Solow
Roger W. Sperry
Wendell M. Stanley
William H. Stein
John Steinbeck
Jack Steinberger (Born in Germany)
Otto Stern (Born in Germany)
George Stigler
James B. Sumner
Earl W. Sutherland Jr.
Albert Szent-Györgyi (Born in Hungary)
Edward L. Tatum
Henry Taube (Born in Canada)
Joseph H. Taylor Jr.
Howard M. Temin
E. Donnall Thomas
Samuel C. C. Ting
James Tobin
Charles H. Townes
Harold C. Urey
Harold E. Varmus
John H. Van Vleck
William Vickrey (Born in Canada)
Selman A. Waksman (Born in Ukraine)
Derek Walcott (Born in St. Lucia)
George Wald
James D. Watson
Steven Weinberg
Thomas H. Weller
George H. Whipple
Eric F. Wieschaus
Elie Wiesel (Born in Romania)
Eugene P. Wigner (Born in Hungary)
Kenneth G. Wilson
Robert W. Wilson
Woodrow Wilson
R. B. Woodward
Rosalyn S. Yalow
Chen Ning Yang (Born in China)

Vietnam
Le Duc Tho

NOBEL PRIZE WINNERS
WHO HAVE DIED SINCE 1991

Carl D. Anderson (*Physics*, 1936) d. January 11, 1991

John Bardeen (*Physics*, 1956, 1972) d. January 30, 1991

Menachem Begin (*Peace*, 1978) d. March 9, 1992

Daniel Bovet (*Physiology or Medicine*, 1957) d. April 8, 1992

Willy Brandt (*Peace*, 1971) d. October 8, 1992

Joseph Brodsky (*Literature*, 1987) d. January 28, 1996

Melvin Calvin (*Chemistry*, 1961) d. January 8, 1997

Elias Canetti (*Literature*, 1981) d. August 13, 1994

Subrahmanyan Chandrasekhar (*Physics*, 1983) d. August 21, 1995

Odysseus Elytis (*Literature*, 1979) d. March 18, 1996

Friedrich A. von Hayek (*Economics*, 1974) d. March 23, 1992

Robert W. Holley (*Physiology or Medicine*, 1968) d. February 11, 1993

Charles B. Huggins (*Physiology or Medicine*, 1966) d. January 12, 1997

Polykarp Kusch (*Physics*, 1955) d. March 20, 1993

W. Arthur Lewis (*Economics*, 1979) d. June 15, 1991

Salvador Luria (*Physiology or Medicine*, 1969) d. February 6, 1991

Barbara McClintock (*Physiology or Medicine*, 1983) d. September 2, 1992

Severo Ochoa (*Physiology or Medicine*, 1959) d. November 1, 1993

Yitzhak Rabin (*Peace*, 1994) d. November 4, 1995

Tadeus Reichstein (*Physiology or Medicine*, 1950) d. August 1, 1996

Isaac Bashevis Singer (*Literature*, 1978) d. July 24, 1991

George D. Snell (*Physiology or Medicine*, 1980) d. June 6, 1996

Roger W. Sperry (*Physiology or Medicine*, 1981) d. April 17, 1994

George Stigler (*Economics*, 1982) d. December 1, 1991

Alexander Todd (*Chemistry*, 1957) d. January 10, 1997

William S. Vickrey (*Economics*, 1996) d. October 11, 1996

Eugene P. Wigner (*Physics*, 1963) d. January 1, 1995

Preface

The original edition of *Nobel Prize Winners* appeared in 1987 and contained biographical sketches of all the 566 men, women, and institutions awarded the Nobel Prize from 1901 through 1986. The first supplement to that book, published in 1992, encompassed biographies of the 49 prize winners from 1987 through 1991. Like those volumes, *Nobel Prize Winners 1992–1996 Supplement*—containing 55 profiles—is intended for students and the general reader, introducing the lives and achievements of the laureates and placing special emphasis on the body of work for which each received the Nobel Prize.

The biographical profiles are arranged alphabetically. Each article traces the development of a laureate's work and assesses its significance. Because the work is often highly technical and has not always been discussed in secondary sources, factual accuracy has been a particular concern. To address this situation, the writers and editors of this book have invited the Nobel laureates to contribute essays in which they explain their work—and in which they reveal what led them to their respective fields. Also, with the permission of the Nobel Foundation, the preparers of this volume have made use of some of the prize winners' autobiographies as published in *Les Prix Nobel*. Additionally, several of the profiles included here appeared originally in another H. W. Wilson Company publication, *Current Biography*, and have been updated or condensed where appropriate.

Each laureate has been given a separate profile, even when a prize has been awarded to two or three persons, as is often the case with the science prizes. While a certain amount of repetition therefore occurs in descriptions of joint work, the reader finds in one place a comprehensive account of an individual laureate's work. As leading members of the literary, scientific, and political community, the Nobel Prize winners have shared in a wide network of mutual influence. To help the reader follow these connections, the names of other laureates appear in small-capital letters when first mentioned in profiles other than their own. This cross-referencing device encourages the reader to explore related profiles, thereby making it possible to trace the development of related ideas.

Bibliographies of works available in English supplement titles cited in the sketches. Works written by the subject appear chronologically by date of first publication in English; those about the subject are listed alphabetically by author or source.

In the text of sketches, foreign titles are given with an English translation of the title and a date. The English translation appears in italics if the work is a book that has been published under that title; in quotation marks if it is a poem, story, or essay published under that title; and in roman type if the editors have supplied the translation. The date is that of first publication of the original work.

By consulting the lists on pages 9–24, the reader can locate subjects (including those who appeared in the original volume and its first supplement) by prize category and year of award and by country of residence. Winners who have died since the publication of the first supplement are also listed, and a short biography of Alfred Nobel as well as a history of the Nobel Prizes and Nobel institutions are also included.

The editor wishes to acknowledge the Nobel Foundation for its generous help in providing information and photographs. Special thanks go to the managing editor, associate editors, and staff writers, who worked diligently in preparing this book.

—Clifford Thompson
1997

ALFRED NOBEL

by Alden Whitman

Alfred Nobel, the Swedish chemical experimenter and businessman who invented dynamite and other explosive compounds and whose will established the prizes that have brought him lasting fame, was a person of many paradoxes and contradictions. His contemporaries in the last half of the 19th century often found him perplexing because he did not quite fit the mold of the successful capitalist of his expansionist era. For one thing, Nobel was fonder of seclusion and tranquility than of ostentation and urban life, although he lived in cities most of his life and traveled widely. Unlike many contemporary barons of business, Nobel was spartan in his habits; he neither smoked nor drank, and he eschewed cards and other games. While his heritage was Swedish, he was a cosmopolitan European, comfortable with the French, German, Russian, and English languages as well as with his native tongue. Despite the heavy demands of his business and industrial affairs, he managed to build a well-stocked library and was well acquainted with the works of such authors as Herbert Spencer, the British philosopher and exponent of social Darwinism; Voltaire; and Shakespeare. Of 19th-century men of letters, he most admired a number of French writers: the Romantic novelist and poet Victor Hugo; Guy de Maupassant, the short-story craftsman; Honoré de Balzac, the novelist whose keen eye pierced the human comedy; and the poet Alphonse de Lamartine. He also liked to read the works of the Russian novelist Ivan Turgenev and the Norwegian playwright and poet Henrik Ibsen. The naturalism of the French novelist Emile Zola, however, left him cold. Above all, he loved the poetry of Percy Bysshe Shelley, whose works inspired in him an early resolve to embark on a literary career. To that end, he wrote a considerable number of plays, novels, and poems, only one of which was published. He then turned instead to a career in chemistry.

Likewise puzzling to his fellow entrepreneurs was Nobel's reputation for holding advanced social views. The notion that he was a Socialist was, in fact, quite undeserved, for he was actually an economic and political conservative who opposed suffrage for women and expressed grave doubts about democracy. Nevertheless, as much as Nobel lacked confidence in the political wisdom of the masses, he despised despotism. As an employer of many hundreds of workers, he took a paternalistic interest in their welfare, without wishing to establish any personal contact. Shrewdly, he realized that a work force with high morale is more productive than a crudely exploited one, which may well have been the basis for Nobel's reputation as a Socialist.

Nobel was quite unassuming and even reticent about himself. He had few confidants and never kept a diary. Yet at dinner parties and among friends, he was an attentive listener, always courteous and considerate. The dinners given at his home in one of the most fashionable neighborhoods of Paris were convivial and elegant, for he was a well-informed host able to call upon a fund of small talk. He could strike off words of incisive wit when the occasion arose, for instance once remarking, "All Frenchmen are under the blissful impression that the brain is a French organ."

He was a person of medium height, dark and slender, with deep-set blue eyes and a bearded face. In the custom of the time, he wore a pair of pince-nez (for nearsightedness) attached to a black cord.

Largely because his health was not robust, Nobel was sometimes capricious, lonely, and depressed. He would work intensely; then, finding it difficult to relax, he would often travel in search of the curative powers of various spas, at that time a popular and accepted part of a healthy regimen. One of Nobel's favorites was the spa at Ischl, Austria, where he kept a small yacht on a nearby lake. He was also fond of Baden bei Wien, not far from Vienna, where he met Sophie Hess. At their introduction in 1876, she was 20 years old, petite, and good-looking; he was 43. There appears to be no doubt that Nobel fell in love with "Sophiechen," a clerk in a flower shop, for he took her to Paris with him and provided her with an apartment. The young woman called herself Madame Nobel, but with time she is said to have become financially demanding. The relationship ended around 1891, only a few years before Nobel's death.

Despite his physical frailty, Nobel was capable of bursts of concentrated work. He had an excellent scientific mind and loved to tackle problems in his chemistry laboratory. Nobel managed his decentralized industrial empire through the board of directors of his many companies, which operated independently of one another and in which Nobel typically owned a 20 to 30 percent interest. Despite his limited financial interest, Nobel personally oversaw many of the details of decisionmaking in the companies that bore his name. According to one of his biographers, "Apart from his scientific and business activities, much of Nobel's time was taken up by voluminous correspondence and paperwork, every detail of which he coped with entirely alone, from duplicating to keeping his private accounts."

In early 1876 he attempted to engage a housekeeper and part-time secretary by advertising in an Austrian newspaper: "A wealthy and highly educated old gentleman living in Paris seeks to engage a mature lady with language proficiency as secretary and housekeeper." One respondent was 33-year-old Bertha Kinsky, then working in Vienna as a governess. Daringly, she came to Paris for an interview and impressed Nobel by her personality and language fluency, but after a week or so, homesickness overtook her and she returned to Vienna to marry Baron Arthur von Suttner, the son of her former employer in Vienna. She and Nobel met again, and in his last 10 years they corresponded about her projects for peace. Bertha von Suttner became a leading figure in the European peace movement and through her friendship with Nobel was able to gain from him substantial financial support for the cause. She received the 1905 Nobel Prize for Peace.

In his final three years, Nobel worked with a private assistant, Ragnar Sohlman, a Swedish chemist in his twenties and a person of great tact and patience. Sohlman functioned as both a secretary and a laboratory aide. Nobel liked and trusted the young man enough to name him chief executor of his will. "It was not always easy to be his assistant," Sohlman recalled. "He was exacting in demands, plainspoken, and always seemingly in a hurry. One had to be wide awake to follow his swiftly leaping thought and often amazing whims when he suddenly appeared and vanished as quickly."

During his lifetime, Nobel often exhibited uncommon generosity toward Sohlman and other employees. When the assistant got married, Nobel impulsively doubled his salary; and, earlier, when his French cook married, he gave her a gift of 40,000 francs, a large sum in those days. Nobel's generosity also often went beyond the realm of personal and professional contacts. For instance, although he was not a churchgoer, Nobel frequently gave money for the parish work of the Swedish church in Paris, whose pastor in the early 1890s was Nathan Soderblöm, later the Lutheran archbishop of Sweden and the recipient of the 1930 Nobel Prize for Peace.

Although he was often called the Lord of Dynamite, Nobel strongly opposed the military uses to which his inventions were frequently put. "For my part," he said three years before his death, "I wish all guns with their belongings and everything could be sent to hell, which is the proper place for their exhibition and use." On another occasion, he stated that war was "the horror of horrors and the greatest of crimes" and added, "I should like to invent a substance or a machine with such terrible power of mass destruction that war would thereby be impossible forever."

Alfred Nobel's distinguished career is all the more remarkable considering his humble origins. The Nobel family came of peasant stock, emerging from obscurity with the surname of Nobelius only late in the 17th century. Alfred's grandfather, a barber-surgeon, shortened it to Nobel in 1775. His eldest son, Immanuel (1801–1872), was Alfred's father. Immanuel, an architect, builder, and inventor, had a precarious business life for several years until the family began to make its fortune in the oil fields of Baku, Russia. He married Caroline Andriette Ahlsell (1803–1879) in 1827; the couple had eight children, only three of whom survived to adulthood: Robert, Ludvig, and Alfred.

Born October 21, 1833 in Stockholm, Alfred Bernhard Nobel was the couple's fourth child. From his first days, he was weak and sickly, and his childhood was marked by chronic illness. Both as a young man and as an adult, Alfred enjoyed an especially close and warm relationship with his mother. No matter how busy he was as an older man, he managed a yearly visit and kept in frequent touch by letter.

After trying his hand at a business making elastic cloth, Immanuel fell on hard times and in 1837, leaving his family in Sweden, moved first to Finland and then to St. Petersburg, where he manufactured powder-charged explosive mines, lathes, and machine tools. In October 1842, when Alfred was nine, he and the rest of the family joined his father in Russia, where his now prosperous family was able to engage private tutors for him. He proved to be a diligent pupil, apt and eager to learn, with a special interest in chemistry.

In 1850, when he was 17 years old, Alfred took an extended trip, traveling in Europe, where he visited Germany, France, and Italy, and the United States. He pursued his chemical studies in Paris, and in the United States he met John Ericsson, the Swedish inventor of the caloric engine, who later designed the ironclad warship *Monitor*.

Returning to St. Petersburg three years later, Nobel was employed in his father's growing business, by then called Fonderies & Ateliers Mécaniques Nobel & Fils (Foundries and Machine Shops of Nobel and Sons), which was producing material for the Crimean War (1853–1856). At the end of the war, the company shifted to the manufacture of machinery for steamboats plying the Volga River and the Caspian Sea. Its peacetime production, however, was not enough to offset the loss of military orders, and by 1858 the company fell into financial trouble. Alfred and his parents returned to Stockholm while Robert and Ludvig remained in Russia to salvage what they could. Back in Sweden, Alfred became engrossed in mechanical and chemical experiments, obtaining three patents. This work sharpened his interest in further experimentation, which he conducted in a small laboratory his father had established on his estate near the capital.

At that time, the only usable explosive for powder-charged mines—either for military or for peaceful uses—was black gunpowder. It was known, though, that the substance nitroglycerin was an extraordinarily powerful explosive compound, which posed extraordinary risks because of its volatility. No one had yet figured out how to control its detonation. After several small experiments with nitroglycerin, Immanuel Nobel sent Alfred to Paris in search of financing in 1861; he succeeded in raising a 100,000-franc loan. Despite some initial failures by Immanuel, Alfred became actively involved in the project. In 1863 he invented a practical detonator, which used gunpowder to set off the nitroglycerin. This invention was one of the primary foundations of his reputation and his fortune.

One of Nobel's biographers, Erik Bergengren, has described the device in this fashion:

In its first form, . . . [the detonator] is so constructed that initiation of the liquid nitroglycerin explosive charge, which is contained in a metal cap by itself or in a blocked-up borehole, is brought about by the explosion of a smaller charge let down into this, the smaller charge consisting of gunpowder in a wooden cap by itself, with a plug, into which a fuse has been inserted.

In order to increase the effect, the inventor altered various details of this construction several times, and as a final improvement in 1865 he replaced the original cap with a metal cap charged with detonating mercury. . . . With the invention of this so-called blasting cap, the Initial Ignition Principle was introduced into the technique of explosives, and this was fundamental to all later developments in this field. It was this principle which made possible the effective use of nitroglycerin and later other violent explosives as independent explosives; it also made it possible to study their explosive properties.

In the process of perfecting the invention, Immanuel Nobel's laboratory was blown up, an explosion that resulted in the loss of eight lives, including that of Immanuel's 21-year-old son Emil. Shortly thereafter, the father suffered a stroke, and remained bedridden until his death eight years later in 1872.

Despite the setback caused by the explosion and the resulting public hostility to the manufacture and use of nitroglycerin, Nobel persevered, and in October 1864 he persuaded the Swedish State Railways to adopt his substance for the blasting of tunnels. In order to manufacture it, he won the financial backing of a Stockholm merchant; a company, Nitroglycerin Ltd., was set up and a factory built in the Swedish countryside. In its first years, Nobel was the company's managing director, works engineer, correspondent, advertising manager, and treasurer. He also traveled extensively to demonstrate his blasting procedure. Among the company's customers was the Central Pacific Railroad in the American West, which used Nobel's nitroglycerin in blasting the line's way through the Sierra Nevadas. After obtaining patents in other countries for his device, Nobel established the first of his foreign companies—Alfred Nobel & Co. in Hamburg—in 1865.

Although Nobel was able to solve the major problems of manufacture, his explosives were sometimes carelessly handled by their purchasers. There were accidental explosions and deaths and even a ban or two on imports. Nonetheless, Nobel continued to expand his business. He won a United States patent in 1866 and spent three months there raising money for his Hamburg plant and demonstrating his blasting oil. Nobel also decided to found an American company that, after some maneuvering, became the Atlantic Giant Powder Company; following Nobel's death, it was acquired by E. I. du Pont de Nemours and Company. The inventor felt badly treated by American businessmen who were eager to float shares in his blasting oil companies. "In the long run I found life in America anything but agreeable," he later wrote. "The exaggerated chase after money is a pedantry which spoils much of the pleasure of meeting people and destroys a sense of honor in favor of imagined needs."

Although blasting oil, correctly used, was an effective explosive, it was nevertheless so often involved in accidents (including one that leveled the Hamburg plant) that Nobel sought some way to stabilize nitroglycerin. He hit upon the idea of mixing the liquid nitroglycerin with a chemically inert and porous substance. His first practical choice was kieselguhr, a chalk-like, absorbent material. Mixed with nitroglycerin, it could be fashioned into sticks and placed into boreholes. Patented in 1867, it was called "Dynamite, or Nobel's safety blasting powder."

The new explosive not only established Alfred Nobel's lasting fame, but it also found such spectacular uses as in the blasting of the Alpine tunnel on the St. Gotthard rail line, the removal of underwater rocks at Hell Gate in New York City's East River, the clearing of the Danube River at the Iron Gate, and the cutting of the Corinth Canal in Greece. Dynamite was also a factor in oil drilling in the Baku fields of Russia, an enterprise in which Nobel's two brothers were so active and became so wealthy that they were known as the Russian Rockefellers. Alfred was the largest single stockholder in his brothers' companies.

Although Nobel held patent rights to dynamite and its later refinements in all the world's major countries, in the 1870s he was constantly harassed by competitors who stole his processes. In these years he refused to hire a secretary or a full-time lawyer, and he was forced to spend much time in patent litigation as his factories steadily increased production.

In the 1870s and 1880s, Nobel expanded his network of factories into the chief European countries, either besting his rivals or forming cartels with them to control prices and markets. Eventually, he established a worldwide web of corporations for the manufacture and sale of his explosives, which, in addition to an improved dynamite, by then included a blasting gelatin. The military uses of these substances began in the Franco-Prussian War of 1870–1871, but during his lifetime, the investments Nobel made in military inventions lost considerable amounts of money. The profits from his industrial ventures came from the use of dynamite in the construction of tunnels, canals, railways, and roads.

Describing the consequences to Nobel of the discovery of dynamite, Bergengren has written:

Not a day passed without his having to face vital problems: the financing and formation of companies; the procuring of trustworthy partners and assistants for managerial posts, and suitable foremen and skilled laborers for a manufacturing process that was extremely sensitive and contained very dangerous ingredients: the erection of new buildings on remote sites, with intricate security measures in accordance with the differing laws of each country. The inventor took part eagerly in the planning and starting of a new project, but he seldom lent his personal assistance to the detailed working of the various companies.

The biographer characterized Nobel's life in the 10 years after the invention of dynamite as "restless and nerve-racking." After his move from Hamburg to Paris in 1873, he was sometimes able to escape to his private laboratories, one a part of his house. To help him there, he employed Georges D. Fehrenbach, a young French chemist, who remained with him for 18 years.

Given a choice, Nobel would have preferred his laboratory to his business, but his companies always seemed to claim a priority as the trade in explosives increased and new factories were established to meet the demands. Indeed, at Nobel's death in 1896, some 93 factories were in operation, producing 66,500 tons of explosives, including ammunition of all kinds as well as ballistite, a smokeless blasting powder that Nobel patented between 1887 and 1891. The new substance could be used as a substitute for black gunpowder and was relatively inexpensive to manufacture.

In marketing ballistite, Nobel sold his Italian patent to the government, an action that aroused the anger of the French. He was accused of stealing the idea for the substance from the French government's monopoly, and his laboratory was ransacked and shut down; his factory was also forbidden to make ballistite. Under these circumstances, in 1891, Nobel decided to close his Paris home and to leave France for a new residence in San Remo on the Italian Riviera. Apart from the uproar over ballistite, Nobel's last Paris years were not totally happy; his mother died in 1889, a year following the death of his older brother Ludvig. Moreover, his French business associate had involved his enterprises in dubious speculations in connection with an unsuccessful venture to build a Panama canal.

At his San Remo villa, which was set in an orange grove overlooking the Mediterranean, Nobel built a small chemical laboratory, where he worked as time permitted. Among other things, he experimented in the production of synthetic rubber and silk. However much he liked San Remo for its climate, Nobel had warm thoughts of his homeland, and in 1894 he bought the Bofors ironworks in Värmland, where he fitted out a nearby manor house for private quarters and built a new laboratory. He spent the last two summers of his life at the Värmland manor house. During the second summer, his brother Robert died, and Nobel himself began to feel unwell.

Examined by specialists in Paris, he was warned that he had angina pectoris, a lack of oxygen supply to the heart, and was advised to rest. He then returned to San Remo, where he worked on a play he hoped to complete and where he drew up a remarkable will in his own hand. Shortly after midnight on December 10, 1896, he suffered a cerebral hemorrhage and died. Except for Italian servants who could not understand him, Nobel was alone at his death, and his final words went unrecorded.

The origins of Nobel's will, with its provisions for awards in a number of fields of human endeavor, are imprecise. The final document is a revision of earlier testaments. Its bequests for science and literature awards, it is generally agreed, are extensions of Nobel's lifelong concern with those fields—physics, physiology, chemistry, and the elevation of the art of writing. Evidence suggests that the award for peace may well have been the fruition of the inventor's long-standing aversion to violence. Early in 1886, for example, he told a British acquaintance that he had "a more and more earnest wish to see a rose red peace sprout in this explosive world."

As an inventor with a fertile imagination and as a businessman with a robust eagerness to exploit the industrial and commercial aspects of his brainchildren, Alfred Nobel was typical of his times. Paradoxically, he was a reclusive and lonely person whose worldly success failed to bring him the consolations of life for which he so avidly yearned.

THE NOBEL PRIZES AND NOBEL INSTITUTIONS
by Carl Gustaf Bernhard

Alfred Nobel died on December 10, 1896. In his remarkable will, written in Paris on November 27, 1895, Nobel stated:

The whole of my remaining realizable estate shall be dealt with in the following way:

The capital shall be invested by my executors in safe securities and shall constitute a fund, the interest on which shall be annually distributed in the form of prizes to those who, during the preceding year, shall have conferred the greatest benefit on mankind. The said interest shall be divided into five equal parts, which shall be apportioned as follows: one part to the person who shall have made the most important discovery or invention within the field of physics; one part to the person who shall have made the most important chemical discovery or improvement; one part to the person who shall have made the most important discovery within the domain of physiology or medicine; one part to the person who shall have produced in the field of literature the most outstanding work of an idealistic tendency; and one part to the person who shall have done the most or the best work for fraternity among nations, for the abolition or reduction of standing armies, and for the holding and promotion of peace congresses.

The prizes for physics and chemistry shall be awarded by the [Royal] Swedish Academy of Sciences; that for physiological or medical works by the Karolinska Institute in Stockholm; that for literature by the [Swedish] Academy in Stockholm; and that for champions of peace by a committee of five persons to be elected by the Norwegian Storting [Parliament]. It is my express wish that in awarding the prizes no consideration whatever shall be given to the nationality of the candidates, so that the most worthy shall receive the prize, whether he be a Scandinavian or not.

The invitation to assume the responsibility of selecting laureates was accepted by the awarding bodies designated in Nobel's will only after considerable discussion. Several members of these organizations were doubtful and, referring to the vague formulation of the will, claimed that it would be difficult to implement. In spite of these reservations, in 1900 the Nobel Foundation was established and statutes were worked out by a special committee on the basis of the will's stipulations.

The foundation, an independent, nongovernment organization, has the responsibility of administering the funds in a manner "destined to safeguard the financial basis for the prizes, and for the activities associated with the selection of prizewinners." The foundation also protects the common interests of the prize-awarding institutions and represents the Nobel institutions externally. In this capacity the foundation arranges the annual Nobel Prize ceremonies on behalf of the awarding institutions. The Nobel Foundation itself is not involved in proposing candidates, in the evaluation process, or in the final selections. These functions are all performed independently by the prize-awarding assemblies. Today, the Nobel Foundation also administers the Nobel Symposia, which since 1966 have been supported mainly through grants to the foundation from the Bank of Sweden's Tercentenary Foundation.

The statutes for the Nobel Foundation and the special regulations of the awarding institutions were promulgated by the King in Council on June 29, 1900. The first Nobel Prizes were awarded on December 10, 1901. The political union between Norway and Sweden came to a peaceful end in 1905. As a result, the current special regulations for the body awarding the peace prize, the Norwegian Nobel Committee, are dated April 10, 1905.

In 1968 the Bank of Sweden at its tercentenary made a donation for a prize in the economic sciences. After some hesitation, the Royal Swedish Academy of Sciences accepted the role of prize-awarding institution in this field, in accordance with the same rules and principles that apply to the original Nobel Prizes. This prize, which was established in memory of Alfred Nobel, is also awarded on December 10, following the presentation of the other Nobel Prizes. Officially known as the Prize in Economic Sciences in Memory of Alfred Nobel, it was awarded for the first time in 1969.

Today, the Nobel Prize—independent of the monetary award—is widely regarded as the highest recognition of intellect that can be bestowed on a man or woman. It is also one of the few prizes known by name to a great part of the nonscientific public, and probably the only prize about which almost every scientist knows. According to the statutes, the Nobel Prize cannot be given jointly to more than three persons. As a consequence, relatively few, however distinguished, can hope to receive the award.

The prestige of the Nobel Prizes depends on the serious work devoted to the selection of the prizewinners and on the effective mechanisms for this procedure, which were instituted from the very outset. It was felt desirable to obtain properly documented proposals from qualified experts in different countries, thereby also emphasizing the international character of the prizes.

For each prize there is a Nobel committee. The Royal Swedish Academy of Sciences appoints three committees, one each for physics, chemistry, and the economic sciences. The Karolinska Institute names a committee for physiology or medicine, and the Swedish Academy chooses a committee for literature. In addition, the Norwegian Parliament, the Storting, appoints a peace prize committee. The Nobel committees play a central role in the selection process. Each consists of five members but may also request temporary assistance from additional specialists in relevant fields.

Nominations of candidates for the prizes can be made only upon invitation, and these invitations are distributed in the fall of the year preceding the award. The recipients are invited to submit a written proposal stating the reasons for their choice. For each prize, more than 1,000 individuals in different parts of the world are invited to submit nominations. Invitations for the science prizes are sent out to active scholars at universities and research institutions. For the literature prize, submissions are invited from academic representatives in the fields of literature and languages as well as from members of distinguished academies and societies of the same character as the Swedish Academy. In order to obtain proposals for the peace prize, representatives from the fields of philosophy, history, and the legal and political sciences, as well as those active in various peace activities, are contacted. Some individuals always receive invitations to submit nominations; among them are previous Nobel laureates and members of the Royal Swedish Academy of Sciences, the Nobel Assembly of the Karolinska Institute, and the Swedish Academy, as well as permanent and active professors in the respective fields from all the Scandinavian countries. Invitations to propose names are confidential, as are the nominations.

Nominations must be received by February 1 of the award year. At that date, the work of the Nobel committees begins, and from then until September committee members and consultants evaluate the qualifications of the nominees. Committees meet several times, with proposals assigned to different committee members as well as to outside experts, all of whom attempt to determine the originality and significance of the nominee's contributions. Several committee members or outside experts may report on various aspects of a single proposal. Every year several thousand persons are involved in the preparatory work. After this work is completed, the committees submit their secret reports and recommendations to the respective prize-awarding bodies, which have the sole right to make the final decisions.

By September or the beginning of October, the Nobel committees are ready with their work. In physics, chemistry, and the economic sciences, they submit their reports to the respective "classes" of the Royal Swedish Academy of Sciences, each of which has about 25 members. The classes then send their recommendations to the academy for the final decision. The procedure for the prize in physiology or medicine is similar, except that the recommendation of the Nobel committee goes directly to the 50-member Nobel Assembly of the Karolinska Institute. In deciding the literature prize, the 18 members of the Swedish Academy make the decision on the basis of the proposal from the Nobel committee. The decision for the peace prize is made by the Norwegian Nobel Committee itself.

In October, final votes are cast in the various assemblies. The laureates are immediately notified of the decisions, which are then announced internationally at a press conference held in Stockholm and attended by representatives of the international news media. The messages contain the names of the laureates and a short statement describing the reasons for the awards. At this occasion, specialists in the various fields are also present to give a more comprehensive explanation of the winners' achievements and their significance.

Subsequently, the Nobel Foundation invites the laureates and their families to the Nobel ceremonies held in Stockholm and Oslo on December 10. In Stockholm the prize ceremony takes place in the Concert Hall and is attended by about 1,200 persons. The prizes in physics, chemistry, physiology or medicine, literature, and the economic sciences are presented by the King of Sweden following a short résumé of the laureates' achievements presented by representatives of the prize-awarding assemblies. The celebration continues at a foundation banquet in the Town Hall.

In Oslo the peace prize ceremony takes place in the Assembly Hall of the University of Oslo in the presence of the King of Norway and the royal family. The laureate receives the prize from the chairman of the Norwegian Nobel Committee. In connection with the ceremonies in Stockholm and Oslo, the laureates present their Nobel lectures, which are later published in the volume *Les Prix Nobel.*

Obviously, a considerable amount of work is devoted to the sifting process by which laureates are selected. In the sciences, the distribution of more than 1,000 invitations for each prize results in 200 to 250 nominations. Since the same scientists are often proposed by several nominators, the number of actual candidates is somewhat less. In literature the Swedish Academy makes the choice from 100 to 150 candidates. Generally, most of the strong candidates are proposed over several years, and very rarely is a laureate selected after having been proposed only once.

The Nobel selections have often been criticized in the international press, as has the secrecy of the selection procedure. As to the complaints about the secrecy, suffice it to say that the statutes mandate that the deliberations, opinions, and proposals of the Nobel committees in connection with the awarding of prizes may not be made public or otherwise revealed. They direct that no protest shall be laid against the award of an adjudicating body and that if conflicts of opinion have arisen, they shall not be recorded in the minutes or otherwise revealed.

As to the singularity of the prizes, it is certainly true that there are many more worthy candidates than prizes. The 1948 Swedish Nobel laureate in chemistry, Arne Tiselius, who served as chairman of the Nobel Foundation for several years, described the situation in the following way: "You cannot in practice apply the principle that the Nobel Prize should be given to the person who is best; you cannot define who is best. Therefore, you are left with the only alternative: to try to find a particularly worthy candidate."

Naturally, the handling of the prizes is based on the principles delineated in the will of Alfred Nobel. In physics, chemistry, and physiology or medicine, the will speaks of an important discovery, improvement, or invention within these fields. Thus, the science prizes are awarded not for the work of a lifetime, but for a specific achievement or a particular discovery. As an experimenter and inventor, Nobel knew very well what a discovery was. Concepts are extremely useful, but concepts change; what remains are the experimental facts—the discoveries. The contributions of some scientists may be of great importance in the development of their fields, but they may not fulfill the specific requirements stipulated by the Nobel Prize rules.

The performance of scientific work and the conditions under which scientists now labor are quite different from those in effect during Alfred Nobel's lifetime, a fact that complicates the selection of laureates. Today, teamwork is common and often results in significant discoveries. The prizes, however, are meant for individuals and not for large groups. This contemporary situation has resulted in a dilemma with which the prize-awarding juries have had to deal in their efforts to fulfill Nobel's intentions.

In his will, Nobel declares that "an idealistic tendency" should be an essential qualification for the prize in literature. This vague expression has caused endless arguments. In *Nobel, The Man and His Prizes* (1962), Anders Österling, a past secretary of the Swedish Academy, writes: "What he really meant by this term was probably works of a humanitarian and constructive character which, like scientific discoveries, could be regarded as of benefit to mankind." Today the Swedish Academy by and large refrains from trying to find guidance from this expression.

To appraise achievements in widely different fields with reference to the phrase "for the benefit of mankind" is, of course, extremely difficult. A glance at the lengthy list of Nobel Prize winners in all fields shows, however, that serious efforts have been made to pay respect to a great variety of claims. For instance, the science prizes have been given for discoveries in pure sciences as well as for advances in applied fields. Lars Gyllensten, a former secretary of the Swedish Academy, has noted, "One has to adopt some sort of pragmatic procedure and take into consideration the basic view in Alfred Nobel's will to promote science and poetry and to distribute prizes in an international perspective to the benefit of mankind, not to distribute empty status awards."

At an early point it became clear that the stipulation that the prizes be awarded for literary or scientific achievements made during the preceding year could not be observed in practice while at the same time maintaining a high standard. To resolve this difficulty, the following rule was inserted in the regulations: "The provision in the will that the annual award of prizes shall refer to works during the preceding year shall be understood in the sense that the award shall be made for the most recent achievements and for the older works only if their significance has not become apparent until recently." The discovery of penicillin, for instance, took place in 1928, but the prize was not given until 1945, when the drug's value had been established by practical use. Likewise, the importance of literary contributions may not be fully appreciated until they can be seen in the context of an entire body of work. Therefore, many laureates in literature have received their prizes late in their careers.

That the choice of laureates for the peace and literature prizes often arouses controversy is self-evident; that there are some unfortunate mistakes in the list of the science prizes must also be admitted. These circumstances reflect the difficulties that the prize juries encounter. It is, however, surprising that criticism is so relatively scarce in the extensive literature that has been written about the Nobel Prizes and the Nobel work.

Very often the Nobel Foundation is criticized for not awarding prizes in other fields. The reason is simply that it was Nobel's wish that only the five specific areas he designated be taken into account. The single exception is the Nobel Prize in Economic Sciences, also administered by the foundation. Nonetheless, contemporary juries are in fact acting within successively widening frameworks. In 1973, for instance, the medicine prize was given to three ethologists for their discoveries concerning organization and elicitation of individual and social behavior patterns, and in 1974 pioneering research in radio astrophysics was honored. The physics prize in 1978, given for the discovery of cosmic microwave background radiation, also provides an example of the increasingly liberal interpretation of the prize field.

For 25 years, while a professor of physiology at the Karolinska Institute, I served as a member and chairman of its Nobel committee. Subsequently, as president and later secretary-general of the Royal Swedish Academy of Sciences, I also had the pleasure of taking part in the Nobel work in physics, chemistry, and the economic sciences for 10 years. During this 35-year period, I saw firsthand the diligence with which the members of the science prize juries fulfilled their delicate mission and witnessed the painstaking work of the specialists in various fields when adjudicating the prize proposals.

While engaged in work relating to the Nobel Prizes, I was often asked by representatives of organizations around the world to discuss the Nobel selection process when some new international prize was going to be created. I usually gave three pieces of advice. First, define the topics carefully so that a proper assessment can be made. We know how extremely difficult it is to make a selection, even in a "hard science" like physics. Second, allow enough time for the selection process. Third, ask for sufficient funds to cover the costs of the selection process, one which may involve a great many specialists and consist of several steps. Actually, the magnitude of the costs of selecting the Nobel laureates and of organizing and conducting the prize ceremonies is more or less the same as that of the Nobel Prizes themselves.

The Nobel Prizes are unique and carry with them considerable prestige. It is frequently wondered why the prizes attract more attention than any other 20th-century award. One reason may be that they were created at the right time and that they epitomize some of the principal historical transformations of the age. Alfred Nobel was a true internationalist, and from the very beginning, the international character of the prizes made an important impression on society. The strict rules of the selection process, which were implemented from the outset, have also been crucial in establishing the importance of the awards. As soon as the prizes are awarded in December, the task of selecting the next year's Nobel laureates begins. This year-round activity, in which so many of the world's intellectuals are engaged, plays a decisive role in directing the interest of society to the importance of the work that is proceeding in the various fields covered by the prizes, for "the benefit of mankind."

ARAFAT, YASIR

(August 24, 1929–   )
Nobel Prize for Peace, 1994 (shared with Shimon Peres and Yitzhak Rabin)

Mohammed Abdel-Raouf Arafat al Qudwa al-Husseini (the most authoritative of numerous reported versions of his full name) was born on August 24, 1929 (some sources give August 4 as his birthday) in Cairo, Egypt. Called Yasir (sometimes spelled Yassir or Yasser) from an early age, he is the sixth of the seven children of Abd al-Raouf al-Qudwa al-Husseini, a successful wholesale merchant who ran businesses in Jerusalem and Cairo, and his first wife, Zahwa Abu Saud, a member of one of Jerusalem's most prominent Arab families. (Contrary to some published reports, his father was unrelated to the Palestinian leader Haz Amin Husseini.) After his mother died, when he was just four years old, Arafat moved in with an uncle who lived in Jerusalem, then the capital of Palestine, which, like much of the Middle East, was under British rule. It was during his years in Jerusalem that Arafat was first exposed to the simmering conflict between the Palestinians and Palestine's émigré Jews, many of whom were intent on forming a homeland there. Following his return to Cairo in about 1937 (one source gives 1942 as the year of his return), Arafat retained an active interest in Jewish-Arab relations, sometimes at the expense of his studies. "He had been back in Cairo only a short time when he started to go to the places and the clubs where the Jews gathered. . . . " his oldest sister, Inam, was quoted as saying by Alan Hart in his book *Arafat: A Political Biography* (1989). "He told us that he wanted to study their mentality." To that end, Arafat also read the works of such Zionists as Theodor Herzl, who founded the Zionist movement in the late 19th century.

By 1946, two years before the British relinquished their mandate over Palestine and the state of Israel was founded, Arafat was already helping to procure arms in Egypt, which would then be smuggled into the territory. As a result of his efforts, he earned a reputation as a man of courage. He also possessed a keen understanding of how to use propaganda to attain one's goals, a talent he demonstrated when, while still a teenager, he persuaded some of his friends to help him push a junked German tank in front of the Egyptian foreign ministry in Cairo, in hopes of convincing the government that it should legalize arms sales to the Palestinians. Although his efforts yielded no tangible benefits, they did serve to spotlight the Palestinians' demand for arms.

When war between the Israelis and the Arab nations of Egypt, Transjordan (now Jordan), Iraq, Lebanon, and Syria as well as the Palestinians began in earnest, in 1948 (the conflict was the first of the five Arab-Israeli wars fought to date), Arafat, then a student in

YASIR ARAFAT

his first year at the University of Fuad I (now Cairo University), was among the first to burn his books as a way of demonstrating his belief that struggling to preserve his homeland was more important than studying. According to some reports, Arafat slipped into Israel to join the fighting. He was dismayed to find that Arab soldiers refused to allow Palestinian irregulars to participate in the fighting and sometimes even confiscated their arms. "I was furious," he was quoted as saying by John and Janet Wallach, the authors of *Arafat: In the Eyes of the Beholder.* "They took our weapons and we began to feel that there was something wrong. There was a betrayal." After Israel emerged victorious, the Palestinians, according to Arafat, suffered another insult at the hands of their fellow Arabs: the Arab states concluded a peace that left more than three quarters of a million Palestinians displaced and stateless. Arafat has since maintained that the Arabs should have accepted the United Nations proposal, made in 1947, to partition Palestine into two independent states—one Jewish and the other Arab.

In the wake of the Arabs' defeat in the 1948 war, Arafat considered attending college in the United States, but by the time his visa application was approved, he had decided to remain in Egypt. He reentered the University of Fuad I, where he majored in engineering. He also remained involved in political activities, received military training at the university's school for reserve officers (the equivalent of the United States ROTC program), and participated in minor sabotage operations against British troops in the Suez Canal Zone. Most significant, Arafat became president of the Palestinian Students' League, a position from which he eventually began to lead discussions about

43

the possibility of forming an independent movement whose aim would be the liberation of Palestine from what he considered to be Israeli occupation.

After receiving his degree in engineering in 1956, Arafat worked briefly in Egypt and then immigrated to Kuwait, where he took a job in the Kuwaiti department of public works. At some point during his stay in Kuwait, he established his own company and, according to John and Janet Wallach, earned a reputation for being a wealthy bachelor who liked fast cars and snappy clothes. At the same time, he became ever more committed to his political activities, and in the mid-1950s he and several other Palestinians formed a movement, which eventually became known as Fatah, dedicated to the liberation of Palestine. Fatah has always been but one of several organizations devoted to reclaiming Palestine for the Palestinians. These groups eventually became subsumed within an umbrella organization, the Palestine Liberation Organization (PLO), which had been formed in 1964 under the sponsorship of the Arab League.

In the early days of its existence, Fatah was viewed as an outlaw organization by the Arab states, partly because, unlike the other, more mainstream groups, Fatah did not promote the then-popular ideal of Arab unity. In keeping with its commitment to liberating Palestine from Israeli rule, in 1959 Fatah launched *Filistinuna* (Our Palestine), a magazine that promoted the cause of armed struggle against Israel. As might be imagined, the magazine was considered by Arab regimes to be thoroughly subversive, and it had to be distributed clandestinely.

By 1963 running Fatah had become Arafat's full-time occupation. He had given up his engineering career, and his overriding concern was launching an armed struggle against Israel. Although some of his comrades urged him to take a more conciliatory course of action, Arafat was bent on initiating an armed struggle, and in about 1965 Fatah guerrillas undertook the first of a number of minor raids into Israeli territory. Although not militarily significant, these incursions had political consequences, just as Arafat had hoped; as word of Fatah's activities spread, it became easier for the group to obtain financial contributions and arms. Also during this period, Arafat took as his nom de guerre the name of a legendary Muslim warrior, Abu Ammar.

A turning point in the history of Arab-Israeli relations was the 1967 Six-Day War, in which Israel captured the Golan Heights from Syria, the West Bank from Jordan, and a smaller parcel of land, the Gaza Strip, from Egypt. Over the next quarter-century, the fate of the territories, especially the latter two, was to be at the center of the wider conflict between the Arabs and Israelis. For several months following the brief and humiliating defeat of Arab nations in the 1967 war, Arafat operated secretly in the West Bank.

He was soon forced to make a quick getaway, and legend has it that he crossed the river Jordan by posing as a woman with a baby. Whether true or not, this was the first of a number of anecdotes illustrating Arafat's sixth sense for danger and his ability to evade it.

While in Jordan, where a large population of Palestinians had found refuge in the decades following the first Arab-Israeli war, Arafat and his colleagues succeeded in recruiting many Palestinians into Fatah. They also continued to mount raids into Israel from Jordan. A particularly important clash occurred on March 21, 1968, when Israeli troops made a retaliatory incursion into Jordan, and Arafat made a historic decision to resist rather than retreat in the face of overwhelming odds. The resulting Battle of Karameh, in which Israeli troops suffered significant losses, was an important victory for Arafat and Fatah. Almost immediately, Arafat received considerable attention from the Middle Eastern and Western presses; in 1968, he was pictured for the first time on the cover of *Time* magazine. Then, in 1969, Fatah "carried out 2,432 attacks on Israel, three times the number of incidents in 1968, and more than 20 times the number carried out in 1967," according to John and Janet Wallach. Arafat's growing reputation as an effective leader and Fatah's emergence as the largest and best-organized of the groups dedicated to the liberation of Palestine led, in turn, to Arafat's election, on February 3, 1969, as chairman of the executive committee of the PLO, which since its founding five years before had languished under ineffective leadership.

In the years following Arafat's elevation to PLO leader, funds began to flow into the organization's coffers, enabling it to sustain its guerrilla war against Israel. Yet its very success on the battlefield also led it to the brink of disaster. For years PLO fighters had been launching attacks on Israel from within Jordan (as they had from other Arab countries near Israel), much to the consternation of that nation's ruler, King Hussein, who was not favorably disposed to radical activity of any sort. Hussein was also troubled by the PLO's role in several hijackings involving international airlines. Then, in September 1970, tensions between the PLO and Jordanians opposed to the organization's activities erupted into civil war. Hussein responded by forcing the Palestinians to leave the country, in what became known as "Black September." Many of the fighters relocated to Lebanon, from which they continued to carry out raids on Israel. As it had in Jordan, the PLO built up a statelike apparatus within Lebanon.

Black September was also the name of a terrorist group, founded in the early 1970s, in which Arafat played an important, albeit not clearly defined, role. A series of terrorist operations conducted by the group—such as the bloody hostage drama at the 1972 Olympics in Munich—stunned the world and indelibly linked the PLO in Western minds with wanton violence. According to most sources, Arafat is thought to have lent his approval to Black September's undertakings, though he was not involved in their actual planning and execution. He also reportedly took pains to disguise the involvement of Fatah in such operations.

Although he was vilified in the Western press because of the PLO's involvement in terrorist activities, Arafat remained a respected figure in the Arab world. At an Arab summit meeting in October 1974, the assembled Arab heads of state recognized the PLO as the "sole legitimate representative" of the Palestinian people. A month later Arafat addressed the United Nations in New York City, concluding his historic speech with the words, "I have come bearing an olive branch and a freedom fighter's gun. Do not let the olive branch fall from my hand." The UN subsequently voted to grant the PLO observer status at the United Nations and formally acknowledged the Palestinians' right to self-determination. The year 1974 was also a turning point in terms of Arafat's strategy regarding his mission to reclaim Palestine for his fellow Palestinians. Previously, he had been committed to bringing about the destruction of Israel as a means to that end. But by 1974 he appeared more willing to try to reach a political settlement with the Israelis.

Meanwhile, in Lebanon, the long-simmering conflict between the country's Muslim and Christian populations, which was exacerbated by the PLO's presence there, had degenerated into sectarian violence, with the country's many militias battling one another. In 1975 the conflict erupted into civil war, and the PLO found itself mired in circumstances as bloody and disastrous as those that had nearly overwhelmed the organization several years earlier, in Jordan. For several years following Syria's invasion of the country, in 1976, the PLO remained based in Beirut, which itself had become a battleground for the warring factions. Then, in June 1982, Israel, provoked by the PLO's cross-border raids into the country, launched an all-out invasion of Lebanon with the intention of crushing the PLO. The Israelis succeeded in achieving that goal, leaving the PLO, and especially Arafat, humiliated in the eyes of the rest of the Arab world. After having been forced to flee Lebanon, Arafat returned to the country later that year, only to be pushed out once again, this time by the combined efforts of Syrian forces, dissident Palestinians, Lebanese factions, and Israelis.

The months following the PLO's expulsion from Lebanon constituted one of the bleakest periods of Arafat's tenure as the organization's chairman. Not only had the PLO lost its base of operations, but its forces were scattered throughout half a dozen Arab countries, and both Arafat and his organization found themselves unwelcome in all the states with which Israel shared a border. He thus had little choice but to reestablish PLO headquarters in Tunis, the capital of Tunisia,

whose culture and political interests were somewhat out of sync with those of the Palestinians. In 1983 Arafat also had to contend with a serious challenge to his leadership mounted by radicals within Fatah who claimed he was too willing to compromise and who remained committed to the complete liberation of Palestine from Israeli rule. Syria reportedly supported the rebels, and in June of the same year Syrian president Hafez al-Assad expelled Arafat and his supporters from the country.

A source of optimism for Arafat was the resumption in 1982 of the United States' efforts to help the Arabs and Israelis reach a negotiated settlement to their decades-old conflict. Over the next few years, Arafat and King Hussein engaged in on-again, off-again talks in which they explored the possibility of including PLO representatives on a Jordanian team in negotiations with Israel. Little of substance resulted from those talks, however. In any event, the peace process was put on hold indefinitely in December 1987, when spontaneous rioting by Palestinians broke out on the West Bank and in Gaza. The revolt shifted international attention away from the talks and onto the plight of the Palestinians inhabiting the occupied territories.

According to Andrew Gowers and Tony Walker, in *Behind the Myth: Yasir Arafat and the Palestinian Revolution*, Arafat was at first perplexed by the uprising, which soon came to be known as the *intifada* (an Arabic word meaning "shaking"), but he and the PLO soon lent it their support. Because many of the young people taking part in the *intifada* were loyal to Arafat and the Fatah faction of the PLO, the international attention that was focused on the uprising also enhanced Arafat's and the PLO's stature within both the Arab world and the West, giving both "the strength and political confidence to offer a more realistic and conciliatory plan," as Scott MacLeod observed in the *New York Review of Books*.

The plan to which MacLeod referred was the Algiers Declaration, adopted in November 1988 by the Palestine National Council, the PLO's parliament in exile, which proclaimed an independent Palestinian state on the West Bank and the Gaza Strip and implicitly recognized Israel's right to exist. Arafat went even further when, on December 13, 1988, in a speech at a special United Nations session held in Geneva, Switzerland (the United States government had refused to allow him to visit the United Nations headquarters, in New York City), he declared that the PLO renounced terrorism once and for all and that it supported "the right of all parties concerned in the Middle East conflict to live in peace and security, including the state of Palestine, Israel, and other neighbors, according to the [United Nations] Resolutions 242 and 338." These words prompted the United States to declare that it was prepared to begin a diplomatic dialogue with the PLO. By the end of the year, some 70 countries had recognized the declared Palestinian state.

However important these developments were, they turned out to be premature harbingers of peace, for the talks broke off in 1990, after the PLO refused to condemn a raid into Israel by one of its factions. Further compromising the strength of the PLO's position was the fact that it supported Iraqi president Saddam Hussein's invasion of Kuwait, which precipitated the 1991 Persian Gulf war. Arafat's decision to back Iraq turned out to be economically disastrous for the PLO, because other Arab nations, having allied themselves with the United States and many other countries in the developed world in their opposition to Hussein, stopped supplying the organization with funds. Following the Gulf war, in late 1991, the peace process was put back on track, and it lurched forward over the next two years. In August 1993 Israel for the first time accepted the participation of the PLO in peace talks, and on September 10, 1993, Arafat and Israeli leader YITZHAK RABIN exchanged letters of mutual recognition. Three days later, on the White House lawn in Washington, D.C., the two men sealed with a handshake a draft agreement, the Oslo Accords, which provided for Palestinian self-rule in Israeli-occupied Gaza and the West Bank town of Jericho and, eventually, in the rest of the West Bank. In October 1994 the Norwegian Nobel Committee awarded Arafat, Rabin, and Israeli foreign minister SHIMON PERES the Nobel Peace Prize, "for their efforts to create peace in the Middle East."

Many political experts and observers have been dubious about Arafat's ability to lead a newly independent state, hold together the various factions of the PLO, maintain popular support, and negotiate with Israel. Debating the issue in *Foreign Affairs*, Amos Perlmutter predicted that "a Palestinian state ruled by Arafat and his PLO cronies will likely be authoritarian, noninclusive, and undemocratic." Other commentators have been more sanguine, noting that no Arab regime in the Middle East is democratic. Arafat himself has said of the era to come, "This is the historical chance. If we lose it, we are criminals."

When Arafat, Rabin, and Peres were awarded the Nobel Peace Prize, it was the second time in a row that opponents had shared the prize—the others being F. W. DE KLERK and NELSON MANDELA of South Africa. In contrast to the situation in South Africa, however, the situation in Israel and Palestine was not to become stable. Although Arafat was the leader of the newly established political entity—not yet a state—in Gaza and Jericho, the assassination of Rabin in November 1995 put paid to peaceful acceptance by Israel of the Oslo Accords. Although Rabin was succeeded by Peres, the Israeli coalition government led by the Labor Party did not last, and Peres was succeeded by a right-wing Likud government in Israel, led by Benjamin Netanyahu.

Arafat triumphed handily in elections held in the West Bank and Gaza in early 1996. He was elected president of the Palestinian Authority. By the end of 1996, however, renewed violence had caused a halt in the peace process. Conflict resumed when a gate to a tunnel for tourists, which Palestinians in Jerusalem called a threat to Muslim holy sites, was reopened by Israeli authorities. Firefights broke out between Israeli soldiers and Palestinian policemen. Throughout 1996 Arafat continued to call for "mass confrontations in all cities and villages." Arafat, thus, rescued his own reputation as miltant leader, but, according to Joel Greenberg in the *New Republic*, Arafat would "still have to grapple with other Palestinian grievances, many of them economic." By December 1996 Arafat termed Israeli Prime Minister Netanyahu's decision to grant economic benefits to Jewish settlements in the West Bank a "time bomb." Tensions eased in January 1997, however, as Arafat and Netanyahu, with the assistance of King Hussein of Jordan, agreed on a plan for Israeli withdrawal from the West Bank in mid-1998.

ABOUT: Foreign Affairs July/August 1994; Gowers, A., and T. Walker. Behind the Myth: Yasir Arafat and the Palestinian Revolution, 1992; Hart, A. Arafat: A Political Biography, 1989; New Republic October 21, 1996; New York Times December 16, 1996; New York Times Magazine August 18, 1985; New Yorker May 16, 1994; Vanity Fair February 1989; Wallach, J., and J. Wallach. Arafat: In the Eyes of the Beholder, 1990.

BECKER, GARY S.
(December 2, 1930–)
Nobel Memorial Prize in Economic Sciences, 1992

Of Jewish descent, the American economist Gary Stanley Becker was born in Pottsville, Pennsylvania, one of the four children of Louis William Becker, a small business owner, and Anna Siskind Becker. Early in his life, the family moved to New York City, where he graduated from James Madison High School in Brooklyn in 1948. He continued his education at Princeton University, where he began his study of economics. The prevailing economic theories of the time did not appeal to Becker—he believed in thinking about economics not merely on an abstract level but in terms of practical applications. As he would later state on the television program *Adam Smith's Money World*, "To me, economics is not subject matter. I mean, it's not dealing with the stock market . . . economics is a way of thinking about life."

Becker graduated summa cum laude from Princeton in 1951 and enrolled in the University of Chicago for postgraduate work. There, he met several individuals who would have profound influences on his work—MILTON FRIEDMAN, Gregg Lewis, THEODORE SCHULTZ, and GEORGE STIGLER. These men were supporters of the practical application of economic theory and "were us-

GARY S. BECKER

ing economics . . . not just to talk in the abstract . . . but to discuss . . . social problems." Becker received his M A in 1953 and his Ph.D. two years later.

When Becker's doctorate work was completed, he was asked to stay on and teach in the economics department—a rare privilege at the exclusive University of Chicago. His doctoral dissertation was written under the tutelage of Professors Friedman and Lewis and was published in 1957 under the title *The Economics of Discrimination*. As stated in *Current Biography* in 1993, the book's major contribution is "to develop a theory of nonpecuniary motivation and to apply it quantitatively to discrimination in the marketplace." In this work Becker suggested that the key to comprehending racial, ethnic, or sexist discrimination is to understand how much people are willing to sacrifice in order to avoid associating with one another. Becker's research found that discrimination is a factor in the marketplace only when the markets are not fully competitive. In a 1993 interview for *Modern Maturity*, he pointed out that "every time I discriminate—if I decline to hire a black and instead hire a white, when they're equally productive but the black is cheaper—I'm losing. I'm [paying] . . . 30 percent [more in wages] to exercise my prejudice. If other people don't have prejudice, they can drive me out by hiring that person and producing goods more cheaply than I do."

In 1957 Becker began his study on the economics of education. He collected data from the United States Bureau of the Census on the incomes of people with varying educational backgrounds and compared it with data from the Federal Office of Education on the exact costs of education. He reasoned that "if education were economically important . . . money rates of return on education ought to be significant." From this modest beginning, he moved into the study of investment in general. In 1962 he partially unveiled his work in an essay for a supplement to the *Journal of Political Economy*. Two years later he published his full analysis in the book *Human Capital*, which the Royal Swedish Academy cited as being his "most noteworthy contribution." In that book, Becker defined human capital as "the skills, the training of individuals . . . the factors that make them more productive in an economy." While he supported the idea that the United States has one of the finest educational systems in the world, he expressed concern for the students of the inner cities who do not excel in school and who, after graduation, usually become part of the lowest quarter of the labor force. Becker proposed that the United States set up a "voucher system for low-end students to let them go to any public or private school that meets certain standards," and also he suggested . . . "an on-the-job training program so students . . . can become productive workers and earn good pay."

In 1968 Becker continued to break with traditional economic thought. He began his analysis on criminal behavior using the principle that people generally act rationally and that, in order to get people to behave correctly, society has to provide the right incentives. With this in mind, he explored the idea that economics have an effect on crime—at a time when most thinkers were focusing on the social causes of crime. He published an article entitled "Crime and Punishment: An Economic Approach," outlining his theories. Becker concluded that a person who commits a crime does so based on a rational decision. The criminal rationally weighs the possibility of getting away with the crime, considers if he or she will get caught and what the punishment will be, and then acts accordingly. Becker has said: "Crime can be deterred by raising the number of police, by increasing the likelihood of conviction, and by punishing criminals more severely."

In 1971 Becker published *Economic Theory*. Three years later he and William M. Landes edited *Essays in the Economics of Crime and Punishment*. Becker's own essay "Crime and Punishment" was among the pieces he brought together in the 1976 volume *The Economic Approach to Human Behavior*. In another essay in this book, "A Theory to the Allocation of Time," Becker departed from the "traditional economic interpretation of the secular decline in hours worked" and instead put forth his assumption that "households are producers as well as consumers."

The book also included his essay "A Theory on Marriage," which suggested that the motivations people have for getting married or divorced can be broken down into quantitative factors—costs and benefits. If it is more beneficial for a couple to stay together, they do so, and if not, they divorce. As Becker wrote, "Why should a couple who don't like each other stay together when they have 30 or 40 years still ahead of them?"

In 1981 Becker published *A Treatise on the Family*, which further explored the changes in marriage and families in the previous hundred years. This book took into consideration the emergence of women into the work force and the increase in divorce rates over the previous few decades. Becker's conclusions were that families have to be productive units in order to stay together. "Marriage, by this logic, is the union of productive factors in which the quantity and type of labor performed by each partner would be determined by economic incentives." The children of any marriage are both goods and potential workers. Parents use the notions of cost and benefit to decide how many children to have and how well to treat them. Also, Becker theorized that the modern family does not have a great deal of time—often, both parents work in order to provide for their children. Education and day care are costly. While, as Becker believes, parents "maximize their well-being, which is affected by children," they may not necessarily want to have more children. Instead, they invest their existing time and resources in fewer children to provide them with better care. This, he concluded, helps to explain the large decline in birth rates in the industrialized world.

Becker, while still a professor of economics and sociology, began writing a column, in rotation with several other economists, for *Business Week* in 1985. His columns have focused on the themes of his life's work, such as deterring crime by increasing the number of police on the streets and imposing harsher prison sentences, and using voucher systems in education to stimulate competition between public and private schools. He has also supported the idea of making prenuptial agreements, easing unemployment by relaxing the minimum wage under certain conditions, and making welfare payments dependent upon such criteria as parents' seeing to it that their children regularly attend school. He has suggested transferring ownership of public housing to the residents of the apartments and charging immigration fees to eliminate possible welfare burdens from abroad.

In 1992 Becker was awarded the Nobel Memorial Prize in Economic Sciences, which carried a stipend of $1.2 million. Becker was the sixth professor from the University of Chicago to receive the prize—two others are his mentors, George Stigler and Milton Friedman. Friedman, upon hearing of Becker's award, stated: "I know of no other economist who comes close to the range of Becker's work."

Since 1992 Becker has been immersed in a study of addictions, including alcohol, nicotine and drug addiction. The subject has been of great interest to him, particularly since he believes that people tend to act rationally and in their best interests. "[Addiction is] so contrary to rational behavior that I wanted to see if we could construct a rational model," he has stated. His work has suggested that economics play a part in ad-

diction. "Would smokers respond if the cost of cigarettes went up?" The results of his study on cigarette addiction were published in *The American Economic Review* in 1994. The article "An Empirical Analysis of Cigarette Addiction," cowritten with Michael Grossman and Kevin M. Murphy, found that a 10 percent increase in the cost of cigarettes reduced the current consumption rate by 7.5 percent in the long run and 4 percent in the short run. In effect, Becker's study showed that there is a rational side to addiction when economics play a factor. This study also demonstrated that, regardless of the federal excise tax that is periodically placed on tobacco products, the tobacco industry itself raised cigarette prices through the 1980s. In a truly competitive environment, this would not be the case—cigarette prices would have to maintain the highest quality at the lowest price. Such pricing, however, is consistent with the monopoly status of the tobacco companies, suggesting that if smoking is addictive and prices are going up, the industry has to increase prices in a faltering market in order to maintain a profit.

Becker has supported the legalization of marijuana, for economic reasons. If marijuana were legalized, Becker argues, the black-market crime surrounding it would diminish. He believes that if the government were to legalize drugs in general, "You would reduce crime, both among criminals—drug dealers shoot each other—and among users, who commit crimes to finance their habits."

Since President Bill Clinton took office in January 1993, Becker, in his column for *Business Week*, has been one of his chief critics in the economics field, writing pieces that appear below with such headlines as "Clinton's Student-Loan Plan Deserves an 'F'" and "The Spending Monster Still Has Too Long A Leash." In an August 1996 column, Becker supported Senator Bob Dole's economic plan. Part of the platform of his 1996 presidential campaign, Dole's plan called for scholarship programs that would enable students in poorer families to attended either private or parochial schools. The plan also suggested tax incentives for companies for the training or retraining of employees. Becker wrote that this approach was " a simple implication of elementary economics taught to freshmen: that powerful changes in incentives have powerful effects on behavior."

From his marriage to Doria Slate, who is now deceased, Becker has two daughters, Judith Sarah and Catherine Jean. In 1979 he married Guity Nashat, a professor of history, with whom he has two sons, Michael Claffey and Cyrus Claffey.

Since 1983, Gary S. Becker has served as University Professor in the Economics Department at the University of Chicago, and he is a senior fellow at the Hoover Institute in Stanford, California. In Chicago, he maintains associate membership in the Economics Research

Center at the National Opinion Research Center. He is an associate member of Japan's Institute of Fiscal and Monetary Policy. He was awarded the University of Michigan's W. S. Woytinsky Award in 1967. In the same year he received the John Bates Clark Medal. He also holds numerous honorary doctorates.

SELECTED WORKS: The Economics of Discrimination, 1957; Human Capital: A Theoretical and Empirical Analysis, 1964; Economic Theory, 1971; The Economic Approach to Human Behavior, 1976; A Treatise on the Family, 1981.

ABOUT: New York Times October 14, 1992; Modern Maturity August/September 1993; Current Biography Yearbook 1993.

BELO, CARLOS FELIPE XIMENES
(February 3, 1948–   )
Nobel Prize for Peace, 1996 (shared with Jose Ramos-Horta)

CARLOS FELIPE XIMENES BELO

The fifth child of Domingos Vaz Felipe and Ermelinda Baptista Felipe, the East Timorese bishop and peace advocate Carlos Felipe Ximenes Belo was born in Wailakama, a village in Vemasse, Baucau, East Timor, then a Portuguese colony. His father, a local schoolteacher, died when Belo was only two years old. Accounts of Belo's childhood and adolescence are, at best, sketchy. It is known that he attended missionary schools in and around Baucau and Dili, East Timor's capital city. He is a devotee of Western classical music and soccer.

In 1973 Belo went to Portugal to study philosophy at Lisbon's Instituto Superior de Estudios Teologicos. It was during this time that he opted to devote his life to religion. After becoming a member of the Salesian Order of the Roman Catholic Church, Belo returned to his home country for a brief teaching stint at Fatumaca College, a Salesian school near Baucau. Upon returning to Lisbon, he studied theology at the Universidade Catolica Portuguesa. He then traveled to Italy to attend the Salesian Pontifical University in Rome, where he received his bachelor's degree in theology. In 1980, Belo was ordained a Catholic priest, and in the following year he again returned to his homeland, to accept a position on the staff of Fatumaca College.

At the time, East Timor was in the midst of a great political and social turmoil, an upheaval that continues to this day. Located in the Indian Ocean on the outskirts of the Indonesian archipelago, the island of Timor has, throughout the ages, undergone change at the hands of various foreign powers. In the 16th and 17th centuries, the Portuguese and Dutch settled the island and divided it in half, with the Portuguese claiming East Timor and the western half of the island becoming a Dutch colony. During World War II the island was host to numerous bloody clashes between Australian and Japanese forces. "We knew misery in the early part of this century, when Portugal cruelly put down a nationalist rebellion. Then came a harsh occupation by Japanese troops . . . when our people paid a severe price for helping Allied forces survive: More than one-tenth of the population . . . perished as a result," Belo wrote in a 1996 New York Times Op-Ed piece.

In 1949 the Netherlands transferred its portion of Timor to Indonesia. A left-wing coup in Lisbon in 1974 resulted in the abandoning of Portugal's various overseas colonies in favor of concentrating on matters closer to home. In the following year, the Portuguese withdrew all troops from East Timor, where a bloody civil war immediately erupted.

At the forefront of East Timor's civil war was the extreme left-wing Revolutionary Front for the Independent East Timor, more commonly known by its Portuguese acronym, Fretilin. Fretilin members, including JOSE RAMOS-HORTA, the man who would one day share the Nobel Peace Prize with Belo, overtook the capital and declared themselves the leaders of the new government of East Timor in November 1975. In the ensuing fighting, Fretilin was responsible for the deaths of members of the four opposing political parties. Indonesia, still wary after a 1965 incident in which its own government was nearly taken over by Communist rebels and fearful of the consequences of a radical left-wing government so close to its borders, invaded East Timor in December 1975. Fretilin leaders, knowing they could not match forces with Indonesian troops, fled the country. In 1976, despite a United Nations request for the withdrawal of troops, the Indonesian government annexed East Timor and declared it Indonesia's 27th province.

Indonesian rule of East Timor only added to the torrent of rage and bloodshed produced by the recent civil war. East Timor's population, of which some 95 percent are Roman Catholics, deeply resented being subjected to the rule of the world's most populous Muslim nation. Within the first five years of Indonesian occupation, between 150,000 and 200,000 of East Timor's estimated 750,000 residents died in the fighting between East Timorese resistance movements and Indonesian forces. Belo, with other East Timorese, has accused Indonesia of numerous human-rights atrocities. In a 1989 statement demanding the end of such violations of human rights, Belo said that interrogations by Indonesian soldiers "accompanied by blows, kickings and beatings" were "the norm in Timor." Additionally, Belo said in a 1993 interview with the *New York Times* that the citizens of East Timor live in constant fear. "We lack the freedom to speak, to walk where we want, to have different opinions. If people talk, they know they will be interrogated. They will be tortured."

His politics notwithstanding, Belo rose in the hierarchy of the Catholic Church. In 1983, the Vatican appointed Belo apostolic administrator of the Dili Diocese, making him the virtual leader of the Catholic church in his homeland. In June 1988 Belo was ordained as a bishop, while continuing to hold his position as apostolic administrator. "I am fully aware of the norms of the Roman Catholic Church, which demands that its religious leaders refrain from activity specific to the field of politicians," he wrote in the *New York Times* in 1996. "But as a bishop I have the moral duty to speak for the poor and simple people who, intimidated and terrorized, cannot defend themselves or make their suffering known."

Belo used his authority and prestige to support traditional East Timorese culture. Rather than conducting religious ceremonies in Bahasa Indonesia, the official language of Indonesia, Belo continued to use Tetum, the East Timorese language, and Portuguese rather than the language used by the Indonesians.

An advocate of social justice, Belo has worked toward improving conditions in East Timor, which, with a per capita income of only $125 per year, remains the poorest province of Indonesia. He initiated the building of numerous secondary schools around the island and set up a system of parish-based clinics that provide basic medical care. Under Belo's guidance, a new seminary and multiple orphanages to house the many East Timorese children left parentless by the country's unrest have been built. To those who claim that Indonesia's developmental impetus has increased East Timor's prosperity, Belo is reported to have responded, "Who is this development for? . . . Not us, the Timorese. It is for the immigrants they are bringing in." Belo was referring to the Indonesian influx into East Timor. He added that the "so-called development" was being used "to change our society, to destroy it."

The combination of Belo's great popularity among the Timorese people, his noted diplomatic skills, and his fluency in a variety of languages, including Tetum, Portuguese, Bahasa Indonesia, English, and Italian, has led to Belo's being called upon to negotiate the end of clashes between the Indonesian military and the Timorese. "He could have stayed outside the country, but he has put his neck on the line and stayed," said Arnold S. Kohen, a journalist and consultant to the United States Catholic Conference on issues involving East Timor, in an interview with the *New York Times*. "He has constantly risked his life—constantly."

Indeed, risking his life has become somewhat commonplace for Belo. In 1991, after the massacre of as many as 200 East Timorese civilians in a Dili cemetery, Belo soundly denounced the Indonesian government. He told the *New York Times* in 1993 that he had proof that several protestors taken into custody on that day were later murdered by Indonesian soldiers. The prisoners, he said, were put to death "with big stones and with iron bars and with injections of a special substance that killed them." Belo added that although the Indonesian army did punish some perpetrators of the massacre, "the behavior is still the same. . . . We know that in the prisons here in Dili all of the political prisoners are tortured." He described prisoners' being dunked in "tubs of water until they nearly drown," burnings with cigarettes, and the psychological torture of mock executions. Belo's willingness to speak out against Indonesia has exacted a great toll. He has survived two assassination attempts, in 1989 and 1991. He is under daily surveillance by Indonesian police. His trips abroad are restricted, and the Indonesian government considered taking action to bar Belo from traveling to Oslo to accept the Nobel Prize, or refusing him a visa that would allow his return to East Timor.

Belo's nomination for a Nobel Prize was supported by several prominent figures, including Archbishop DESMOND TUTU and the Irish human-rights activist Maired Maguaire. In 1996 Belo received the Nobel Prize for Peace. He shared the prize, along with the $1.1 million monetary award, with East Timorese activist Jose Ramos-Horta. The academy praised the pair for their "sustained and self-sacrificing contributions for a small but oppressed people." Belo, who received the news of his award while saying Mass in Dili, said it was an honor that should be shared by all the people of East Timor. "It honors all of those who work for peace, for reconciliation, for openness and for the defense of human rights," he said in a statement issued the day he received the prize.

ABOUT: East Timor Estafeta November 3, 1996; New York Times January 2, 1989, April 21, 1993, November 22, 1994, October 12, 1996, November 19, 1996, December 10, 1996; Royal Swedish Academy of Sciences 1996 Nobel Prize Announcement; Time October 21, 1996.

BROCKHOUSE, BERTRAM N.

(July 15, 1918–   )
Nobel Prize for Physics, 1994 (shared with Clifford G. Shull)

The quoted material that follows was taken from the autobiography of Bertram Brockhouse, as it appeared in *Les Prix Nobel* in 1994.

Bertram Neville Brockhouse was born in Lethbridge, Alberta, Canada, the son of Israel Bertram Brockhouse, who had settled with the rest of his family in Alberta in 1910, and Mable Emily (Neville) Brockhouse. Brockhouse's family included a sister, Alice Evelyn, and two brothers: Robert Paul, who died in infancy, and Gordon Edgar, who later became a railroad civil engineer. Some of Brockhouse's earliest memories are of the farm, near Milk River, where his family lived. In the winter of 1926–1927, the Brockhouse family moved to Vancouver, British Columbia, the city in which he spent the remainder of his childhood.

Before the family moved to Vancouver, Brockhouse had attended school somewhat irregularly in a one-room schoolhouse near the family's farm. However, when he attended elementary school, and later King George High School, he received a "good basic education" and generally found the experience enjoyable, excepting some problems which came from the fact that—despite his formerly spotty school attendance— he was more academically advanced than most of the children his age. He has cited these early school years as having a great influence on him. He has also credited his older cousin Wilbert B. Smith with contributing to an early interest he had in radio.

With the onset of the Great Depression in 1929, the family faced serious financial problems. Brockhouse delivered newspapers through most of his teens to help make ends meet. In 1935 the family was forced to move again, this time to Chicago, hoping that they could better their situation. By this time, Brockhouse had graduated from high school and was attending night classes at Central YMCA College (now Roosevelt University). At that time, as he explained: "I was interested in the technical aspects of radio and learned to repair and design and build them. This and my facility with mathematics were, I suppose, what pointed me eventually in the direction of physics." For part of the time that the family was in Chicago, he worked in a small electronics firm called Aubert Controls Corporation, but the company went bankrupt in 1937, and in the next year the family returned to Vancouver. In Chicago, Brockhouse had begun to repair radios as a small side business, a practice he continued in Vancouver.

As he wrote in his autobiography, something else had begun to interest him in Chicago. "I had always been interested in politics, but now I began to take part as an active member of the leftist party of the era . . .

BERTRAM N. BROCKHOUSE

and continued for many years, in fact until I became an employee of the Dominion Government in the shape of the Chalk River Laboratory . . . I was profoundly antitotalitarian and hence anti-Communist, so that when World War II erupted I was motivated from many sides to join the military."

In September 1939 he joined the Royal Canadian Navy with the idea of becoming a radio telegrapher. He spent several months at sea as a radio operator; most of his six years in the navy, however, were spent servicing equipment at a shore base. In 1944 he enrolled in a six-month course in electrical engineering at Nova Scotia Technical College. While still in the navy, he was appointed to the test facilities at the National Research Council in Ottawa. In Ottawa, he met Doris Miller, who would later become his wife.

When the war ended in August 1945, the Department of Veterans' Affairs was ready to provide returning servicemen with a number of options: money for a small land-holding or training or education. Brockhouse enrolled immediately at the University of British Columbia, wanting to study physics and mathematics. He recalled: "The university life was probably not typical because many of us were older than would normally have been the case. It was not all study; I operated also a (very) small business which eased our financial problems, and I owned a motorcycle for transportation and enjoyment."

Brockhouse completed his B.A. in April 1947 and traveled to Ottawa to his new summer job in the National Research Council in the laboratory of the electronics standards section. In that summer he and Doris were formally engaged; they were married in May of the next year. Also in 1948, Brockhouse completed his master's degree in solid state physics at the Low Temperature Laboratory of the University of Toronto. He planned on continuing his education. "Being already 29 years of age, I was very anxious to embark on my physics career . . . I started work under the guidance of Professors Hugh Grayson-Smith and James Reekie on the effects of stress and temperature on ferromagnetism and finished a master's program in the then normal period of eight months."

For most of the summer of 1948, Brockhouse and his wife lived in Ottawa. Doris worked as a film technician at the National Film Board while Brockhouse worked as a summer student in the acoustics section of the National Research Council. A phase of Brockhouse's life was now complete, the "more passive phase" of his education, and he looked forward to working on his Ph.D. The Low Temperature Laboratory at Toronto was a long-established institution and was well-equipped for the research Brockhouse had to conduct for his thesis work. Sir Edward Bullard, an expert in the Earth's magnetism, assumed leadership in the department just as Brockhouse began his doctoral toil. Brockhouse's thesis subject was an experiment in solid-state physics involving both high and low temperatures. He received his doctorate in 1950, and he was offered a position at Chalk River working in the field of nuclear energy.

In that same year, Brockhouse moved his family—then consisting of his pregnant wife and baby daughter, Ann—to Deep River. Though Brockhouse and his wife thought they would stay for only a few years before moving on, they wound up staying for 12 years and had four more children there. A main reason for this was the work that they were doing in Chalk River. As Brockhouse described, "the major advance at this time in early 1951 was the realization that phonons could be studied by studying inelastic scattering and that evocative experiments to do so might be feasible at Chalk River.

"The first actual experiments studied the scattering of neutrons by highly absorbing elements, in the process verifying the famous Breit-Wigner formula. This work . . . was done in collaboration with Myer Bloom and D. G. Hurst and was published in *Physical Review* (1951) and in the *Canadian Journal of Research* (1953). The apparatus was later much modified and used to study the inelastic scattering from several materials (aluminum, graphite and diamond) by absorption methods. This was the first quantitative experiment in slow neutron spectroscopy and was published in *Physical Review*. Other experiments by absorption methods were done at about the same time at Harwell by R. D. Lowde and P. A. Egelstaff; that by Ray Lowde was particularly significant as it went far to establish the concept 'spin wave' on a microscopic basis.

"Preparations were underway to attempt proper (differential) studies of inelastic scattering, and some almost futile attempts had been made when our work was terminated by an accident to the NRX high flux reactor, which was the source of the neutrons we used. This occurred in November 1952, and I did not resume actual experiments at NRX until the summer of 1954. Fortunately, I was invited to go to Brookhaven National Laboratory and was able to spend most of one year there with my family, returning to Deep River in February 1954. The time was very profitable for me, I worked on several experiments . . . But I did not do any spectroscopic work, though I met Donald Hughes and Harry Palevsky, now also thinking about inelastic scattering and in particular thinking about the 'Cold Neutron' or (Beryllium) Filter-Chopper method. And I met Leon Van Hove and learned about the new generalized (time-dependent) correlations which Noel K. Pope and I were later to put to good use.

"After NRX was available to us again in August 1954, things progressed rapidly . . . we had metal monochromators of greatly improved efficiency compared with the NaCl crystals which we were using in 1952. Alec T. Stewart was rapidly getting the Be/Pb Filter-Chopper apparatus together and the primitive Triple-Axis spectrometer was functioning. So I was able to present a paper with substantial (if primitive) results at the New York meeting of the American Physical Society at the end of January 1955. Publications followed soon after, in *Physical Review* and in the *Canadian Journal of Research*.

"In 1956 we were able to complete the first true Triple-Axis crystal spectrometer, though only for operation at constant incoming energy. The flexibility of operation and the accuracy of the results were both greatly improved. The 'Constant Q Method' was invented in 1958, and at about the same time new apparatus allowing operation with variable incoming energy was installed at the new high-flux reactor NRU. . . . With the considerable improvements in both the neutron flux and the operating conditions afforded by NRU, the subject entered a new phase in 1959. The Triple-Axis spectrometer thereby reached nearly full development. Visitors from other countries were now arriving to spend time working in the group. . . . From about 1958 on the interest shifted, from the neutron physics and the methods and the validity of the theory to the specific results and interpretation for the specific specimen material.

"In 1956 also Alec Stewart completed the Filter-Chopper apparatus. This was an equipment similar in general to that of Hughes and Palevsky; it was used in experiments on Aluminium and Vanadium, both chosen for the same good technical reasons that others chose to work on them. . . . I converted the instrument to the first 'Rotating Crystal Spectrometer'. . . . This instrument was used principally to study liquids and polycrystals, as was its improved successor at the NRU reactor.

"Three other major technological initiatives were taken. Filters of (large, perfect) single-crystals (quartz), preferably cooled to low temperatures, enabled major improvement in the ratio of slow neutrons to fast in the primary beam and thus in the signal to background ratio. The 'Beryllium-Detector' method was developed by enabling the Triple-Axis spectrometer to accept Beryllium polycrystalline filters in the scattered beam and thus, with incoming neutrons of variable energy, to get energy distributions in a different and sometimes advantageous manner—an inverse of the Filter-Chopper method. Finally profitable uses of the new material, pyrolitic graphite, were found as filters and as crude monochromators."

Because of this work, Brockhouse was invited to give lectures around the world. In 1957 he made his first trips to England and then Europe, speaking at many conferences and seminars. In October 1960 he returned to Europe to give lectures at two scientific conferences in Vienna. One of these was the first Conference on Inelastic Scattering, and his lecture helped the development of that branch of physics.

In 1958 Brockhouse's research group was joined by A. D. B. (David) Woods, who for a time became his closest collaborator. Four years later, however, Brockhouse left the group after taking a position as a physics professor at McMaster University in Hamilton, Ontario. Now that the research program he had helped to found was well established, he wanted to take up a university position, which had been his intention for some time, and McMaster had a swimming-pool reactor which made his transition easier in regards to research. While teaching at McMaster, he still had ties with Chalk River because, according to Brockhouse, "the Laboratory facilitated our transfer and encouraged my plans to continue a research program based at McMaster and to use the reactor there for training students and preliminary work on experiments to be carried out at Chalk River. This arrangement was, I think, very successful. . . . At McMaster a talented group of students put together a neutron diffractometer and a Triple-Axis instrument, and these were available from 1965 on—and indeed are still in use. For the first years we used the existing equipment at Chalk River, but about 1971 we installed our own spectrometer at NRU, and the smaller group now working with me used it (as did others) until I completely left neutron scattering about 1979."

During the 1970s Brockhouse realigned his intellectual interests, exploring different avenues. One was what he termed the "philosophy of physics." Another was a consideration of energy supply, economics, and the related ethical ramifications. Very little of this work was made public. In 1984 Brockhouse retired from teaching at McMaster University after 22 years. Exactly a decade later, he and his fellow physicist CLIFFORD G. SHULL of the Massachusetts Institute of

Technology were presented with the Nobel Prize for Physics by the Royal Swedish Academy of Sciences. Other than the Nobel Prize, Brockhouse has received numerous awards and distinctions for his work over the years. In 1962 he was made a fellow of the Royal Society of Canada and received the Oliver S. Buckley Prize of the American Physical Society. In 1965 he became a fellow of the Royal Society of London. He received an achievement award from the Canadian Association of Physics and the Centennial Medal of Canada in 1967, and he was presented with the Tory Medal of the Royal Society of Canada in 1973. He has been given a number of honorary doctorates from various universities, including the University of Waterloo in 1969. He has published more than 90 articles, mostly pertaining to neutron physics.

From his 1948 marriage to Doris Miller, Brockhouse has six children: Ann, Gordon, Ian, James, Alice, and Charles. Brockhouse and his wife also have eight grandchildren.

ABOUT: Les Prix Nobel, 1994.

CHARPAK, GEORGES
(August 1, 1924–   )
Nobel Prize for Physics, 1992

The French scientist Georges Charpak was born in Dabrovica, Poland, to Anna Szapiro and Maurice Charpak. The family moved to France when Charpak was seven. Charpak began his education in France at the Lycee Saint-Louis in Paris, just before the start of World War II. During the war, he attended the Lycee de Montpellier for a time, before joining the French resistance. In 1943 he was imprisoned by the Nazi-controlled Vichy authorities and was consequently deported to the German concentration camp at Dachau. When the camp was liberated by the Allied forces in 1945, Charpak went back to school, this time at the Ecole des Mines de Paris. In 1946 he became a naturalized French citizen. Two years later, he graduated from the Ecole des Mines with a bachelor's degree in science.

He then attended the College de France to work on his Ph.D. in physics. While studying there, he also worked at the Centre National de la Recherche Scientifique (CNRS), in the laboratory of FRÉDÉRIC JOLIOT. He began his work as a graduate student for Joliot, according to Physics Today, by building nuclear particle detectors. In an interview with the New York Times, Charpak explained how he became interested in this work, for which he would win the Nobel Prize: "I got into the habit of building my own instruments. We didn't have very many instruments back then, so we had to make them, even though I was not very good at it. But at least if something went wrong I knew why and could get others to help me fix it." From 1950 to 1954, Charpak worked on perturbing electron shells

GEORGES CHARPAK

by using beta radioactivity. By the time he finished that work, he had received his Ph.D. in experimental nuclear physics from the College de France.

Starting in 1956, Charpak spent about a year trying to perfect the world's first fully functioning spark chamber. At that time, bubble chambers were the predominant instruments for studying particles. *Science* described bubble chambers as "tanks full of superheated liquid hydrogen, which form a telltale trail of bubbles wherever a particle streaks through." According to *Physics Today*: "Bubble chambers produced beautiful pictures with superb spatial resolution. But they had two serious limitations: they couldn't be triggered on promising events, and their output was in the form of photographs. The only way to find interesting collisions was to look through thousands of pictures by eye." Another limitation was that the bubble chamber could only take one picture per second, greatly limiting the amount of specific information a scientist could look for. Charpak sought to find a better way of observing interesting particle collisions. Spark chambers, though they relied on photographs, had a microsecond of memory which enabled the device to decide, "on the basis of signals from scintillation counters as in radioactive emissions," whether or not something was worth recording.

Charpak did not become the inventor of the spark chamber. That distinction went to Shuji Fukui and S. Miyamoto of Japan in 1958. In that same year, Charpak went to work for LEON M. LEDERMAN at the European Organization for Nuclear Research (CERN) in Geneva, who suggested that he work on the first precise measurement of the magnetic moment to the muon— an unstable particle that exists in both positive

and negative forms. Begrudgingly, Charpak did so, abandoning his research on spark chambers. Lederman related a comical story to *Physics Today* about how "one day a few months later [Charpak] came storming in, waving these beautiful spark chamber pictures Fukui had just published. From then on he always blamed me for having stopped him from inventing the spark chamber." Charpak confirmed his mentor's story, adding: "But of course it was in jest."

Still at CERN between 1962 and 1967, he invented several types of spark chambers that recorded particle activity without the use of photography. They, too, had their drawbacks. According to the *Larousse Dictionary of Scientists*, it was Charpak who, in early 1968, created a wire proportional chamber for particle detectors, using a multiwire system. This meant that large-area detectors could be built at a smaller expense than before. Single-wire proportional chambers had been around for quite some time but had long been considered obsolete, even by Charpak's own high-energy physics group. Recalling that he had built single-wire proportional chambers for his thesis experiment in Joliot's lab, he set out to build a multiwire proportional chamber. Armed with this knowledge, something that most high-energy physicists didn't possess, he began his work. One of the first things Charpak did in building his device was to replace the camera with a gas-filled chamber "containing a network of closely spaced charged wires linked to amplifiers and recorders." This chamber tracked both the paths and the energies of charged particles that spray out from a collision, but did so considerably faster than any other device. It allowed researchers, according to *Science News*, "to pinpoint individual particle trajectories with improved precision while handling hundreds of thousands of such events per second. Thus researchers could sift through billions of interactions to focus on rare but particularly interesting examples of exotic particles." *Computers in Physics* cited the fact that Charpak's multiwire chamber records up to 1 million tracks per second with accuracy. It then sends the data directly to a computer for analysis.

All particle detectors since that time have in one way or the other descended from Charpak's original model. The *New York Times* has suggested that his wire chamber helped to capture two Nobel Prizes in the 1970s and 1980s, contributing as it did to the discoveries of the charm quark and the W and Z particles. The *Science* reporter theorized that "if more particles are waiting to be discovered in the next generation of accelerators . . . they'll likely be detected by variants of Charpak's original invention."

In 1974 Charpak used another type of detection chamber—a drift chamber—to measure the spherical drift in the study of protein structure by X ray diffraction. In 1978 he channeled high-energy particles in crystals at the University of Aarhus. He spent the next

12 years developing avalanche multistep chambers for the study of particles, including luminous avalanche chambers. From 1985 to 1991, he concerned himself with moving his work from the world of high-energy physics to biological research. He had single-handedly weaned physics from its need for photographic results and iniciated the use of particle detectors, and he wanted to do the same for biology. "Open any biological journal," *Science* quoted Charpak as saying, and "you see all these ugly pictures obtained with film. Why? Because we physicists haven't given biologists a detector that can localize electrons."

Since winning the Nobel Prize for Physics in 1992, Charpak has attempted to give biologists just such a detector. According to the Agence France Presse, Charpak has indeed succeeded in creating a new detector for biological uses: the staff at Saint Vincent de Paul Hospital in Paris call it the Charpak system. As of 1996, the equipment was being evaluated. Its supporters believe that "patients will be subject to 100 fewer X rays than before. The system also increases the amount of information conveyed by the image and provides direct digital acquisition." It scans though slices of anatomy at varying speeds, depending on the physical depth of the area being scanned. The Charpak system has only one drawback—a patient can be scanned only in a standing position, which poses a problem for invalids or unconscious individuals. A table that will not interfere with the workings of the detector is currently in development.

Finally, because of the sheer amount of information that passes through all of Charpak's various detectors, he has, indirectly, helped the intergration of computers into the data-acquisition process and also helped the memory capacity of computers themselves. According to *Computers in Physics*, "it is estimated . . . that at the Superconducting Super Collider some 40 trillion bytes of information per second will flow out of the detector monitoring the proton-proton interactions taking place."

Charpak has received many awards from all over the world. In 1977 he received an honorary degree from the University of Geneva. Three years later, he was given the Paul Ricard Prize of the French Society of Physics, and in 1985 he became a member of the French Academy of Sciences. He became a foreign associate of the National Academy of Sciences of the United States of America in the following year and a member of Austria's Academy of Sciences in 1993. He visited Canada in October 1994 to deliver a lecture in Ottawa. When he returned a year later, he was made an honorary doctor of the University of Ottawa. For the occasion, he sponsored a Canada-Israel research grant, created by the French embassy. In 1995, he also became a corresponding member of the Lisboa Academy of Sciences.

ABOUT: Agence France Press November 1996; Computers in Physics September/October 1992; International Who's Who 1996-97; Larousse Dictionary of Scientists, 1994; New York Times October 15, 1992; Physics Today January 1993; Science October 23, 1992; Science News October 24, 1992.

CRUTZEN, PAUL
(December 3, 1933–)
Nobel Prize for Chemistry, 1995 (shared with Mario J. Molina and F. Sherwood Rowland)

The Dutch chemist Paul Josef Crutzen was born in Amsterdam to Jozef Crutzen, a waiter, and the former Anna Gurk. In an autobiographical statement for *Nobel Prize Winners*, Crutzen wrote: "My six years of elementary school largely overlapped with the Second World War. Our elementary school class had to move between different premises in Amsterdam after the German army had confiscated our original school building." He added that "normal school education only became possible again with the start of the new school year in the fall of 1945." For his five years of middle school, Crutzen attended the Hoger Burger School (HBS), which prepared him for University entrance. He finished middle school in 1951 with natural sciences as his focal subjects. Unfortunately, a "heavy" fever during the final exam period at HBS kept Crutzen from qualifying for a university stipend and led him instead to attend Middlebare Technische School (MTS) to train as a civil engineer. Crutzen recalled that "although the MTS took three years, the second year was a practical year during which we earned a modest salary, enough to live for about two years. From the summer of 1954 until February 1958, with a 21-month interruption for compulsory military service in the Netherlands, I worked at the Bridge Construction Bureau of the City of Amsterdam." During this period Crutzen met Terttu Soininen, who became his wife in February 1958. They settled in Gavle, a little town about 200 kilometers (120 miles) north of Stockholm, where Crutzen found a job in a building-construction bureau. Their first child, Ilona, was born there in December 1958. In March 1964, the Crutzens had another daughter, Sylvia.

Crutzen recalled that "all this time I had longed for an academic career." The chance came in the beginning of 1958, when he applied for an opening for a computer programmer at the Department of Meteorology of Stockholm Hogskola. At this time, the Meteorology Institute of Stockholm University (MISU) and the associated International Meteorological Institute (IMI) were at the forefront of meteorological research. "The great advantage of being at a university department was that I got the opportunity to follow some of the lecture courses that were offered at the university. By 1963, I could thus fulfill the requirement for the *filosofie kandidat* (corresponding roughly to a master

PAUL CRUTZEN

of science) degree, combining the subjects mathematics, mathematical statistics, and meteorology." Crutzen added that "being employed at the meteorological research institute, it was quite natural to take a meteorological topic for my *filosofie licentiat* thesis (comparable to a Ph.D thesis). Originally, further work on the further development of a numerical model of a tropical cyclone had been proposed to me. However, around 1965 I was given the task of helping a scientist from the U.S. to develop a numerical model of the oxygen allotrope distribution in the stratosphere, mesosphere, and lower thermosphere. This project got me highly interested in the photochemistry of atmospheric ozone, and I started an intensive study of the scientific literature. This gave me an understanding of the status of scientific knowledge about stratospheric chemistry by the latter half of the 1960s, thus setting the 'initial conditions' for my scientific career. I preferred research on stratospheric chemistry, which was generously accepted. At that time the main topics of research at the Meteorological Institute at the University of Stockholm were dynamics, cloud physics, the carbon cycle, studies of the chemical composition of rainwater, and especially the 'acid rain' problem which was largely 'discovered' at MISU through the work of Svante Oden and Erik Eriksson." Although acid rain was being examined in depth at the institute, Crutzen was not interested in the issue. Rather, he "wanted to do pure science related to natural processes." Therefore he picked the stratospheric ozone as his subject.

Ozone, first noted in 1840 by the German chemist Friedrich Schonbein, is created above 12.4 miles, when shortwave solar radiation is absorbed by molecular oxygen (O_2). The process of absorption causes the dissociation of molecular oxygen into two oxygen atoms (O), which then mostly recombine with other molecular oxygen, yielding ozone (O_3). Ozone can also be created through electrical discharges in molecular oxygen or in air. The first estimates of the level of ozone in the atmosphere were obtained in 1913, and by 1930 the first systematic global observations of ozone were begun. These observations soon revealed the vital nature that ozone plays in keeping the planet habitable. By absorbing solar ultraviolet radiation before it reaches the ground, ozone helps to protect humans from DNA damage that can lead to skin cancer, cataracts, and injury to the immune system. At the equator, where the ozone layer is thinnest, the greater amount of short-wavelength light that reaches the Earth's surface is believed to account for the high incidence of skin cancer there. The presence of ozone is also indispensable to the existence of all forms of plant and animal life.

In his *filosofie licentiat* thesis of 1968 (he was awarded his doctorate degree five years later), Crutzen discarded earlier theories regarding stratospheric ozone chemistry by concluding that at least part of the solution to the problem of the ozone distribution might be the introduction of additional photochemical processes not yet discovered. He noted that "the influence of nitrogen compounds on the photochemistry of the ozone layer should be investigated." Crutzen was able to confirm his thoughts about the potential role of nitrogen compounds in stratospheric chemistry after he joined the Department of Atmospheric Physics at the Claredon Laboratory of Oxford University as a post-doctoral fellow of the European Space Research Organization. The head of the research group, Dr. John Houghton, after hearing about Crutzen's idea on the potential role of nitrogen compounds, handed him a solar spectrum taken on board a balloon by Dr. David Murcray and coworkers at the University of Denver. After some analysis of the solar spectrum, Crutzen was able to derive the approximate levels of stratospheric HNO_3, including a rough idea of its vertical distributions. According to Crutzen, "with this information, I knew that NOx should also be present in the stratosphere." This, in turn, gave him the confidence to submit his paper on catalytic ozone destruction by NO and NO_2. In a paper submitted in 1970, Crutzen showed how the balance of the ozone layer, created naturally through the interaction of sunlight with oxygen, was being destroyed by nitrogen oxides that react chemically with ozone. In addition, he showed the link between the thickness of the ozone layer and chemicals released by bacteria in the soil, indicating that Earth operates as a system in which ocean, air, and land are all tied together.

Although Crutzen's finding was not generally accepted for a decade, it helped pave the way for research by MARIO J. MOLINA and F. SHERWOOD ROWLAND, which showed how depletion of the global ozone shield by human-made chemicals such as chloroflouro-carbons (CFCs) was theoretically possible. In its citation, the Royal Swedish Academy said that the work by Crutzen, Molina, and Rowland has "contributed to our salvation from a global environmental problem that could have catastrophic consequences." The academy added that largely because of the three scientists, "it has been possible to make far-reaching decisions on prohibiting the release of gases that destroy ozone." In response to their findings, and to the discovery of a hole in the ozone layer above Antarctica, the United States and 70 other countries signed the Montreal Protocol to phase out synthetic CFC gases by the year 2000. The Nobel Prize awarded to Crutzen and his colleagues was the first given for work on a specific environmental problem.

Crutzen is a member of the Royal Swedish Academy of Sciences, the Royal Swedish Academy of Engineering Sciences, and Academia Europaea.

ABOUT: New York Times October 12, 1995, October 15, 1995.

CURL, ROBERT F., JR.
(August 23, 1933–   )
Nobel Prize for Chemistry, 1996 (shared with Harold W. Kroto and Richard E. Smalley)

The American chemist Robert Floyd Curl Jr. was born in Alice, Texas, the second child of Robert Curl, a Methodist minister, and Lessie (Merritt) Curl. Because of his father's vocation, the Curl family was forced to relocate several times throughout Curl's childhood and adolescence. He lived in a succession of mostly small towns in southwest Texas: Alice, Brady, San Antonio, Kingsville, Del Rio, Brownsville, McAllen, Austin, then back to San Antonio.

In an autobiographical sketch submitted for use in *Nobel Prize Winners*, Curl described himself as a child who was a "not particularly able but fairly hardworking student." When he was nine years old, his parents gave him a chemistry set for Christmas. Within a week of receiving this gift, he had resolved to pursue a career as a chemist, a decision from which he never wavered. Curl's interest in chemistry further blossomed under the tutelage of his high-school chemistry teacher, Lorena Davis, who provided him with encouragement and extra assignments to challenge the budding chemist. In 1950, at the age of 16, he graduated from Thomas Jefferson High School in San Antonio.

Curl then went on to major in chemistry at Houston's Rice Institute. There, he found himself drawn to mathematics and physics as well as chemistry. Because of these additional interests, he decided to pursue a career in physical chemistry. At Rice one of his professors praised Kenneth Pitzer's work in discovering barriers to internal rotation. In 1954, Curl, aided by a National Science Foundation graduate fellowship, began his

ROBERT F. CURL JR.

graduate studies under Pitzer at the University of California at Berkeley. While there, Curl concentrated on the development of Pitzer's extension of the Theory of Corresponding States and conducted what he described in his autobiographical essay as "an experimental project using matrix isolation infrared spectroscopy to obtain an estimate of the Si-O-Si bond angle in disiloxane." In 1957 Curl was awarded his Ph.D in chemistry.

With Pitzer's help, Curl then obtained a research fellowship with E. B. Wilson at Harvard. Working with Wilson, Curl was able to research new methods for determining methyl group internal rotation barriers by microwave spectroscopy. Curl credits Wilson with teaching him "the value of a healthy skepticism and how careful you must be to be sure that you are drawing the correct conclusions."

In 1958 Curl was offered a faculty position at Rice, where he acquired a working microwave spectrometer and a research group. Most importantly, Curl inherited "an excellent frontier problem in microwave spectroscopy, the treatment of fine and hyperfine structure in the rotational spectra of asymmetric rotors, and a superb graduate student, James L. Kinsey." The work of Curl and Kinsey, on the microwave spectrum of ClO and the theory of fine and hyperfine structure, provided a solid foundation for an intensive study and interpretation of the spectra of stable free radicals, which earned him a promotion and tenure in 1963.

In that same year, he went to the Mathematical Institute at Oxford on a NATO postdoctoral fellowship. While there, Curl researched "the relationship between electron spin-rotation interaction constants and the anisotropy in electronic g-values that bears Curl's name."

Upon returning to Rice in 1964, in addition to maintaining his research program in microwave spectroscopy, he began a new collaboration with his old mentor, Kenneth Pitzer, who was then president of Rice. "One fruit of this collaboration was the recognition that in cases of spin isomers more complex than hydrogen and deuterium, new mechanisms for nuclear spin species conversions will be present," Curl explained. The pair soon developed a theory for nuclear spin isomerization rates in these cases. In 1967 Curl was promoted to full professor. He became the first master of Lovett, a new residential college at Rice, in 1968.

Three years later, Curl began working with Frank Tittel of the Rice electrical engineering department in the field of laser spectroscopy. This research involved the use of "continuous wave dye lasers to explore high resolution electronic spectra of small molecules. Specialized techniques, including intermodulated fluorescence and microwave-optical double resonance, allowed the resolution of nuclear hyperfine structure in both the upper and lower state of the transition." In 1973, while on sabbatical with Takeshi Oka at the National Research Council of Canada, Curl and Tittel were able to observe "radio frequency transitions allowed by the centrifugal distortion induced dipole moment of methane using infrared-radio frequency double resonance."

In 1979 Curl began collaborating with Philip R. Brooks "to explore the electronic spectrum of a molecule in the process of chemical reaction by direct excitation of the reaction complex followed by fluorescence emission from an atom produced by this excitation." Included in this work were some of the first spectroscopic experiments probing systems in the process of chemical reaction.

In 1984 Curl, along with RICHARD E. SMALLEY and Frank Tittel, began an intensive study of semiconductor clusters. Smalley had developed a method for making small clusters, aggregates of molecules or atoms, by laser vaporization. The clusters "were then cooled to a few degrees kelvin by supersonic expansion into a vacuum, skimmed into a molecular beam, and probed by laser photoionization mass spectrometry." Smalley had been using this approach to study clusters of various metals. Curl, Smalley, and Tittel decided to join in a program investigating clusters of silicon, germanium, and gallium arsenide. That same year, HAROLD W. KROTO of the University of Sussex visited Curl at Rice and learned of the group's work. Kroto became intensely interested in examining carbon clusters. He wanted to prove that certain carbon chain molecules that exist in space, such as HC_3N, could be formed by condensing carbon atoms that had been ejected from carbon stars. The process of laser vaporization followed by condensation, the same process through which Curl, Smalley, and Tittel had investigated a variety of other materials, seemed a reasonable laboratory simulation of this situation. Curl soon "began pushing to study carbon, but more from the aspect that it might be possible to study the electronic spectra of carbon chain molecules using a technique called resonance enhanced two photon ionization."

In August 1985 Kroto arrived in Houston to participate in an investigation of carbon clusters. The results of that investigation were quite unexpected. "It was observed that, when the cluster chemistry was given a long time to occur, the mass spectrometer peak for C60 became enormously prominent. One structural isomer of C60 has a symmetrical, spherical closed-cage structure in the form of a truncated icosahedron, which would be expected to be highly unreactive and thus survive intense clustering conditions. The inevitable conclusion was that the prominent peak in the mass spectrum must consist of this isomer, which was somehow forming out of the chaos of condensing carbon vapor." This cage, which was dubbed a "buckminsterfullerene," or, more informally, "buckyball," in honor of R. Buckminster Fuller, the man who designed the geodesic dome for the 1967 Montreal World Exposition, was but one of a whole family of closed-cage carbon compounds (fullerenes) formed in condensing carbon vapor.

In 1996 the Royal Swedish Academy of Sciences awarded Curl the Nobel Prize for Chemistry. He shared the prize, along with the $1.12 million award, with Richard E. Smalley and Harold W. Kroto, the codiscoverers of fullerenes.

By the time of the Nobel Prize announcement, Curl had already abandoned his study of fullerenes. "By 1991, the fullerene research field became so large and active that it became burdensome to keep up with developments, much less to contribute," he explained. In the ensuing years, Curl collaborated with numerous scientists, including Frank Tittel and Graham Glass, on a variety of research projects, including "the development of compact, portable, rugged tunable infrared laser sources for atmospheric monitoring" and "the application of high-resolution infrared kinetic spectroscopy to the investigation of the structure and chemical kinetic behavior of transient free radicals."

Curl lives in Houston with Jonel Whipple, his wife since 1955. They have two children and two grandchildren. Outside of the laboratory, Curl enjoys participating in tournament bridge and squash.

In addition to the Nobel Prize, Curl has won the Clayton Prize of the Institute of Mechanical Engineers (1958, jointly with Pitzer), the Humboldt Prize (1984), and the American Physical Society International Prize for New Materials (1992, jointly with Kroto and Smalley). He is a fellow of the American Optical Society.

SELECTED WORKS: Probing C60 (with R. E. Smalley), Science November 18, 1988; Rate and Measurement of the Recombination Reaction $C_3H_3+C_3H_3$ (with C. L. Morter, S. K. Farhat, J. D. Adamson, and G. P.

Glass), Journal of Physical Chemistry 1994; The Reaction of NH₂ with O (with J. D. Adamson, S. K. Farhat, C. L. Marter, G. P. Glass, and L. F. Phillips), Journal of Physical Chemistry 1994.

ABOUT: Aldersey-Williams, H. The Most Beautiful Molecule, 1995; American Men and Women of Science, 1996; Baggott, J. Perfect Symmetry, 1994; Science October 18, 1996; Time October 21, 1996; Who's Who in America, 1997.

DE KLERK, F. W.
(March 18, 1936–   )
Nobel Prize for Peace, 1993 (shared with Nelson Mandela)

The son of Jan de Klerk and Corrie (Coetzer) de Klerk, Frederik Willem de Klerk was born on March 18, 1936 in Johannesburg in the Transvaal province of South Africa. He and his brother, Willem, born seven years earlier, grew up in an Afrikaner family of prominent politicians. The Afrikaners, who constitute approximately 60 percent of South Africa's white minority population, first settled in the area in the 17th century. Descended from Dutch, German, and French Huguenot settlers, Afrikaners dominated national politics for many years. De Klerk's father, Jan de Klerk, was a school principal and the National Party secretary for the Transvaal before his appointment to the cabinet of J. G. Strijdom. Jan de Klerk subsequently served in the cabinets of Hendrik Verwoerd (prime minister from 1958 to 1966) and John Vorster (prime minister from 1966 to 1978); he was briefly acting president and once presided over the Senate, which was abolished on January 1, 1981.

Known by his initials since childhood to distinguish him from his maternal grandfather, F. W. de Klerk graduated from Monument High School in Krugersdorp before enrolling in Potchefstroom University for Christian Higher Education. In college he edited the campus newspaper, served as vice-president of student government, and joined the National Party's student organization, the Afrikaanse Studentebond. He also joined the highly influential Broederbond, a once secret Afrikaner society open only to well-connected white male Protestants. After graduating cum laude with a law degree in 1958, he spent six weeks in England on an Abe Bailey Travel Bursary. Determined to improve his English-language skills, he joined a South African firm of English-speaking lawyers on his return to the Transvaal.

From 1961 to 1972, de Klerk practiced law in Vereeniging, a mining town near Johannesburg. Meanwhile, he became active in National Party politics, serving on Vereeniging's divisional council. In 1972 he was about to take the chair of administrative law at his alma mater when the National Party selected him to stand for Parliament in a by-election after the Veree-

F. W. DE KLERK

niging seat was vacated unexpectedly. Since he had not yet occupied his academic post, he decided to enter politics full-time after consulting his wife, the former Marike Willemse, whom he had married in 1958 or 1959. "She was the one who said, 'O.K., let's do it,'" de Klerk told Christopher S. Wren in an interview in the *New York Times Magazine*.. His wife supported his campaign by working as a bookkeeper for a firm of undertakers.

The Vereeniging seat was then safely Nationalist, and de Klerk won easily. After serving for several years on the back benches of the 178-member House of Assembly, 166 of whose members were then directly elected by white voters, de Klerk was appointed minister of posts and telecommunications and social welfare and pensions in 1978 by Prime Minister Vorster. Under P. W. Botha, he held a succession of junior-level posts, including posts and telecommunications and sports and recreation (1978–79); mines, energy, and environmental planning (1979–80); mineral and energy affairs (1980–82); internal affairs (1982–85); and national education and planning (1984–89). In 1985 he became chairman of the Ministers' Council in the House of Assembly. On December 1, 1986 he became the leader of the House of Assembly.

Although he was once described as "one of the cabinet's most vocal right-wingers," de Klerk has indicated that his outlook was broadened by a trip he made in 1976 to the United States—a visit sponsored by the United States Information Agency in an effort to acquaint him, as a foreigner with potential for national leadership, with the American system of government. He remained firmly within the ideological confines of the National Party, however, which began to suffer defections to the left and to the right in the early 1980s as a result of Botha's proposals for constitutional reform. Initiated in 1982, Botha's reforms, which took effect in 1984, included the creation of a powerful state presidency to supplant what had been a largely titular post and a tricameral Parliament enabling Asians and coloreds to take part in national politics for the first time, though blacks remained excluded entirely. Fearing that even those limited reforms would lead to power-sharing with blacks, a number of right-wing members of Parliament opposed Botha's efforts and were expelled from the party in March 1982. Among them was the party's provincial leader, Andries Treurnicht, who promptly founded the Conservative Party to accommodate those who opposed any compromise with a policy of strict apartheid, the white-supremacist system of racial separation. De Klerk was selected to replace Treurnicht as party leader in the Transvaal, where the Conservatives enjoyed so much support that de Klerk managed to hold on to his own seat by a margin of only 1,500 votes in the election of May 1987.

In an effort to stem the exodus from the National Party to the Conservative Party, de Klerk presented Botha's reforms in a conservative light to his constituents, leaving open the question of whether his motives were primarily ideological or pragmatic. His actions as minister of white education went beyond the call of pragmatism, however. A series of measures known as the de Klerk bills, which would have authorized the expulsion of university students for political activism, proved to be so unpopular that they had to be withdrawn, and his efforts to tie subsidies of universities to the successful restraint of campus unrest were struck down by the courts. De Klerk also tried to limit the enrollment of black students in previously all-white universities.

An interpretation of de Klerk's politics that emphasizes his pragmatism and flexibility is supported by two policy statements that he made in 1987. Andrew Bilski of *Maclean's* quoted him as telling a provincial party congress, "A balance has to be struck between political emancipation of nonindependent blacks [those who did not live in the nominally self-governing homelands] and the effective protection of existing rights and freedoms of our own people." The London *Times* quoted de Klerk as acknowledging in a preelection meeting that the momentum of reform could be slowed, but not reversed: "[A more conservative government] might possibly keep the lid on the pot for another five years. But after that the pot will explode and blow us and our future into the air. . . . After 14 years in Parliament, nine of these years as a minister, I can tell you we tried hard to make this [the old system] work. But we have now come to the realization that it cannot work. Our theory is on the rocks. People want a vote where they live."

Despite de Klerk's realization that changes in South Africa's political system were inevitable, he was considered the most conservative of the four contenders for the National Party leadership following Botha's mild stroke and subsequent resignation. The party caucus elected de Klerk by a vote of 69 to 61 in the last of three ballots on February 2, 1989, but Botha's clinging to the presidency rendered de Klerk powerless to execute policy. On April 6, 1989 Botha finally agreed to resign following parliamentary elections that were to be held in the fall. Preparing to lead his party to victory in those elections, de Klerk outlined the differences between the Nationalists and the two opposition parties in a speech that he delivered to the House of Assembly on May 12. "The contrast is clear," he said. "The Conservative Party stands for a minority government in a South Africa that will, by their own admission, in perpetuity be populated by a majority of people of color. It is unfair and does not pass the test of justice. The Democratic Party stands for a majority government. In a country with such a massive and wide diversity as ours, this is unfair toward the smaller peoples and population groups. Their policy, too, fails the test of justice." The Nationalists, de Klerk implied, would secure justice for all by protecting "group rights" (widely perceived as a euphemism for continued white rule) as well as individual rights under a two-tiered system of self-governance and consensus.

De Klerk campaigned abroad in an effort to repair South Africa's international relations, which were burdened with economic sanctions imposed in 1986 after Botha had declared a nationwide state of emergency. He visited Prime Minister Margaret Thatcher in London and West German chancellor Helmut Kohl in Bonn in June 1989, Mozambican leader Joaquim Chissano in July, and Zaire's Mobutu Sese Seko and Zambia's Kenneth Kaunda in August. Those meetings not only enhanced his image as a statesman but also provided him with the clout to force a showdown with Botha. Objecting to de Klerk's meeting with Kaunda on the grounds that the outlawed African National Congress (ANC) was headquartered in Lusaka, Zambia, Botha tried unsuccessfully to prevent the meeting from taking place, though his case was not aided by the fact that he himself had recently met with NELSON MANDELA, the long-imprisoned leader of the ANC. Nor did Botha's autocratic style, which contrasted markedly with de Klerk's easygoing affability and willingness to listen to his subordinates, endear him to his former cabinet. On August 14 Botha resigned, and de Klerk was sworn in as acting president on the following day.

"History, I believe, offers us a unique opportunity for peaceful solutions," de Klerk declared at his swearing-in ceremony. "I trust the people of South Africa will, in these times, show the courage and vision required to break the cycle of conflict, tension, and isolation which has gripped us for so long—the courage and vision to work for a new, strong, and just South Africa."

Even as he spoke, the country was in the midst of a campaign of civil disobedience launched that month by the Mass Democratic Movement, a loose coalition of antiapartheid activists protesting the exclusion of blacks from the general election held in September. On September 15, 1989 F. W. de Klerk was elected the ninth white leader of South Africa since the country was formed in 1910. Aligning himself with the Democrats, de Klerk noted that 70 percent of white voters had voted for change and proclaimed a mandate for reform. But the death toll during election-night violence, which reportedly climbed to 29, represented one of the largest single-day killings by police in South Africa's history. "Mr. F. W. de Klerk's presidency now sits in a pool of blood," observed the Reverend Allan A. Boesak, the president of the World Alliance of Reformed Churches.

Less than one week after the election, de Klerk announced that peaceful protests would thenceforth be tolerated, even though they were technically illegal under the state of emergency. Two rallies held by about 20,000 protesters each proceeded without incident in Cape Town and Johannesburg, but a third march, of black and white women that was scheduled for September 23 in Pretoria, was prevented by police. One month later, however, a rally of 70,000 people was allowed to take place near Soweto in celebration of the October 15 release of eight prominent black leaders, seven of whom belonged to the ANC, including Walter Sisulu, the organization's former secretary general.

Meanwhile, de Klerk met with antiapartheid leaders, including Boesak and Archbishop DESMOND TUTU, the Anglican primate of southern Africa and a 1984 Nobel laureate, to discuss the possibilities for eventual negotiations with the ANC and other black groups, such as the Zulu chief Mangosuthu Gatsha Buthelezi's Inkatha movement. In one memorable exchange often cited by Tutu during interviews with reporters, de Klerk insisted that "the purpose of government is the establishment of law and order." Boesak countered, "In our religious tradition, the purpose of government is the establishment of justice." De Klerk astounded the clerics by assenting, "Yes, you are right." The ANC's key preconditions for talks, which were approved by many in the international community, included the lifting of the state of emergency and of the ban on outlawed organizations and the release of Nelson Mandela and other political prisoners.

Many of those conditions were met during de Klerk's first year in office. On February 2, 1990 the 30-year ban on the ANC and about 60 other political groups was lifted, and Mandela was released from prison on February 11, after serving for 27 1/2 years (26 of which were for a life sentence for high treason, imposed when Mandela was already serving time on a lesser charge). On June 7 de Klerk declined to renew

the state-of-emergency regulations in the Transvaal, the Cape Province, and the Orange Free State. On August 6 de Klerk and Mandela signed the Pretoria Minute, the first document to result from the process of talks about negotiations leading to a new South African constitution. The ANC agreed to a cease-fire (it had long refused to abandon armed struggle as one of its methods for ridding the country of apartheid) in exchange for the gradual release of political prisoners. Such measures, in themselves, might have meant little were it not for de Klerk's acquiescence, announced during a visit to the United States in September, to the principle of one person, one vote, a demand that opponents of apartheid had vowed never to relinquish.

The task of establishing a truly democratic government in South Africa fell to the multiparty Convention for a Democratic South Africa, which began in December 1991. The negotiations that ensued, led by Mandela and de Klerk, were not without conflict and were broken off at various points. A major hurdle was crossed on September 26, 1992, when Mandela and de Klerk signed a Record of Understanding, which formalized their agreement that a single, freely elected constitutional assembly would both serve as the transitional legislature and draft a new constitution. Another milestone was reached on June 3, 1993, when it was agreed that the first elections open to all South African citizens would take place on April 27, 1994.

In 1993 de Klerk shared the Nobel Prize for Peace with his old antagonist, Nelson Mandela. At a news conference in December 1993, just before receiving the award, de Klerk and Mandela shared a podium. Showing a degree of expansiveness and optimism, according to the New York Times, de Klerk, still president of South Africa, spoke of a prosperous new era and "suggested that he and Mandela had laid a 'foundation for understanding' that could serve as a model for racial reconciliation for the whole country." De Klerk added, "We must in South Africa make real reconciliation work. We cannot build the future on a revival of conflicts from the past. We cannot build a future on hate and we cannot build a future on retribution."

Few were surprised when Mandela became a candidate for president in those elections. As expected, the ANC won handily, capturing 62.6 percent of the popular vote. By 1994 de Klerk was a cabinet member in Nelson Mandela's government. He maintained the position of quasi-apologetic reconciliation, saying in a Time magazine interview about the apartheid past: "I don't think it was a good idea to tell people where to live and to kick people out of particular townships. It became forced removals. That is where apartheid became morally unjustifiable. . . . People's dignity was being impaired, and it brought humiliation. I have said time and again, 'We are sorry that that happened.'"

His position in the new government of South Africa

proved untenable for de Klerk when, in May 1996, a new constitution was adopted. The National Party, headed by de Klerk, formally left the coalition, and de Klerk announced that South Africa's "first nonracial democracy was strong enough for a robust opposition party and that he intended to lead it," according to the *New York Times*.

ABOUT: London Observer March 12, 1989; Macleans September 18, 1989; New York Review of Books October 26, 1989, October 20, 1994; New York Times March 23, 1989, December 10, 1993, May 10, 1996; Time January 3, 1994.

DOHERTY, PETER C.
(October 15, 1940–)
Nobel Prize for Physiology or Medicine, 1996
(shared with Rolf M. Zinkernagel)

The immunologist Peter C. Doherty was born in the Australian state of Queensland and raised there in Oxley, a working-class suburb of Brisbane. A dislike of his childhood surroundings led the young Doherty to concentrate on the one sure way of escaping from Oxley—getting an education. He chose to attend the University of Queensland, where, despite his admission in the *Weekend Independent* that his "best subjects were literature and writing," he pursued a career in veterinary science. He received his bachelor's degree in 1962 and his master's degree in 1966. Doherty then traveled to the United Kingdom, where, in 1970, he received his Ph.D. in animal pathology from the University of Edinburgh.

By 1971 Doherty had completed a term as a veterinary officer at Brisbane's Animal Research Institute (1963–1967) and worked as scientific officer at Edinburgh's Moredun Research Institute's department of experimental pathology (1967–1971). In 1972 he received a research fellowship in the microbiology department of the John Curtin School of Medical Research, part of the Australian National University, in Canberra. At the Curtin School Doherty, along with fellow researcher ROLF M. ZINKERNAGEL, probed the inner workings of the human immune system and made a discovery that would one day provide new insight into immune response against a variety of diseases, including cancer and HIV, the virus that causes AIDS.

Prior to the work of Doherty and Zinkernagel, relatively little was known about the signaling and recognition mechanisms of the cellular immune system. It was understood that T lymphocytes, or T cells, were the part of the cellular immune system responsible for recognizing cells infected with various viruses and destroying them. Plaguing immunologists was the question of exactly how these T cells were able to detect and attack only infected cells while leaving healthy cells completely untouched. "There were a number of different people who had been snuffling around this

PETER C. DOHERTY

problem, but they couldn't reach a conclusion," Philippa Marrack, an immunologist at the National Jewish Center for Immunology and Respiratory Medicine, told the *New York Times*. She further explained that many of these previous attempts had been hindered by extremely complicated experimentation systems that yielded information that was nearly impossible to interpret.

Doherty and Zinkernagel, who collaborated not out of a strong desire to work with one another, but rather because of a shortage of space at the John Curtin School of Medical Research, decided to conduct experiments on the immune system reactions of mice exposed to the virus that can cause meningitis. After injecting mice with the virus, the pair mixed samples of both the virus-infected cells and T cells from the mice in a test-tube. The results led to a very surprising discovery: the T cells would recognize and kill the infected cells only if they were from the same strain of mice. Infected cells from different strains of mice would simply be ignored. Doherty and Zinkernagel deduced that the T cells would attack an infected cell only after it recognized two key factors: a set of certain molecules known as the major histocompatibility antigens that indicate that the cell is, indeed, part of the self, and not foreign matter; and a fragment of the virus itself, indicating that the cell is infected.

This discovery immediately solved a mystery that had puzzled immunologists for years. The major histocompatibility antigens, which had actually been discovered by scientists studying transplantation biology, differ in each individual and quickly label transplanted organs as foreign, thus provoking the immune system to attack and reject them. But why, since transplants do not occur in nature, did these major histocompatibility antigens exist? The hypothesis presented by Doherty and Zinkernagel provided a much-needed answer to this question. The major histocompatibility antigens exist because they are an integral part of the body's two-step process in recognizing infected cells. Suddenly, from the pair of scientists whom Dr. Ronald Schwartz, chief of the laboratory of cellular and molecular immunology at the National Institute of Allergy and Infectious Diseases, described in an interview with the *New York Times* as having appeared "out of left field," came an answer to one of immunology's fundamental questions. "Then they took over leadership in the field," Schwartz added.

The implications of the pair's discovery are extremely broad. Already, their work has been vital in helping to avoid rejection in organ transplants. Further, Doherty and Zinkernagel have provided a strong foundation upon which scientists may be able to expand the knowledge and, one day, treat such diseases as rheumatoid arthritis and non-insulin-dependent diabetes, illnesses in which the body loses the ability to differentiate between self and nonself and the immune system attacks the body's own tissues. As T cells are one of the body's foremost defenses against HIV, there is much hope that the work of Doherty and Zinkernagel may lead to better treatments for AIDS. Additionally, their work is being applied to the development of new vaccines for a variety of illnesses. "Already it has led to successful vaccines for animals, and if one has such a vaccine for animals, then it must not be far away before you can do the same with humans," said Sten Grillner, chairman of the Nobel medicine committee.

After the conclusion of the pair's work at the John Curtin School of Medical Research, Doherty, the man who had once harbored aspirations of becoming a "country vet," now found that he was one of the world's premier immunologists. "It's not really what I expected to do with my life, but that's just the way it turns out," he said in a 1996 interview with Reuters.

In 1975 he left Australia to become an associate professor and later a professor at Philadelphia's Wistar Institute, where he remained until 1982. He then returned to Australia to head the experimental pathology department in the very place where he had conducted his research with Zinkernagel, the John Curtin School of Medical Research. In 1988 Doherty accepted a position as chairman of the Department of Immunology at St. Jude Children's Research Hospital in Memphis, Tennessee. Four years later he became an adjunct professor in both the pathology and pediatrics departments of the University of Tennessee's College of Medicine.

In 1996, more than 20 years after shedding new light on the responses of the body's immune system, Peter C. Doherty was awarded the Nobel Prize. He shared his award, along with the $1.12 million prize, with the codiscoverer of the body's two-pronged recognition of infected cells, Rolf Zinkernagel. The academy praised the pair for work that has "fundamentally changed our understanding of the development and normal function of the immune system." Fellow immunologists were very pleased with the announcement. "Most of us in the field felt this was an award that was coming, and it was only a question of when they would get it," said Dr. Philip Greenberg, an immunologist and cancer specialist at the University of Washington School of Medicine. "It's all very exciting and gratifying," Doherty said upon receiving the news of his award. "It's very satisfying to have had some responsibility for triggering an enormous area of research."

Doherty has been the recipient of numerous other awards, including the Paul Ehrlich Prize (1983), the Gairdner Foundation International Award (1986), and the Albert Lasker Medical Research Award (1995). Also, Doherty has been a fellow of the Australian Academy of Science (1983) and the Royal Society of London (1987).

SELECTED WORKS: Restriction of In Vitro T Cell–Mediated Cytotoxicity in Lymphocytic Choriomeningitis Within a Syngenic and Semiallogeneic System (with R. M. Zinkernagel), Nature 248, 1974; Immunological Surveillance Against Altered Self Components by Sensitized T Lymphocytes in Lymphocytic Choriomeningitis (with R. M. Zinkernagel), Nature 251, 1974; A Biological Role for the Major Histocompatibility Antigens (with R. M. Zinkernagel), Lancet, 1975; MHC Restricted Cytotoxic T Cells: Studies on the Biological Role of Polymorphic Major Transplantation Antigens Determining T Cell Restriction Specificity (with R. M. Zinkernagel), Advances in Immunology, 1979.

ABOUT: Los Angeles Times October 8, 1996; New York Times October 8, 1996; Newsday October 8, 1996; Reuters October 8, 1996; Royal Swedish Academy of Sciences 1996 Nobel Prize Announcement; Weekend Independent November 1996.

FISCHER, EDMOND H.

(April 6, 1920–)
Prize for Physiology or Medicine, 1992 (shared Nobel with Edwin G. Krebs)

The American biochemist Edmond Fischer was born in Shanghai, China, in 1920, the third son of Oscar and Renée (Tapernoux) Fischer. Fischer's father had come to Shanghai from Vienna, Austria, after studying law and business. His mother had come by way of Hanoi with her parents from France. His grandfather, a prominent figure in Shanghai, helped to established the first French newspaper in China, *Courrier de Chine*, and established the first school that

EDMOND H. FISCHER

Fischer attended. At the age of seven, Fischer, along with his two older brothers, Raoul and Georges, moved to Switzerland to attend the Swiss Federal Polytechnical Institute, in Zürich. He began his study of chemistry at the University of Geneva in 1939, and he was awarded his Ph.D. in 1947, after completing his doctoral thesis, entitled "Purification and Crystallization of Hog Pancreas $\propto$ Amylase." From 1948–1950 he was a fellow of the Swiss National Foundation, and from 1950–1953 he was a fellow of the Rockefeller Foundation.

Fischer came to the United States in 1953, first spending a year at the California Institute of Technology as a research associate in the division of biology. He then joined the faculty of the University of Washington in 1954. It was there that he met his research partner, the American physiologist EDWIN G. KREBS. In the autobiography Fischer wrote for *Les Prix Nobel,* he recollected his first days at the University of Washington: "Within six months of my arrival, Ed Krebs and I started to work together on glycogen phosphorylase. He had been a student of [CARL F. CORI and GERTY T. CORI] in St. Louis. They believed that AMP [adenosine monophosphate] had to serve some kind of cofactor function for that enzyme. In Geneva, on the other hand, we had purified potato phosphorylase, for which there was no AMP requirement. Even though essentially no information existed at that time on the evolutionary relationship of proteins, we knew that enzymes, whatever their origin, used the same coenzymes to catalyze identical reactions. It seemed unlikely, therefore, that muscle phosphorylase would require AMP as a cofactor but not potato phosphorylase. We decided to try to elucidate the role of this nucleotide

in the phosphorylase reaction. Of course, we never found out what AMP was doing: that problem was solved 6–7 years later when Jacques Monod proposed his allosteric model for the regulation of enzymes. But what we stumbled on was another quite unexpected reaction: i.e. that muscle phosphorylase was regulated by phosphorylation-dephosphorylation. This is yet another example of what makes fundamental research so attractive: one knows where one takes off but one never knows where one will end up.

"These were very exciting years, when just about every experiment revealed something new and unexpected. At first we worked alone in a small, single laboratory with stone sinks. Experiments were planned the night before and carried out the next day. We worked so closely together that whenever one of us had to leave the laboratory in the middle of an experiment, the other would carry on without a word of explanation. Ed Krebs had a small group that continued his original work: determining the structure and function of DPNH-X, a derivative of NADH. I was still studying the $\propto$ amylases with Eric Stein. In collaboration with Bert Vallee, we were able to demonstrate that these enzymes were in reality calcium-containing metalloproteins."

In 1992, more than 40 years later, Fischer and Krebs were awarded the Nobel Prize for this work, which led to the accidental discovery of a basic process in human cells that regulates most of the biochemical processes of life. The process of reversible protein phosphorylation controls how chemical reactions within cells are turned on and off. It is now known to be a prominent player in most, if not all, normal cellular phenomena. It also may play a major role in the treatment of most diseases, including cancer and AIDS.

Fischer and Krebs began this work with a grant from the National Institutes of Health to study the problem of how adrenalin causes the breakdown of glycogen, giving muscles the energy to contract in the "fight or flight" response. They were concentrating on an enzyme called phosphorylase, which Fischer had previously worked with in plant studies at the University of Geneva. It was known that both active and inactive forms of the enzyme were present in muscle cells, but how the two forms differed was not understood.

Proteins have a defined three-dimensional structure that dictates molecular interactions. An enzyme's ability to act on other proteins depends on an elaborate "lock and key" mechanism by which the enzyme and the protein upon which it acts fit together perfectly; thus each has the ability to act only on specific molecules. Fischer and Krebs's research proved that a phosphate molecule attached to the inactive form of phosphorylase at a key location activated the enzyme. The removal of the phosphate group rendered the enzyme inactive. The scientists thus discovered that proteins could be regulated by having their structure modified in a reversible way.

The process by which a phosphate group is added to an enzyme is called phosphorylation. The enzymes that carry it out are called protein kinases. The reverse process, called dephosphorylation, is carried out by enzymes called phosphatases. The overall process is referred to as reversible protein phosphorylation.

"We stumbled on it," said Fischer. "We had no idea how widespread this reaction would be." The process turned out to be responsible for regulating a huge variety of metabolic processes, including the action of hormones in the body, muscle contraction, immune responses, cell growth and division, blood pressure, inflammatory reactions, and signals in the brain. The Nobel Academy's statement on the prize states that an estimated 1 percent of the genes in human DNA are devoted to blueprints for the production of phosphorylating enzymes. Fischer was modest on the subject of the prize. "So much superb work has been carried out by so many investigators . . . you wonder why we were selected," he said. "You can think of literally dozens of other people who would deserve it."

One of the most important applications for the study of phosphorylation is oncology. More than half of the cancer-causing cells are known to encode protein kinases. Some biologists have theorized that blocking phosphorylation in cancer cells could halt tumor growth. Continued study of the phosphorylation process in cancer cells may lead to the development of new and different types of anticancer drugs.

Some immunosuppressant drugs, such as cyclosporine, utilize the reverse process of dephosphorylation to block the activation of white blood cells that would attack transplanted organs. Researchers are currently working on a possible role for dephosphorylation in the fight against diabetes. Since the original discovery, further research has shown that many phosphorylation reactions are considerably more complicated than they first appeared. Some kinases phosphorylate other kinases, which in turn phosphorylate still other kinases, producing a biochemical cascade. A corresponding number of phosphatases work against the cascade, creating a regulatory mechanism that is more like a dimmer than a mere on/off switch. Each time enzymes act upon each other in sequence, their effect is amplified one millionfold to 20 millionfold. The cascade effect in hormone reactions, for instance, allows a tiny amount of hormone to exert an enormous influence and yet still be very closely regulated.

Initially, the discovery of reversible protein phosphorylation by Fischer and Krebs gathered little attention in the scientific community. It was not until the mid-1970s that the wide application of the process was appreciated and research in the area blossomed. A whole new field of research has been initiated concerning the signaling processes that control cellular events; a particularly large area in recent years is the role of kinases and phosphatases in growth control. Un-

official estimates have suggested that up to 10 percent of articles published in the field of biochemistry deal with this topic.

As of 1996, Fischer was a senior researcher and professor emeritus at the University of Washington, where he continued to carry out research in the field he helped to found almost 40 years earlier. Around the time he was awarded the Nobel Prize, his research involved studying the process of cell transformation in cancer.

Fischer has two sons, FranDcois and Henri, from his first wife, Nelly Gagnaux, who died in 1961. He married Beverley Bullock in 1963. Fischer also has two grandsons.

In addition to the Nobel Prize, Fischer has received numerous awards from various institutions including the Swiss Chemical Society, the Guggenheim Foundation, the University of Geneva, and the University of Washington. He is the recipient of honorary doctorates from both the University of Montpellier in France and Switzerland's University of Basel. Additionally, he is a member of the American Academy of Arts and Sciences, the National Academy of Sciences, and the Venice Academy of Sciences, Arts and Letters, and a foreign associate of the Spanish Royal Academy of Sciences.

ABOUT: Los Angeles Times October 13, 1992; New York Times October 13, 1992; Science October 23, 1992; Seattle Post-Intelligencer October 13, 1992; Wall Street Journal October 13, 1992; Washington Post October 13, 1992; Who's Who in America, 1992.

FOGEL, ROBERT W.
(July 1, 1926–)
Nobel Memorial Prize in Economic Sciences, 1993 (shared with Douglass C. North)

The American economist Robert William Fogel was born in New York City to Harry G. and Elizabeth Fogel, both Russian immigrants. He received his bachelor's degree from Cornell University in 1948. When he entered Columbia University in the 1950s to study statistics, as Sylvia Nasar reported in the *New York Times*, he had already established himself as being "both brilliant and something of a bomb thrower." "By the time he arrived at Columbia University," Nasar wrote, he "had spent several years as a Communist youth organizer."

He served as an instructor at Johns Hopkins University (where he received his Ph.D. in 1963) in 1958 and 1959 and as an assistant professor at the University of Rochester from 1960 to 1964. In the latter year he joined the faculty of the University of Chicago and remained there until 1975, when he became professor of economics and history at Harvard. In 1981 he returned to the University of Chicago, where he has remained since.

ROBERT W. FOGEL

Fogel and DOUGLASS C. NORTH, with whom he shared the 1993 Nobel Prize, are credited with founding the science of cliometrics, which applies rigid statistical methodology to the study and interpretation of history. In 1964 Fogel published his groundbreaking work, *Railroads and American Growth: Essays in Econometric History*, in which he disputed the common notion that railroads were largely responsible for the growth of the American economy in the late 19th century. He began by examining the raw materials that were used to create railroads: iron, coal, machinery, and other commodities. By devising a mathematical model to account for the materials that went into railroad construction, Fogel showed that only 10 percent of American production involved the use of crude iron. Because American railroad manufacturing relied primarily on the recycling of scrap metals and on British imports, Fogel asserted, the impact of railroad-building on the economy was not as great as had been previously believed. Fogel also documented the importance of other means of transport, such as waterways, further downplaying railroads' economic importance.

Fogel's next major work, written with Stanley L. Engerman, was his most controversial: *Time on the Cross: The Economics of American Negro Slavery*, published in 1974. Written both for academics and for educated lay readers, *Time on the Cross* was read widely and touched off heated debates about the role of slavery in the American economy before the Civil War. By meticulously examining records of all sorts, from plantation medical documents to crop outputs to slave auction reports, Fogel challenged the accepted belief that slavery as a system was economically ruin-

ous. Asserting that the antebellum North's free-labor system was less productive than that of the South's slave-based economy, Fogel presented, as Stephen D. Engle wrote in the *Historian*, "loads of statistics" to corroborate his thesis. Fogel wrote, "There is no evidence that economic forces alone would have soon brought slavery to an end without the necessity of a war or some other form of political intervention. Quite the contrary; as the Civil War approached, slavery as an economic system was never stronger and the trend was toward even further entrenchment." Fogel also dispelled the notion that slaves were lazy, unmotivated, and unproductive. Instead, he says, the average slave was "harder working and more efficient than his white counterpart." The final sentence of the work reads, "It's time to reveal, not only to blacks but to whites as well, that part of American history which has been kept from them—the record of black achievement under adversity."

"Seldom has the advent of a historical study been greeted with such publicity and ballyhoo," the critic Nathan Irvan Huggins declared in *Commonweal*. "Despite its argumentative style," Naomi Bliven wrote in the *New Yorker*, *Time on the Cross* "is continually interesting, even absorbing. And still more important for any contribution to historical understanding, it is productive of reflection." Still, some critics saw the work as a justification for slavery and assailed it as racist.

Continuing on the same theme, *Without Consent or Contract: The Rise and Fall of American Slavery* appeared in four volumes from 1989 to 1992. William N. Parker wrote in *Business History Review* about *Without Consent or Contract*, "As the tumult and shouting died, Fogel surveyed the flooded scene and placed a rainbow in the sky in the form of a final work." In the second volume, Fogel and coeditors Ralph A. Galantine and Richard L. Manning compiled 74 pieces by 18 scholars discussing their interpretations of slavery and the emancipation movement as well as the methodologies that led the scholars to their respective conclusions. This volume, Winifred B. Rothenberg wrote in *Reviews in American History*, is "a window on the state of the art of quantitative social science history." In the third and fourth installments, Fogel (with Engerman again as coeditor) included papers that revisited some of the controversial assertions of *Time on the Cross*, employing new data sets and new methods of historical demography to probe further into the institution of slavery, which is denounced in the volumes. Rothenberg wrote that Fogel's work contained "the finest statement of the moral problem of slavery that I have ever seen."

Fogel and Douglass C. North were credited by the Royal Swedish Academy of Sciences for "applying economic theory and quantitative methods" to historical questions and for their pioneering work in cliometrics.

According to Claudia Rosen, a Harvard University economic historian, "Fogel leans more in the direction of the empirical. . . . He tries to find a fact, prove it's a fact, and then prove it is a fact a hundred times over."

Fogel is currently investigating the phenomena of hunger and extended life spans in both America and Europe. He has found, for example, that France had a lower rate of food consumption during the French Revolution than India did more than 100 years later, and he asserts that large-scale starvation became a significant problem more recently than is generally believed.

As a winner of the Nobel Memorial Prize in Economic Sciences, Fogel became one of the 21 American winners in that category and one of the seven from the University of Chicago. He has been named a fellow by numerous groups, including the American Academy of Arts and Sciences, the Econometric Society, the American Association for the Advancement of Science, and the Royal Historical Society. Other awards and honors include many National Science Foundation grants, a Fulbright grant, and the Bancroft Prize in American History from Columbia University. He was the honorary vice-president of the Economic History Society of Glasgow in 1967 and president of the Economic History Association in 1977 and 1978. His other books include *The Union Pacific Enterprise*, published in 1960, and *The Dimensions of Quantitative Research in History*, published in 1972. He has also written numerous essays and articles for various publications. Fogel has lectured all over the world, and his works have been published in Italy, Spain, the United Kingdom, and Japan. He and his wife since 1949, the former Enid Morgan, have two sons, Steven Dennis and Michael Paul.

ABOUT: Business History Review Winter 1993; Contemporary Authors, 1979, 1984; Historian Winter 1994; NBER Reporter Fall 1993; New York Times October 13, 1993, November 7, 1993; Reviews in American History December 1993; Wall Street Journal October 13, 1993; Washington Post October 13, 1993.

GILMAN, ALFRED G.

(July 1, 1941–   )
Nobel Prize for Physiology or Medicine, 1994
(shared with Martin Rodbell)

The American pharmacologist Alfred Goodman Gilman was born in New Haven, Connecticut, the son of Alfred and Mabel (Schmidt) Gilman. Gilman's father was the founding head of pharmacology at New York's Albert Einstein School of Medicine and a member of a Yale Medical School research team that developed nitrogen mustard as a treatment for cancer. Gilman credits his father with igniting his interest in science and medicine by taking the then 10-year-old

ALFRED G. GILMAN

boy to visit his laboratory. The son's love of medicine would continue into his adulthood and eventually take him to the apex of the field.

Gilman was educated at Yale University, where he received his bachelor's degree in 1962. He then left the East Coast for Cleveland, Ohio, where he received both his M.D. and his Ph.D. in pharmacology from Case Western Reserve University in 1969. Upon graduation, Gilman accepted a position as a research associate at the National Institutes of Health in Bethesda, Maryland. In 1971, Gilman left the NIH to embark on a teaching career at the University of Virginia in Charlottesville, where he would eventually serve as director of the university's Medical Science Training Program. It was during his years at the University of Virginia that Gilman immersed himself in the work that would one day earn him the Nobel Prize, the study of how cells within the human body receive and communicate outside stimuli.

In the early 1970s, much of what was known about the process of cellular signaling was based on work conducted by EARL W. SUTHERLAND JR. According to the Sutherland model, when a person is startled or suddenly frightened, the individual's body produces adrenaline that quickly arrives at the liver. Receptors, which are dotted across the liver's outside lining, were believed to capture the adrenaline and somehow convey the message of the adrenaline's presence to the enzyme inside the cell. Thus notified, the enzyme would signal the liver cell to release glucose, allowing the body to respond to the adrenaline surge.

Despite the wide acceptance of this theory, one man, sparked by a Sutherland lecture that encouraged researchers to "tear apart a cell and isolate its component parts," decided to challenge it. Believing that nature rarely operates in such an orderly and compact manner, MARTIN RODBELL thought that Sutherland's model of cellular communication lacked a vital step. Through his research, he eventually concluded that after a receptor grabs the adrenaline or other chemical messenger, it changes shape. This shape change causes the molecule next to the receptor to change shape as well. This second molecule then acts as a transducer, a chemical messenger that is powered by the receptor and, in turn, stimulates another molecule. In the case of an unexpected scare, the molecule stimulated by the transducer then causes the liver to produce glucose. The existence of this transducer molecule was neither mentioned nor suspected in the Sutherland model. Unfortunately, few scientists took much notice of Rodbell's theory. He became the victim of a scientific community unwilling to accept a more complicated version of Sutherland's well-accepted theory. "I would go to meetings and people would say, 'Oh Marty, not again,'" Rodbell recalled in an interview with *Newsweek.* For Rodbell's theory to be accepted by the scientific community, he needed the one thing he could not find—solid proof of the existence of a transducer molecule.

In 1980, while working completely independently of Rodbell, Gilman discovered the much-needed proof. Gilman, who, ironically, had once been a student of Sutherland, was conducting experiments on leukemic cells with mutated genes. He found that cells with normal receptors that generated acceptable levels of cyclic adenosine monophosphate, or AMP, a messenger chemical found in all humans, did nothing when exposed to outside stimuli. Realizing that the mutated cells lacked a transducer, he tried injecting the cells with various proteins found in normal cells. Eventually, he found a protein that, when injected into the mutated cells, restores the normal transduction function. This protein, called the G protein because it binds with a nucleotide known as guanosine triphosphate (GTP), acts as a "biological traffic light" that processes a variety of external signals such as neurotransmitters, light, and smell and converts them into specific cellular responses, all in about four or five seconds.

Gilman's work with G proteins has led to numerous advances in the understanding of cellular signalizing in the human body. Each of the nearly 20 known varieties of G proteins is activated by certain receptors and, in turn, sets in motion specific responses. For example, a specific G protein in the eye reacts when the retina is exposed to light. The G protein then stimulates an enzyme, which, in turn, starts a flurry of activity that results in sight. Similarly, certain G proteins located in the nose and tongue activate enzymes that transmit the sensations of smell and taste to the brain.

Gilman's work with G proteins has also increased understanding of certain diseases. It is now known that an upset in the normal functioning of G proteins can be disastrous. Scientists have found in a variety of cancerous tumors G proteins that have mutated or have suddenly become overactive. The extreme loss of salt and water suffered by cholera victims is a direct result of a toxin secreted by the bacteria that attaches itself to a G protein and forces the protein to remain in an "on" position. This, in turn, prevents the intestines' normal absorption of salt and water, causing often-fatal dehydration and diarrhea. Further, some symptoms of diseases such as diabetes and alcoholism have their roots in a faulty transduction of signals through G proteins.

The increased understanding of the connection between certain diseases and G proteins has also opened up a new realm of possibilities for the treatments of these diseases. Currently, scientists are trying to dissect the complex wiring of cells and discover which receptors activate which G proteins. As there are more than 300 receptors that communicate with the nearly 20 known G proteins, the extremely time-consuming task of sorting them all out has been likened to untangling the wires of an old-fashioned telephone switchboard. Upon completion, however, the understanding of cells' inner wiring would enable scientists to develop drugs that are extremely efficient. "You'll be able to design a drug that works only on the molecule you want and no other molecule in the body," Gilman said in an interview with the *New York Times.* "It will happen. I just can't tell you when."

In 1994 Gilman, who had been working as a professor of pharmacology and chairman of the pharmacology department at the University of Texas Southwestern Medical Center since 1981, was awarded the Nobel Prize for Physiology or Medicine. He shared the award, along with the $930,000 prize, with Martin Rodbell. When asked about his reaction to the news that he had received the Nobel Prize, Gilman responded in terms appropriate to his research. "First, I activated my receptor, then my G protein," he said. "I was obviously extremely excited. I think I secreted all the adrenaline I had."

Gilman lives in Dallas with Kathryn (Hedlund) Gilman, his wife since 1963. They have three children.

In addition to the Nobel Prize, Gilman has received numerous other awards, including the Norwegian Pharmacology Society's Poul Edvard Poulsson Award (1982), the Albert Lasker Basic Medical Research Award (1989), the American Heart Association's Basic Scientific Research Prize (1990), and the Durham, North Carolina City of Medicine Award (1991). Also, Gilman is a member of organizations that include the American Society of Pharmacology and Experimental Therapeutics, the American Society of Biological Chemistry, the National Academy of Sciences, and the American Academy of Arts and Sciences.

SELECTED WORKS: The Pharmacological Basis of Therapeutics (ed.), 1975, 1980, 1985, 1990; more than 150 articles in professional journals.

ABOUT: Boston Globe October 11, 1994; Newsweek October 24, 1994; New York Times October 11, 1994; Royal Swedish Academy of Sciences 1994 Nobel Prize Announcement; Science June 23, 1995; Science News October 15, 1994; Who's Who in America, 1997.

HARSANYI, JOHN C.

(May 20, 1920–   )
Nobel Memorial Prize in Economic Sciences, 1994 (shared with John F. Nash and Reinhard Selten)

The Hungarian economist John Charles Harsanyi was born in Budapest, the only son of pharmacists Charles and Alice Harsanyi. His early life was spent comfortably in Hungary. He graduated in 1937 from the Lutheran Gymnasium, one of the best high schools in the country. While in high school, Harsanyi developed a fondness for mathematics, a subject that would become the basis for his life's work. In an autobiographical essay in the *American Economic Review*, he proudly recalled winning "the First Prize in Mathematics at the Hungary-wide annual competition for high school students." Though he preferred mathematics and philosophy, Harsanyi chose to study to be a pharmacist to please his parents—and also to gain a military deferment just as Europe was entering World War II. Being of Jewish origin, his family was particularly fearful of Adolf Hitler's murderous campaign, which was spreading from Germany throughout Europe. When the German army occupied Hungary in March 1944, Harsanyi lost his military deferment and had to serve in a labor unit. From November 1944 to January 1945, he was in hiding from the Nazis in a Jesuit monastery. These good priests, Harsanyi wrote, "probably saved my life."

After the war, he studied philosophy at the University of Budapest, and in 1947 he received his Ph.D. For the next year he was a faculty member at the University Institute of Sociology. It was there that he met his future wife, Anne Klauber, with whom he would have a son, Tom. In 1948 he had to resign from the Institute when it became commonly known that he strongly opposed Marxist doctrine, which had become the norm since Hungary had become a Communist state. Harsanyi and his wife decided to leave their native land, believing that this was the only way he could have an academic career. They traveled to Australia in 1950. There Harsanyi found that his degrees were not recognized by the Australian academic community, and that his English was too poor to enable him to teach. The couple struggled for three years as Harsanyi worked in factories. In the evenings he studied economics at Sydney University, where he received his

JOHN C. HARSANYI

M.A. in 1953. For the next two years he stayed in Australia, as lecturer in economics for the University of Queensland in Brisbane.

Harsanyi first became interested in game theory economics in the 1950s, describing it in his autobiographical essay as "a theory of strategic interaction . . . of rational behavior in social situations in which each player has to choose his moves on the basis of what he thinks the other players' counter moves are likely to be." Game theory analyzes the different interactions among economic players—whether they be individuals, corporations, banks, or governments—and accounts for the entire range of possible options. The ultimate goal of game theory economics is to help to understand why, according to *Business Week*, "existing economic and social arrangements are stable, and what the alternatives might be." In 1944 the mathematician John von Neumann and the economist Oskar Morgenstern put forth the first ideas on game-theoretic tools as applied to a varied group of economic systems. Though Harsanyi wrote several articles on the use of the von Neumann–Morgenstern utilities in welfare economics and in ethics, it was JOHN F. NASH's work, published later, that piqued his interest. Harsanyi explained: "My interest in game-theoretic problems in a narrower sense was first aroused by John Nash's four brilliant papers . . . on cooperative and noncooperative games, on two-person bargaining games, [and] on mutually optimal threat strategies in such games." By 1950, John Nash had developed the formal mathematical principles of the game theory, but his work was limited by one major assumption—that each side would have perfect knowledge of rivals' motives and resources. Seeing this as a major flaw,

Harsanyi elaborated on Nash's original theory and set out to prove that "nothing need be known for certain so long as it is predictable in terms of chance." An example of this new aspect of game theory might be that if two rival companies were figuring out pricing strategies, each would need only to figure out the *probability* of the rival's responses and counter responses.

In 1956 Harsanyi received a Rockefeller Scholarship and also accepted a position as visiting assistant professor at Stanford University, in California, where he completed work on his Ph.D. in 1959. Harsanyi's dissertation supervisor was KENNETH ARROW, an economist who would have a great influence on his economic work. As Harsanyi wrote: "I benefited very much from discussing many finer points of economic theory with [Arrow]. But I also benefited substantially by following his advice to spend a sizable part of my Stanford time studying mathematics and statistics. These studies proved very useful in my later work in game theory."

Harsanyi spent several years in a research position in the Australian National University in Canberra. By 1961, however, he had returned to the United States, feeling quite isolated from his peers in the field: "At that time in Australia, there was not much interest in game theory." On the recommendation of his mentors, Arrow and JAMES TOBIN, he became a professor of economics at Wayne State University. Once back in the United States, he continued his work on game theory. In 1963, he published an article that "extended the Shapely value [a game with incomplete information] to games without transferrable utility" and also showed that his new theory "was a direct generalization both of the Shapely value and of Nash's bargaining solution with variable threats."

In 1964 Harsanyi became a professor of business administration at the University of California at Berkeley. Around the same time, the German economist REINHARD SELTEN helped the Nash model of game theory by suggesting that game outcomes could be either reasonable or unreasonable—and that one could mathematically distinguish between the two catagories. In 1967-68, Harsanyi published a three-part paper entitled "Games with Incomplete Information Played by 'Bayesian' Players." The paper outlined the way in which to convert a game with incomplete information into one with complete, but imperfect, information. He found that there is a mathematical technique for deciding when the outcome of an economic interaction is in equilibrium. This technique, though first ridiculed by the economic community, has in recent years become the standard tool in many areas of economic theory—from deciding the fluctuation of banks' interest rates to tracking the spending patterns of the largest corporations. By 1973 Harsanyi had proved that nearly every one of the "mixed-strategy Nash equilibria can be reinterpreted as pure-strategy equilibria of a suitably chosen game with randomly fluctuating payoff functions."

In 1976 Harsanyi gathered the numerous journal articles he had written over the years in the volume *Essays on Ethics, Social Behavior and Scientific Explanation*. The next year he published *Rational Behavior and Bargaining Equilibrium in Games and Social Situations*, which unified game theory by extending the use of bargaining models from cooperative games to noncooperative games. In 1982 he and Reinhard Selten brought their work together for the book *Papers in Game Theory*. In 1988 they coauthored *A General Theory of Equilibrium Selection in Games*. These latter two books are often used as the blueprint for game theory today.

In 1990 Harsanyi retired from the staff at Berkeley as professor emeritus. In 1993 and 1994 he wrote two papers in which he proposed a new theory on equilibrium selection. This theory is grounded in the thesis of his 1988 book with Selten, yet it is, according to Harsanyi, "a simpler theory and is in my view an intuitively more attractive one." In 1994 Harsanyi, Selten and Nash were jointly awarded the Nobel Memorial Prize in Economic Sciences for their work through the years in game theory, and they shared the $930,000 award equally. In the October 1994 issue of *Science*, Robert Pool suggested that the work of Nash, Harsanyi, and Selten goes beyond economic theory into the realm of evolutionary biology: "Many of the ideas and mathematical techniques they pioneered are at the cutting edge in understanding competition within and among biological species." Reporting on the announcement of the 1994 Economics Nobel Prize, the *New York Times* quoted Barry Nalebluff of the School of Organization and Management at Yale: "Harsanyi gave shape to the fog in real-world games." The *American Economic Review* praised him in these terms: "In all his work, John Harsanyi exhibits a true scholar's care and temper. He probes deeply and incisively into problems that others see as hopeless muddles, and he pulls out brilliant structures that help us see through the muddle."

In addition to being the author of four books and of numerous journal articles dating back to the 1950s, Harsanyi has received many fellowships and awards, including a fellowship of the Center of Advanced Study in Behavioral Sciences in Stanford, California. He is also a fellow of the Econometrics Society and the American Academy of Arts and Sciences and a member of the American Economic Association.

SELECTED WORKS: Essays on Ethics, Social Behavior and Scientific Explanation, 1976; Rational Behavior and Bargaining Equilibrium in Games and Social Situations, 1977; Papers in Game Theory (with Reinhard Selten), 1982; A General Theory of Equilibrium Selection in Games (with Reinhard Selten), 1988.

ABOUT: American Economic Review June 1995; Business Week October 24, 1994; New York Times October 12, 1994; Science October 21, 1994; Who's Who in America, 1996.

HEANEY, SEAMUS
(April 13, 1939–   )
Nobel Prize for Literature, 1995

SEAMUS HEANEY

Seamus Justin Heaney, Irish poet, essayist, translator, and professor, was born in County Derry in Northern Ireland. The eldest of Patrick and Margaret Heaney's nine children, he grew up among farms and villages that had surrounded the home of his Catholic family for generations. His upbringing in that boggy region, rich in ancestral lore, where his father worked the earth as his father and grandfather had worked it before him, instilled in Heaney a deep regard for inherited tradition and for history. "In the names of its fields and townlands," he wrote in "Mossbawn," the first essay in his prose anthology *Preoccupations* (1980), "in their mixture of Scots and Irish and English etymologies, this side of the country was redolent of the histories of its owners." Those histories, as Heaney came to understand, were often bitter chronicles of religious and social animosities.

Despite the anxieties and challenges of growing up in "the split culture of Ulster," Heaney's childhood on Mossbawn, the family farm, was essentially happy. He has recalled with affection his pleasure in digging in the garden, and the rhymes and limericks he sang with classmates. He recited before relatives and friends patriotic ballads or "sometimes, a Western narrative" like Robert Service's, verse much different from the classic English poems he was learning in school, whose literary language did not reflect his experience or echo his own speech. Conversely, the lyrics he recited for his family gave poetry "a place in the life of the home, made it one of the ordinary rituals of life."

In 1951 Heaney left Mossbawn to enroll in St. Columb's College in Londonderry, under the 1947 Education Act, which enabled promising students from rural areas to attend secondary schools and universities on scholarships. During his six years as a boarder at St. Columb's, Heaney's interest in reading blossomed into a love of literature: "When I read in *Lorna Doone* how John Ridd stripped the muscle off Carver Doone's arm like a string of pith off an orange, I was well on the road to epiphanies."

Only after his introduction to the larger world of letters at Queen's University in Belfast, an experience that he regards as crucial to the emergence of his talent, did Heaney feel inspired to write poetry. Fascinated with words for their own sake, he tried at first to imitate "the bumpy, alliterating music, the reporting sounds and ricochetting consonants" that he heard in the verse of Gerard Manley Hopkins. As a Queen's student, he joined the University Gaelic Society, belonged

to a local amateur dramatic society, and contributed pieces to the university literary magazine.

"At school I studied the Gaelic literature of Ireland as well as the literature of England," he explained in "Belfast," "and since then I have maintained a notion of myself as Irish in a province that insists it is British." In an interview for the *New York Times*, he reaffirmed his commitment to his Irish heritage in more forceful terms: "The basis of my cultural allegiance is an Irish island of Ireland with an Irish integrity and sensibility." In his discussion of Heaney's work in the *New York Review of Books*, however, Irvin Ehrenpreis argued that self-definition is the dominant theme of Heaney's poetry and that in the process of self-definition "what the poet means to accomplish is a union of the two traditions"—the Irish and the English.

Following his graduation with first-class honors in English from Queen's University in 1961, Heaney attended for one year St. Joseph's College of Education in Belfast. There he met Michael McLaverty, a dynamic teacher who encouraged the fledgling poet: "Go your own way./Do your own work." In 1962 McLaverty lent him *A Soul for Sale* by Patrick Kavanagh, the most important, Heaney has said, of the seven contemporary writers whose poetry he read at that time.

The arrival in Belfast of the English writer and teacher Philip Hobsbaum in the mid-1960s had a profound impact on Heaney and his peers, whom he helped to transform into serious and dedicated poets. He gave, in Heaney's account, "a generation a sense of themselves" and, in weekly workshops at his apartment, emboldened members of "the Group" to write

71

about the things, places, and people they knew, encouraged them to become, as Heaney put it, "genuine parochials." His encouragement strengthened Heaney's belief in the validity of Kavanagh's dictum—"Parochialism is universal: it deals with the fundamentals." Thus convinced of the primacy of personal experience in the creative process, Heaney turned with newfound vigor and confidence to writing about his heritage, childhood, and rural background. While learning his craft, he supported himself by teaching at St. Thomas' Secondary School in 1962–63 and by lecturing in English at St. Joseph's College of Education from 1963 to 1966.

Heaney's early poetry appeared in pamphlet form in *Eleven Poems* in 1965 and in book form in *Death of a Naturalist*. Critics in general responded favorably, impressed by the honesty and courage with which poems like "Digging," "Follower," "Mid-Term Break," and "The Diviner" confronted and commemorated Heaney's youthful experiences, and his direct, private contact with nature.

The outcome of Heaney's struggle to find "a voice," *Death of a Naturalist* earned Denis Donoghue's appraisal as a "book of promise," an endorsement surpassed by its winning the Eric Gregory Award in 1966, the Cholmondeley Award in 1967, and the Geoffrey Faber Memorial Prize and the Somerset Maugham Award in 1968.

Similarly disposed toward Heaney's next book, *Door into the Dark* (1969), Donoghue concluded in his comments in the *New York Times Book Review* that the poems in both collections are the efforts of an inexperienced talent striving to express itself in effective ways: "In a few poems the young poet's veins bulge more than the occasion warrants, but mostly the rhetoric is true, well-earned. The poet in these books is walking the land, training his eyes, getting the measure of things right."

Several of Heaney's early poems reflect his preoccupation with technique and with the creative process of writing poetry, in which he sees analogies to digging and water divining. "When I called my second book *Door into the Dark*," he recounted in "Feeling into Words," "I intended to gesture towards the idea of poetry as a point of entry into the buried life of the feelings or as a point of exit for it." The phrase "buried life of the feelings" refers to the image introduced in Heaney's first book in "Digging" and elaborated upon most revealingly in "Bogland" of the later collection. That is, the poet must dig deep into his subconscious to discover the source of the "unnameable energies that . . . hovered over certain bits of language and landscape." For, Heaney maintained in "Belfast," "the secret of being a poet, Irish or otherwise, lies in the summoning of the energies of words. But my search for definition . . . is conducted in the living speech of the landscape I was born into."

Two months after the publication of *Door into the Dark*, in the summer of 1969, the eruption of long-smoldering hostilities between Protestants and Catholics in Northern Ireland into violence and bloodshed became pivotal in the life and career of the poet, who was at the time vacationing in Spain, an experience he recorded in "Summer 1969": " While the Constabulary covered the mob / Firing into the Falls, I was suffering / Only the bullying sun of Madrid." "From that moment," he related in "Feeling into Words," "the problem of poetry moved from being simply a matter of achieving the satisfactory verbal icon to being a search for images and symbols adequate to our predicament." His objective was poetry that would "encompass the perspectives of a humane reason and at the same time . . . grant the religious intensity of the violence its deplorable authenticity and complexity." "The question, as ever, is 'How with this rage shall beauty hold a plea?'" he went on to explain. "And my answer is, by offering 'befitting emblems of adversity.'"

Ideas for "befitting emblems of adversity" occurred to Heaney that same summer, after he had read the English translation of P. V. Glob's *The Bog People*. Glob's study of the bodies of men and women preserved in Northern European bogs since the Iron Age aroused Heaney's curiosity and imagination. Considering that some of them had been murdered in fertility ceremonies, he concluded that "taken in relation to the tradition of Irish political martyrdom . . . , this is more than an archaic barbarous rite: it is an archetypal pattern." So he began to explore the contemporary, historical, and ethnic implications of that "archetypal pattern" in a number of poems about the "Bog People."

Among the poems of *Wintering Out* was "The Tollund Man," in which Heaney vows to visit Jutland to see the remains of one of the sacrificial victims preserved in the bogs: "In the old man-killing parishes / I will feel lost, / Unhappy and at home." In the dedication of his third volume, Heaney dealt directly for the first time with the "Troubles": "This morning from a dewy motorway / I saw the new camp for the internees: / a bomb had left a crater of fresh clay / in the roadside, and over in the trees / machine-gun posts defined a real stockade." Several critics were disappointed that the book did not contain a greater number of similar poems. But Heaney has resisted pressure to indulge in "public celebrations or execrations of resistance or atrocity" because "it would wrench the rhythms of writing procedures to start squaring up to contemporary events with more will than ways to deal with them."

Shortly before *Wintering Out* appeared, Heaney resigned the teaching position at Queen's University that he had held since 1966 and, in the summer of 1972, moved to rural Glanmore, County Wicklow, in the

Irish Republic. Some people saw his departure as an abdication of his responsibilities as an Irish-Catholic poet. When he had returned in 1971 to Belfast from a year of lecturing at the University of California at Berkeley, "it was assumed," Donoghue wrote in the *New York Times*, "that he would become the spokesman, in poetry, for the Catholics, his own people." Heaney declined that role. He admitted that the violence had infiltrated his daily life and his dreams, but he was determined not to let it infiltrate his poetry any more than it already had—determined not to let his poetry become a "diagram of political attitudes."

Heaney remained at Glanmore for the next three years, working as a freelance writer of essays and as a coeditor of poetry anthologies. To *Soundings: An Annual Anthology of New Irish Poetry* he added *Soundings II* in 1974. His purpose at Glanmore, "to put the practice of poetry more deliberately at the center of [his] life," was aided in 1973 by an American Irish Foundation grant of $7,000 and in 1975 by the E. M. Forster Award, the former awarded to give artists "freedom in which to work," the latter presented by the National Institute of Arts and Letters and the Academy of Arts and Letters to help finance the stay in the United States of a writer of the English language.

Resuming his career in teaching in 1975, Heaney took a position as a lecturer at Caryfort College, a teacher-training college in Dublin, where he later became head of the English department. By the time he left County Wicklow he had probably completed the poems that make up his widely acclaimed *North*. Recipient of the W. H. Smith Award and the Duff Cooper Prize and, like *Door into the Dark*, a choice of the Poetry Book Society, *North* was hailed as Heaney's "best book" by A. Alvarez in an otherwise skeptical essay in the *New York Review of Books* and by Anthony Thwaite in the *Times Literary Supplement*. Critics recognized that Heaney had at last achieved the necessary balance between the public and private demands of his craft. "Balance is in fact what Heaney's writing heroically exemplifies," R. B. Shaw asserted in *Poetry*, "refusal to hold his talent aloof from public concerns and at the same time a refusal to allow commitment to degenerate into fanaticism."

"*North* was a superb volume," but its successor was "even better," according to Donald Hall, who enthusiastically greeted the publication of *Field Work* (1979). "The voice," he went on to say in his review for the *Nation*, "speaks of love with an astonishing and wholly captivating tenderness. It speaks as well of violence, desire, and memory, and it speaks with deliberate intelligence—willful, diligent and playful. For all the qualities I list, the most important is song." As Heaney works with verse forms, metrics, and half-rhymes and internal rhymes that are traditional in English poetry, he achieves through his sensitivity to patterns of vowels and consonants and the cadence of words what Marjorie Perloff in *Book World* described as his "gorgeously crafted sound structures."

Heaney attained a solid reputation among such respected critics as Hall, Donoghue, and Helen Vendler, who called Heaney "the best poet now writing in Ireland." In response to interest in his work, Farrar, Straus, & Giroux published in 1980 *Poems 1965–1975*, a collection of all the poems in the books that preceded *Field Work*, and *Preoccupations; Selected Prose, 1968–1978*, an anthology of 10 essays and 11 reviews dealing with the composition of his own poetry and the poetry of Wordsworth, Keats, Hopkins, Yeats, Theodore Roethke, and others.

From 1982 Heaney was a visiting professor and Boylston Professor of Rhetoric and Oratory at Harvard University. He was Professor of Poetry at Oxford University in England from 1989 to 1994.

Heaney's more recent books include the prose works *The Government of the Tongue* (1988) and *The Place of Writing* (1989) and the poetry collections *Seeing Things* (1991), *Sweeney's Flight* (1992), and *The Spirit Level* (1996).

In 1995, the year he published *The Redress of Poetry*, Heaney was awarded the Nobel Prize in Literature for "works of lyrical beauty and ethical depth." In an interview in *Publishers Weekly*, he declared that "literature is there to open the spaces, not to erect tariff barriers." He observed "that the sense of proportion, the sense of joy, the sense of irony, depends upon a certain amphibiousness between what we can conceive of and what we have to put up with."

Although by the time Heaney won the Nobel Prize he was recognized as being richly deserving of it, controversy remained among critics as to Heaney's dedication to the role of the poet in society. In the *New Yorker*, Helen Vendler dubbed Heaney "the Irish poet whose pen has been the conscience of his country." She interpreted Heaney's work in the light of decades "of unrelenting bloodletting," which "forced a poet whose deepest impulse was celebration into an unsparing examination of violence—one conducted in prose as well as in the lyrics of *North* . . . and subsequent volumes. Essays and lectures have served Heaney as vehicles for considering not only poetry but also political and ethical issues."

J. D. McClatchy, however, writing in the *New York Times Book Review*, although he felt that the Nobel Prize committee had given the award to Heaney "to nudge the peace talks between London and the IRA," considered that "Heaney's poems have all along concerned themselves with something else. The fractious, often deadly politics of his homeland . . . flicker through his poems. But his ambitions have always been more private, and his gift essentially lyric."

Heaney himself explains in "The Government of the Tongue," in the book of the same name, that poetry "does not propose to be instrumental or effective. Instead, in the rift between what is going to happen and whatever we would wish to happen, poetry holds attention for a space, functions not as distraction but as pure concentration, a focus where our power to concentrate is concentrated back on ourselves." The Nobel Prize committee deemed him successful in producing that focus when it lauded him for works "which exalt everyday miracles and the living past."

SELECTED WORKS: Poetry—Death of a Naturalist, 1966; Door into the Dark, 1969; Wintering Out, 1972; North, 1979; Selected Poems 1965-1975, 1980; Sweeney Astray: A Version from the Irish, 1984; Station Island, 1984; The Haw Lantern, 1987; New Selected Poems 1966-1978, 1990; Seeing Things, 1991. Essays—Preoccupations: Selected Prose 1968-1978, 1980; The Government of the Tongue, 1988; The Place of Writing, 1989; A Collection of Critical Essays, 1993; The Redress of Poetry, 1995.

ABOUT: America June 20, 1981; Contemporary Authors, 1980; Heaney, S. Preoccupations, 1980; New York Times Book Review December 2, 1979, December 24, 1995; New Yorker September 28, 1981, October 23, 1995; Newsweek February 2, 1981; Publishers Weekly December 4, 1995.

HULSE, RUSSELL A.

(November 28, 1950–   )
Nobel Prize for Physics, 1993 (shared with Joseph H. Taylor Jr.)

The American physicist Russell Alan Hulse was born in New York City, the son of Earle and Betty Joan (Wedemeyer) Hulse. Hulse's interest in science developed very early in his life. He attended New York's Bronx High School of Science before enrolling at the Cooper Union for the Advancement of Science and Art, where he received his bachelor's degree in physics in 1970. Like all students accepted to Cooper Union, Hulse received a full-tuition scholarship. After graduation, he left New York to attend the University of Massachusetts for his graduate studies. He received his master's degree in 1972 and his Ph.D. in 1975.

Hulse's decision to leave his home state for further schooling was one that had been a long time in the making. "For graduate school I chose the University of Massachusetts because of its radioastronomy group," he said. "I had actually fooled around with building an amateur radiotelescope in high school." While at the University of Massachusetts, Hulse came under the tutelage of radioastronomer JOSEPH H. TAYLOR JR. Together, the pair made a discovery that would eventually earn them the Nobel Prize and shatter previously held beliefs about the existence and behavior of mysterious, light-emitting celestial anomalies called pulsars—all while Hulse was still a graduate student.

Much of Hulse's work at the university centered on

RUSSELL A. HULSE

the search for new pulsars. In 1973, six years after the discovery of the first pulsar by British astronomer ANTONY HEWISH and his graduate student Jocelyn Bell, nearly 100 pulsars were known to exist. It was understood that a pulsar was a dead or dying star of nearly unfathomable mass that had collapsed upon itself into a surface area of only a few kilometers. Pulsars have a gravitational field so intense that a human weighing 150 pounds on Earth would weigh 15 trillion pounds standing on a pulsar's surface. Additionally, pulsars constantly spin and emit two beams of radio waves in opposite directions. To earthbound scientists using radiotelescopes, pulsars appear as regular flashes of light, much like celestial lighthouses. The timing of the flashes directly relates to the pulsars' rotation speed. The extreme regularity of these flashes makes pulsars among the most precise and accurate time-keepers in the universe.

With Taylor, Hulse embarked on a project to execute the largest and most systematic search for pulsars ever attempted. "We wanted to get the greatest possible search sensitivity by doing the best possible signal processing," Hulse said. With this goal in mind, Hulse gathered such unorthodox materials as chicken wire, discarded telephone poles, government surplus parts, and wire mesh ordered from a department store catalog. He then used these items to help build a powerful radiotelescope next to the Quabbin Reservoir, in Amherst, Massachusetts. In order to maximize the telescope's efficiency, however, the receiver needed to be moved to Arecibo, Puerto Rico, home of the world's largest radiotelescope reflector.

Armed with a small computer, a rarity in the early 1970s, Hulse and Taylor set out for Arecibo in hopes of fine-tuning the established algorithm used to search for pulsars. The success of this algorithm relied on the user's knowing at least one of the three parameters that characterize all pulsars—pulse width, period, and frequency dispersion. "The problem is, you don't know these parameters when you're looking for new pulsars," Hulse said. "So we had to search not only the sky but also this three-dimensional parameter in space." While the telescope swept the sky in an attempt to locate a pulsar, Hulse analyzed the collected data for information that indicated the possible existence of a pulsar's characteristic radio-wave flashes. Once such information was found, the confirmation process included an agonizing wait of several days or weeks to collect more data and see if the object still emitted the same pattern of flashes.

On August 25, 1974, while examining data collected from a possible pulsar that he had observed several weeks earlier, Hulse detected something highly unusual. According to his analysis, the time between flashes at the beginning of the two-hour observation period differed from those at the end of the period by about 30 microseconds. Given that pulsars are such notoriously accurate clocks, something was definitely wrong. "I thought the problem might be that our time resolution was too slow for such a fast pulsar," Hulse said. "So I reconfigured the hardware to sample the data faster, and I wrote a new dispersion algorithm that had to run on a mainframe. Our minicomputer was too slow." Despite the hardware improvements, the pulse differences remained. Even more puzzling than the pulse differences was the fact that these differences seemed to follow a regular pattern of alternately speeding up and slowing down. "I noticed that if I shifted the second day's curve forward by about 45 minutes, it fell neatly onto the previously day's data," he said. "And then the next day's data turned out to be 45 minutes behind the second day. It looked as if I was seeing the Doppler variation of a pulsar in a binary system with an orbital period just 45 minutes shy of commensurability with the Earth's daily rotation."

After some additional testing, Hulse concluded that the only plausible cause of the pulsar's alternating pulses was that the pulsar was part of a binary system, and, hence, subject to the gravitational pull of another large object, presumably another pulsar. In this situation, while traveling around its orbit, the smaller pulsar would emit signals at a constant rate. The signals, however, would appear to be much faster and closer together as the pulsar moved toward the Earth. Similarly, as the pulsar moved away from Earth, the signals would appear to be much slower. Binary systems, though very common in stars, were unheard of in pulsars. The pulsar, PSR 1913+16, was the first of its kind ever discovered.

The importance of Hulse's discovery extended far beyond the significance of finding the first binary pulsar. PSR 1913+16 quickly came to be something of a testing ground for ALBERT EINSTEIN's theories of relativity. According to Einstein, such a system would emit gravitational rays that would drain some of its energy, eventually causing it to slow down. Hulse's adviser in the pulsar project, Taylor, tracked the pulsar over the next several years and found that it slowed down exactly as much as Einstein had predicted. Unfortunately, despite several attempts, the existence of these gravitational waves was never proven. The work of Hulse and Taylor, however, provided some very strong support both for the existence of such waves and also for Einstein's theories. "I don't think you'd find any physicist who wouldn't say it's a very precise confirmation of general relativity," said astrophysicist John Bahcall, professor of natural science at Princeton University.

In 1975, less than a year after his discovery, Hulse was awarded his Ph.D. He subsequently took a position as a research associate at the National Radio Astronomy Observatory, where he remained until 1977. He then accepted a position as a research physicist at Princeton University's Plasma Physics Lab.

In 1993, nearly 20 years after Hulse discovered the binary pulsar, he was awarded the Nobel Prize for Physics. He shared his prize, along with the $825,000 monetary award, with his mentor, Joseph H. Taylor Jr. Awarding the Nobel Prize to both Taylor and Hulse was seen by many experts as a compensation of sorts for the academy's 1974 decision to award the Nobel Prize for Physics solely to Antony Hewish, despite the fact that it was his graduate student, Jocelyn Bell, who had actually made the crucial discovery.

Since 1994, Hulse has headed Princeton University's Advanced Modeling Sciences Laboratory. Quite the outdoorsman, he actively pursues a variety of hobbies, including canoeing, cross-country skiing, hiking, and bird-watching.

Hulse is a member of both the American Astronomy Society and the Society of Industrial and Applied Math. He has been a recipient of a fellowship from the American Physical Society.

ABOUT: Boston Globe October 14, 1993; Physics Today December 1993; Science News October 23, 1993; Who's Who in America, 1996.

KREBS, EDWIN G.
(June 6, 1918–)
Nobel Prize for Physiology or Medicine, 1992
(shared with Edmond H. Fischer)

The American biochemist Edwin Gerhard Krebs was born in Lansing, Iowa to William Carl Krebs, a Presbyterian minister, and Louise Helena (Stegeman) Krebs, a former teacher. By the time he reached his mid-teens, his family had moved from Lansing to Newton, Illinois and then on to Greenville, Illinois.

EDWIN G. KREBS

When Krebs was 15, the death of his father led to yet another move within the state, this time to Urbana. He remained there during high school and throughout his years at the University of Illinois, where he received his A.B. degree in chemistry in 1940. Krebs's decision to pursue a career in the medical field was a direct result of coming of age during the melancholy years of the Great Depression. "The Depression of the 1930s influenced me not to be too complacent and strengthened my desire to know how to do something specific—like being a scientist," he said in a statement for *Nobel Prize Winners*.

Upon completing his undergraduate work, Krebs left Illinois to attend Washington University School of Medicine, in St. Louis, Missouri, where he received his M.D. in December 1943. He then served as an intern and assistant resident in internal medicine at St. Louis's Barnes Hospital. Krebs's respect and admiration for numerous "academically oriented faculty members" in medical school led him to a career in medical research rather than medical practice. After a brief stint in the United States Navy, Krebs returned to Washington University, where he became a research fellow in biological chemistry. In 1945 he married Virginia Frech. It was at this time that Krebs had the opportunity to work with CARL F. and GERTY T. CORI, a husband-and-wife team whose work on enzymes and carbohydrate metabolism earned them the Nobel Prize for Physiology or Medicine in 1947.

Much of the Coris' work, particularly their discovery of phosphorylase, an enzyme that assists a resting muscle in deriving from glucose the energy necessary for contraction, would soon become an intrinsic part of Krebs's research. The Coris knew that phosphoryl-

ase existed in two forms—active and inactive. They were unsure, however, of the way in which these forms differed. In 1947 Krebs, then working as an assistant professor at Seattle's University of Washington, joined forces with EDMOND H. FISCHER to tackle this question. Funded by the National Institutes of Health, Krebs and Fischer set out to discover exactly how inactive phosphorylase was activated by the substance adenosine monophosphate, or AMP. As fate would have it, however, the two young scientists' work would soon take on another direction, as they would inadvertently discover a completely different type of reaction.

The reaction they stumbled upon involved the activation of the inactive phosphorylase enzyme by the addition of a phosphate from the compound adenosine triphosphate (ATP) to the protein. Similarly, they found that the removal of the phosphate converted the phosphorylase back to its inactive state. Knowing that all cellular biochemical reactions are the result of enzyme activity, Krebs and Fischer set out to discover the enzyme or enzymes responsible for the addition and removal of the phosphate. The pair soon discovered protein kinase, the substance that transfers phosphate from ATP to proteins. Additionally, the pair went on to discover phosphatase, the enzyme responsible for the removal of the phosphate. These discoveries not only gave the scientific community further insight into the transmission of signals and chemicals to muscles, but also expanded upon the known processes involved in the inner workings of biological cells. "It's a widespread mechanism," Fischer said. "This is how hormones work, it's how a cell grows, how a cell differentiates, how a cell dies, how cancer proceeds and so forth." For Krebs, the idea that their work would have such numerous and far-reaching ramifications was no surprise. "I always said that glycogen metabolism revealed innumerable biological principles," he said in an interview with *Science*.

The fact that such a small amount of protein kinase or other substance can have such a tremendous impact on a wide array of human functions results from a cascade system. "First, when an enzyme acts on an enzyme which acts on yet another enzyme, one has a huge amplification system—in this instance, something of the order of a million, 10- or 20-millionfold," Fischer wrote. "This is why extremely low concentrations of a circulating hormone can bring about the mobilization of very large quantities of a reserve compound like glycogen in a very short time."

After the discovery, Krebs continued working with Fischer at the University of Washington. He scaled the ranks of the university's faculty, eventually becoming a professor of biochemistry and dean for planning in the school of medicine. In 1968 Krebs left Seattle to become chairman of the biological chemistry department at the University of California at Davis's school of medicine, where he remained until 1976. In that year, he returned to the University of Washington to chair the Department of Pharmacology. Additionally, he worked as a Seattle-based investigator for the Howard Hughes Medical Institute, in Bethesda, Maryland, and in the early 1980s he was promoted to senior investigator. At this time, he also resumed his teaching duties in the University of Washington's biochemistry department. In 1988 Krebs retired and was awarded professor emeritus status. Three years later he was awarded senior investigator emeritus status from the Howard Hughes Medical Institute.

In 1992 Edwin G. Krebs was awarded the Nobel Prize. He shared the prize and the $1.2 million award with his longtime colleague, Edmond H. Fischer. The academy praised the pair's work for pioneering "a research area which today is one of the most active and wide-ranging." Joan Brugge, one of the researchers attempting to expand upon the work started by Krebs and Fischer, stated that the scientists had "initiated a whole field of research that concerns signaling processes that control cellular events that are central to human life and death." Krebs's receiving the news that he had won the Nobel Prize was somewhat hindered by a hearing problem that rendered him oblivious to telephone calls and to the messages left on his answering machine. He first received the good news when a reporter knocked on the door of his home in Seattle early one morning. "I was in disbelief at first," Krebs said in an interview with the *New York Times*. "I hadn't been up that long, and I guess I was dreaming a bit."

In addition to the Nobel Prize, Krebs has received numerous other awards, including the Washington University, St. Louis, Alumni Citation for Outstanding Professional Achievement (1972), the Gairdner Foundation Award (1978), the American Heart Association's Research Achievement Award (1987), and the Robert A. Welch Award in Chemistry (1991). He has been awarded honorary degrees from various universities, among which are the Medical College of Ohio (1993), the Universidad Nacional De Cuyo, Argentina (1993), and the University of Illinois (1995). Krebs has served as an editorial adviser to *Biochemistry* (1971 to 1976), *Molecular Pharmacology* (1972 to 1977), and *Molecular and Cellular Biochemistry* (1987 to the present), and he was an associate editor of the *Journal of Biological Chemistry* from 1972 to 1993. Additionally, throughout his career, he has been active in such professional organizations as the Board of Scientific Counselors of the National Institute of Arthritis, Metabolism and Digestive Diseases, NIH (1979-84), Scientific Advisory Board, Sam and Rose Stein Institute, University of California, San Diego (1994), the American Academy of Arts and Sciences (since 1971), the American Society of Pharmacology and Experimental Therapeutics, and L'Academie Royale de Medecine de Belgique, Brussels (since 1994).

SELECTED WORKS: Protein Phosphorylation (ed.,

with O. M. Rosen), 1981; Role of the Cyclic AMP—Dependent Protein Kinase in Signal Introduction, Journal of the American Medical Association October 6, 1989; The MAPK Signaling Cascade (with R. Seger), The FASEB Journal June 1995.

ABOUT: New York Times October 13, 1992; Science October 23, 1992; Science News October 17, 1992; Who's Who in America, 1997.

KROTO, HAROLD W.
(October 7, 1939–)
Nobel Prize for Chemistry, 1996 (shared with Richard E. Smalley and Robert F. Curl)

The English chemist Harold Walter Kroto was born in Wesbech, Cambridgeshire, in 1939 and was brought up in Bolton, Lancashire. He attended the University of Sheffield, where he received his bachelor of science degree in 1961. He continued his studies at the university and acquirred his Ph.D. in 1964. During the years leading up to his doctorate, he conducted research with R. N. Dixon on high-quality electronic spectra of free radicals occurring through flash photosynthesis. After he received his doctorate, he journeyed to Canada for postdoctoral work in electronic and microwave spectroscopy at the National Research Council in Ottawa. In 1966, after only two years in Ottawa, he moved to the Bell Telephone Laboratories in New Jersey, where, according to *Larousse's Dictionary of Scientists*, "he carried out Raman spectroscopic studies of liquids and quantum chemistry calculations." Though after only a year at Bell he would return to academic life at the University of Sussex in Brighton, England, this early research would significantly help him in the work for which he would later receive the Nobel Prize for Chemistry.

Before he began that work, however, he was involved with microwave spectrography, a branch of radio astronomy. Microwave spectrography is used for analyzing gases found in the cold of space. Kroto's first fascination was with carbon-rich giant stars. While studying such giants, he came across and soon investigated what the Nobel announcement called "spectrum lines in their atmospheres and found that they could be ascribed to a kind of long-chained molecule of only carbon and nitrogen, termed cyanopolyynes." Cyanopolyynes can also be found in gas clouds in space. Kroto wanted to get a better look at these carbon compounds because he was curious to see if they could be reproduced in an atmosphere like Earth's.

At Rice University in Houston at the same time, RICHARD E. SMALLEY and ROBERT F. CURL JR., along with their graduate students James Heath, Sean O'Brien, and Yuan Liu, were studying clusters of molecules with a complex machine that Smalley had built. These were clusters of atoms that existed only briefly and only in certain situations. They were not like normal

HAROLD W. KROTO

molecules in that very little was known about the exact arrangement of the atoms and the bonds between them. According to *Technology Review*, they are "typically unstable" and are "significant because they represent a mysterious intermediate scale of matter." To take the example of aluminum: scientists know a great deal about that substance's atoms—including the fact that they contain 13 electrons—and also about aluminum in bulk, with its vast number of atoms. However, when it comes to what exists between those two ends of the spectrum—between one atom and many—scientists know little. Clusters simply don't exist for a long enough period of time for researchers to do a great deal of investigation.

Smalley had been investigating clusters for years, creating them by using a laser to burn through pieces of metal or semiconductors. The vapor that resulted from this action came into contact with a colder gas that froze the clusters as they were created, thereby giving Smalley and his fellow researchers something to study.

In 1984 Kroto took his first trip to Rice University, knowing that the school had the best system in the world for studying vaporized atoms. During an interview on the television program *Nova*, Kroto and Smalley discussed their meeting. Kroto stated that he had wanted to substitute carbon for the silicon material they were using to see, in his own words, if "we could simulate that chemistry and perhaps make the carbon chains that we had detected a few years earlier in space." Smalley said on *Nova* that though they had found "all that astrophysical stuff" interesting, it wasn't what they wanted to do in the laboratory at the time. So Smalley suggested to Kroto that they might

possibly do that experiment on some other occasion. Smalley was hesitant because such an experiment had been done at the Exxon labs some time before, and, as Andy Kaldor, speaking on behalf of Exxon Research and Engineering, told *Nova*, "Carbon was a horrendous mess. It made the machine absolutely filthy. But one of the interesting benefits of it was that we ended up seeing a very unusual mass spectrum." The mass spectrum readings suggested unusual carbon chains and high numbers of carbon-60 (C60) clusters. However, though the scientists at Exxon reported their findings, they did not conclude that the clusters were stable and did not venture to propose they had found a new form of carbon.

About a year and a half after Kroto first visited Houston, he received a call from Robert Curl, who said that Smalley had agreed to do the experiment. Kroto immediately flew back to Houston. When he arrived at Rice on September 1, 1985, he and Smalley and Curl began their work on carbon molecules, with no funding from any company, foundation, or endowment. Some of the experiments they conducted at Rice resulted in the types of molecules Kroto had predicted. He found the long chains of carbon which he believed existed in space. However, these three scientists found themselves involved with an entirely new prospect almost right away. The C60 clusters that Exxon had seen kept reappearing, along with a smaller number of carbon-70 clusters. The C60s seemed to be stable. According to *Technology Review*, the persistent rate at which the mass spectrometer registered a 60-atom peak suggested only one thing—that they were not dealing with a cluster but with a stable carbon molecule consisting of 60 atoms. Before this time, it had been previously though that only two forms of carbon existed in molecular form—diamond and graphite. From this point the three researchers attempted to analyze the structure of this new form of carbon. After a great deal of debate and by using paper models, the group finally constructed a closed sphere, since that was the only way to tie up all the dangling bonds between atoms and create a form stable enough for them to exist as a molecule. The construction was an arrangement of 12 hexagons and 12 pentagons in the shape of a soccer ball. The Nobel Committee's announcement stated that the scientists named the new form of carbon buckminsterfullerene, after the American architect R. Buckminster Fuller, who designed the geodesic dome with that structure. The molecules are affectionately nicknamed "buckyballs," according to the *Boston Globe*.

When this research was completed after 11 days of intense study, Kroto, Curl, and Smalley had a very plausible theory but no real proof. The reason for this was that their equipment could only produce several billion molecules at a time—far fewer than were needed in order to illustrate the carbon molecule's structure authoritatively by chemical reactions or spectroscopy.

From 1985 to 1990, Kroto and Smalley attempted to prove that their theoretical buckyballs existed, using various compounds to discover their reactions. According to the Nobel Prize Committee's announcement, they injected several gases such as hydrogen, nitrous oxide, carbon monoxide, sulphur dioxide, oxygen, and ammonia into the helium gas stream, but no effect on the carbon-60 molecules could be found, suggesting that the molecule was a slow-reacting compound. Some evidence to support their theory was that they were able to identify carbon clusters that enclosed one or more metal atoms, owing to the fact that C60 and C70 molecules are hollow, allowing other atoms to be placed inside them.

In 1990, the buckyball theory was finally proven by two scientists cited by the Nobel Committee, though they did not share in the award. The two scientists, Donald R. Huffman of the University of Arizona and Wolfgang Kratschmer of the Max Planck Institute for Nuclear Physics in Heidelberg, Germany, created an arc using two graphite rods that burned in a helium atmosphere. They then extracted the carbon condensate and retreived a mixture of C60 and C70 to determine their structures. The scientific community could now study the chemical properties of C60 and C70 and create buckyballs in vast quantities easily. As stated in the Nobel Committee's announcement: "An entirely new branch of chemistry developed, with consequences in such diverse areas as astrochemistry, superconductivity and materials chemistry/physics." The benefits are enormous. Because buckyballs are so strong for their size, it is theoretically possible that they will be able to conduct electricity without any resistance or loss of power, and they could also be used as a delivery system for medicine to the human body. Buckyballs have also been useful in many other branches of science, including synthetic chemistry, solid state chemistry and physics, cluster beam studies, and astrophysical studies.

In 1985 Harold Kroto became a full professor at the University of Sussex. As of 1996 he was still chairman of the editorial board of the Chemical Society Reviews, a position he assumed in 1990. In 1991 he was made a Royal Society Research Professor. He has received many awards for his work, including the International Prize for New Materials by the American Physical Society and the Italgas Prize for Innovation in Chemistry. In 1993 he received the Royal Society of Chemistry Longstaff Medal, and he was honored with the Hewlett Packard Europhysics Prize in 1994. The same year he won another award—the Moet Hennessy/Louis Vuitton Science pour l'Art Prize—for his other interest, graphic arts. In 1996 he and his partners in the buckyball discovery, Robert Curl and Richard Smalley, were honored with the 1996 Nobel Prize for Chemistry.

ABOUT: Boston Globe October 10, 1996; Economist May 23, 1992; Larousse Dictionary of Scientists, 1994; New York Times October 10, 1996; Nova (PBS), December 19, 1995; Royal Swedish Academy of Sciences 1996 Nobel Prize Announcement; Technology Review January 1994.

LEE, DAVID M.
(January 20, 1931–)
Nobel Prize for Physics, 1996 (shared with Douglas D. Osheroff and Robert C. Richardson)

The American physicist David Morris Lee was born in Rye, New York, the son of Annette Franks and Marvin Lee. After graduating from Rye High School in 1948, he attended Harvard University and graduated cum laude in 1952. He then served in the United States Army for two years; upon being discharged, he continued his education at the University of Connecticut, where he received his master of science degree in 1955. He moved to New Haven in that same year to join the doctoral program at Yale. While at Yale he was a Dupont Graduate Fellow for the school year 1957–1958, before finishing his doctoral work and receiving his Ph.D. in 1959.

That same year he accepted a position as a physics instructor at Cornell University, in Ithaca, New York. He married Dana Thorangkul—with whom he would later have two sons, Eric Bertel and James Marvin—in 1960. At Cornell, Lee established himself quickly and moved to full tenured professor in fewer than 10 years. He also met and worked alongside ROBERT C. RICHARDSON, an associate professor at Cornell and a fellow physicist, and DOUGLAS D. OSHEROFF, then a physics graduate student. Lee would later be awarded the Nobel Prize for Physics with these two men for their work in superfluid helium-3.

Helium is the second most abundant element in the universe, making up 28 percent of all known matter. It is second only to hydrogen, which accounts for 70 percent. Hydrogen is most abundant in stars, and it also turns into helium with the release of a star's energy. However, helium gas is quite rare in Earth's atmosphere, owing to the fact it is so light that the gravitational field cannot hold onto it. Helium was first understood to be a new element in 1868 by Pierre Jules Cesar Janssen while he was on an expedition to India to observe a solar eclipse. His spectroscopic study of the sun revealed a yellow line, which he first thought to be sodium. In 1871 Janssen proved that this line was not sodium, and he speculated that it was not any element found on Earth. Almost 25 years would pass before the scientific community discovered that helium could naturally occur on our planet. In 1895, WILLIAM RAMSAY, working separately from but at about the same time as the Swedish chemists Per T. Cleve and Nils Langlet, proved that helium is present in the gas released when the mineral cleveite is heated. Just a year later, Heinrich G. J. Kayser discovered that

DAVID M. LEE

small amounts of helium are present in our atmosphere. By 1906, helium had been discovered in natural gas and in the alpha particles emitted by natural and other radioactive elements.

Helium is an odorless, colorless, and tasteless gas which does not combine with itself or any other element. It is also the only material on the Earth which remains in a liquid form when cooled to absolute zero. Helium's most common isotope has two protons and two neutrons in its nucleus. It is called helium-4 because its atomic mass number is four. An isotope with two protons and one neutron was discovered in 1939 by LUIS W. ALVAREZ and R. Cornog. It is called helium-3 and is rare in nature as compared with helium-4. It is usually obtained from tritium that is undergoing radioactive decay. Tritium is used in thermonuclear fusion weapons.

Lee, Richardson, and Osheroff worked with helium-3 beginning in 1972. They made an unexpected discovery: helium-3 could achieve superfluidity at about two one-thousandths of a degree above absolute zero (approximately minus 459.67 degrees Fahrenheit). The scientific community had already speculated that such a condition could exist in helium-3, especially since it had been shown to occur in helium-4 in the 1930s by the Russian scientist PYOTR KAPITZA, who was awarded the 1978 Nobel Prize for Physics for his discovery. Superfluid helium, according to the *New York Times*, "loses the viscosity associated with ordinary fluids and flows without resistance. It can climb the walls of containers and flow down the outside, among many other strange tricks." The three physicists discovered that helium-3 in such a superfluid condition was also magnetic. This was so surprising

to the scientific community that it refused to publish the results of their research, insisting that such a condition was not possible. Douglas Osheroff, recollecting that incident to the *New York Times*, stated, "It was because our results were so unexpected that our paper reporting the discovery was initially rejected by *Physical Review Letters*." That publication, one of the top physics journals in the world, later reassessed the paper and printed it. A new kind of sound—zero sound—was also uncovered during the three scientists' research on superfluidity. Zero sound occurs only at temperatures near absolute zero and is akin to waves that arise in ionized gases, known as plasmas. Finally, superfluid helium-3 shows effects ordinarily associated with microscopic phenomena, such as molecules or other such subatomic particles.

A superfluid such as helium-3 can function as a quantum microscope, which researchers can use to better understand the field of quantum mechanics—a field in which the rules of everyday physics do not apply. An example that the *New York Times* used is as follows: "Vortices formed by swirling these superfluids appear or disappear in abrupt quantum jumps, rather than smooth progressions, as they would be in ordinary water." On the quantum level, Lee and his fellow scientists at Cornell discovered that helium-3 behaves quite differently from helium-4 in the state of superfluidity. Due to superfluidity, the group was able to observe on a large scale the properties of microscopic phenomena. According to Lee, the nuclei of superfluid helium-3 "dance around each other in pairs." However, the nuclei are not so close that other particles are unable to pass between them. Lee also noted that a continued study of superfluid helium-3 could help humanity better understand the rotational neutron stars.

The study of superfluid helium-3 has other benefits. According to the *Los Angeles Times*, "since superfluid helium-3 is quite similar to superconducting materials, in which electric currents can flow forever without losing energy, understanding it could help physicists develop practical superconductors for use in power lines and motors." *Newsday* reported in its article about the 1996 Nobel Prize for Physics that the research conducted by Lee, Richardson, and Osheroff has brought new insights into the first moments of the universe. "The physical transactions that occur as helium becomes frictionless are similar to processes believed to have taken place a fraction of a second after the Big Bang." The superfluidity of helium may have had a direct effect on the condensation of matter into galaxies.

After completing his work with Richardson and Osheroff, Lee continued teaching at Cornell, with which he is still affiliated. During the 1974–1975 school year, he was a visiting professor at the University of Florida. For the month of October 1981, he was a visiting lecturer at Peking University in China. In 1988, he was twice a visiting professor—first at the

University of California in San Diego and then at the University of Grenoble (Joseph Fourier University) in France.

David Lee has been associated with many groups in the United States which have recognized him for his outstanding work in the field of physics. In 1982 he was a member of the Optical Society of America. In the same year he was granted fellowships from the American Physical Society and the American Association for the Advancement of Science. In 1990 he was a fellow of the American Academy of Arts and Sciences, and in 1991 he became a member of the National Academy of Sciences. He joined the American Physical Society Committee to Evaluate Reviews of Modern Physics in 1992. Finally, in both 1993 and 1995, he was given Class Membership in the National Academy of Sciences.

With Robert Richardson and Douglas Osheroff, David Lee was awarded three prizes for the discovery of superfluid phases of liquid helium-3: the Sir Francis Simon Memorial Prize (1976), the Oliver E. Buckley Solid State Physics Prize of the American Physical Society (1981), and the 1996 Nobel Prize for Physics, for work that the Nobel Committee suggested "may offer some insights into cosmic mysteries."

ABOUT: American Men & Women of Science, 1995-96; Collier's Encyclopedia, 1996; Los Angeles Times October 10, 1996; New York Times October 10, 1996; Newsday October 10, 1996; Royal Swedish Academy of Sciences 1996 Nobel Prize Announcement; Who's Who in America, 1997.

LEWIS, EDWARD B.

(May 20, 1918–)
Nobel Prize for Physiology or Medicine, 1995 (shared with Christiane Nüsslein-Volhard and Eric F. Wieschaus)

The American geneticist Edward B. Lewis was born in Wilkes-Barre, Pennsylvania, to Laura Histead and Edward B. Lewis. While he attended high school in Wilkes-Barre in the 1930s, he became interested in the natural mutations of fruit flies, which produced such abnormalities as extra sets of wings. This early fascination with a normally overlooked development would lead him to become a geneticist and a Nobel Prize winner. Still, Lewis had other interests—he attended Bucknell University for a year in his native state of Pennsylvania on a music scholarship before transferring to the University of Minnesota. In 1939, he earned his B.A. in biostatistics from Minnesota, then moved on to the California Institute of Technology for graduate work. He received his Ph.D in genetics from Caltech in 1942, and the next year he received a master's degree in meteorology. Lewis stayed on at Caltech in Pasadena, joining the staff as an instructor of biology in 1946. He became a full professor in 1966.

EDWARD B. LEWIS

In 1910 the first work on fruit fly mutations was undertaken by THOMAS HUNT MORGAN, an early Nobel Prize winner. However, it was not until the 1930s that scientific researchers began to use X rays, and later chemicals, to cause mutations purposely. This work was done to investigate the inheritance factor in such mutations, not necessarily to comprehend the development of individual specimens. In the 1940s Michael Ashburner, a geneticist at Cambridge University in England, suggested that such mutations—which also occur naturally— were not just interesting abnormalities but were the key to unlocking the code of genetic development, and he believed that this work would be "interesting in a biological sense." It turned out that Ashburner was correct in his assertion—fruit flies are classic genetic specimens, and the basic structure of their genetic codes is similar to those for higher life forms, including humans.

According to the Nobel Committee, the work Lewis began in the early 1940s on fruit flies "laid the foundation for what is now known about the genes that regulate the development of specific regions of the body." His work led first to a new study of genetic development and later to the understanding that most life forms are controlled by a set of master regulatory genes. The mutations he studied are termed "homeotic" mutations, *homeotic* coming from the Greek word for likeness. Upon careful observation, he discovered that these mutations, like the duplicate sets of wings on the fruit flies, occurred because the body was missing a section which was replaced by a duplicate section. Because of this, he concluded that the genes of the body were segmented and ordered, even in the embryo stage. Genes play an important part in the ordering of the body plan, and each section is controlled by a specific group of genes. According to the *New York Times*, Lewis discovered that groups of genes "were arranged in the same order on the chromosomes as the body segments they controlled." The first genes control the head section, the next control the torso, the next the tail region, and so on.

Lewis chose the fruit fly not only because it has a genetic structure similar to that of human beings but also because it develops from fertilized egg to embryo in only nine days. The fertilized egg divides quickly into two cells, then four, then six, and so on. The Nobel Prize Committee in their announcement described how, up until the 16-cell cycle, all the cells are equal; however, "beyond this point, cells begin to specialize and the embryo becomes asymmetrical. Within a week it becomes clear what will form the head and tail regions and what will become the ventral and dorsal sides of the embryo. Sometime later in development the body of the embryo forms segments, and the position of the vertebral column is fixed." Lewis, and later CHRISTIANE NUSSLEIN-VOLHARD and ERIC F. WIESCHAUS, sought to discover which genes control this development and whether their control of each region is independent or if the genes work in unison.

Lewis increased humanity's understanding of genetics tremendously. He demonstrated that genes are ordered and are assigned to separate sections of the developing body, and he proved that duplication occurs in order to create a segment of the body when a needed gene is missing. His findings were published in *Nature* in 1978 as a paper entitled "A Gene Complex Controlling Segmentation in Drosophila." Other scientists, however, were critical because they were not convinced that he was dealing with genes. Peter A. Lawrence, a geneticist, was quoted by the *New York Times*: "Nowadays, Lewis might have lost his grant, but those were more permissive times; he was undeterred and faced up to the daunting task of understanding" the gene complexes he was researching. Shortly after his findings were released, however, two scientists, working out of the European Molecular Biology Laboratory in Heidelberg in what was then West Germany, began to pursue a deeper understanding of the genes he had researched for so long.

Eric Wieschaus, an American, and Christiane Nüsslein-Volhard, a German, wanted according to the *Boston Globe*, "to go far beyond Lewis's work, hoping to discover all the genes that determine embryo development in the fruit fly." They took a trial-and-error approach to finding out which genes started the process of development. They bred 40,000 fly families, only to discover that the majority of the mutations were minor. However, they did discover that of the fruit fly's 20,000 genes, 5,000 were important to development, and 139 were absolutely necessary. The *New York Times* reported that some of the mutations were

bizarre as well as fascinating—from the lack of muscles throughout some of the bodies to the skin of others being comprised solely of nerve cells. Categorizing these various mutant reactions proved to be daunting for the pair of researchers. *Science* reported that they found some illumination when they observed that "their mutant flies fit into three distinct categories—which they named 'gap,' 'pair-rule,' and 'segmented-polarity'—and proposed that the three corresponding sets of genes each act at a different level to progressively subdivide the embryo into segments."

Theoretically this work will produce benefits for humanity. Already, researchers have a better understanding of which genes are most important in fruit flies—that is, which genes have remarkable correlations to those of human beings. Also, this research can be used to explore the flaws in human embryos that account for some of the nearly 40 percent of birth defects with no known cause. The work done on the fruit fly by these three scientists has been instrumental in providing a better understanding of congenital malformations in mankind, including Waardenburg's syndrome, a rare disease that involves deafness, defects in the facial skeleton, and abnormal pigmentation in the iris. The trio has also discovered that another gene mutation causes aniridia, or the complete loss of the iris.

Lewis retired from teaching in 1988 and became a professor emeritus at Caltech. In October 1995, the Royal Swedish Academy announced that Lewis, Wieschaus, and Nüsslein-Volhard were the winners of the Nobel Prize in Physiology or Medicine for their work in genetics. The Nobel Committee in its announcement stated that "these three scientists have achieved a breakthrough that will help explain congenital malformations in man. It is likely that mutations in such important genes are responsible for some of the early, spontaneous abortions in man and for some of the 40 percent of the congenital malformations that develop due to unknown reasons." Upon hearing the announcement, Edward Lewis refused credit for himself or his work, maintaining that the award was simply "a recognition of the power of pure genetics."

For his contributions to his field, Edward B. Lewis has received numerous awards from around the world. Among those are: the honorary doctorate of philosophy from the University of Umea in Sweden in 1981, the Thomas Hunt Morgan Medal of the Genetics Society of America in 1983, the Gairdner Foundation International Award of Canada in 1983, and the 1987 Wolf Prize in Medicine from Israel. He also became an honorary member of the Genetical Society of the United Kingdom in 1990, and received an honorary doctorate from the University of Minnesota in 1993.

SELECTED WORKS: Clusters of Master Control Genes Regulate the Development of Higher Organisms, Journal of the American Medical Association,

March 18, 1992; Sequence Analysis of the Cis-Regulatory Regions of the Bithorax Complex of Drosophila, Proceedings of the National Academy of Sciences of the United States of America, August 29, 1995.

ABOUT: Boston Globe October 10, 1995; New York Times October 10, 1995; Royal Swedish Academy of Sciences 1995 Nobel Prize Announcement; Science October 20, 1995; Science News October 14 1995; Who's Who in America, 1997.

LUCAS, ROBERT E., JR.
(1937–   )
Nobel Memorial Prize in Economic Sciences, 1995

The American economist Robert E. Lucas Jr. was born in Yakima, Washington. A Proctor & Gamble Scholar from 1955 to 1959, he was educated at the University of Chicago and received his B.A. in history there in 1959. When he decided to continue his education, he switched majors from history to economics— the subject for which he would eventually win the Nobel Prize. While working on his doctoral degree as a Woodrow Wilson Fellow, he was also a lecturer at the University of Chicago. He received his Ph.D. in economics in 1964.

After attaining his doctoral degree, he accepted a position at Carnegie-Mellon University in Pittsburgh. During this period, a battle was raging between the two great economic think tanks in the United States — the Massachusetts Institute of Technology, which was the cornerstone of microeconomics (the study of markets), and Lucas's alma mater, the University of Chicago, which supported the application of macroeconomics (the study of the whole of an economy). MIT's economists followed the traditional modes of study that flourished in the 1950s and 1960s, accepting the idea that economists could predict such phenomena as next year's expected inflation rate by studying past trends. Their goal was simple: to fine-tune the economy to work more effectively. This proved not always to be the outcome, however, when the methods were applied to real-life problems. The economists at the University of Chicago, disagreeing with the assumptions put forth at MIT, chose to follow the ideas of John Muth, the father of rational expectation in macroeconomics. In 1961 Muth, according to the Economist, "argued that it would be better to assume that people have 'rational expectations' . . . [which are] forward-looking, in that they are based upon all data to hand; expectations that are persistently wrong will be discarded."

Lucas supported the ideas put forth in Muth's work and sought to develop them further. Not only did he help to mathematically confirm Muth's theory that expectations come from all the data at hand and not from

ROBERT E. LUCAS JR.

past trends alone, but he also had a surprising policy solution: that the economy is essentially self-correcting, and that government-made corrections in the economy only make matters worse. Rational expectations, Lucas argued, are genuinely forward-looking. The Royal Swedish Academy of Sciences, in announcing that Lucas had won the Nobel Memorial Prize in Economic Sciences, stated: "The rational expectations hypothesis means that agents exploit available information without making the systematic mistakes implied by earlier theories. Expectations are formed by constantly updating and reinterpreting this information."

The first article Lucas wrote on the subject of rational expectations was considered too controversial to be published in any mainstream economic journals. It was finally published in a new periodical, the Journal of Economic Theory, in 1970. The editor of that journal, Karl Shell, told David Warsh of the Boston Globe that Lucas's work, considered a bombshell at the time, was constructed on "three giant predecessors: the notion of rational expectations itself . . . by John Muth; the overlapping generations model of PAUL SAMUELSON; and an early use of the idea of asymmetric information from the island model of Edmund Phelps." This first article was followed by a series of others on the subject of rational expectations. The most notable of these were "Expectations and the Neutrality of Money," published in the Journal of Economic Theory in 1972, and "Econometrics Policy Evaluation: A Critique," published in the Carnegie-Rochester Conference Series on Public Policy in 1976.

Lucas went further than all of his predecessors in explaining the ramifications of rational expectations theory. He challenged many economic assumptions in this series of articles in the 1970s, including the Phillips curve, which had been named for the economist from New Zealand. A. W. H. Phillips had argued that there is a stable relation between the rate of unemployment and the rate of inflation. By the 1960s economists had reinterpreted this theory to suggest that policymakers could lower unemployment by allowing higher inflation. However, as the inflation problems of the 1970s demonstrated, this did not prove to be the case. When, in that period, unemployment went up, inflation rose at the same time, producing "stagflation." Lucas's work was instrumental in moving economists away from thinking of this type and into predicting trends by using all available information.

According to the *New York Times*, Lucas and his colleagues challenged this common misconception about the correlation between unemployment and inflation. If a government gives in to demand and cuts taxes, "higher potential revenues will induce employers to pay higher wages to attract more workers. But prices rise too, eventually erasing the impact of the wage increase and disappointing the workers." Though workers will be fooled for a while, Lucas argued, the number of persons employed will slip back. In fact, Lucas argued, if the government continues to trick its citizens with these tax breaks, the consumers will know how to predict the coming inflation and the Phillips curve will flatten.

In 1974 Lucas left Carnegie-Mellon University and returned to the University of Chicago, where he continued to teach and to challenge accepted economic thought. He supported the idea that the U.S. economy "is in excellent shape" and has also stated that the federal government is finally "not trying to do things with economic policy that it isn't capable of doing." Unlike most leading economists, Lucas refused to get involved with politicians by offering them advice during campaigns and in committees. Unlike his fellow Nobel laureate and University of Chicago professor, GARY S. BECKER, he did not write a column in which he second-guessed politicians. For the most part he has stayed away from the political fray. Describing Lucas as a modest man, the *New York Times* quoted him as giving credit to his former colleagues at the University of Chicago: "Ed Prescott and Tom Sargent applied the ideas [of rational expectations] at about the same time." Still, Lucas was the one cited by the Royal Swedish Academy Committee as being "the economist who has had the greatest influence on macroeconomic research since 1970."

Lucas has expressed some regret about his work, believing that it has done more to wreck the older strains of economic thought than to create a replacement for those rules. Many economists agreed with Lucas's expression of regret, even though his work forced a more disciplined look at the usual assumptions made by

economists who study human behavior by means of economic principles. Yet by giving Lucas, a man whose work only emerged in the 1970s, the Nobel Prize, the academy itself acknowledged the division between the different generations of economists. According to the *Boston Globe*: "In making the award, the committee of the Swedish Academy of Sciences leapfrogged over some serious work of the 1950s and 1960s and pinned the medal to the leading figure of the 1970s—thereby signaling their view of discontinuity between the older generation of economists and the new."

In 1981 Lucas published two books on his theories in economics: *Rational Expectations and Econometrics Practice*, with T. J. Sargent, and *Studies in the Business Cycle Theory*. The latter book is a compilation of the research he conducted in the 1970s. During that same year he left the University of Chicago for Northwestern, only to return to Chicago a year later. Also in 1981, he became a Guggenheim Foundation Fellow. In 1987 he published the relatively accessible volume *Models of Business Cycles*, detailing his views on business cycle theory.

After being awarded the Nobel Prize in 1995, Lucas had to split the $1 million prize with his ex-wife, Rita, whom he had divorced seven years previously. As of 1996, Lucas was living with his second wife, Nancy Stokey, and was working on the latest subject to preoccupy him: new growth theory, which concerns the forces that drive economic development. In an article in the *New Yorker*, John Cassidy summed up the criticism that Lucas's work has drawn both in real-world and academic terms. Studies attempting to substantiate Lucas's claim that "changes in monetary policy did not have any systematic impact on the economy . . . found that . . . the actions of the Fed did have substantial and long-lasting effects on output, unemployment, and numerous other economic variables. . . . whether the policy changes were expected or unexpected." From the theoretical viewpoint it was found that Lucas's assumption that the supply of workers equals the demand for workers is unrealistic, "but if the supply-equals-demand assumption is dropped, few of Lucas's conclusions hold up."

Lucas told Cassidy that monetary shocks are no longer the cornerstone of his theory of what causes recessions and booms. "There's no question that's a retreat in my views," he said.

SELECTED WORKS: Rational Expectations and Econometrics Practice (with T. J. Sargent), 1981; Studies in Business Cycle Theory, 1981; Models of Business Cycles, 1987.

ABOUT: Boston Globe October 11, 1995, October 21, 1995; Cambridge Journal of Economics April 1995; Economist October 14, 1995; New Yorker December 2, 1996; New York Times October 11, 1995; Royal

Swedish Academy of Sciences 1995 Nobel Prize Announcement; Who's Who in Economics 1700-1986, 1987.

MANDELA, NELSON
(July 18, 1918–   )
Nobel Prize for Peace, 1993 (shared with F. W. de Klerk)

The antiapartheid activist and president of South Africa was born Rolihlahla Dalibhunga Mandela in the village of Mvezo in the Transkei, a region on South Africa's southeastern coast. His father, Gadla Henry Mphakanyiswa, was the chief of Mvezo and a member of the royal house of the Thembu tribe; his mother, Fanny Mandela, was one of his father's four wives. Following his father's death, when he was nine, young Mandela came under the guardianship of Jongintaba Dalindyabo, the powerful regent of the Thembu people, who groomed him for tribal duties as counselor to the chief and whom he came to admire greatly.

Mandela's mature ideas about leadership, especially his belief in the importance of leading by consensus, were inspired by the example set by the regent, as Mandela revealed in his autobiography: "I always remember the regent's axiom: A leader, he said, is like a shepherd. He stays behind the flock, letting the most nimble go out ahead, whereupon the others follow, not realizing that all along they are being directed from behind."

As a youth Mandela was also influenced by certain Western cultural values that prevailed at the Methodist primary and secondary schools he attended. The schools were modeled after British schools, and Mandela and his classmates were taught to aspire to be "black Englishmen," he has recalled somewhat ruefully. Mandela's identification with British interests remained strong at the University College of Fort Hare in Alice, which he entered at the age of 21 at the urging of his guardian. Indeed, when the South African government entered World War II on the side of the Allies to help liberate Europe from German domination, Mandela and his classmates heartily supported the move—"forgetting," he wrote, "that we did not have that freedom here in our own land."

Mandela's exposure to Western culture also distanced him from Thembu traditions, to the extent that he could not bring himself to submit to marrying a woman of the guardian's choosing, in accordance with custom. To avoid marrying the woman, in 1941 Mandela fled to Johannesburg, where, with the help of Walter Sisulu, a prominent black businessman from the Transkei, he soon got a job as a law clerk in the office of a liberal Jewish law firm. Concurrently, he began a correspondence course from the University of South Africa, which awarded him a B.A. degree in 1942.

During his early years in Johannesburg, Mandela

NELSON MANDELA

was surrounded by people of all political persuasions, but he did not allow himself to feel pressured to embrace any one particular philosophy. Instead, he carefully considered all points of view, including not only those of friends who belonged to the Communist Party and the African National Congress (ANC), many of whose members were students at the University of the Witwatersrand, which Mandela entered in 1943 with the aim of obtaining a bachelor of law degree, but also those of his white employers, who did their best to discourage him from pursuing a career in politics.

After much thought, Mandela found that he had the greatest affinity for ideas promoted by the ANC, whose principal goal was the liberation of black South Africans from the shackles of racism. "I had no epiphany, no singular revelation, no moment of truth, but a steady accumulation of a thousand slights, a thousand indignities, a thousand unremembered moments, produced in me an anger, a rebelliousness, a desire to fight the system that imprisoned my people; instead, I simply found myself doing so, and could not do otherwise."

Mandela joined the ANC in 1944, and shortly after that he and others helped establish the ANC Youth League, which eventually came to dominate the ANC and whose aims were nothing less than "the overthrow of white supremacy and the establishment of a truly democratic form of government," as Mandela has described them. Those goals became more elusive than ever after the Afrikaner dominated National Party came to power in 1948. In the following years, the Nationalists passed a series of sweeping laws that transformed from custom into law the system of racial segregation known as apartheid. In addition to requiring each of South Africa's racial groups to live in separate, designated areas, the laws prohibited marriage between people of different races, mandated that all South Africans be registered according to their race, and outlawed the Communist Party in terms so broad that almost anyone could be considered a member.

In response to the new measures, the ANC leadership felt compelled to rethink its strategy to protest the oppression of black South Africans. That rethinking ultimately prompted the ANC to demand, in a letter to the prime minister in 1952, that the government repeal the discriminatory laws. When the demand was rebuffed, as expected, the ANC launched the Campaign for the Defiance of Unjust Laws, which Mandela helped organize. Those involved in the campaign committed such nonviolent—and, according to the new laws, illegal—acts as entering proscribed areas without permission, using "whites only" facilities, including toilets and railway station entrances, and taking part in strikes. Because of his role in the campaign, Mandela, along with many others, was found guilty of "statutory communism," despite the fact that he did not even belong to the party. As a punishment, he was "banned," which meant that he was prohibited from attending rallies or other gatherings (even nonpolitical ones) for several months. (In 1952 Mandela, having already qualified to practice law, established the first black-run law practice in South Africa, with his friend Oliver Tambo.) Mandela was later banned again, and as a result he did not return to the public eye until 1955.

On December 5, 1956, Mandela was among 156 resistance leaders charged with high treason—specifically, committing acts aimed at toppling the government and replacing it with a Communist regime—an offense punishable by death. The acts in question included the Defiance Campaign of 1952 and similar challenges to the government's legitimacy. In the trial, which did not begin until 1959 (Mandela was free on bail during the interim), the government was unable to show that Mandela or the ANC had plotted any sort of violent revolution, and on March 29, 1961 he and his comrades were acquitted. Mandela was pleased by the verdict, though he regarded it not as "a vindication of the legal system or evidence that a black man could get a fair trial in a white man's court," as he wrote in *Long Walk to Freedom*, but rather "as a result of a superior defense team and the fair-mindedness of the panel of these particular judges." Not long after his acquittal a warrant for his arrest was issued, the ANC having been banned by the government in 1960. In the following months Mandela thus lived as a fugitive, posing variously as a chauffeur, cook, or gardener.

Throughout his years of involvement with the ANC, Mandela was committed to fighting to end apartheid through nonviolent means. By the early 1960s, however-

er, he, along with other ANC leaders, began to question the effectiveness of this approach, for increasingly the government was responding to the ANC's actions with violence. One of the more infamous instances in which the government resorted to violence occurred in the town of Sharpville in 1960, when 69 protesters were killed by police. Mandela was the keynote speaker at the Allin African Conference at Pietermaritzburg in March of 1961, which helped galvanize public opinion against apartheid in the new Republic of South Africa. Whether or not to launch an armed struggle subsequently became the subject of heated debate, especially at an ANC meeting in June 1961. For his part, Mandela, having become convinced that "it was wrong and immoral to subject [his] people to armed attacks by the state without offering them some kind of alternative," argued that the ANC had no choice but to take up an armed struggle against the state. Notwithstanding his lack of military experience, Mandela was given the task of organizing an armed wing of the ANC, Umkhonto we Sizwe (Spear of the Nation), whose mission was to organize acts of sabotage against the state with the aim of overthrowing the white-minority government. Mandela now had more reason than ever to be mindful of his movements around the country. His uncanny luck and success in evading capture earned him the nickname "the Black Pimpernel," after the Scarlet Pimpernel, the title character of a book by Emmuska Orczy who eludes capture during the French Revolution.

Mandela's underground existence came to an end on August 5, 1962, when he was arrested on charges of inciting workers to strike and leaving the country without valid travel documents. In the trial that followed, in which he conducted his own defense, he never denied the government's charges, for he had indeed organized workers to strike and left the country without proper papers. Instead, he argued that the state had no jurisdiction over his activities since its laws had been made by a government in which he had no representation, and that it was merely his natural desire to live as a free man in a state that denied him freedom that had put him on the wrong side of the law. "There comes a time," he declared to the court at the trial's conclusion, "as it came in my life, when a man is denied the right to live a normal life, when he can only live the life of an outlaw because the government has so decreed to use the law to impose a state of outlawry upon him." On November 7, 1962 he was sentenced to five years in prison with no chance of parole.

Eight months later South African authorities raided the ANC's headquarters at a farm in Rivonia and seized documents outlining the organization's plans to wage guerrilla warfare in South Africa. That discovery enabled the state to try Mandela, along with several other top ANC officials, on new and more serious charges. The Rivonia Trial, as it became known, ended with the defendants being convicted of treason. Although their crime was punishable by death—an outcome that Mandela fully expected—the court sentenced them to life in prison, with no chance of parole, on June 12, 1964. The trial was the subject of considerable media attention around the world, and appeals for clemency were received in South Africa from abroad. An editorial writer for the *New York Times* predicted that history would judge that "the ultimate guilty party is the government in power—and that is already the verdict of world opinion."

For the next 18 years, Mandela was confined to the maximum-security prison on Robben Island, off South Africa's coast. His first cell there was seven feet square, with a single light bulb and a mat on the floor for sleeping. He had the right to receive only one brief letter and one visitor every six months. But in spite of the harsh conditions, Mandela was determined not to surrender to despair. Indeed, he has said that he never seriously considered the possibility that he would not one day walk on South African soil as a free man.

Within a year or two, conditions at Robben Island improved somewhat, in part through the efforts of the International Red Cross. Mandela was permitted to take correspondence courses from the University of London, and he and the other prisoners were eventually provided with desks and, later, stools. Still, virtually all conversation among the prisoners was forbidden, and they were not allowed to read newspapers, which they nevertheless felt duty-bound to try to do (and which they succeeded in doing), so as to keep abreast of political developments in South Africa. Beginning in the 1970s, as conditions permitted, Mandela and his ANC comrade Walter Sisulu led political study groups. Mandela also drafted judicial appeals for other inmates, often piecing together the details of a case as information came slowly to him through the prison grapevine.

In 1980, at the urging of several top ANC officials, the *Johannesburg Sunday Post* launched a campaign to free Mandela by printing a petition that readers could sign to demand that he and other political prisoners be released. Although it had strong resistance from the government—newspapers had long been barred from printing Mandela's photograph or citing his words—the campaign established him more firmly as the embodiment of black South Africans' fight for freedom.

In 1982 Mandela was transferred to Pollsmoor Maximum Security Prison. By then the effort to end apartheid had taken on greater urgency among the younger generation of black South Africans and as a result was gaining attention and sympathy abroad. There were also signs that the South African government was not impervious to the mounting international criticism of its policies, and that, more important, it realized it might eventually have to accommodate at least some of the concerns of the country's increasingly militant black majority.

One such sign came in 1985, when President P. W. Botha offered to free Mandela and all other political prisoners if they agreed to "unconditionally" repudiate violence. Mandela refused, for the same reason that he had committed himself to the armed struggle against apartheid more than two decades before—namely, that the government, by resorting to violent means itself, had left the ANC with no other course of action. But he saw in Botha's offer a change in attitude and decided to take a chance. Later that year, on his own initiative, he began exploring the possibility of conducting secret talks with the government. Such an effort, not coincidentally, had only then become logistically feasible, because in that year Mandela was moved to a cell where he had little contact with his colleagues and could thus speak with government officials privately.

Mandela at first told no one about his plan. "There are times when a leader must move ahead of the flock, go off in a new direction, confident that he is leading his people the right way," he wrote in his memoir. He took some consolation in the fact that his "isolation furnished [his] organization with an excuse in case matters went awry; the old man was alone and completely cut off, and his actions were taken by him as an individual, not as a representative of the ANC."

By 1987 Mandela had had several secret discussions with the minister of justice, Kobie Coetsee, the upshot of which was that the government appeared to be interested in reaching some sort of compromise with the ANC. In late 1988 Mandela was transferred to Victor Verster Prison, also near Cape Town, where he was provided with a cottage with a swimming pool and allowed to keep his own schedule. There, the talks continued.

In 1989 Botha stepped down both as head of the National Party and as president; he was succeeded by F. W. DE KLERK. At first Mandela, like most political observers both within and outside South Africa, viewed de Klerk as simply a party man, but he soon came to see the new president as "a man who saw change as necessary and inevitable." Change was not long in coming. Shortly after taking office, de Klerk overturned many of the laws that constituted petty apartheid (such as those segregating parks and restaurants and other public facilities), released a number of black leaders from prison, and met personally with Mandela. Then, in a speech before Parliament on February 2, 1990, de Klerk lifted the ban on the ANC as well as on other opposition organizations, declaring, "The time for negotiations has arrived." The following week he told Mandela that his release was imminent.

Mandela's release from prison, on February 11, 1990, was one of the most dramatic news events of the year. A few months later Mandela embarked on a world tour, making stops in major cities throughout North America and Europe, where he was welcomed as a hero and world leader. In Great Britain he met with Prime Minister Margaret Thatcher. In the United States he addressed a joint session of Congress and conferred with President George Bush.

The task of establishing a truly democratic government in South Africa fell to the multiparty Convention for a Democratic South Africa, which began in December 1991. The negotiations that ensued, led by Mandela and de Klerk, were not without conflict and were broken off at various points. A major hurdle was crossed on September 26, 1992, when Mandela and de Klerk signed a Record of Understanding, which formalized their agreement that a single, freely elected constitutional assembly would both serve as the transitional legislature and draft a new constitution. Another milestone was reached on June 3, 1993, when it was agreed that the first elections open to all South African citizens would take place on April 27, 1994. For their efforts in bringing South Africa to that point, Mandela and de Klerk were awarded the 1993 Nobel Peace Prize.

Few were surprised when Mandela became a candidate for president in those elections. As expected, the ANC won handily, capturing 62.6 percent of the popular vote. "The images of South Africans going to the polls that day are burned in my memory," Mandela recalled in his autobiography. "Great lines of patient people snaking through the dirt roads and streets of towns and cities; old women who had waited half a century to cast their first vote saying they felt like human beings for the first time in their lives; white men and women saying they were proud to live in a free country at last. The mood of the nation during those days of voting was buoyant. The violence and bombings ceased, and it was as if we were a nation reborn."

In his inaugural speech in May 1994, Mandela declared, "Our deepest fear is not that we are inadequate. Our deepest fear is that we are powerful beyond measure. It is our light, not our darkness, that most frightens us . . . as we let our own light shine, we unconsciously give other people permission to do the same. As we are liberated from our own fear, our presence automatically liberates others."

In the months that followed, Mandela and the Government of National Unity began to draft a program of reconstruction and development aimed at both satisfying the demands of long-disenfranchised blacks and attracting new investments from abroad. Mandela has been credited with significantly advancing the cause of mutual understanding and tolerance among his country's diverse ethnic and political groups. As a result, he has succeeded in gaining the confidence of the more conservative elements of South Africa's electorate. "Even if Mandela achieves little more before he retires, he will have won a special niche in South African history as the dignified, white-haired patriarch

who won the respect of his political enemies," wrote Patrick Laurence in *Africa Report* in 1994. As it turned out, South Africa, under Mandela's leadership, adopted a new constitution in 1996—one that guarantees freedom of speech and political activity, grants employees the right to strike, and gives citizens the right to restitution for land seized by the government under apartheid, among other measures.

From his marriage to Evey Mase, a nurse, which lasted from 1944 until 1956, Nelson Mandela has three children (a fourth died in infancy). In 1958 he married Nomzamo Winnie Madikizela, then a young social worker. The couple had two daughters in the four years they lived together before Mandela's imprisonment. Winnie Mandela became her husband's principal supporter and spokesperson during his years in prison, and she ultimately developed a political power base of her own. Her reputation was later marred by charges of criminal behavior. Following Mandela's release, the couple became estranged, and they separated in April 1992.

In addition to the Nobel Prize, over the years Mandela has received numerous honors and awards. He won the Bruno Kreisky Prize for Human Rights in 1982 and was named an Honorary Citizen of Rome in 1983. He received the Sakharov Prize in 1988 and the Gaddaff Human Rights Prize in 1989 and shared the Houphouet Prize in 1991. He has received a great number of honorary doctorates, including a joint honorary degree from 38 traditionally black American universities, which he accepted in 1990 during a ceremony at Morehouse College, in Atlanta.

"The policy of apartheid created a deep and lasting wound in my country and my people," Nelson Mandela concluded in his autobiography. "All of us will spend many years, if not generations, recovering from that profound hurt." Mandela nevertheless remains full of hope that such a recovery will eventually take place. "My country is rich in the minerals and gems that lie beneath his soil, but I have always known that its greatest wealth is the people, finer and truer than the purest diamonds."

SELECTED WORKS: Long Walk to Freedom, 1994; Mandela: An Illustrated Autobiography, 1996; Nelson Mandela Speaks: Forging a Democratic, Nonracial South Africa (S. Clark, ed.,), 1993; Nelson Mandela Speeches 1990: Intensify the Struggle to Abolish Apartheid, 1990; The Struggle is My Life, 1990.

ABOUT: Benson, M. Nelson Mandela: The Man and the Movement, 1986; Current Biography Yearbook 1995; Ebony August 1994; Mandela, W. A Part of My Life Went With Him (A. Benjamin and M. Benson, eds.), 1985; Meer, F. Higher Than Hope, 1990.

MARCUS, RUDOLPH A.
(July 21, 1923–)
Nobel Prize for Chemistry, 1992

The American chemist Rudolph Arthur Marcus was born in Montreal, Quebec to Myer and Esther (Cohen) Marcus. He was educated in Montreal at McGill University, earning his bachelor of science degree in 1943 and his Ph.D. in 1946. For the next three years, he served as a postdoctoral fellow at the National Research Council of Canada in Ottawa. During this first postdoctoral work he studied unimolecular reactions. He returned to that study after doing the work for which he would win the Nobel Prize in 1992—on the way in which an electron moves from one molecule to another. After completing his work in Ottawa in 1949, he went to the United States to continue his work as a postdoctoral fellow, at the University of North Carolina. In August of that same year, he married Laura Hearne, with whom he would later have three sons. In 1958 he became a naturalized American citizen.

After completing his postdoctoral work at the University of North Carolina, Marcus began to teach at the Polytechnic Institute of Brooklyn, in New York City. At Polytech Marcus first began to consider the problem of electron transfers between molecules. The chemist Brian Hoffman of Northwestern University, upon hearing that Marcus had won the Nobel Prize for work undertaken nearly 40 years earlier, exclaimed: "What could be simpler than one electron going from here to there? [And then again] what could be more complicated?" Marcus, like many scientists of his day, was puzzled at first as to how electrons could leap from one molecule to another without breaking their chemical bonds. According to Barbara Levi in *Physics Today*, by the time Marcus began to do his initial work in this subject, he "had already read 11 books and published two papers on electrolytes, his interest in the subject having been stimulated by a question posed by a student in his class." He began to pore over WILLARD F. LIBBY's work on the transfer of electrons between molecules and discovered that something had been overlooked by Libby—"the role played by fluctuations in the dielectric polarization."

From 1956 to 1965 Marcus published his findings in a series of papers on electron transferral. Marcus, according to a 1992 issue of *Science News*, "found simple mathematical expressions for the way changes in the molecular structure of reacting molecules and their neighbors affect the energy of a molecular system. He could then calculate the rates of electron-transfer reactions and explain the surprisingly large differences in the rates at which various reactions occur in terms of these molecular rearrangements." What he had created was a mathematical analysis from which he could measure the overall energy through the system of interacting molecular changes. He was also able mathe-

RUDOLPH A. MARCUS

matically to deduce how much energy is created for an electron to jump from one molecule to another.

Marcus sought to test these mathematical calculations. While at Polytech, he would frequently visit his associate at Brookhaven National Laboratory, Norman Sutin. The laboratory had an active program in electron transfers and did various experiments on molecules. Marcus discussed his predictions and calculations on electron transfers with Sutin, who then proceeded to test these theories. Sutin encouraged Marcus to continue his work, feeling that the experiments they were doing, along with the theory itself, could be quite beneficial to the scientific community. As it turned out, the Marcus theory shed light on many complex chemical reactions, including corrosion and photosynthesis in plants.

The end result of all of Marcus's papers is now called the Marcus Theory. The theory, according to *Physics Today*, uses simple yet extremely useful equations to predict how electron energy transfer rates vary within specified parameters. In addition, these equations can show rates for self-exchange transfers in molecules and those for corresponding cross-reactions. Therefore, in the Marcus theory, "electron transfer between the reacting molecules can only occur when the system is at the intersection of the reactant and product free energy curves." Although his work was thorough and he had explained each of his simple equations in detail, one aspect of his work proved to be harder than most for other chemists to accept. Marcus theorized that by increasing molecular force, one would actually slow down chemical reactions. Some experimental research in the 1980s, however, proved even this aspect of his theory to be correct.

In 1964 Marcus left Polytech to teach physical chemistry at the University of Illinois, Urbana-Champaign. He stayed there for 12 years and continued his work on his theory of electron transfer but also worked on other chemical projects. From the days of his first postdoctoral work, he studied unimolecular reactions and attempted to measure them mathematically. He also continued to study the semiclassical theories of bound vibrational states and of collisions. In 1978 Marcus left the University of Illinois to join the staff at the California Institute of Technology, in Pasadena, where he still worked as of 1996.

In 1992 Rudolph Marcus received the Nobel Prize for Chemistry for the work he had done throughout the years with electrons. The *New York Times* announced the prize, worth $1.2 million dollars, on October 15, 1992, stating that Marcus's "achievement provided a mathematical explanation for some otherwise puzzling chemical interactions involving the transfer of electrons between molecules." The Royal Swedish Academy cited as the basis for the award his "contributions to the theory of electron transfer reactions in chemical systems." Brian Hoffman suggested that Marcus's work in the study of electron transfer "is one of the central kinds of reactions of all chemical and biological systems."

Since 1992 Marcus has led a research team of seven graduates and research associates who continue his work on electron transfers at his Caltech laboratory. According to a 1992 article by Ivan Amato in *Science*: "A current focus . . . is on reactions in which electron transfer occurs over distances of a billionth of a meter or so—quite long in the molecular world— in cytochrome C and other proteins important in photosynthesis and cellular respiration. Such studies should reveal how energy flows through these large molecules and perhaps point toward possible spin-offs, such as improved devices for tapping solar energy."

Rudolph Marcus has been honored by various institutions all over the world. He has been a member of several commissions and research committees for chemistry and served as the chairman of the Committee on Chemical Reactions from 1975-1977. Among his other distinctions, he has been an Alfred P. Sloan Fellow (1960-1961) and a Fulbright-Hays Scholar (1972). He was the recipient of the Senior U.S. Scientist Alexander von Humbolt-Stiftung Award in 1976 and of the Robinson medal for the Royal Society of Chemistry in 1982. In addition, he was awarded the Wolf Prize in Chemistry in 1985, the National Medal of Science in 1989, the Evans Award at Ohio State University in 1990, and the Hirschfield Prize in Theoretical Chemistry by the University of Wisconsin in 1994. He has held a Fudan University Honorary Professorship in Shanghai, China and an Honorary Fellowship at University College of Oxford University. His scientific papers have been published in numerous journals, and

he has also served on the editorial boards of several periodicals, including *Laser Chemistry, Advances in Chemistry and Physics, World Science Publications,* and *International Reviews in Physical Chemistry.*

ABOUT: New York Times October 15, 1992; Physics Today January 1993; Science October 23, 1992; Science News October 24, 1992, Who's Who in America, 1996.

MENCHÚ, RIGOBERTA
(1959–   )
Nobel Prize for Peace, 1992

Rigoberta Menchú is a member of the Quiché, one of 22 groups of Mayan Indians who constitute 60 percent to 80 percent of Guatemala's population of 10 million. The sixth of the nine children of Vicente Menchú, a catechist and community leader, and Juana Menchú, a midwife and traditional healer, Rigoberta Menchú was born in 1959 in the village of Chimel, near San Miguel de Uspantán, the capital of the northwestern province of El Quiché, Guatemala. Like many other families of the Altiplano, a mountainous region in northern Guatemala, where farmers subsist on the beans and corn that they grow on small plots of land, the Menchús spent the months of October to February picking coffee beans or cotton on the *fincas*, or plantations, on the south coast. By the age of eight, Menchu was toiling in the fields from 3:00 A.M. until dusk alongside her mother for subsistence wages.

Working conditions on the coffee plantations approximated those of slavery. Menchú's eldest brother, Felipe, whom she never knew, died from inhaling fumes from the pesticides that were sprayed on the coffee crops while the family was working. When Menchu was eight, her youngest brother, Nicolas, died of malnutrition. The family was not allowed to bury him, and Menchú, her mother, and another brother, who had been looking after Nicolas, were evicted from the plantation without being paid for the previous 15 days of work. "From that moment, I was both angry with life and afraid of it, because I told myself: 'This is the life I will lead, too; having many children, and having them die,'" Menchú said in her autobiography, *I, Rigoberta Menchú* (1983), which was recorded, transcribed, edited, and introduced by Elisabeth Burgos-Debray, a Venezuelan-born anthropologist. "It's not easy for a mother to watch her child die and have nothing to cure him with or help him live. Those 15 days working in the *finca* was one of my earliest experiences, and I remember it with enormous hatred. That hatred has stayed with me until today."

At the age of 12 Menchú went to Guatemala City to work as a maid for a landowning family. As she recounted in her autobiography, she slept on a straw mat next to the family dog, which was treated better than she was. After four months of back-breaking labor and

RIGOBERTA MENCHÚ

humiliation, Menchú returned to her home village in the Altiplano, only to learn that her father had been imprisoned for organizing the resistance to the government-sanctioned effort to oust the Maya from their homelands. For years Vicente Menchú had been trying to prevent the appropriation of Indian farms by wealthy landowners, who hired soldiers to mount raids on Chimel and other villages, apparently with the cooperation and approval of governmental authorities. Again and again, armed men destroyed the Indians' homes and their few belongings, raped their young women, and killed their dogs, which in the Mayan faith is tantamount to murdering human beings. At first, Vicente Menchú had sought to redress the Indians' grievances legally, but after exhausting all his options, he and his neighbors resorted to guerilla tactics. Despite their efforts, the village of Chimel was virtually eradicated, its population reduced from 400 to 12 by 1992.

It took Rigoberta Menchú and her family over a year to obtain Vicente's freedom. Three months later, he was kidnapped near his home by the landowners' guards, who tortured him and left him for dead in the road. As soon as he recovered, he resumed his organizing activities, this time with Rigoberta in tow. She traveled everywhere with him, learning some Spanish and making contacts with Europeans and others who wanted to help. He often told Rigoberta, his favorite child, that she would have to carry on his work when he was no longer around.

In 1977 Vicente Menchú was incarcerated again and sentenced to life imprisonment for Communist subversion. In response to community protests, he was released after 15 days, but not without threats from the authorities that he or one of his children would be assassinated. In prison, Vicente had encountered another political prisoner, who spurred him to found, with others, the Committee of Peasant Unity, which is known by its Spanish acronym, CUC. Going into hiding in 1977 to protect his family, Vicente Menchú returned sporadically to teach them and others in the community about the political aspects of their struggle for land rights, which he himself had only recently come to understand, as Rigoberta reported in her autobiography: "We started thinking about the roots of the problem and came to the conclusion that everything stemmed from the ownership of land. The best land was not in our hands. It belonged to the big landowners. Every time they see that we have new land, they try to throw us off it or steal it from us in other ways." In 1979 Rigoberta and her brothers joined the CUC, which had emerged from underground activity in May 1978. It was around the same time that she decided to learn to speak, read, and write Spanish in order to break out of the cultural isolation that had simultaneously sheltered her and prevented her from exercising her legal rights. She also learned three other Indian dialects—Mam, Cakchiquel, and Tzutuhil—to facilitate her organizing work for the CUC in other communities.

With the entire Menchú family branded as Communists, none of them was safe. On September 9, 1979 Rigoberta's 16-year-old brother, Petrocinio, who had become a catechist and community leader, was turned in to the army by a villager. Literally dragged from the village, he was tortured for 16 days before being flayed and burned alive with other prisoners in view of the entire community, including Rigoberta and her parents, who had been forced to watch. In January 1980 Vicente Menchú and other activists, among them Indian peasants, students, and trade unionists, took control of radio stations in El Quiché to broadcast the news of the human rights abuses. Then, on January 31, they occupied the Spanish Embassy in Guatemala City, where they thought the presence of high-ranking Spanish officials would ensure their safety. Ignoring the pleas of the Spanish ambassador, Guatemalan soldiers lobbed several hand grenades into the building. The explosions killed all 39 people inside, including Vicente Menchú. On April 19, 1980 Rigoberta's mother was kidnapped. After being repeatedly raped and tortured for many weeks, she was left to die on a hillside, where her body was eventually devoured by predators.

By the time of her mother's death, Rigoberta Menchú had broadened her organizing activities to include labor strikes. In February 1980 some 8,000 peasants went on strike on the sugar and cotton plantations on the southern coast of Guatemala. The strike drew as many as 80,000 supporters and lasted for 15 days. In the following year Menchú's CUC led the peasants in forming the 31 January Popular Front, in memory of the massacre at the Spanish Embassy. Composed of many smaller organizations of students, peasants, and workers, the front carried out such actions as the Labor Day commemoration, beginning on May 1, 1981, in which demonstrators erected barricades, distributed leaflets, and delivered bomb threats to factories in order to force the owners to give workers some time off.

From then on, Menchú was wanted by the government for her subversive activities. Sheltered by her supporters, she managed to evade arrest until she ventured out on the street for the first time in weeks and was spotted by some soldiers. Knowing that she would meet the same fate as her parents and brother if she did not run, Menchú ducked into a nearby church and disguised herself by letting her hair down and hid among the kneeling worshipers. The soldiers searched the church but failed to recognize her. Even though the town was surrounded by security forces who had been alerted to her presence, she was able to escape and make her way to Guatemala City, where she went to work anonymously as a maid for some nuns. Three weeks later, upon learning that a young Nicaraguan the nuns were harboring worked for the Guatemalan secret police, Menchú was forced to find another hiding place. Shortly thereafter, she fled to Mexico, where she was protected by members of the Guatemalan Church in Exile, a liberal Roman Catholic group. There, through a chance encounter, she was briefly reunited with her two younger sisters, who had joined the guerrillas in the mountains a few years earlier. The three of them met Europeans who wanted to help them and who offered them the opportunity to live in Europe. Menchú and her sisters declined the offer, as she explained in her autobiography. "[My sisters] said: 'If you want to help us, send us help, but not for ourselves, for all the orphans who've been left.'"

It was during a trip to Europe in 1982 that Menchú recounted the story of her life to Elisabeth Burgos-Debray, while spending a week in Paris. Published in Spanish in 1983 and in English translation in 1984, *I, Rigoberta Menchú* has since been translated into 12 languages, including a pirated edition in Arabic, and it has become well known among American college students of multicultural literature. Menchú concluded her experiences with a justification of her role as a revolutionary leader: "The only road open to me is our struggle, the just war. The Bible taught me that. . . . We have to defend ourselves against our enemy but, as Christians, we must also defend our faith within the revolutionary process."

Menchú's nomination for the 1992 Nobel Peace Prize was sponsored by two Nobel laureates, ADOLFO PÉREZ ESQUIVEL of Argentina and Bishop DESMOND TUTU of South Africa, who won the peace prize in 1980 and 1984, respectively. In protest, the Guatemalan government nominated its own candidate, Elisa Molina de Stahl, who works with the deaf and blind. Menchú's nomination was highly controversial not only because it coincided with the celebrations of the 500th anniversary of the "discovery" of the Americas by Christopher Columbus but also because she was accused of actively supporting violence. In an interview with Tim Golden of the *New York Times*, Menchú declared, "When there is already a war, when there is already a conflict, when there are two parties involved, the way to bring about a solution is not merely to condemn it. It is a matter of contributing so that the causes of the war are resolved."

On October 16, 1992, during a visit to the city of Quetzaltenango, in western Guatemala, Menchú was informed that she had been chosen from among a record 130 candidates to receive the Nobel Peace Prize. In presenting the Nobel peace medal and diploma to her, Francis Sejersted, the chairman of the Norwegian Nobel Committee, said, "By maintaining a disarming humanity in a brutal world, Rigoberta Menchú appeals to the best in us. She stands as a uniquely potent symbol of a just struggle." Accepting the honor, Menchú replied, "I consider this prize not as an award to me personally, but rather as one of the greatest conquests in the struggle for peace, for human rights, and for the rights of indigenous people who, along all the 500 years, have been the victims of genocides, repression, and discrimination."

Not everyone was pleased with the Norwegian Nobel Committee's decision. Although a spokesperson for the Guatemalan government was quoted by a Norwegian news agency as stating that "the government recognizes Menchú for her efforts and agrees with her that the prize is a recognition of the indigenous peoples and their efforts to achieve better economic and political conditions," Guatemala's chief military spokesman, Captain Julio Yon Rivera, had said, a few days before the announcement in October, "She has only defamed the fatherland," and the Guatemalan foreign minister, Gonzalo Menendez Park, flatly declared that she should not have won the prize. Shortly after Menchú accepted her award, the Guatemalan army launched reprisals against leftist rebels in the northern regions of the country.

Menchú's reaction to the widespread opposition to her winning the award was philosophical. In her interview with Evelyn Blanck for Guatemala City's *Cronica*, which was reprinted in *World Press Review*, she said, "Perhaps I would have been offended once, but now I understand that one must respect other people's opinions. Moreover, those criticisms are not personal but are addressed to an ideal that does not belong to me alone."

With her $1.2 million Nobel cash award, Menchú set up a foundation in memory of her father. Headquartered in Mexico City, with branch offices in Guatemala City, New York City, and Berkeley, California, the Vicente Menchú Foundation works to ensure the human rights and education of indigenous peoples in Guatemala and throughout the Americas. In addition to her work with the Vicente Menchú Foundation, Rigoberta Menchú has continued her efforts on behalf of the Committee of Peasant Unity and the United Representation of the Guatemalan Opposition—a group made up largely of exiles and allied with the guerrillas. She is also a member of the American Continent's Five Hundred Years of Resistance Campaign and the United Nations International Indian Treaty Council. In 1993 she served as the goodwill ambassador to the United Nations for the Year of Indigenous Peoples.

In the years since her Nobel win, Rigoberta Menchú and the Vincente Menchú Foundation have aided the return of thousands of indigenous Guatemalans exiled in southern Mexico since the early 1980s. Menchú's foundation has established a variety of programs designed to improve education, health care, housing conditions, and job training in her native country. After an October 1995 incident during which a Guatemalan army patrol killed 11 villagers from Xamán, a new refugee village organized by the Vincente Menchú Foundation, Menchú was named the official plaintiff in the landmark trial against the soldiers. "These were the people we loved," Menchú told the *Village Voice*. "We normally run from a massacre, but this is the first time in the history of Guatemala that we are seeking legal recourse."

ABOUT: Guardian February 4, 1992, October 17, 1992; International Who's Who, 1993–94; Lazo, Caroline. Rigoberta Menchú, 1994; Menchú, Rigoberta. I, Rigoberta Menchú: An Indian Woman in Guatemala, 1983; Partnoy, Alicia, ed. You Can't Drown the Fire: Latin American Women Writing in Exile, 1989; People December 21, 1992; Progressive January 1993; Time October 26, 1992; Village Voice October 24, 1995.

MIRRLEES, JAMES A.
(July 5, 1936–)
Nobel Memorial Prize in Economic Sciences, 1996 (shared with William Vickrey)

The Scottish economist James Alexander Mirrlees was born in Minnigaff, Scotland, the son of George B. M. Mirrlees and Gillian M. (Hughes) Mirrlees. He was educated at the University of Edinburgh, where he received his master's degree in mathematics in 1957. For his doctoral studies, Mirrlees moved to England, where he received his Ph.D. from Trinity College, University of Cambridge, in 1963.

Mirrlees's professional career in economics actually started while he was in his final year at Cambridge. At that time, he served as an adviser to the Massachusetts Institute of Technology Center for International Studies in New Delhi, India. After graduation, Mirrlees remained at Cambridge, where he accepted a position as an assistant lecturer in economics. In 1965 he was promoted to lecturer. He became a research asso-

JAMES A. MIRRLEES

ciate at the Pakistan Institute for Developmental Economics in the following year, and in 1968 he returned to the United Kingdom to serve as Edgeworth Professor of Economics at Oxford University, a position he would hold for more than a quarter-century.

Mirrlees conducted much of his best-known work, that which would one day earn him the Nobel Prize, during his years at Oxford. Central to this work and to the majority of Mirrlees's theories and economic models is the concept of asymmetric information. Informational asymmetries occur whenever one party has information that is incomplete or is different from that held by another party. Car vendors who possess far more information about cars than do the potential buyer, auctioneers who know little about bidders' willingness to pay, and banks that lack complete information about the future income of their lenders are all holders of asymmetric information. Research into informational asymmetries revolves around designing contracts and organizations to prevent the parties with the most information from exploiting their advantages. Such research has yielded new insight into a variety of areas, including political institutions, auctions, insurance and credit markets, and tax systems.

Of particular interest to Mirrlees was the idea of creating an "optimal" income tax, one that is both extremely efficient and fair. An optimal tax could easily be created if the government knew each worker's capacity for production at various levels of exertion. In such a case, the government could distribute taxes fairly by requiring each individual to pay a fixed amount. Ideally, this would have little or no effect on a person's desire to work and be productive. In reality, however, the government is a victim of asymmetric information.

It has no way of knowing an individual's capacity for production and instead must rely on the only information it has: each person's yearly earnings. Thus, the current system taxes people according to this incomplete information by taking a portion of every dollar earned. This system perpetuates a cycle in which individuals' incentives to work harder and earn more are reduced because of the knowledge that increased income results in increased taxes.

The questions surrounding optimal income taxation have long plagued economists. Nearly 50 years ago, WILLIAM VICKREY, who would one day share the Nobel Prize with Mirrlees, devised such a tax by working out a rough equation involving a trade-off between tax equity and efficiency. Twenty years after Vickrey first struggled with the optimal income tax problem, Mirrlees decided to try his hand at developing an improved solution. "The solution came in a flash," he told Reuters news service. Utilizing extremely advanced mathematics, the Mirrlees model of optimal income tax produces a result equal to that produced in a situation in which all individuals have reported their productivity levels and the government has adjusted taxes accordingly. Central to Mirrlees's equation is the single-crossing condition, which, in part, states that two level curves cannot intersect more than once. "In more economic terms, the essential requirement of this condition is that if increased effort is imposed on an individual, then in order for the individual to remain indifferent, he needs a greater increase in consumption as compensation, the higher his initial effort," the Royal Swedish Academy of Sciences 1996 Nobel Prize announcement stated. Though Mirrlees was the first to identify the single-crossing condition and explain its economic meaning, it has now become commonplace in a variety of economic theories about incentives. "Mirrlees's work on the optimal income tax was a starting point for a vast amount of research," said Bengt Holmstrom, an economist at MIT, in an interview with the New York Times. In addition to its uses in research, Mirrlees's tax model has found a niche in the political arena. "Every member of the House Ways and Means Committee and every lobbyist has been practicing Jim Mirrlees's tax theory for years as they have argued about the efficiency of various tax policies. . . . He provided the first mathematically rigorous treatment of efficiency and equity that is central to modern economic policy debate," said Deputy Treasury Secretary Lawrence H. Summers in an interview with the Washington Post.

Much to the surprise of Mirrlees, a former adviser to Britain's Labour Party, his model of optimal income tax proved that a progressive tax system is inherently flawed. In such a system, the incentive for very high earners to increase productivity falls. This decline outweighs the benefits derived from increased revenue. In terms of the idea that a progressive tax system is significantly less than ideal, Mirrlees's model is remarkably similar to the theories of modern supply-side economists.

Mirrlees, in collaboration with Peter Diamond, also spent much time analyzing taxes in a variety of situations, including a "second-best" world. In a second-best world, due to an unavoidable social cost, the optimal setup for taxes or economic structure must be avoided in favor of the second-best setup available. Mirrlees and Diamond proved that under such conditions, to avoid a decline in production efficiency, it is most beneficial to avoid levying taxes on any factor of production. This and other results obtained from the pair's work on second-best economies have been repeatedly used in forming economic policy in developing countries around the world.

In 1996 James Alexander Mirrlees was awarded the Alfred Nobel Memorial Prize in Economic Sciences. The prize, along with the $1.12 million award, was given jointly to Mirrlees and Columbia University economist William Vickrey. Fellow economists praised the academy's choice of recipients. "They broke ground on the practical side of game theory; how economic actors can anticipate the reaction of others in formulating their actions," said Barry Nalebuff, a Yale School of Management economist, in an interview with the New York Times.

Since leaving Oxford in 1995, Mirrlees has been professor of political economy at Cambridge University. He has a reputation for being quiet and mild-mannered. "He is a very English person," Holmstrom told the New York Times, "a very pleasant person, but a very private one." In his spare time, Mirrlees indulges his interests in music, travel, and computers, and he also enjoys reading detective stories.

Mirrlees has lectured as a visiting professor at the Massachusetts Institute of Technology, the University of California at Berkeley, and Yale University. He has been a member of the Treasury Committee on Policy Optimization (1976–1978) and an honorary member of both the American Academy of Arts and Sciences and the American Economic Association. He is also a past president of both the Econometric Society (1982) and Royal Economic Society (1989–1992).

SELECTED WORKS: Project Appraisal and Planning for Developing Countries (with I. M. D. Little), 1974; Private Constant Returns and Public Shadow Prices (with P. Diamond), Review of Economic Studies, 1976; The Optimal Structure of Incentives and Authority Within an Organisation, Bell Journal of Economics, 1976; The Economic Uses of Utilitarianism, Utilitarianism and Beyond (A. K. Sen and B. Williams, eds.), 1982.

ABOUT: International Who's Who, 1996-1997; New York Times October 9, 1996; Royal Swedish Academy of Sciences 1996 Nobel Prize Announcement; Time October 21, 1996; Washington Post October 9, 1996; Who's Who in Economics, 1986.

MOLINA, MARIO J.

(March 19, 1943–)
Nobel Prize for Chemistry, 1995 (shared with F. Sherwood Rowland and Paul Crutzen)

The American chemist Mario J. Molina was born in 1943, in Mexico City, Mexico. The following quoted sections are taken from the autobiographical essay he provided for inclusion in *Nobel Prize Winners*.

"My parents were Roberto Molina Pasquel and Leonor Henriquez de Molina. My father was a lawyer; he had a private practice, but he also taught at the National University of Mexico . . . (UNAM). In his later years, he served as Mexican ambassador to Ethiopia, Australia and the Philippines.

"I attended elementary school and high school in Mexico City. I was already fascinated by science before entering high school; I still remember my excitement when I first glanced at paramecia and amoebae through a rather primitive toy microscope. I then converted a bathroom, seldom used by the family, into a laboratory and spent hours playing with chemistry sets. With the help of an aunt, who was a chemist, I continued with more challenging experiments along the lines of those carried out by freshman chemistry students in college. Keeping with our family tradition of sending their children abroad for a couple of years, and aware of my interest in chemistry, I was sent to a boarding school in Switzerland when I was 11 years old, on the assumption that German was an important language for a prospective chemist to learn. I remember I was thrilled to go to Europe, but then I was disappointed in that my European schoolmates had no more interest in science than my Mexican friends. I had already decided at that time to become a research chemist; earlier, I had seriously contemplated the possibility of pursuing a career in music—I used to play the violin in those days. In 1960 I enrolled in the chemical engineering program at UNAM, as this was then the closest way to become a physical chemist, taking math-oriented courses not available to chemistry majors.

"After finishing my undergraduate studies in Mexico in 1965, I decided to obtain a Ph.D. degree in physical chemistry. At first I went to Germany and enrolled at the University of Freiburg. After spending nearly two years doing research in kinetics of polymerizations, I returned to Mexico as an assistant professor at the UNAM, and I set up the first graduate program in chemical engineering. In 1968 I left for the University of California at Berkeley to pursue my graduate studies in physical chemistry.

"I joined the research group of Professor George C. Pimentel, with the goal of studying molecular dynamics using chemical lasers, which were discovered in his group a few years earlier. My graduate work involved the investigation of the distribution of internal energy in the products of chemical and photochemical reac-

MARIO J. MOLINA

tions; chemical lasers were well suited as tools for such studies.

"My years at Berkeley have been some of the best of my life. I arrived there just after the era of the free-speech movement. I had the opportunity to explore many areas and to engage in exciting scientific research in an intellectually stimulating environment. It was also during this time that I had my first experience dealing with the impact of science and technology on society. I remember that I was dismayed by the fact that high-power chemical lasers were being developed elsewhere as weapons; I wanted to be involved with research that was useful to society, but not for potentially harmful purposes. It was also at that time that I met Luisa Tan, who was a fellow graduate student in Pimentel's group and who later became my wife and close scientific collaborator.

"After completing my Ph.D. degree in 1972, I stayed for another year at Berkeley to continue research on chemical dynamics. Then, in the fall of 1973, I joined the group of Professor F. SHERWOOD (Sherry) ROWLAND as a postdoctoral fellow, moving to Irvine, California, with my wife, Luisa. Professor Rowland had pioneered research on 'hot atom' chemistry, investigating chemical properties of atoms with excess translational energy and produced by radioactive processes. He offered me a list of research options; the one project that intrigued me the most consisted of finding out the environmental fate of certain very inert industrial chemicals—the chlorofluorocarbons (CFCs) which had been accumulating in the atmosphere and which, at that time, were thought to have no significant effects on the environment. This project offered me the opportunity to learn a new field—atmospheric chemistry—about which I knew very little; trying to solve a challenging problem appeared to be an excellent way to plunge into a new research area. The CFCs are compounds similar to others that Professor Rowland and I had investigated from the point of view of molecular dynamics; we were familiar with their chemical properties, but not with their atmospheric chemistry.

"Three months after I arrived at Irvine, Professor Rowland and I developed the 'CFC ozone depletion theory.' We published our findings in *Nature*, in a paper which appeared in the June 28, 1974 issue. The years following the publication of our paper were hectic, as we had decided to communicate the CFC-ozone issue not only to other scientists but also to policymakers and to the news media; we realized this was the only way to ensure that society would take some measures to alleviate the problem. Soon after, we published several more articles on the CFC-ozone issues; we presented our results at scientific meetings, and we also testified at legislative hearings on potential controls on CFC emissions.

"In 1975 I was appointed as a member of the faculty at the University of California, Irvine. I set up an independent program to investigate chemical and spectroscopic properties of compounds of atmospheric importance, focusing on those that are unstable and difficult to handle in the laboratory, such as hypochlorous acid, chlorine nitrite, chlorine nitrate, peroxynitric acid, etc. It was in those years that Luisa, my wife, began collaborating with me, providing invaluable help in carrying out those difficult experiments. We also started then to raise a family; our son, Felipe, was born in 1977. Initially, Luisa had a teaching and research position at Irvine; however, after Felipe was born, she decided to work only part-time so that she could devote more time to Felipe. Throughout the years, she has been very supportive and understanding of my preoccupation with work and the intense nature of my research.

"In 1982 I decided to move to a nonacademic position and joined the Molecular Physics and Chemistry Section at the Jet Propulsion Laboratory. Around 1985, after becoming aware of the discovery by Joseph Farman and his coworkers of the seasonal depletion of ozone over Antarctica, my research group at JPL investigated the peculiar chemistry which is promoted by polar stratospheric clouds, some of which consist of ice crystals. We were able to show that chlorine-activation reactions take place very efficiently in the presence of ice under polar stratospheric conditions; thus, we provided a laboratory simulation of the chemical effects of clouds over the Antarctic. Also, in order to understand the rapid catalytic gas phase reactions that were taking place over the South Pole, Luisa and I carried out experiments with chlorine peroxide, a new compound which had not been reported previously in the literature and which turned out to be important in providing the explanation for the rapid loss of ozone in the polar stratosphere.

"In 1989 I returned to academic life, moving to the Massachusetts Institute of Technology, where I have continued with research on global atmospheric chemistry issues. After taking off for a few years, Luisa rejoined my research group. Our son is now in college: besides science, he also has an interest in music; he has been playing piano for over 10 years."

In 1995 Mario Molina, F. Sherwood Rowland, and Paul Crutzen of the Max Planck Institute of Chemistry were honored by the Nobel Committee for their continuous and influential work in the study of the ozone layer. The Nobel Committee's citation stated that these three scientists "have contributed to our salvation from a global problem that could have catastrophic consequences." Though initially their work caused a great deal of controversy with the CFC industry and policymakers alike, eventually both of these groups relented in their criticism. Molina told the *New York Times* that the CFC industry was convinced of the usefulness of the scientists' work once "the scientific evidence was good enough to work with us and the scientific community and the policymakers to formulate regulations."

"When I first chose the project to investigate the fate of chlorofluorocarbons in the atmosphere," Molina wrote in his essay, "it was simply out of scientific curiosity. I did not consider at that time the environmental consequences of what Sherry and I had set out to study. I am heartened and humbled that I was able to do something that not only contributed to our understanding of atmospheric chemistry, but also had a profound impact on the global environment."

Mario Molina has received numerous honors and awards for his work in the study of the ozone. In 1976 he received special recognition from the University of California, Irvine for Contributions in Basic Research. In 1977 he was presented with the Newport Democratic Club Public Service Award for Service to the Environment. From 1976 to 1978 he was an Alfred P. Sloan Foundation fellow. In 1983 he received the Tyler Ecology & Energy Award and was presented with the Society of Hispanic Professionals Engineers Award for Achievement in Science and Technology. He was given the American Chemical Society Esselen Award in 1987 and elected a member of the National Academy of Sciences in 1989. His native country awarded him membership in the Academia Mexicana de Ingenieria in the following year. Molina has also held positions in numerous professional societies, including the American Chemical Society and the American Physical Society. As of 1996 he was a member of the President's Committee of Advisors on Science and Technology (PCAST).

ABOUT: New York Times October 12, 1995.

MORRISON, TONI
(February 18, 1931–   )
Nobel Prize for Literature, 1993

The second of the four children of George and Ramah (Willis) Wofford, the American novelist Toni
Morrison was born Chloe Anthony Wofford in Lorain,
Ohio, a steel town 25 miles west of Cleveland. During
the worst years of the Depression, her father worked
as a car washer, a welder in a local steel mill, and road-
construction worker, while her mother, a feisty, determined woman, dealt with callous landlords and imper-
tinent social workers. "When an eviction notice was
put on our house, she tore it off," Morrison remembered, as quoted in *People*. "If there were maggots in
our flour, she wrote a letter to [President] Franklin
Roosevelt. My mother believed something should be
done about inhuman situations."

In an article for the *New York Times Magazine*,
Morrison discussed her parents' contrasting attitudes
toward white society and the effect of those conflicting
views on her own perception of the quality of black life
in America. Ramah Wofford believed that, in time,
race relations would improve; George Wofford dis-
trusted "every word and every gesture of every white
man on Earth." Both parents were convinced, however, that "all succor and aid came from themselves and
their neighborhood." Consequently, Morrison, although she attended a multiracial school, was raised in
"a basically racist household" and grew up "with more
than a child's contempt for white people."

After graduating with honors from high school in
1949, Toni Morrison enrolled at Howard University in
Washington, D.C. Morrison devoted most of her free
time to the Howard University Players, a campus theater company she has since described as "a place where
hard work, thought, and talent" were praised and
"merit was the only rank." She often appeared in campus productions, and in the summers she traveled
throughout the South with a repertory troupe made up
of faculty members and students.

Morrison took her B.A. degree in 1953 and then
went on to Cornell University for graduate work in
English. In 1955, on submission of what she has since
called a "shaky" thesis on the theme of suicide in the
works of William Faulkner and Virginia Woolf, she received an M.A. degree. After two years of teaching
English "theory, pronunciation, and grammar" to un-
dergraduates at Texas Southern University in Houston,
she joined the faculty of Howard University as an instructor in English, a post she held until 1964. While
at Howard, she met and married a Jamaican architect
with whom she had two sons, Harold Ford and Slade
Kevin

Unhappy in her marriage, Morrison began to write
fiction in the early 1960s as an escape of sorts. "It was
as though I had nothing left but my imagination," she

TONI MORRISON

said in an autobiographical sketch submitted to
Current Biography. "I had no will, no judgment, no
perspective, no power, no authority, no self—just this
brutal sense of irony, melancholy, and a trembling respect for words. I wrote like someone with a dirty habit. Secretly. Compulsively. Slyly." She eventually
drifted into a small, informal group of poets and writers who met once a month to read, discuss, and criti-
cize each other's work. For a while, Morrison took the
"old junk" that she had written in high school, but one
day, finding herself without a sample of writing to
take to the meeting, she dashed off "a little story about
a black girl who wanted blue eyes," which was the gen-
esis of her first novel.

In 1964 Morrison resigned from Howard and, after
a divorce, moved with her children to Syracuse, New
York, and then to New York City, where she worked
as an editor for Random House. There, partly to alleviate her loneliness, she developed the short story she
had written at Howard into a novel, and in 1969 Holt
published *The Bluest Eye*, the story of two young sisters living in a tiny, provincial black community in
Ohio in 1941 and of their friendship with Pecola
Breedlove, a homely, outcast little girl so mercilessly
victimized by her parents and narrow-minded neighbors that she eventually retreats into insanity.

Described by Toni Morrison as a book about "the
absolute destruction of human life because of the most
superficial thing in the world—physical beauty," *The
Bluest Eye* is, on one level, a treatment of the universal
theme of the loss of innocence and, on another, an in-
dictment of the physical and emotional poverty of
middle-class black life during World War II. "Morrison expresses the negative of the Dick-and-Jane-and-

Mother-and-Father-and-Dog-and-Cat photograph that appears in our reading primers, and she does it with a prose so precise, so faithful to speech, and so charged with pain and wonder that the novel becomes poetry," John Leonard wrote in his review for the *New York Times.* "I have said 'poetry.' But *The Bluest Eye* is also history, sociology, folklore, nightmare, and music."

The Bluest Eye established Morrison as a brilliant observer of contemporary black America, and she was often asked to write social commentary for mass-market publications. As a senior editor at Random House she took a special interest in black fiction. "I want to participate in developing a canon of black work," she told Sandra Satterwhite in an interview for the *New York Post.* "We've had the first rush of black entertainment, where blacks were writing for whites, and whites were encouraging this kind of self-flagellation. Now we can get down to the craft of writing, where black people are talking to black people."

Toni Morrison's own writing career took another step forward in late 1973 with the publication of *Sula,* an examination of the intense, 40-year friendship between two women: Nel, who accepts the conventional mores and rigid moral code of the insular black community that is her hometown, and Sula, who defies them. Much of the largely favorable critical response to *Sula* focused on Morrison's spare, precise language, economical, life-like dialogue, and convincing characterizations. To Sara Blackburn, who reviewed *Sula* for the *New York Times Book Review,* the main characters seemed "almost mythologically strong and familiar" and had the "heroic quality" of the characters of GABRIEL GARCÍA MÁRQUEZ. Other reviewers, including Ruth Rambo McClain in *Black World,* Jerry H. Bryant in the *Nation,* and Fath Davis in the *Harvard Advocate,* seconded Blackburn's assessment and singled out for special praise Morrison's masterful creation of Sula, a complex woman who is at once self-reliant, amoral, predatory, alluring, and ruthless.

For Jonathan Yardley, the most fully realized character in *Sula* was the tiny black community of Bottom. "Toni Morrison is not a Southern writer, but she has located place and community with the skill of a Flannery O'Connor or Eudora Welty," Yardley commented in the *Washington Post.* "Thus the novel is much more than a portrait of one woman. It is in large measure an evocation of a way of life that existed in the black communities of the small towns of the 1920s and 1930s, a way of life compounded of such ingredients as desperation, neighborliness, and persistence." *Sula* was named an alternate selection of the Book-of-the-Month Club and was nominated for the 1975 National Book Award in the fiction category.

Morrison's third novel, *Song of Solomon,* the personal odyssey of Macon Dead Jr., presented a different kind of challenge. "I had to think of becoming a whole person in masculine terms," she explained to Mel Watkins for a *New York Times Book Review* profile. "I couldn't use the metaphors I'd used describing women. I needed something that suggested dominion—a different kind of drive."

The central metaphor in *Song of Solomon* is flying—"the literal taking off and flying into the air, which is everybody's dream." Inspired by his great-grandfather Solomon's escape from slavery a century earlier ("My great granddaddy could flyyyyyy . . . He left everybody down on the ground and he sailed off like a black eagle . . . He didn't need no airplane. He just took off; got fed up."), Macon, known as Milkman because his mother nursed him well past infancy, leaves his middle-class Midwestern home for the South, ostensibly to search for a secret cache of gold, but ultimately to find his family heritage.

Song of Solomon was inevitably compared to Ralph Ellison's classic *Invisible Man,* to Alex Haley's *Roots,* and to Maxine Hong Kingston's *The Woman Warrior.* A few reviewers quibbled about the occasional vanished character and the myriad subplots; most, however, were overwhelmingly enthusiastic. Perhaps the most rapturous was John Leonard, who declared in his paean for the *New York Times* that *Song of Solomon* had been "a privilege to review." He was particularly taken by the evocative, poetic descriptions of places "where even love found its way with an ice pick" and where the "heavy, spice-sweet smell . . . made you think of the East and striped tents and the sha-sha-sha of leg bracelets." "From the beginning . . . Toni Morrison is in control of her book, her poetry," Leonard wrote. "Out of the decoding of a children's song, something heroic is regained; out of terror, an understanding of possibility and a leap of faith; out of quest, the naming of our fathers and ourselves."

In 1978 *Song of Solomon* received the National Book Critics' Circle Award as the best work of fiction in 1977. It was the first novel written by a black author to be chosen as a full selection of the Book-of-the-Month Club since Richard Wright's *Native Son* in 1940.

Morrison's *Tar Baby* is cast in the form of allegory. It begins on a French island in the Carribbean, at the home of a wealthy white man, Valerian and his wife, Margaret. The pair have black servants, including a couple, Sydney and Ondine, whose light-skinned daughter—Jadine—has been sent by Valerian to study at the Sorbonne. A beauty and model, Valerian's creation, Jadine has little relation to her black heritage. The edgy tranquility of the house is suddenly disrupted by the appearance of a young runaway black man, Son, who suggests a primitive black past. Jadine and Son attempt to relate to each other but cannot. The novel thus becomes an exploration of the boundaries white society has created between black men and women. Reviewers generally praised *Tar Baby* as a novel of ideas, with Wilfred Sheed mentioning "the thrumming poetry, the animistic sense that clouds and trees are onto something big," but faulting the stereotypical characters and the too-obvious political message.

With *Beloved*, Morrison's next novel, her reputation soared again. Margaret Atwood, writing in the *New York Times Book Review*, was highly impressed by this tale of a runaway slave, Sethe, who is forced to kill her two-year-old daughter in order to escape recapture. Later a young woman, who does not know where she comes from and who calls herself Beloved, appears and attaches herself to Sethe. According to Atwood, Morrison's "versatility and technical and emotional range appear to know no bounds." She added: "Through the different voices and memories of the book . . . we experience American slavery as it was lived by those who were its objects of exchange."

Calling the novel "a masterpiece," Walter Clemons in *Newsweek* remarked that "Morrison casts a formidable spell. The incantatory, intimate narrative voice disarms our reluctance to enter Sethe's haunted house." Stanley Crouch, writing in *The New Republic*, however, differed with the chorus of lavish praise, saying that *Beloved* "is designed to placate sentimental feminist ideology and to make sure that the vision of black woman as the most scorned and rebuked of the victims doesn't weaken."

Jazz, published by Morrison prior to her winning the Nobel Prize for Literature, again has a historical—but more recent—setting. The book, whose action takes place in Harlem in 1926, has characters—a door-to-door salesman, who murders his young lover, and his wife, who disfigures the corpse—who seem controlled by circumstance. Edna O'Brien in the *New York Times Book Review* called them "people who are together simply because they were put down together." O'Brien, although she praised Morrison's virtuosity, complained that she "hesitates to bring us to . . . a predicament that is both physical and metaphysical, and which in certain fictions, by an eerie transion, becomes our very own experience. Such alchemy does not occur here." Jane Mendelsohn in the *Voice Literary Supplement*, on the other hand, remarked that the novel "replays the old plot of rupture and reconciliation and still it surprises, lifting at the end to a moment of beauty."

It was the beauty of Morrison's language that won her the Nobel Prize in 1993: "She delves into the language itself, a language she wants to liberate from the fetters of race. And she addresses us with the luster of poetry," the Swedish Academy declared in its citation. Morrison, in turn, brought the Academy and assembled guests to their feet when she delivered her lecture, one that was compared to William Faulkner's. In what the *New York Times* reporter John Darnton described as "a lovingly wrought paean to language and

to the sublime vocation of 'word work,'" she declared: "We die. That may be the meaning of life. But we do language. That may be the measure of our lives."

Toni Morrison is a visiting lecturer at Yale University and other colleges and since 1987 has been a Robert F. Goheen Professor in the Humanities Council at Princeton University. She teaches Studies in American Africanism, creative writing workshops, and courses on the works of such black women writers as Angela Davis, Alice Walker, Gwendolyn Brooks, Bessie Head, and, occasionally, Toni Morrison. She herself feels a special kinship with the Spanish American authors García Márquez and MIGUEL ASTURIAS because they effectively combine myth and political sensitivity. She has also expressed admiration for NADINE GORDIMER and Eudora Welty because those two women, in her words, "write about black people in a way that few white men have ever been able to write. It's not patronizing, not romanticizing. It's the way they should be written about.".

SELECTED WORKS: The Bluest Eye, 1970; Sula, 1974; Song of Solomon, 1977; Tar Baby, 1981; Beloved, 1987; Jazz, 1992; Playing in the Dark: Whiteness and the Literary Imagination, 1992

ABOUT: Contemporary Authors, 1972; Gates, H. L. And Appiah, A., eds. Toni Morrison: Critical Perspectives Past and Present, 1993; Contemporary Authors, 1972; Newsweek September 28, 1987; New York Times October 10, 1993, December 8, 1993; New York Times Book Review September 13, 1987, April 5, 1992; New York Times Magazine May 20, 1979; People January 2, 1978; Voice Literary Supplement May 1992; Washington Post September 30, 1977; Who's Who in America, 1978–79; World Authors 1975-1980, 1985.

MULLIS, KARY B.
(December 28, 1944–   )
Nobel Prize for Chemistry, 1993

The second of four sons, Kary Banks Mullis was born on December 28, 1944 in Lenoir, North Carolina, and was raised in Columbia, South Carolina. His father, Cecil Banks Mullis, was a salesman, and his mother, Bernice Alberta Barker Mullis, was a real-estate broker. Mullis's interest in science and technological innovation can be traced to his youth. Among other anecdotes, he has recounted how at 17 he learned to make rocket fuel out of potassium nitrate and sugar. With the fuel and a rocket, he launched various small objects a mile and a half into the sky. In a more practical vein, he once built a door opener that enabled him to let his dog out of the house without having to leave his bed.

While at the Georgia Institute of Technology, in Atlanta, which he attended with the help of a National Merit Scholarship, Mullis put his flair for innovation

KARY B. MULLIS

to still other uses. In addition to setting up a chemical-manufacturing company, he reportedly developed a device that used brain waves (which he generated by having his subjects look at pictures of scantily clad women) to turn lights on. After taking his B.S. degree in chemistry in 1966, he entered the University of California at Berkeley, where, besides studying biochemistry, he immersed himself in the then-flourishing counterculture. He conferred a measure of legitimacy on his extracurricular passions when, as a student lecturer, he taught a neurochemistry course on hallucinogens. His adviser, Joe Nielands, rightly described him as "very undisciplined and unruly—a free spirit."

After he obtained his Ph.D. in 1972, Mullis's adventurous spirit led him to Kansas City, where he settled with his first wife, Richards Haley. While there, he temporarily abandoned his scientific career and tried his hand at writing fiction. When he realized that his literary gifts were limited, he accepted a postdoctoral fellowship at the University of Kansas Medical School. He then returned to California to begin a second fellowship, at the University of California at San Francisco. He soon lost interest in his research yet again, though, and began working at a local restaurant.

Thanks at least partly to the encouragement of his graduate school adviser, Mullis picked up the threads of his scientific career in about 1979, when he accepted a job as a biochemist at the Cetus Corporation, in Emeryville, California. Mullis was hired to synthesize oligonucleotide probes, or short stretches of single-stranded DNA, which other Cetus scientists could then use to isolate target genes or nucleotide sequences from a sample of DNA.

In early 1983, thanks to improvements in the proce-

dure for synthesizing oligonucleotides, Mullis found himself with a good deal of free time on his hands, which he filled with a project of his own design: figuring out how to determine the identity of a nucleotide at a specific point in a given stretch of DNA. A technique for doing so would be extremely useful because it would constitute a first step in learning the sequence of the nucleotides in, or the code of, an entire DNA fragment.

Mullis seemed to be close to achieving his goal one Friday evening in April 1983, as he drove to his home in California's redwood country for the weekend. By that time he had already come up with an experiment and had only to work out the details. In the experiment, heated DNA—heated so as to separate the double-stranded DNA molecule into two strands—would be combined with three other ingredients: an oligonucleotide "primer"; DNA polymerase, the enzyme found in cells that adds nucleotides to a growing strand of DNA during DNA synthesis; and, most important, four dideoxynucleotide triphosphates (ddNTP) that correspond to the four different types of nucleotides, the so-called building blocks of DNA. In the first step of the reaction, the primer would bind to a complementary nucleotide sequence on one of the two DNA strands. Next, through the action of the DNA polymerase, one of the ddNTPs would be added to the primer. Since nucleotides—and ddNTPs—bind with other nucleotides in a predictable fashion, and since just one of the ddNTPs would be radioactively labeled, the identity of the target nucleotide could easily be deduced when the radioactively labeled fragments were separated from the unlabeled ones.

Although the basic outlines of the experiment were in place, there were several problems Mullis needed to work out, and it was to these concerns that he turned his thoughts during his drive home. How, for instance, could he ensure that one or several stray nucleotides would not be added to the primers before the addition of the ddNTP, an effect that would distort his results? It was upon asking himself this question that Mullis had a revelation: the addition of several, or indeed many, nucleotides to the primers might pose a problem for his sequencing effort, but it was the key to inventing a technique for synthesizing large quantities of DNA. To achieve the latter goal, he already had all the necessary ingredients; he could even omit the ddNTPs and in their stead use the four types of nucleotides.

In the new experiment he envisioned, Mullis planned to combine DNA (which, as in his earlier formulation, would be heated to separate the two strands) with the oligonucleotide primers, the DNA polymerase, and all four types of nucleotides. In a reaction that mimics the process of DNA synthesis as it occurs in nature, the nucleotide building blocks would be added, one by one, to the primer until a new strand of DNA, complementary to the original, was synthesized. The reaction, he realized with mounting excitement, would double the amount of the target DNA fragment or gene in the sample. Moreover, the mixture could then be reheated and the reaction permitted to run its course all over again—and in the process again double the amount of target DNA in the sample. In other words, if he continued to repeat the reaction—a chain reaction catalyzed by DNA polymerase, or, as it came to be called, the polymerase chain reaction (PCR)—he could synthesize as many as a billion copies of an entire strand of DNA in a relatively short period of time.

By the end of that Friday evening in 1983, Mullis knew that if he could make his idea work in the lab, it would have the power to transform biological research. Other techniques had already been developed to clone DNA, but such techniques were not always useful because they resulted in the replication of the entire genome; Mullis's method, on the other hand, seemed likely to yield a significant amount of a discrete DNA fragment both quickly and cheaply.

Notwithstanding the conceptual simplicity of the polymerase chain reaction, it took Mullis several months to design an experiment to see if it would work. "I had to decide what concentration of chemicals to add to the solution, what temperature to heat it at, how long to cool it down, and so forth," he explained to Richard A. Marini in an interview for Popular Science. "It was like trying to bake a chocolate cake without a recipe." Eventually, Mullis came up with a simple test-tube experiment that, as he had expected, quickly amplified his target DNA fragment exponentially.

Mullis first published a description of the technique in the December 20, 1985 issue of Science, and in 1986 he described it in a paper published in the Cold Spring Harbor Symposia on Quantitative Biology. When he read the paper at the symposium, which was attended by many eminent molecular biologists, Mullis received a standing ovation. The patent for the process was granted in 1987, and soon after that Cetus announced the invention of the Thermal Cycler, a relatively inexpensive and automatic system for using the PCR.

Although Cetus credited him with helping to develop several of the practical applications of the PCR, and though his name was on the PCR patent, in the following years Mullis did not receive the recognition he believed he deserved. For instance, according to Robert Fildes, the CEO of Cetus at the time, Mullis felt that he should have been listed as the lead author, rather than as a coauthor, of papers describing work that relied on his technique. Another source of frustration for Mullis was the fact that instead of trusting him to pursue areas of research that he thought were likely to lead to other important inventions, his superiors insisted on closely monitoring his research efforts. "When they finally realized that someone among them had discovered something royally good, every . . . administrator who wanted to make a name for himself suddenly decided he wanted to be my boss . . . " Mullis told Anthony Liversidge in an interview for Omni. "They all started proposing experiments for me to do, treating me like a grad student."

Finally, in 1986, Mullis left the company. Although there was little love lost between them, Mullis and Cetus joined forces three years later, when the Du Pont Corporation mounted a patent challenge against the PCR. Du Pont claimed that HAR GOBIND KHORANA had in 1971 invented the polymerase chain reaction. Concerned that if Du Pont were successful, he would lose his credit for the invention of the PCR, Mullis agreed to testify in behalf of Cetus. In its verdict, handed down in 1991, a federal jury disallowed Du Pont's claim and asserted that Mullis was the sole inventor of the PCR. Meanwhile, Cetus, which had paid Mullis a $10,000 bonus for the invention of the PCR, later sold the rights for part of the application to the Swiss firm Hoffmann-LaRoche for $300 million.

After leaving Cetus Mullis took a job as the director of molecular biology at Xytronyx Inc., a San Diego-based biotech firm, where, among other things, he developed a type of light-sensitive plastic. In about 1987 he set up shop for himself as a freelance consultant. Since then, he has worked on a variety of projects, one of which involved developing a method to quickly extract DNA from blood cells. Another of his ideas has been to found a company, StarGene, to sell fragments of DNA extracted from the cells of rock stars and other cultural heroes. "Originally we were thinking about jewelry," he told a New York Times reporter. "But now we are thinking more about cards. Something a little classier than a baseball card, with the person's picture and some of their DNA worked right into the card, and some sequence information printed on the back."

Meanwhile, the PCR, whose importance was recognized as soon as it was published, had become as fundamental to biological research as the screwdriver is to carpentry. Indeed, it has facilitated the work of researchers of all stripes—from forensic scientists interested in learning the identity of a person whose blood was found at the scene of a crime to paleontologists wanting to compare DNA derived from the bones of extinct animals with that of their living relatives to physicians wishing to test fetuses for such hereditary diseases as sickle-cell anemia and beta thalassemia. The technique has also led to the development of a new, more reliable test for AIDS that detects the presence of the virus rather than the antibody. "Fairly quickly it was apparent that [the PCR] was a very important development," John Gibbs of the Baylor College of Medicine, in Houston, was quoted as saying in the New York Times. "But we have continually been surprised at how important it has become."

The extent of the PCR's significance was formally recognized in October 1993, when Mullis was awarded the Nobel Prize for Chemistry. The award, which Mullis shared with MICHAEL SMITH, a Canadian who also developed a new means of manipulating DNA, carried a cash prize of $825,000, split between the two winners. Mullis's receipt of the award surprised many people, including some who know him well, because Mullis has a reputation for being sexist and a womanizer, for harboring outlandish ideas (including the notion that AIDS is not caused by the HIV virus), and for not taking his work seriously enough. "He doesn't fit the normal mold of a Nobel Prize winner," Robert Fildes told Emily Yoffe. "He's a wild man. There's a certain amount of politicking involved, and I was not sure his personality and his lifestyle would have allowed him to win." At the traditional reception following the Nobel banquet, Mullis revealed himself to be as unorthodox as ever: among other stunts, he reportedly sang and improvised a comedy routine in which he parodied the king of Sweden.

His unorthodox style again caused controversy in 1995 when he testified as a defense witness in the O. J. Simpson murder case. Mullis argued for the defense that PCR does not uniquely identify a person but rather calculates the probability that two people will match coincidently— though there is little likelihood of a mismatch, the possibility, however small, still exists. The prosecution challenged his credibility on the basis of his lifestyle, arguing that his "personal and professional life have caused many members of the scientific community to disregard his opinions about forensic PCR applications."

Kary B. Mullis has been married and divorced three times. Through his marriage to Richards Haley, he has a daughter, Louise. His second marriage was to Gail Hubbell; his third, to Cynthia Gibson, produced two sons, Christopher and Jeremy. He divides his time between a beachfront apartment in La Jolla, California and a ranch that he owns in California's Mendocino County and that he has dubbed "The Institute for Further Study," because, he has explained, scientific papers frequently end with the words "This work warrants further study." Aside from biochemistry, his interests include cosmology, mathematics, artificial intelligence, virology, chemistry, hallucinogenics, and photography. He also enjoys gardening, surfing, skiing, and in-line skating.

In addition to the Nobel Prize, Kary Mullis has received numerous honors, including the Allan Award from the American Society of Human Genetics (1990), the biochemistry prize of the German Society of Clinical Chemists (1990), the Gairdner Foundation International Award (1991), the National Biotechnology Award (1991), the Robert Koch Award (1992), and the biotechnology research award of the American Society of Microbiology (1992). He was also named scientist of the year by *R&D Magazine* in 1991. After the Nobel, the most lucrative award he has won (in 1993) is the Japan Prize, which is the Japanese version of the Nobel and which carried a cash prize of about $400,000.

ABOUT: Current Biography Yearbook 1996; Science April 7, 1995.

NASH, JOHN F.
(June 13, 1928–   )
Nobel Memorial Prize in Economic Sciences, 1994 (shared with John C. Harsanyi and Reinhard Selten)

John Forbes Nash Jr., the American economist, was born in Bluefield, West Virginia to John Forbes Nash, an electrical engineer, and Margaret Nash, a Latin teacher. Growing up during the Great Depression did not affect young Nash or his sister, Martha, in the way one might expect. In fact, the town of Bluefield had the highest per capita income for the entire state of West Virginia through the 1930s and 1940s. With its handful of millionaires Bluefield prospered, and so did the Nashes. At the height of the Great Depression, the Nash family was living in a white frame house down the street from the local country club.

Nash was a good student who read constantly and played chess. When he was in elementary school, a teacher told his mother that he was having some problems in math; as it turned out, he was simply beginning to see mathematics on a completely different level from most people his age. In 1945, when he entered college at the Carnegie Institute of Technology, in Pittsburgh (now Carnegie-Mellon University), he was labeled a genius by his instructors. One of Nash's mathematics professors called him "a young Gauss," a comparison to the great German mathematician. In his freshman year, Nash switched his major from chemistry to mathematics. By the end of two years, he had already acquired his B.S. and was working toward his master's degree.

In 1948 Nash entered the doctoral program at Princeton University. The university was a prestigious scientific center—ALBERT EINSTEIN and John von Neumann, the mathematician who developed the computer as well as the mathematical theory behind the hydrogen bomb, were both on campus. Nash was eager to prove himself among such great minds. When not pacing furiously, Nash talked a great deal about mathematical theories with his fellow students in the common room of Fine Hall. In that common room, using markers and hexagonal bathroom tiles, Nash invented a clever mathematical game which the other students then named after him. (The same game was later independently invented by Piet Hein in Denmark.) Students and professors alike were fascinated by him, describing him as "odd as well as brilliant." Sylvia Nasar, in the *New York Times*, recounted an anecdote

JOHN F. NASH

about young Nash: "His graduate professor, R. J. Duffin, recalls Nash . . . [came] to him one day and described a problem he thought he had solved. Professor Duffin realized with some astonishment that Mr. Nash, without knowing it, had independently proved Brouwer's famed theorem. The professor's letter of recommendation for Mr. Nash had just one line: 'This man is a genius.'"

In 1950, Nash published his Ph.D. thesis, "Noncooperative Games," in the journal *Annals of Mathematics*. His 27-page work is now considered the cornerstone of the mathematical principles of game theory—the analysis of interactions among various economic players that accounts for the entire range of their options. Game theory itself, however, was the invention of von Neumann and Oskar Morgenstern. Nash chose von Neumann's theory for further study because he felt he was able to correct its major flaw and elaborate on its principles. Von Neumann's theory accounted only for the type of rivalry in which one side's gain is the other's loss. Nash's doctoral thesis focused on the rivalries in which both sides could benefit. It also showed that there were stable solutions to game theory problems, in which no player would be able to do better than any other player, even if he or she knew what the other players were doing. He invented what is now called the "Nash equilibrium," which occurs when no player wants to change his or her strategy, even when full knowledge of other players' strategies is divulged. Finally he showed that a distinction is possible between cooperative games, in which binding agreements are made, and noncooperative games, in which binding agreements are not feasible. According to the *Economist*: "These days, no economics student

can hope to graduate without knowing the rudiments of [Nash's game theory]."

In 1950 Nash received his doctorate from Princeton. For the next year he divided his time between teaching at Princeton and consulting for the Cold War think tank, the Rand Corporation. In 1951 he left Princeton to teach at the Massachusetts Institute of Technology. Just as he did in Princeton, he arrived at MIT wanting to show his zeal for mathematics and prove that he could solve seemingly impossible problems. Sylvia Nasar reported on his days at MIT: "Nash was in the common room knocking, as he often did, other mathematicians' work. An older professor . . . challenged him to solve one of the field's most notorious problems . . . considered virtually insoluble. But . . . Nash wound up solving it. To do so, he invented a completely new method for approaching the problem that turned out to unlock a difficulty encountered in a far larger class of problems." The students and professors in the common room were stunned. In fact, every time Nash presented his findings, people simply could not believe what they were observing.

In the mid-1950s Nash was extremely productive, lecturing at MIT and publishing papers. When he was bored with mathematics, he would go over to the economics department to discuss various issues with professors ROBERT M. SOLOW and PAUL SAMUELSON. It was also during this period that Nash met Alicia Larde, a Salvadorean physics student at MIT. Larde recalled to Sylvia Nasar her first impressions of her future husband: "He was very, very good-looking, very intelligent. It was a little bit of a hero-worship thing." They were married in 1957, the year Nash spent on leave at the Institute of Advanced Study.

The year 1958 appeared to be a good one for the Nashes. Nash was awarded tenure at MIT and in July was named by *Fortune* the "most promising young mathematician in the world." Alicia was back at graduate school and working part-time in the computer center when she became pregnant with their son, John Charles Martin Nash. Nash would also publish the last of his academic papers that year.

In spring of 1959, at the age of 30, John Nash was admitted to the psychiatric ward at McLean Hospital in Belmont, Massachusetts, where he was diagnosed with paranoid schizophrenia. In the months preceding his hospitalization, Nash had been a changed man, his behavior erratic, his lectures nonsensical. He had occasionally walked out in the middle of his lectures and had written bizarre letters to various public officials. In a paper delivered at the 1996 World Congress of Psychiatry, Nash explained how he began to feel that "the staff at . . . the Massachusetts Institute of Technology, and later all of Boston, were behaving strangely towards me . . . I started to see crypto-Communists everywhere . . . I started to think I was a man of great religious importance and to hear voices all the time. I began to hear something like telephone calls in my head, from people opposed to my ideas . . . The delirium was like a dream from which I never seemed to awake."

The months in the hospital did little good for Nash. In the late 1950s the drugs that were used to treat the symptoms of schizophrenia were only starting to come into vogue. Initially, Nash was treated by psychoanalysis. Nash's psychiatrists believed that the cause of his illness was his wife's pregnancy, that he was suffering from "fetal envy," and that the problems would subside after she gave birth.

The paranoia did not subside, however, and Nash had to resign his post at MIT. He spent a period of time wandering around Europe, fearing that he was being spied on and sending unusual postcards, encrypted with number-filled messages, to his wife and colleagues. At one point he tried to give up his American citizenship. In 1963 the Nashes divorced, and Nash went to live with his mother and sister in Roanoke, Virginia. For the next 20 years, he spent his time between hospitals and his family's home. Nash also would increasingly return to Princeton over the years, to wander around the campus or to read in the library. Eventually, Alicia Nash allowed her former husband to live with her and their son again, and she supported them by working as a computer programmer. The couple never remarried, however.

Nash's work was not forgotten by the economic community. REINHARD SELTEN and JOHN C. HARSANYI, working independently, continued to refine Nash's game theory. In the late 1960s, Harsanyi elaborated on Nash's original theory. In Nash's work, each player is aware of the other players' intentions, a circumstance that does not occur in real life. Harsanyi proposed games in which players do not have complete information on each other, and he came up with a mathematical formula allowing such games to work. In 1965 Selten came up with the idea of "subgame perfection"—a refinement that suggests that players act rationally in all situations. According to the *Economist*, since "virtually all interesting economic games involve continual interaction between players . . . [Harsanyi and] Selten extended the Nash equilibrium to such settings." By doing this, Harsanyi and Selten helped to fine-tune game economics into a system used in everyday business practice, one that has "revolutionized the economics of industrial organization and has influenced many other branches of the subject, notably the theories of monetary policy and international trade."

After many years, without any drugs or treatment, John Nash started to overcome his paranoia. He was also able to learn how to use computers in ingenious ways. His skill at mathematics had continued to flourish, even after so much time in hospitals. On the subject of his condition, Nash stated: "I would not treat myself as recovered if I could not produce good things in my work." Some have suggested that Nash's paranoid schizophrenia evolved from his brilliant mathematical work. To this theory, John Nash has responded: "I would not dare say that there is a direct relation between mathematics and madness, but there is no doubt that great mathematicians suffer from maniacal characteristics, delirium, and symptoms of schizophrenia."

In 1985 the Nobel Prize Committee began looking at Nash's achievements and took into account his mental illness. Though there is no written rule which states that the award cannot go to someone with a history of mental illness, the committee was fearful that such a recipient might have difficulty giving a Nobel lecture or addressing the king of Sweden in an appropriate manner at the ceremony. Also—and there is no offical rule on this either—there has never been a prize winner who has not held a university post or maintained an active career in the field in which he or she has been awarded the prize.

Princeton rallied around Nash once the administration got a suggestion that the award might go to him. Most young game theorists urged that he receive the prize, knowing that his work was the rock on which game theory was built. Professor Harold W. Kuhn, Nash's friend and a game theorist in his own right, had Princeton create the title of visiting research specialist for Nash, in case a question ever came up with regard to his affiliation. In 1994 Nash, along with his fellow game theorists, Selten and Harsanyi, were jointly awarded the Nobel Memorial Prize in Economic Sciences. Upon hearing the news of Nash's award, an economist at Princeton, Avinash Dixit, said that Nash was "the first guidepost for predicting the consequences of rivalries."

ABOUT: Business Week October 24, 1994; Economist October 15, 1994; New York Times October 12, 1994, November 13, 1994; Science October 21, 1994.

NORTH, DOUGLASS C.
(November 5, 1920–   )
Nobel Memorial Prize in Economic Sciences, 1993 (shared with Robert W. Fogel)

The American economist Douglass Cecil North was born in Cambridge, Massachusetts, the son of Henry Emerson and Edith (Saitta) North. He was educated at the University of California at Berkeley, where he received his bachelor's degree in 1942. Throughout his college years he considered himself a Marxist. After graduation, North served in the merchant marine. Additionally, he spent nine months as a photographer, documenting California farm life for the government.

After returning to Berkeley for graduate studies, North was awarded his Ph.D. in 1952. By this time he had already been an assistant professor of economics

DOUGLASS C. NORTH

at the University of Washington in Seattle for nearly two years, and his career as an educator at that institution continued for more than three decades. For three years (1967–1969), North served as chairman of the university's economics department. In 1983 North retired and was granted professor emeritus status. His retirement, however, did not end his teaching career. North accepted a position as professor of law and liberty and economics at Washington University in St. Louis in 1983.

Very early in his career, North began to form economic theories that differed greatly from those of most traditional, or neoclassical, economists. Along with ROBERT W. FOGEL, the economist with whom North shared the 1993 Nobel Prize, North is credited with founding cliometrics. Named for Clio, the muse of history in Greek mythology, cliometrics is the application of economics theory to history, a subject ignored for many years by most economists. "Economists generally believe that markets, not institutions, are what matters," Claudia Goldin, professor of economics at Harvard, told the New York Times. "What North pointed to is economic historians' keenest insight, which is that markets are embedded in institutions. And that institutions change slowly over time, and therefore, that history matters."

North's theory is that the past is an ideal testing ground for hypotheses about economics and the various forces that propel economic development. "Economic history is about the performance of economies through time," he said in his Nobel Prize lecture. "The objective of research in the field is not only to shed new light on the economic past, but also to contribute to economic theory by providing an analytical framework that will enable us to understand economic change." Much of North's early work, which helped bring recognition to cliometrics, dealt with American history. This subject was examined in great detail in two of North's earliest published works, The Economic Growth of the U.S. 1790-1860 (1961) and Growth and Welfare in the American Past (1966).

Deeply embedded in his theories about economic history is the belief that technical innovations alone are not enough to affect economic development; institutions, such as laws, constitutions, and norms of behavior, play a vital role. "Institutions form the incentive structure of a society, and the political and economic institutions, in consequence, are the underlying determinants of economic performance," North said. Further, he theorized that it is the interaction among such institutions and organizations as political parties, schools, churches, and trade unions that shapes the evolution of an economy. "That is, if the institutional framework rewards piracy, then piratical organizations will come into existence; and if the institutional framework rewards productive activities, then organizations—firms—will come into existence to engage in productive activities." In 1968 North applied this theory to the great upswing in productivity experienced by the shipping industry in the 19th century. He showed that the boom was caused not by technical improvements, but rather by efforts to reduce piracy and improve emergency services.

North also devoted much time to using his theories to address the question, "Why do some countries become rich while others remain poor?" He found that even to begin to answer this question, it is essential to understand that history repeatedly demonstrates that the evolution of phenomena including prejudice, myths, and ideologies all play a great role in explaining societies and change. In examining the history and development of western Europe from the 10th to the 18th centuries, North wondered what had transformed the region from one of relative chaos to the leading economic power in the world. He determined that the development of western Europe was the "story of a gradually evolving belief system in the context of competition among fragmented political/economic units producing economic institutions and political structure that produced modern economic growth." Further, North pointed out that even among the relatively small group of civilizations, individual cultural experiences were diverse enough to produce both successes (Britain) and failures (Portugal and Spain).

Attempting to explain "path dependence," the tendency for economies on a path of growth or decline to continue on the same path, is another vital part of North's work on the wealth-of-nations question. While neoclassical theory holds that nations with failing economies can be revitalized if those with political power simply change the rules of operation, history does not show that this is true. "It is not that rulers have been unaware of poor performance," North said. "Rather the difficulty of turning nations around is a function of the nature of political markets and, underlying that, the belief systems of the actors." North viewed his work as merely laying the foundation upon which the study of economic history will eventually rise. "We have just set out on the long road to achieving an understanding of economic performance through time," he concluded in his Nobel Prize lecture. "The ongoing research embodying new hypotheses confronting historical evidence will not only create an analytical framework enabling us to understand economic change through time; in the process it will enrich economic theory, enabling it to deal effectively with a wide range of issues currently beyond its ken."

North has spent much time counseling leaders of developing nations in Eastern Europe and South America. The ever-evolving political, social, and economic status of these nations has given him reason to ponder further the applications of cliometrics. "We cannot account for the rise and decline of the Soviet Union and world communism with the tools of neoclassical analysis, but we should with an institutional/cognitive approach to contemporary problems of development," he said.

In 1993, after devoting nearly half a century to the study of economics, Douglass C. North was awarded the Nobel Memorial Prize in Economic Sciences. He shared his prize, along with the $825,000 monetary award, with the cofounder of cliometrics, Robert W. Fogel. The academy praised both North and Fogel for creating immense computer data bases and finding large amounts of new data. The recognition of these two men, said experts, showed the public that economics is not only about numbers. "Economic history has a lot to contribute to understanding how the world works," said North.

North lives in St. Louis with Elisabeth Willard (Case) North, his wife since 1972. He has three children from a previous marriage. The Norths named their dog Clio.

In addition to the Nobel Prize, North has been the recipient of many grants from a variety of institutions, including the Social Science Research Council (1962), the Rockefeller Foundation (1960–1963), the Ford Foundation (1961, 1966), and the Bradley Foundation (1986). He has been awarded fellowships by several organizations, including the Center for Advanced Study on Behavioral Sciences (1987–1988) and the American Academy of Arts and Sciences. Also, North is a past director of the Institute for Economic Research (1960–1966) and a current member of both the American Economic Association and the Economic History Association.

SELECTED WORKS: The Economic Growth of the U.S. 1790-1860, 1961; Growth and Welfare in the American Past, 1966; Institutional Change and American Economic Growth (with L. Davis), 1971; The Economics of Public Issues (with R. Miller), 1971, 1974, 1976, 1978, 1980; The Rise of the Western World (with R. Thomas), 1973; Structure and Change in Economic History, 1981; Institutions, Institutional Change and Economic Performance, 1990.

ABOUT: American Economic Review June 1994; Boston Globe October 13, 1993; New York Times October 13, 1993; Newsweek October 25, 1993; Science October 22, 1993; Who's Who in America, 1996.

NÜSSLEIN-VOLHARD, CHRISTIANE
(October 20, 1942–)
Nobel Prize for Physiology or Medicine, 1995 (shared with Eric F. Wieschaus and Edward B. Lewis)

The German biologist Christiane Nüsslein-Volhard was born in Magdeburg to Rolf Volhard, an architect, and Brigitte (Haas) Volhard, an artist and musician. She was the only one of four siblings, and apparently the only female in her immediate surroundings, to pursue a career in science. "My family got used to it, my teachers got used to it," she explained. "It was not a big deal. They thought, why not?" She did graduate work at the University of Tubingen and was a research associate at the Max Planck Institute for Virus Research from 1972 to 1974. She received postdoctoral fellowships in Basel, Switzerland from 1975 to 1976 and at the University of Freiburg in 1977.

In the late 1970s, still in the early years of her career, Nüsslein-Volhard teamed up with the American biologist ERIC WIESCHAUS. Together, as young group leaders at the European Molecular Biology Laboratory in Heidelberg, they sought to continue the research in fruit-fly genetics that EDWARD B. LEWIS had begun. Lewis, of the California Institute of Technology, began his groundbreaking study of the fruit fly, *Drosophila Melanogaster*, during the 1940s. His main contribution to fruit-fly genetics analysis was his discovery of the bithorax gene complex. After fruit-fly embryos have divided into segments that are to become the fly's head, thorax, and abdomen, genetic movement causes these segments to be developed further into appendages such as legs and wings. The genes of the bithorax gene complex are the puppet masters of this stage of fruit-fly development—each gene tugs at the strings of hundreds more, either mobilizing or demobilizing their contacts, to produce the network of organs in a fruit fly's body. By creating mutant fruit flies, interbreeding them, and examining their offspring, Lewis discovered this family of genes, which is vital to the development of fruit-fly organs.

Nüsslein-Volhard and Wieschaus focused their

CHRISTIANE NÜSSLEIN-VOLHARD

work on the genes that function earlier in embryonic development than do the bithorax complex—those that alter a sphere of similar-looking cells into the semblance of an animal. Like Lewis, they worked with the fruit fly, adding DNA damaging chemicals to the sugar water they fed to adult males. They then mated these mutant males with females, who often produced dead embryos. Using a trial-and-error method, the pair bred a total of 40,000 fruit-fly families, each with a single defect. Over the span of one year, using a special dual microscope, they scanned thousands of embryos and dead larvae of the fruit fly, looking for defects in the cuticle construction of the fly and trying to assess which of its 20,000 genes were significant to the developmental process and which were absolutely essential. In describing their mission, Wieschaus explained, "We would ask, do the embryos of a given stock look abnormal in the same way? Is there a mutant phenotype that did something constant during development? Then we would try to classify the defects."

In categorizing the defects, they were attempting to discover how the affected genes function under normal conditions. Using this classification technique, they narrowed their gene pool to approximately 5,000 they deemed as significant and to 139 that were essential. By linking the genes to the effects of various mutations, such as the lack of muscles or skin composed of nervous cells, they were able to learn which of the genes were necessary for the developmental process to take place.

Their method of categorization, as explained by Mark Peifer, a developmental biologist who studied in Wieschaus's lab at Princeton, was "a phenomenally well-organized frontal assault on a problem, and rela-

tively shortly into it they already knew they'd hit the jackpot." They discovered that their mutant flies could be classified into three separate categories corresponding to the three different sets of genes that act to subdivide the embryo. They named these categories "gap," "pair-rule," and "segment polarity." According to their research, gap genes are first sparked into action by a maternal gene product and divide the embryo into general regions. Then the pair-rule genes work to segment these regions, and the segment polarity genes finalize the division process by ordering anterior-to-posterior arrangements in each segment.

The work of Lewis, Wieschaus, and Nüsslein-Volhard has had a widespread impact. Because embryonic development in humans occurs much like that of insects, worms, and other primitive organisms, their research has proven to be relevant to the study of human life. Many human disorders, for example, can be traced back to mutations in genes that are related to those in fruit flies. According to *Time*, "scientists now believe that flawed copies of these genes in humans underlie some miscarriages and perhaps 40 percent of the birth defects that have no apparent cause." Says Richard Losick, a developmental biologist at Harvard University, the work of these Nobel recipients "has had a huge impact on the field. . . . It's made it possible to understand how you get from a fertilized egg to a multicellular creature with specialized types of cells."

Wolfgang Driever, a developmental geneticist at Massachusetts General Hospital, also attests to the importance of their work. "If you went through a textbook in developmental genetics and took out all the pages that couldn't have been written if these three people hadn't been around, there wouldn't be much left."

In granting the prize to Nüsslein-Volhard and Wieschaus, the Nobel committee declared, "It was a brave decision by two young scientists at the beginning of their scientific careers. . . . Nobody before had done anything similar, and the chances of success were very uncertain," due, in part, to the fact that "the number of genes involved might be very great."

The first Nobel Prize given for basic developmental research since 1935, Nüsslein-Volhard's award has held great meaning to her in more ways than one. Now, she says, the word is out that "basic research . . . is really worth doing. And if you have a Nobel Prize, I guess people listen a bit more carefully to what you say." She is also the first German woman to win the prize. Natalie Angier of the *New York Times* wrote that when Nüsslein-Volhard discovered that she had won the Nobel, "she was hugely happy. . . . People had been predicting Dr. Nüsslein-Volhard's Nobel for years, and nobody could doubt the importance of her contributions or the ferocity of her intelligence or drive."

Nüsslein-Volhard has been the director of the Department of Genetics at the Max Planck Institute for Developmental Biology since 1990 and has continued her research there. She applied the results of her studies of *Drosophila* to a new specimen, the zebra fish, in an attempt to grasp its stages of development. Some have expressed doubts about the usefulness of her jump to the study of the zebra fish, a vertebrate, for, in contrast to the fruit fly, the value and implications of studying it have not been proven. Nüsslein-Volhard asserts, however, that vertebrates must be studied if scientists are to understand human development. Her institute furnished her with a fish laboratory, where she can keep her 7,000 tanks and study the same process of mutation in the zebra fish that she examined in *Drosophila*. Judith Kimble, a developmental biologist at the University of Wisconsin in Madison, deems Nüsslein-Volhard's move to zebra fish "bold" and says that Nüsslein-Volhard "sets her sights on a truly big question." Nüsslein-Volhard phrases it this way: "I must say, I'm easily bored."

Nüsslein-Volhard, known as "Janni" by those close to her, describes herself as "normal . . . I'm modest, but I'm also proud. I'm also a perfectionist, and so I'm insecure. I get frustrated with myself easily." Her renown can also be wearisome. "The more famous you get, the more prizes you win, the more humble you have to be. . . . You have to put others at their ease. You have to assure them you're just like them, and that can be tedious sometimes."

Among other honors, Nüsslein-Volhard has received the Lasker Prize, the Rosensteil Medal from Brandeis University, and the Franz-Vogt Prize from the University of Giessen, and she has been named an honorary doctor of science by Yale University. She has also published more than 50 scientific articles. Nüsslein-Volhard lives in a peaceful area of Tubingen in the millhouse of a 14th-century monastery. Because this environment is so beautiful, she says, she seldom takes vacations. Married briefly as a young woman, she retained the surname Volhard for the sake of her career.

ABOUT: Economist October 14, 1995; International Who's Who 1996-97, 1996; New York Times October 10, 1995, December 5, 1995; Science October 20, 1995; Science News October 14, 1995; Time October 23, 1995; Washington Post October 10, 1995.

OE, KENZABURO

(January 31, 1935–   )
Nobel Prize for Literature, 1994

Kenzaburo Oe, the third of seven children, was born in Ose, a remote village on Shikoku, the smallest of the four main islands of Japan. The village of Ose, which has since been annexed to a neighboring town, was home to generations of his ancestors. By his own ac-

KENZABURO OE

count, Oe's approach to his craft is inseparably bound to his origins in what he has labeled a "peripheral, marginal, off-center region." Both his parents nurtured a love of literature in their son: His father, Kotaro Oe, who died in 1944 while serving in the Japanese armed forces, introduced him to Chinese poetry; his mother, Koseki Oe, gave him a copy of Mark Twain's masterpiece, *The Adventures of Huckleberry Finn*, which remains among the works he most cherishes and admires. Another of Oe's favorite stories during his youth was *The Wonderful Adventures of Nils* by the Swedish writer Selma Lagerlöf. During the countless hours that Oe spent daydreaming in the dense forest surrounding Ose, where he felt "a sense of security which [he] could never find indoors," he often fantasized that someday, like Nils, he would fly away with a flock of wild geese.

Oe's childhood was spent in a Japan that had mobilized itself to extend its military and economic hegemony over eastern Asia. When he was two, Japan invaded China and began its occupation of Manchuria; shortly after he entered a local public school in 1941, Japan and the United States went to war. Oe told Rioji Nakamura, an interviewer for *Reforma*, that pupils were given nothing but "military propaganda texts" to read. "We . . . practiced charging with bamboo spears at straw dolls lashed to stakes," he reported in a reminiscence for the *New York Times Magazine*. "That all Japanese, including children, would fight to the death with bamboo spears [if an enemy invaded] was an ideology set in stone in our classroom and every classroom in the land."

In his essay "A Portrait of the Postwar Generation," Oe described how people in his village reacted to the emperor's surrender, broadcast on August 15, 1945, days after the atomic bombings of Hiroshima and Nagasaki: "The adults sat around their radios and cried," he wrote; "The children gathered outside in the dusty road and whispered their bewilderment. We were most surprised and disappointed that the emperor had spoken in a human voice. . . . How could we believe that an august presence of such awful power had become an ordinary human being on a designated summer day?" Many of the essays Oe wrote in his adult years would examine from ethical, political, sociological, and psychological perspectives the consequences of the atomic bombings and Japan's abrupt, forced transformation from a totalitarian, militaristic state to a democracy in which the emperor remains primarily a cultural symbol.

At war's end, Oe's feelings of betrayal, anger, helplessness, and humiliation became mixed with relief and gratitude when the American soldiers who entered his village did not "crush [people] beneath the wheels of their tanks," in his words, but, rather, handed out gifts of chocolate bars and chewing gum. In his introduction to *Warera no kyōkai o ikiru michi o oshieyo (Teach Us to Outgrow Our Madness, 1977)*, a collection of four of Oe's novellas, translator John Nathan wrote that "those potent feelings have remained entangled in [Oe] and, as he has said himself, defy his efforts to sort them out."

According to *World Authors*, Oe entered in 1951 a high school in Matsuyama, in northwestern Shikoku, and then spent a year at a preparatory school in Tokyo. Other sources report that he never left Shikoku until he enrolled at the University of Tokyo, in 1952 or 1953. "I went through real torment at being torn from my community," he acknowledged to Rioji Nakamura. Part of his anguish stemmed from his speech: he knew only a dialect of Japanese and, ashamed of his rural accent, developed a stutter. Writing (and, for a while, tranquilizers and alcohol) helped him "exorcise [his] demons," as he put it. "I still have the feeling that I am separated from my true community," he told Nakamura. "But, at the same time, if I returned to life in the village, perhaps I would also feel the need to flee. I'm always in doubt."

Oe began his university career with a concentration in science and mathematics, but later changed his major to French literature, receiving his B.A. degree from the University of Tokyo in 1959. He came under the tutelage of Kazuo Watanabe, an expert in the French Renaissance, whose translations of Rabelais encouraged Oe in his literary studies, leading him eventually to conclude that Rabelaisian grotesque realism was "the most effective literary technique with which to tackle the problems of the modern world," Sanroku Yoshida wrote in *World Literature Today*. Oe himself, in his Nobel lecture, "Japan, the Ambiguous, and Myself," said that he had adopted Watanabe's human-

istic philosophy as a means of helping readers "to recover from their own sufferings and the sufferings of their time and to cure their souls of the wounds." Oe was also profoundly influenced by the ideas of ALBERT CAMUS and other French existentialists: for his senior thesis he examined the philosophy of JEAN-PAUL SARTRE, whom he interviewed in Paris in 1961.

Oe has dismissed his earliest fictional works as failed attempts to copy the style of the avant-garde writer Kobo Abe. He soon found his own voice, as in his short story "Kimyō na shigoto" ("A Strange Job"), which won a Tokyo University May Festival Prize and was later nominated for an Akutagawa Prize, the most important literary award given in Japan to relatively unknown writers.

"Kimyō na shigoto" is about an apathetic college student who works part-time in a laboratory, where he kills dogs for researchers. The plight of the dogs, which are "helplessly leashed together, looking alike, hostility lost and individuality with it," strikes him as foreshadowing the fate of "ambiguous Japanese students" like himself.

With the novella "Shiiku" ("Prize Stock," also translated as "The Catch"), Oe won the coveted Akutagawa Prize in 1958. The title refers to a black American pilot who, having survived the downing of his plane, is being held in a Japanese mountain village during World War II. One summer afternoon, a group of boys blissfully bathe with the aviator in the village spring. The narrator, who was then one of the group, says, "How can I describe how much we loved him . . . how can I convey the repletion and rhythm of it all? To us it seemed that the summer which had bared those resplendent muscles, the summer that suddenly and unexpectedly geysered like an oil well, spewing happiness . . . , would continue forever." His joy ends abruptly, for the American takes him hostage when he tells the aviator that he is about the be turned over to the authorities, and the boy is injured when his father kills the man with an axe.

Oe's first novel, *Memushiri kouchi saiban*, was published in 1958 and translated into English as *Nip the Buds, Shoot the Kids*. This powerful story of evacuated reform-school boys who are manipulated and abandoned by villagers is evocative of WILLIAM GOLDING's *The Lord of the Flies* and Albert Camus's *The Plague*. It was one of a series of stories by Oe in which "young Japanese struggled to survive with dignity on the margins of a violent, desecrated, meaningless society," in the words of John Nathan in a *Japan Quarterly* article. Among these works are *Warera no jidai* (1959, translated as *Our Age* or *Our Times*) and *Okurete kita seinen* (1962, translated as *The Youth Who Arrived Late* or *A Youth Who Came in Late*). "In these largely pessimistic early books," Nathan observed, "Oe conveys his longing for, and begins to conjure, a kind of mythic homeland beyond time and the constraints of history, where innocence and joy remained within reach."

In 1960 Oe traveled to the People's Republic of China as a representative of young Japanese writers. There, he met with the Communist leader Mao Zedong and Zho Enlai, then China's foreign minister. Also in 1960 he cofounded the Young Japan Group to protest the terms of renewal of the 1951 United States–Japan security treaty, which he feared might someday cause Japan to be drawn into another war. In October 1960, after months of sometimes violent mass demonstrations by supporters and opponents of the treaty, Otoya Yamaguchi, a 17-year-old right-wing fanatic, assassinated Asanuma Inejira, the chairman of the Japanese Socialist Party; a few weeks later, while in police custody, he committed suicide. The murder and suicide inspired Oe to write the novella "Seventeen" and its sequel, "Death of the Political Youth," which appeared in two successive issues of the Japanese literary journal *Bungakukai*. Thinly fictionalized accounts of the actual events, they "equate right-wing ideology with masturbation—both are temporary escapes from the pain of life," James Ryan observed in *Japan Quarterly*. The stories provoked right-wing groups to threaten both Oe and *Bungakukai*'s publisher with death. In response, the editor printed a full-page apology for causing offense. According to James Ryan, "Oe never personally apologized for the stories, a stance that he admirably reaffirms to this day." With a lack of inhibition rare in a Japanese, Oe again explored sexual themes in a social context in several novels that followed. In the *Nation*, Masao Miyoshi reported that "throughout the [1960s], Oe's work relentlessly criticized Japan's history of war, suppression, provincialism, its political—especially imperial—system, and its bourgeois sexual hypocrisy."

Despite his prodigious literary output and political activities, Oe began to feel that he had "lost all sense of identity," as he recalled to David Remnick, who profiled him for the *New Yorker*, and that his "life [was] dark and negative, with no thought toward the future." That preoccupation ceased in June 1963, with the birth of his first child—Hikari, nicknamed Pooh—who was born with what Oe told Remnick was a massive growth on his head. (In *Japan Quarterly*, January-March 1995, John Nathan wrote that Oe "has varied his description of Hikari's condition but has always avoided precise medical terminology.") Doctors told the Oes that their only chance of saving the baby's life was through surgery that would cause permanent brain damage.

In August 1963, still in the agony of indecision, Oe went to Hiroshima on a writing assignment and made his first visit to a hospital where some victims of atomic-bomb radiation were undergoing treatment. The courage and perseverance of the patients and physicians amazed him. "I began to create in my mind a new image of human suffering," Oe told David Remnick. "It is difficult to explain, but my thinking was changing." The profound experience was transformative for Oe the writer. His 1964 novel *Kojinteki na taiken* (*A Personal Matter*) includes a hero (some say antihero) named Bird, who undergoes a similar transformation. Horrified by the prospect of raising a "monster baby" (his newborn son's "brain hernia" gives him the appearance of having two heads), Bird leaves his wife and tries to distract himself through sex, liquor, and fantasy. He arranges to have the baby killed, but before the deed is done, he rescues his son, having realized that the child's death would mean his own destruction as well, and that, for his own good, he must assume responsibility for him. "I kept trying to run away," Bird says. "And I almost did. But it seems that reality compels you to live properly when you live in the real world."

A Personal Matter won the Shincho Literary Prize. When the English translation appeared in 1968, American reviewers responded enthusiastically. At Oe's request, *A Personal Matter* was published at the same time as *Hiroshima Notes*, which grew out of his interviews and observations at a hospital where victims of the atomic bombing were treated.

Oe returned to the theme of a father and his impaired son in *Sora no kaibutsu Agui* (*Aghwee the Sky Monster*, 1964). In that story the ghost of a baby whose death the parent engineered appears before the father as a large, nightie-clad, kangaroo-like apparition that floats down from the sky. The father has learned from an autopsy report that his son's brain tumor was actually operable, and he repeatedly summons the ghost in an effort to reconstruct the past. In the story "Warera no kyōki o ikinobiru michi o oshieyo (Teach Us to Outgrow our Madness, 1969)," which won a Noma Literary Prize, the Fat Man, as the father is called, identifies so completely with his son that he "was convinced that he experienced directly whatever physical pain his son was feeling." "When he read somewhere that the male celatius, a deep-sea fish common to Danish waters, lived its life attached like a wart to the larger body of the female, he dreamed that he was the female fish suspended deep in the sea with his son embedded in the body like the smaller male, a dream so sweet that waking up was cruel." The Fat Man's awareness of his "madness" begins when he and his son get separated during a visit to the zoo and he discovers, to his astonishment, that the boy is not helpless without him. During the 1970s, as Hikari was growing up, Oe returned to this theme with two other major novels in which he doggedly pursues his obsession: the growing-up of this insecure father paired with his double, "the idiot son." His 1973 work *Kōzui wa waga tamashii ni oyobi* (*The Waters Have Come in unto My Soul*), which won the Noma Literary Prize, was followed in 1976 with *Pinchi rannā chōsho* (*The Pinch-Runner Memorandum*).

During the 1970s Oe's literary imagination and technique matured greatly. He had already experimented with polyphony and multilayered texts in *Chichi yo anata wa doko e ikuno ka?* (*Father, where are you going?*, 1968) and *Ma'nen gannen no huttobōru* (The Football Game of the First Year of Manen, 1967, translated as *The Silent Cry.*) Oe made several significant intellectual rediscoveries in the course of his habitual voracious reading: Mikhail Bakhtin's "grotesque realism" and "carnivalization," Victor Turner's "communitas" and "marginality," Mircea Eliade's concept of the dyad of death and rebirth, trickster tales, and semiotics. Oe synthesized all of these ideas in one of the most ambitious and politically explicit of his novels, *Dōjidai geemu* (*The Game of Contemporaneity*, 1979). This long narrative takes the reader back to Macondo, the imaginary village of "Prize Stock", a location that would reappear in several of Oe's works. In his 1971 short story "Mizukara waga namida o nugui-tamō hi," Oe expressed his reaction against Yukio Mishima's ultraconservative vision of Imperial Japan, a vision that had propelled Mishima to suicide in 1970.

In the stories that followed, Oe suggested that a recreation of Japan's mythical past—"when grass, trees, rocks and fierce *kami* [deities] uttered words"—would generate "a culturally creative force" and "rearrange the Japanese cultural paradigm." In his novel *M/T to mori no hushigi no monogatari* (The Tale of Marvel, M/T, and the Forest), Oe used an oral-tradition format and an unusual colloquial style to relate a long story about the village in the valley. In this work "M" stands for matriarchy and "T" for trickster. The novel ends with a retarded boy named Hikari describing his musical composition entitled "The Forest of Marvel".

Oe's 1983 novel *Atarashii hito you mezame yo* (*Rouse Up, O Young Men of the New Age!*) won an Osaragi Jiro Prize. In this work, a mixture of autobiography and invented narratives, Oe experiences a shock similar to that of the Fat Man's, when the nearly 20-year-old Hikari, apparently for the first time, proclaims his personhood by refusing to respond to his nickname. Overwhelmed at first by a feeling of loss, Oe realizes that "the time was ripe" to start addressing his son by his given name. He then envisions Hikari and Hikari's younger brother as "young men of a new age, a baleful, atomic age," and imagines himself beside them in a glorious scene of rebirth and redemption. The title of *Rouse Up* is from a poem by William Blake that, Oe wrote, he "had often read aloud" and that "seemed to surge up" in him during his pivotal experience with Hikari.

Throughout his literary career, Oe has maintained a lively interest in Western literature. William Blake, Charles Dickens, W. H. Auden, and T. S. Eliot are among the British writers whose works have strongly influenced him. A self-described "diligent reader of the totality of American literature" as well as of European, Latin American, and Asian literary works, Oe has also cited as inspirational the writings of WILLIAM BUTLER YEATS, Norman Mailer, WILLIAM FAULKNER, SAUL BELLOW, and Philip Roth, among others. Impatient with the vagueness of classical Japanese prose, starting early on Oe wrote with the goal of reconstructing the Japanese language to make it more suitable for the new age that had dawned in his country.

Until the award of the Nobel Prize for Literature in 1994, which came as a surprise to many, Oe was relatively unknown in the United States, and much of his writing remains untranslated. He was only the second Japanese writer to receive the prize, after YASUNARI KAWABATA in 1968. Several days after his Nobel award was announced, Oe was offered Japan's highest cultural honor, the Imperial Order of Culture, conferred by the Emperor, but Oe refused the award because of its associations with the imperial system that he believed responsible for World War II. Explaining his decision, Oe said "The reason I declined the cultural award was that I would not recognize any authority, any value, higher than democracy. This is very simple but very important."

In 1960, he married Yukari Itami, daughter of the writer Mansaku Itami and younger sister of film director Juzo Itami. Oe and his wife live in Tokyo. Their younger children are a son, Sakurao, and a daughter, Natsumiko.

SELECTED WORKS IN ENGLISH TRANSLATION: A Personal Matter (tr. by J. Nathan), 1969; The Silent Cry (tr. by J. Bester), 1974; Teach Us to Outgrow Our Madness (tr. by J. Nathan), 1977; The Pinch-Runner Memorandum (tr. by M. N. and M. K. Wilson), 1994; Hiroshima Notes (tr. by D. Swain and T. Yonezawa), 1995; Japan: The Ambiguous and Myself: The Nobel Prize Speech and Other Lectures, 1995; Nip the Buds, Shoot the Kids (tr. by P. Mackintosh and M. Sugiyama), 1995; An Echo of Heaven (S. Shaw, ed., tr. by M. Mitsutani), 1996; The Catch and Other War Stories, 1995; A Healing Family (S. Shaw, ed., tr. by S. Snyder), 1996; A Quiet Life (tr. by K. Yanagishita and W. Wetherall), 1996; Seventeen (The Political Being) & J (The Sexual Being), 1996.

ABOUT: Georgia Review Spring 1995; Japan Quarterly January-March 1995; New York Times October 14, 1994, November 6, 1994; Publishers Weekly August 7, 1995; World Authors 1980–1985, 1991.

OLAH, GEORGE A.

(May 22, 1927–)

Nobel Prize for Chemistry, 1994

A refugee from the 1956 Hungarian uprising, the American chemist George A. Olah settled first in Canada before moving to the United States in 1964. He was born in Budapest, the son of Julius Olah, a lawyer,

GEORGE A. OLAH

and Magda Krasznai. "To my best knowledge nobody in my family before had interest in science," he has recalled. "I grew up between the two World Wars and received a rather solid general education, the kind middle-class children enjoyed in a country whose educational system had its roots dating back to the Austro-Hungarian monarchy." Olah attended a gymnasium in Budapest run by the Piarist Fathers, a Roman Catholic order. There, he endured "a strict and demanding curriculum" that included eight years of Latin and required courses in German and French. "Although we had an outstanding science teacher who later became a professor of physics at the University of Budapest, I cannot recollect any particular interest in chemistry during my school years," he wrote in 1996. "My main interest was in the humanities, particulary history, literature, etc. I was (and still am) an avid reader and believe that getting attached too early to a specific field frequently shortchanges a balanced, broad education. Although reading the classics in Latin in school may not be as fulfilling as it would be at a more mature age, few scientists can afford the time for such diversion later in life."

After graduating from high school, he entered the Technical University of Budapest, where he began to study chemistry despite the school's limited laboratory facilities. "At the same time the laboratory training was thorough," he recalled. "For example, in the organic laboratory we did some 40 Gatterman preparations. It certainly gave a solid foundation." Olah became particularly interested in organic chemistry and became a research assistant to Geza Zemplen, a specialist in carbohydrates and glycosides and the senior professor of organic chemistry in Hungary, who

himself was a student of EMIL FISCHER in Berlin. He later recalled: "Zemplen expected his students to pay their own way and even [pay] for the privilege to work in his laboratory. Becoming an assistant to him . . . meant no remuneration but also no fee. Zemplen had a formidable reputation, and working for him was quite an experience. He also liked partying, and these remarkable events in neighboring pubs lasted frequently for days. Certainly one's stamina developed through these experiences."

The relationship between mentor and student was sometimes contentious. "Early in our association," Olah stated, "it became clear that my ideas and interest were not always closely matching his. When I suggested that flourine containing carbohydrates may be of interest in coupling reactions, his reaction was not unexpectedly very negative. To try to pursue fluorine chemistry in postwar Hungary was indeed far-fetched. Eventually, however, he gave in." Olah and his colleagues had to work in an environment in which basic chemicals needed for their research were unavailable, so the resourceful chemist made them himself. Because of the scarcity of venting equipment, Olah and his colleagues were forced to carry out their experiments on an open balcony that they enclosed and ventilated. "I am not sure that Zemplen even set foot in it," he recalled. "We enjoyed, however, our new quarters and the implicit understanding that our fluorine chemistry and related study of Friedel-Crafts reactions and their intermediates was now officially tolerated."

When Communists came to power in Hungary in the late 1940s, wrote Olah, "university research was deemphasized and research institutes were established under the auspices of the Academy of Sciences. I was invited to join the newly established Central Chemical Research Institute of the Hungarian Academy of Sciences in 1954 and was able to establish a small research group in organic chemistry, housed in temporary laboratories of an industrial research group. With my group, which now included my wife, we were able to expand our work and made the best of our possibilities." Olah had married Judith Lengyel in 1949; she later enrolled in the Technical University as a chemistry student after having first worked there as a technical secretary. Their older son, George John, was born in Budapest in 1954.

From 1954 to 1956 Olah served as the head of the Department of Organic Chemistry and associate scientific director of the Institute. After the ill-fated uprising in Budapest in October 1956, Olah and his family fled to London, where his wife had relatives. In his brief stay there, he was able to establish personal contact with some of the organic chemists whose work he knew and admired—particularly Christopher Ingold and ALEXANDER TODD, to whom he was always grateful for their "extended efforts on behalf of a young, practically unknown Hungarian refugee chemist." In the spring of 1957 the Olahs moved to Montreal, Canada, where his mother-in-law lived. Soon afterward, he began work with Dow Chemical's newly established exploratory research laboratory in Sarnia, Ontario. Packing all their worldly possessions in two cardboard boxes, they "started [their] new life" in Sarnia, where their younger son, Ronald Peter, was born in 1959. Judith Olah devoted herself to bringing up their children, returning to research work with her husband a decade later.

"The Sarnia years at Dow were productive," Olah wrote. "It was during this period in the late 1950s that my initial work on stable carbocations was started. Dow was and is a major user of carbocationic chemistry, such as the Friedel-Crafts type manufacture of ethylbenzene for styrene production. My work thus also had practical significance and helped to improve some industrial processes. In return I was treated well and given substantial freedom to pursue my own ideas. Eventually, I was promoted to company scientist, the highest research position without administrative responsibility."

In the spring of 1964, Olah moved to Dow's Eastern Research Laboratories in Framingham, Massachusetts, which later relocated to Wayland, just outside Boston. In the summer of 1965, he was invited to join the faculty of Western Reserve Univeristy in Cleveland, as professor and chair of the Department of Chemistry. "My Cleveland years were both scientifically and personally most rewarding," he later wrote. "My wife, Judy, was able to rejoin me in my research, and my research group grew rapidly." Olah oversaw the merging of the chemistry departments at Western Reserve and the neighboring Case Institute of Technology and served as chair of the joint department. In the fall of 1976, he joined the faculty at the University of Southern California in Los Angeles. "The challenge of trying to build up chemistry in a dynamic university and the attractiveness of life in Southern California convinced us to move. We fell in love with California and we still are," he wrote some 20 years later. "As USC had limited chemistry facilities, it was offered to establish a research institute [now the Loker Hydrocarbon Research Institute] in the broad area of hydrocarbon research and provide it with its own building and facilities. We moved in May of 1977. Some 15 members of my research group joined the move west. By arrangements worked out we were able to take with us most of the laboratory equipment, chemicals, etc."

After he received the Nobel Prize for Chemistry in 1994, Olah wrote: "As rewarding as the Nobel Prize is personally to any scientist, I feel it is also recognition of all my past and present students and associates (by now numbering close to 200) who contributed over the years so much through their dedicated hard work to our joint effort. It also recognizes fundamental contri-

butions by many colleagues and friends from around the world to a field of chemistry [that] is not frequently highlighted or recognized."

The saturated-hydrocarbon research for which Olah won his Nobel Prize has enormous implications for the development of new fuels that can be created from such substances as petroleum, coal, or methane and for the improvement of existing fuels such as gasoline. For some two decades he focused his study on the stabilization and recombination of carbocations— short-lived, positively charged fragments of hydrocarbon molecules that had eluded detailed study because of their instability. By using superacids to split the hydrocarbon molecles, Olah was able to isolate and stabilize their carbocations and study them with conventional techniques such as magnetic resonance spectroscopy. Describing his own research, Olah wrote for this volume, "One of the foundations of organic chemistry (i.e., that of carbon compounds) is the tetra valency of the carbon atom formulated by the German chemist Kekule in the 1850s. This meant the realization that carbon is capable [of binding] simultaneously only to four other atoms, although some of these bonds can be multiple bondings to the same atom." Olah's work starting in the 1960s centered on the study of ionic organic reactions and their intermediates. He was for the first time able to obtain cations of carbon compounds (concations) as persistent, long-lived species and to study their chemical structure and reactivity. This was made possible by using extremely strong acid systems (superacids) whose acidity can be billions of times stronger than that of 100 percent sulfuric acid.

"The chemistry in superacids," he continued, "opened up new vistas and showed that carbons in some concations can bind simultaneously to five or even six other atoms . . . , involving, besides the usual two electron–two center bonds, two electron–three center bonds. This represents the foundation for the chemistry of saturated hydrocarbon at high acidities, where such transformation as alkylation and isomerization (to produce high-octane gasoline) and even conversion of methane (natural gas) to higher hydrocarbons can be readily carried out."

Olah is the author of more than 1,000 published scientific papers as well as several books, and he holds 100 patents. Over the years, he has received much recognition for his work. From the American Chemical Society, he won the Award in Petroleum Chemistry (1964), the Award for Creative Work in Synthetic Organic Chemistry (1979), and the Roger Adams Award in Organic Chemistry (1989). He was a Guggenheim fellow in 1972 and 1988 and a fellow of the Society for the Promotion of Science, Japan, in 1974. In 1979 he received the Alexander von Humbolt-Stiftung Award for Senior U.S. Scientists. The American Chemical Society Inc. presented him with its Chemical Pioneers Award in 1993. In 1990, his native Hungary inducted him as an honorary member of the Hungarian Academy of Sciences. He holds memberships in both the U.S. National Academy of Sciences and the European Academy of Arts, Sciences, and Humanities; and honorary memberships in the Italian Chemical Society and the Hungarian Academy of Sciences. Olah has also been awarded honorary degrees from the University of Durham, England; the Technical University of Budapest; the University of Munich; the University of Crete; the University of Jozsef Attila, Szeged, Hungary; the University of Veszprém, Hungary; the University of Southern California, Los Angeles; and Case Western Reserve University.

SELECTED WORKS: Introduction to Theoretical Organic Chemistry (in German), 1960; Friedel-Crafts and Related Reactions (four volumes), 1963-65; Carbonium Ions (four volumes, with P. V. R. Schleyer), 1968-73; Carbocations and Electrophilic Reactions, 1973; Friedel-Crafts Chemistry, 1973; Halonium Ions, 1975; Superacids (with G. K. Surya Prakash and J. Sommer), 1985; Hypercarbon Chemistry (with G. K. Surya Prakash, K. Wade, L. D. Field, and R. E. Williams), 1987; Nitration: Methods and Mechanisms (with R. Malhotra and S. C. Narang), 1989; Cage Hydrocarbons (ed.), 1990; Electron Deficient Boron and Carbon Clusters (ed., with R. E. Williams and K. Wade), 1991; Chemistry of Energetic Materials (ed., with D. R. Squire), 1991; Synthetic Fluorine Chemistry (ed., with R. D. Chambers and G. K. Surya Prakash), 1992; Hydrocarbon Chemistry (with A. Molnar), 1994.

ABOUT: New York Times October 13, 1994.

OSHEROFF, DOUGLAS D.

(August 1, 1945–   )
Nobel Prize for Physics, 1996 (shared with David M. Lee and Robert C. Richardson)

The American physicist Douglas D. Osheroff was born in Aberdeen, Washington, the son of William Osheroff, a physician, and Bessie Anne (Ondov) Osheroff, a nurse. As a child, Osheroff loved to take apart his toys and tinker with their inner workings. His parents generally encouraged this behavior, despite incidents during which young Osheroff's mechanical experimentation went awry, such as the time he built a muzzle-loading rifle that accidentally went off in the house.

Osheroff was educated at the California Institute of Technology, where he received his bachelor of science degree in 1967. For his graduate studies, he attended Cornell University, in Ithaca, New York. He obtained his master's degree in 1969. At Cornell, Osheroff met and eventually worked with DAVID M. LEE and ROBERT C. RICHARDSON, both faculty members in the physics department. While Osheroff was still working toward his Ph.D., the trio embarked on an in-depth study of

DOUGLAS D. OSHEROFF

a rare form of helium that would eventually earn them the Nobel Prize.

Helium is the second most abundant element in the universe. It was first identified in 1868 by Pierre Jules Cesar Janssen while he was in India observing a solar eclipse. Janssen's spectroscopic study of the sun revealed a yellow line, thought to be sodium until, in 1871, Janssen proved that it was not. He speculated that it was not any element found on Earth. Almost a quarter of a century later, WILLIAM RAMSAY, working separately from—but at about the same time—as the Swedish chemists Per T. Cleve and Nils Langlet, found that helium is present in the gas expelled when the mineral cleveite is heated. Helium was subsequently identified in the Earth's atmosphere, natural gas, and a host of other earthbound substances.

Helium is a colorless, odorless, and tasteless gas that cannot be combined either with itself or with other elements. With the exception of hydrogen, it is the least dense gas known. Helium's weak interatomic force and extremely light mass combine to make it the only element on Earth that remains liquid when cooled to absolute zero (O degrees kelvin or -273.15 degrees centigrade). Additionally, helium has the lowest boiling point of any known substance. Its most common isotope, or form, is helium-4, which has two protons and two neutrons in its nucleus.

In the last half of the 1930s, the Russian physicist PYOTR KAPITZA discovered that, when cooled to a temperature near absolute zero, liquid helium-4 exhibits a phenomenon known as superfluidity. Superfluid helium, according to the New York Times, "loses the viscosity associated with ordinary fluids and flows without resistance. It can climb up the walls of containers and flow down the outside, among many other strange tricks." The apparent loss of viscosity in superfluid helium is caused by helium atoms that line up in such a way that they effectively begin to behave as a single atom. Practical applications for superfluid helium-4 include its use as a coolant fluid for particle accelerators.

In 1939 a helium isotope with only one neutron and two protons, helium-3, was discovered by LUIS W. ALVAREZ and R. Cornog. Obtained from the radioactive decay of tritium, an isotope of hydrogen used in some thermonuclear fusion weapons, helium-3 constitutes only 10 to 15 percent of all helium on Earth. Though theorists had predicted that helium-3, like helium-4, could exist in a superfluid state, all attempts to demonstrate this had failed.

Then, in 1972, while attempting to discover an antiferromagnetic phase in solid helium-3, Osheroff, Richardson, and Lee inadvertently discovered helium-3 superfluidity. While conducting experiments on the behavior of helium-3 when it had been cooled to a temperature near absolute zero, Osheroff saw very subtle signs that the helium had changed phases. Further experiments yielded the conclusion that this change in phase was, indeed, the manifestation of superfluidity. The three physicists discovered that helium-3 in a superfluid state had some unexpected magnetic properties. These properties were so different from those predicted by theorists that the trio's original paper reporting the discovery of helium-3 superfluidity was rejected. Douglas Osheroff, in an interview with the *New York Times*, stated, "It was because our results were so unexpected that our paper reporting the discovery was initially rejected by the prominent physics journal *Physical Review Letters*." The journal later conducted a subsequent reevaluation of the paper, which resulted in its publication.

In a superfluid state, helium-3 and helium-4 exhibit quantum characteristics normally associated only with molecules, atoms, and subatomic particles. Superfluid helium can, thus, be used as a sort of quantum microscope that allows researchers to better study quantum mechanics—a field in which the rules of everyday physics gives way to strange statistical laws. For example, when a superfluid liquid is rapidly stirred, it tends to form waves or swirls that appear and disappear in rapid jumps rather than in the gradual progression associated with ordinary liquid. Studies of some of these unusual characteristics of superfluid helium-3 may one day lead to an increased knowledge of neutron stars, mysterious celestial anomalies that continue to puzzle researchers.

The benefits of superfluid helium-3 are numerous. According to the *Los Angeles Times*, "since superfluid helium-3 is quite similar to superconducting materials, in which electric currents can flow forever without losing energy, understanding it could help physicists de-

velop practical superconductors for use in power lines and motors." Further, it is hoped that an in-depth study of the transition phase during which regular helium-3 is transformed into superfluid helium-3 may eventually give scientists some answers to a plethora of questions regarding the origin of the universe. Researchers speculate that the transition process that occurs as helium becomes superfluid is similar to the process that took place seconds after the big bang and led to the formation of galaxies.

In 1973, one year after the discovery of helium-3 superfluidity, Osheroff received his Ph.D. from Cornell. By that time, he had already been working as a staff member at AT&T Bell Laboratories in New York, a position that he would hold in one capacity or another for the next 15 years. In 1982 Osheroff was named the head of AT&T Bell Laboratory's solid state physics department. Five years later, a California biotechnology firm made an irresistible offer to protein biochemist Phyllis S. K. Liu, Osheroff's wife since 1970, that lured the couple west. Also in 1987, Osheroff became the J. G. Jackson and C. J. Wood Professor in Physics at Stanford University. In 1993, he became the head of Stanford's physics department.

Douglas Dean Osheroff was awarded the Nobel Prize in 1996. He shared the award, along with the $1.12 million prize, with the codiscoverers of helium-3 superfluidity, Robert C. Richardson and David M. Lee. After learning of his award, Osheroff told Stanford News Service that he was surprised and very pleased. "There is so much good work in physics that is never recognized by a Nobel, I feel very lucky," he said. Colleagues praised the academy's decision. "It couldn't have happened to a nicer guy," said Stanford physics professor Alexander Fetter in an interview with Stanford News Service. "And he is such a great teacher, too."

In addition to the Nobel Prize, Osheroff has received numerous other awards, including the Simon Memorial Prize from the British Institute of Physics (1976), the John D. and Catherine T. MacArthur Prize (1981), and the Oliver E. Buckley Solid State Physics Prize (1981). He is also a member of the American Physical Society, the American Academy of Arts and Sciences, and the National Academy of Sciences.

SELECTED WORKS: Novel Magnetic Properties of Solid Helium-3 (with M. C. Cross); Physics Today February 1987

ABOUT· Colliers 1996 Encyclopedia CD-ROM; Los Angeles Times October 10, 1996; New York Times October 10, 1996; Newsday October 10, 1996; Royal Swedish Academy 1996 Nobel Prize Announcement; Stanford News Service Press Release October 9, 1996.

PERES, SHIMON
(August 16, 1923–   )
Nobel Prize for Peace, 1994 (shared with Yasir Arafat and Yitzhak Rabin)

Shimon Peres, the son of Yitzhak and Sarah Persky, was born in a small village in what was then Poland and is now Belarus. His parents were nonreligious Jews who embraced Zionist ideals, and according to one source Shimon was involved in the Zionist youth movement in Poland. In 1931 his father emigrated to Palestine, and two years later the rest of his family joined him. On settling in Palestine, Shimon attended the Balfour primary school in Tel Aviv, where he was an average student. As he grew older he flourished in his studies, becoming an accomplished writer, rhetorician, and speaker. He also continued his involvement in Zionist youth organizations, including Hano'ar Ha'oved (Working Youth). He received a scholarship to the Ben Shemen Agricultural School, where he was sent by the Hano'ar Ha'oved to continue his education and to acquire the agricultural skills so highly valued by Palestine's Jewish settlers. Peres also found time to read poetry and study the works of Karl Marx.

While at Ben Shemen, Peres came under the influence of Berl Katznelson, an intellectual in the Jewish Labor movement. In his book *From These Men: Seven Founders of the State of Israel* (1979), Peres described his relationship with his mentor and discussed his ideological development: "[Katznelson] was the cornerstone of the Labor movement; he showed the way, and he was the fountain from which flowed the original and constructive spirit of the Labor movement in our country." Katznelson's lectures, Peres wrote, "left an indelible impression on many of us. They implanted in us a negative attitude toward the Communist revolution and Marxist dialectic, an attitude more interested in the values of the human race than in the study of Soviet Russian statistics." Also during high school, Peres joined the Haganah, the underground Jewish self-defense organization, which would later play a crucial role in Israel's winning the Arab-Israeli War of 1948 (also known as the Israeli War of Independence).

After leaving Ben Shemen in 1941, Peres continued his training at Kibbutz Geva and then went on to found Kibbutz Alumot, in the Jordan Valley, of which he was elected secretary. He devoted most of his energy, though, to his work with Hano'ar Ha'oved. "I traveled around the organization's farms, persuading the young people to lend their support to the unity of the movement," he recounted in *From These Men.* During this period he also joined the Mapai, the Israel Worker's Party, then the dominant political party in Palestine. According to Matti Golan, the author of *The Road to Peace: A Biography of Shimon Peres* (1989), "He was seen as a pusher in those early days, both in the field of action and in the realm of ideas. . . . He loved

SHIMON PERES

public affairs, felt driven to achievement, and sought positions which enabled him to implement his ideas."

In 1946 Peres attended the 22nd World Zionist Congress in Switzerland, at which he proved himself to be a firm supporter of David Ben-Gurion, who was already a legendary figure in the Zionist movement and who was to become the first prime minister of Israel. In 1947, at the bequest of another key Israeli politician, Levi Eshkol, Peres became the director of manpower in the Haganah, in the Tel Aviv offices of the General Staff. Peres's duties included weapons procurement, which soon became his area of specialization. Not long after Ben-Gurion declared Israel a sovereign state, on May 15, 1948, Peres, along with the other members of the Haganah, was sworn in as a member of the Israel Defense Forces. During the War of Independence that followed, Peres served as the head of the defense ministry's naval department. Once the war had ended, in 1949, Prime Minister Ben-Gurion asked Peres to head a mission to continue to acquire arms for Israel. Because of the United States embargo on arms sales at that time, this task was an especially difficult one. Nevertheless, Peres accomplished his assignment. He also found time to attend the New School for Social Research and New York University, both in New York City, and Harvard University.

In early 1952, after returning to Israel, Peres was appointed deputy director-general of the ministry of defense, and several months later he was promoted to director-general. During his seven years in that position, Peres was responsible for developing Israel's government-owned weapons industry. He devoted special attention to nuclear research and weapons procurement, and, in the process, he became known for both his formidable negotiating skills and his conviction that Israel's survival depended on its technological development. One of his most notable accomplishments in that post was his success in forging a relationship between Israel and France at a time (the mid-1950s) when Israel had few dependable allies. Israel's friendship with France, which supplied the newly independent country with much-needed weapons, was crucial to its success in capturing the Sinai Peninsula from Egypt in 1956. France remained Israel's principal supplier of arms for the next decade. Equally significant, Peres conducted secret negotiations with West Germany on Israel's behalf in 1957, despite the fact that at that time diplomatic relations between the two countries did not exist. According to the Toronto *Globe & Mail*, the German-Israeli relationship proved to be important to Israel during the 1967 Six-Day War, by the time of which France had greatly reduced its commitment to Israel's defense. (After the Six-Day War, Israel occupied the West Bank and the Gaza Strip, populated mainly by Palestinian Arabs.) As a result of these achievements, Peres was regarded as a member of the "Young Mapai," a group that consisted of influential members of the younger generation of Israeli politicians.

Peres had entered a new phase of his career in 1959, when he was elected to a seat in the Knesset, as a member of the Mapai Party. The party itself continued its domination of Israeli politics, with the result that Ben-Gurion remained prime minister. Ben-Gurion chose as his deputy minister of defense Peres, who held the position until 1965. One of the more notable events of his tenure was his visit to the United States in 1962, when Peres helped persuade the Kennedy administration to sell Israel its Hawk antiaircraft missile system. The purchase marked the beginning of a new phase in Israel's relationship with the United States, which after 1967 became Israel's main supplier of arms.

By the mid-1960s a rift had developed between David Ben-Gurion and several other key Israeli politicians, including Levi Eshkol, who became prime minister following Ben-Gurion's resignation from that post in 1963. Two years later the conflict between Ben-Gurion and Eshkol came to a head, with Eshkol declaring that Ben-Gurion supporters had no place in the government. As a result, Ben-Gurion resigned from the Mapai Party and formed one of his own—Rafi, or the Worker's List Party. He was joined by a number of his supporters, including Shimon Peres, who became the newly formed party's secretary-general. Within a few years, though, it became clear that Rafi was unlikely to win widespread popular support, and in 1968 it merged with other pro-labor groups (including the Mapai Party) to form the Israel Labor Party, of which Peres became deputy secretary-general.

In 1969 Peres was reelected to the Knesset and was appointed to the cabinet of the new prime minister,

Golda Meir. Over the following four years, he held a variety of cabinet portfolios, including immigration absorption (1969), transport and communications (1970–1974), and information (1974); he also served as minister without portfolio with responsibility for economic development in the occupied territories.

Labor's fortunes—as well as those of Peres— changed dramatically after Israel's defeat in the Yom Kippur War of 1973. The loss of the war shook the Israeli public, which responded by placing the blame with the Labor-led government, whose members were widely viewed as having shirked their responsibility to defend the nation from its hostile Arab neighbors. Israelis' dissatisfaction with the Labor-led government was compounded by rising inflation and generally poor economic conditions. Finally, in April 1974, continued public criticism of the government prompted Golda Meir to resign from the prime ministership, a move that required new elections to be held. Peres, who was then involved in a power struggle with YITZHAK RABIN—a military hero who, despite his recent entry into domestic politics, was extremely popular among the electorate—lost the party chairmanship to Rabin, who was elected the new Israeli prime minister in the 1974 elections. In a gesture of conciliation, Rabin appointed Peres minister of defense. During his three years in that position, Peres concentrated his efforts on reinvigorating the Israeli defense forces.

The rivalry between Peres and Rabin developed into a much-publicized feud for a period during the 1970s. According to the historian Howard Sachar, writing in his book *A History of Israel*, their inability to work together harmoniously "led to a near paralysis of executive responsibility. . . . The animus between [then-Prime Minister Rabin] and Peres became all but uncontrollable, intruding in ministerial discussions, even undermining the line of command in the defense establishment." Despite their difficulty in getting along, the two men put aside their differences and worked together on the dramatic rescue of the hijacked airline passengers in Entebbe, Uganda, in 1976. Peres was also involved in the negotiations that resulted in the 1975 disengagement agreement between Israel and Egypt.

In January 1977 Peres challenged Yitzhak Rabin for the chairmanship of the Labor Party, and for a second time he lost his bid to defeat his rival. Rabin went on to lead Labor to victory in the general elections, but several months later, following revelations that his wife had maintained a foreign bank account, a violation of Israeli law, he was forced to resign as both prime minister and party chairman. Rabin's indiscretion in turn cleared the way for Peres's election as Labor Party chairman in June 1977. If Labor had triumphed in the elections later that year, Peres would have become prime minister. But voters, frustrated with the continued high rate of inflation and lacking confidence in Labor's ability to defend the country against its enemies, gave the right-wing Likud Party, headed by MENACHEM BEGIN, the right to lead the country. Likud went on to dominate Israeli politics for the next seven years, a period during which Peres served as leader of the opposition.

Although he lacked a portfolio, Peres remained active on the foreign-policy front during the late 1970s, and in the process he succeeded in cultivating an image as a statesman. Traveling frequently outside Israel, he met with Egyptian president Anwar Sadat and leaders of both Communist and non-Communist nations. In 1978 he supported the Camp David agreement, which Begin worked out with Sadat. Whereas Peres had long been regarded as a hawk in defense issues, when compared to members of the Likud he was decidedly dovish, for he was markedly more open to the idea of reaching a negotiated settlement with Israel's Arab neighbors and its Palestinian population. Peres also worked hard to breathe new life into the party so as to increase its appeal among the Israeli electorate.

The resignation of Menachem Begin in 1983 provided Labor with an opportunity to recapture its control of the government, and in fact Peres succeeded in leading Labor to a narrow victory over Likud, with Labor winning 44 seats in the Knesset and Likud taking 41. Nevertheless, Peres was unable to form a government, with the result that the two parties came up with a novel power-sharing arrangement: they agreed to form a National Unity government, in which cabinet posts would be evenly divided between them and the leader of each would serve half a term as prime minister. Under this arrangement, Peres served as prime minister of Israel from 1984 until 1986.

According to many political observers, Peres was an unusually effective prime minister. His greatest achievement was his deft handling of the economic crisis in which Israel was mired. "We have to turn first of all to ourselves, control our standard of living, reduce our expenses, and make Israel self-reliant from an economic point of view," he declared soon after taking office, as quoted in *Time*. In addition to devaluing the shekel, he cut government spending, persuaded Israel's dominant labor federation to cut real wages, and persuaded employers to freeze prices. The net result of these initiatives was that inflation dropped from an annual rate of about 445 percent (some sources give a much higher rate) in 1984 to 25 percent two years later. "Israel's success in halting inflation, with virtually no increase in unemployment, is almost unprecedented," Stanley Fischer, an economics professor at MIT, told Thomas L. Friedman of the *New York Times*. "Argentina and Brazil both tried to do it at the same time as Israel, with nowhere near the same results."

Another of Peres's achievements as prime minister was his success in coordinating Israel's withdrawal from Lebanon, which the country had invaded in 1982. Its continued presence there was unpopular not only within the international community but also among Israelis. Peres also developed important diplomatic relationships. For instance, he made an official visit to Morocco, where he met with King Hassan II, an event that made him the first Israeli prime minister to be invited to an Arab country other than Egypt. He also met with President Hosni Mubarak of Egypt.

The principal disappointment of Peres's term as prime minister, according to most observers, was his failure to make any significant progress in the effort to resolve the Arab-Israeli conflict. A major stumbling block to any resolution of the conflict was that Labor and Likud were fundamentally divided on how to negotiate a peace settlement. While Peres and other members of the Labor Party were willing to consider the possibility of turning over to Jordan the administration of the occupied territories in return for guarantees of Israel's security, Likud was adamantly opposed to relinquishing territory. Despite the near impossibility of the two parties' seeing eye to eye on the issue, Peres received the most criticism for the government's failure to advance the peace process. Notwithstanding that perception, when Peres turned over the prime ministership to Yitzhak Shamir in October 1986 according to the previously agreed upon power-sharing arrangement, he ended what Abraham Rabinovich, writing in the Toronto *Globe & Mail*, called "one of the most successful terms of office ever served by an Israeli prime minster." Also according to the two parties' agreement, Peres at the same time became vice-premier and foreign minister.

In the campaign that preceded the 1988 elections, Peres and the Labor Party adopted a strategy that many observers considered to be risky: the party promised to resolve the conflict with the Palestinians—which had worsened considerably since late 1987, when the *intifada*, or uprising, erupted in the Israeli-occupied territories—by trading land for peace. While the Israeli electorate was anxious to conclude a negotiated settlement with the Palestinians, in the end it was persuaded by Likud's argument that a dovish Labor-led government could not be trusted to protect Israel's security interests, and Likud scored a razor-thin victory over Labor, with Likud and Labor winning 40 and 39 Knesset seats, respectively. The outcome of the election left the two parties with little choice but to form another coalition government, though, in a departure from the arrangement devised in 1984, Yitzhak Shamir was to serve as prime minister for the full four-year term. Peres, in addition to remaining leader of the opposition, served as vice-premier and finance minister.

By the early 1990s Israeli public opinion in regard to the Palestinian problem had changed dramatically. With the *intifada* continuing unabated, Israelis were growing increasingly dissatisfied with Likud's apparent unwillingness to advance the peace process. Moreover, the 1991 Persian Gulf war changed the geopolitics of the region in such a way that the United States had begun to exert considerable pressure on Israel to make peace with its Arab neighbors and the Palestinians. "We had reached one of those rare critical junctures," Peres wrote in *The New Middle East* (1993), "that enable discerning statesmen to make a quantum leap in their thinking—and perhaps turn the tide of history." Although officially out of power, during this period Peres took part in a series of high-level meetings with PLO officials, meetings that were conducted in secrecy because all contact between Israelis and members of the PLO was prohibited by Israeli law.

Meanwhile, in 1992, the Labor Party elected Yitzhak Rabin as its new chairman, marking the end of Peres's 15-year-long leadership of the party. Rabin had emerged as a more attractive candidate for prime minister than Peres at least partly because of his reputation as a military hero: under his leadership, it was widely thought, Israel's national security would not be jeopardized. Following Rabin's election as prime minister in June of that year, Peres was named foreign minister.

According to an article in the *National Review* that chronicled the secret PLO-Israeli negotiations that were conducted in the early 1990s, Peres spent the months following the 1992 election taking part in high-level discussions with the PLO. Then, in Oslo in the summer of 1993, an agreement between the two parties was reached, though it was not made public at that time. According to Mark Perry, writing in *A Fire in Zion* (1994), in August 1993 Peres secretly held an eight-hour telephone conversation with YASIR ARAFAT, and he later met with PLO officials to initial a "Declaration of Principles on Interim Self-Government Arrangements." This agreement was formally endorsed by both Israel and the PLO on September 13, 1993, on an occasion of state in Washington, D.C.

On October 14, 1994 Shimon Peres, Yitzhak Rabin, and Yasir Arafat were jointly awarded the Nobel Prize for Peace. The announcement of the prize was to some extent overshadowed by continuing violence in Israel, and when the award was presented to the three recipients, on December 10, 1994, the peace process was at a standstill. Nevertheless, each of the three recipients of the prize remained committed to implementing the hard-won agreements. "There was a time," Shimon Peres declared on accepting the prize, "when war was fought for lack of choice; today it is peace that is the 'no choice' for all of us."

When Yitzhak Rabin was assassinated by an Israeli right-wing extremist on November 4, 1995, Peres succeeded him as prime minister. In the election held on May 29, 1996, Israelis chose the Likud Party candidate, Benjamin Netanyahu—who had campaigned on a platform of security for Israel—over Peres, who had stressed his desire to continue the peace process.

Shimon Peres married Sonia Gelman on May 1, 1945. They have a daughter, Zvia, two sons, Jonathan and Nechemia, and numerous grandchildren. In addition to the Nobel Prize, Peres has received a number of awards, including the French Legion of Honor. A poised, handsome man with a receding hairline and a cleft chin, Peres is not considered to be a charismatic politician. "Deep in my heart," he has said, "I'm convinced that I'm incorrigibly shy, but I must reconcile myself to the fact that many claim that I'm also a man who tried to leap forward—almost an arrogant man."

SELECTED WORKS: From These Men: Seven Founders of the State of Israel, 1979; The New Middle East, 1993.

ABOUT: Globe & Mail September 13, 1986; Golan, Matti. The Road to Peace: A Biography of Shimon Peres, 1989; International Who's Who, 1994–1995; National Review March 7, 1994; New York Times October 13, 1986, September 19, 1993; Political Leaders of the Contemporary Middle East and North Africa, 1990.

PERL, MARTIN L.
(June 24, 1927–)
Nobel Prize for Physics, 1995 (shared with Frederick Reines)

Born in Brooklyn, New York, Martin L. Perl is the son of parents who, in 1900, came to the United States as children from what was then the Polish area of Russia. His father, Oscar Perl, was a clerk and salesman for a printing/stationery firm; his mother, Fay Rosenthal, was a secretary and bookkeeper for a firm of wool merchants. They also had a daughter, Lila. By the time of Martin Perl's birth, his father had established the Allied Printing Company, which, as the Nobel laureate wrote in an autobiographical essay published in *Les Prix Nobel*, "brought the four of us into the middle class and kept us in the middle class through the Depression of the 1930s. We lived in the better neighborhoods of the borough of Brooklyn, not the fanciest neighborhoods, but quite good neighborhoods, and so we went to quite good schools."

Perl graduated from James Madison High School in Brooklyn in 1943. He credits his early school experiences with helping establish a positive foundation for his later work. In his 1995 work *An Autobiographical Memoir on the Discovery of the Tau Lepton*, he wrote: "These schools and the attitude of my parents toward these schools were important in preparing me for the work of an experimental scientist. Going to school and working for good marks, indeed working for very good

MARTIN L. PERL

marks, was a serous business. My parents regarded school teachers as higher beings, as did many immigrants. School principals were gods to be worshiped but never seen by children or parents. . . . The remoteness of my parents from the schools, so unfashionable today, was often painful for me; but I learned early to deal with an outside and sometimes hard world. Good training for research work! The experimenter dealing with nature faces an outside and often hard world. Nature's curriculum cannot be changed."

Although Perl now believes that his high-school curriculum was unsophisticated, he studied two foreign languages, four years of English, four years of mathematics, and a year of physics. He indulged his love for reading by checking out the maximum number of books allowed from his local public library. "This reading had only partial approval from my parents," he recalled. "They wanted me to play more sports because they were acutely sensitive to their children being 100 percent American, and they believed that all Americans played sports and loved sports. They felt that too much reading interfered with my going outside to play sports." The books that most influenced the young Perl were two by Lancelot Hogben—*Mathematics for the Millions* and *Science for the Citizen*—that he borrowed from the library over and over again, making summaries of them for his own study. Perl was also fascinated by all things mechanical, though he had to share an Erector set with his cousin since "one Erector set per extended family was considered quite enough." "I loved to build with the Erector set, I loved to build toys and models out of wood, I loved to draw mechanical devices, even those I could not build. I loved to read the magazines *Popular Mechanics* and *Popular*

Science . . . Before leaving this subject I must mention that since I never owned an Erector set as a child, I have compensated in my adult years by collecting old European, English, and American construction sets; and even by devising and starting prototype production of a modern wooden construction set called BIG-NUT.

"I was also interested in chemistry, but my parents were not willing to buy me a chemistry set. I had some chemicals, but when I bought sulfuric acid and nitric acid my father confiscated the acid on grounds of safety. As every child knows, chemistry with nothing stronger than vinegar soon becomes dull."

In spite of this early fascination with science and mechanics, Perl admits that he never thought of becoming a scientist because, "as the children of immigrants, my sister and I were taught that we must use our education to 'earn a good living'" in fields such as medicine, dentistry, accounting, law, or—Perl's choice—engineering. He enrolled in the chemical engineering program at the Polytechnic Institute of Brooklyn (now Polytechnic University).

"This was an unusual choice for a Jewish boy in the early 1940s," he recalled, "because there was still plenty of anti-Semitism in engineering companies." But Americans in those days had an optimistic faith in the ability of science to provide them with nylon, radio, automobiles, and other consumer products, and Perl sensed that studying chemistry could provide a reliable source of income. He was also bored by the required coursework in classical physics, which to him amounted to nothing more than "pulleys and thermometers," but he later credited the skills and knowledge he acquired there as "crucial in all my experimental work." His studies at Polytechnic were interrupted by World War II. In 1944 he left to become an engineering cadet in the program at the Kings Point Merchant Marine Academy. He wrote: "But when I went to sea for six months as part of the training, I was on a Victory ship with a sealed turbine and electrically driven auxiliary machinery. Very boring. Therefore when the war ended with the atom bomb, I left the merchant marine and went to work for my father while waiting to return to college. I knew so little about physics that I didn't know even vaguely why the bomb was so powerful." Perl was soon drafted into the army and spent a "pleasant year at an army institution in Washington, D.C., doing very little."

Returning to civilian life, he received a bachelor's degree summa cum laude from Polytechnic in 1948. He then joined General Electric as an engineer in its Schenectady, New York electron-tube production factory in the early days of the television industry. He went to nearby Union College for courses in atomic physics and advanced calculus. There he came under the influence of professor Vladimir Rojansky, who encouraged him to enter the doctoral program in physics at Columbia University. With I. I. RABI as his thesis mentor, Perl researched the problem of using the atomic beam resonance method to measure the quadruple moment of the sodium nucleus, using "boldly mechanical" apparatus such as a brass vacuum chamber, submarine storage batteries, and a wall galvanometer. In so doing, Perl developed much of his style in experimental science. He wrote: "In designing experiments and in thinking about the physics, the mechanical view is always dominant in my mind. More important, my thinking about elementary particles is physical and mechanical . . . I see the positron . . . and electron . . . as tiny particles which collide and annihilate one another. I see a tiny cloud of energy formed, and then I see that energy cloud change into two tiny particles of new matter, a positive tau lepton . . . and a negative tau lepton . . . ."

"In my thesis experiment," he continued, "I first experienced the pleasures, the anxieties, and sometimes the pain that is inherent in experimental work: The pleasure when an experiment is completed and the data safely recorded, the anxiety when an experiment does not work or breaks, the pain when an experiment fails or when an experimenter does something stupid . . . I learned things more precious than experimental techniques from Rabi. I learned the deep importance of choosing one's own research problems . . . [and] I learned from Rabi the importance of getting the right answer and checking it thoroughly. . . . It is far better to be delayed, it is better to be second in publishing a result, than to publish first with the wrong answer."

It was I. I. Rabi who sparked Perl's life's work in particle-physics research. Perl received his Ph.D. in 1955 and considered job offers from the physics departments at Yale University, the University of Illinois, and the University of Michigan. He deliberately chose Michigan because, of the three, it had the weakest reputation in elementary particle physics. In so doing, he wrote, "I followed a two-part theorem that I always pass on to my graduate students and postdoctoral research associates. First: don't choose the most powerful experimental group or department, choose the group or department where you will have the most freedom. Second: there is an advantage in working in a small or new group, then you will get the credit for what you accomplish."

As an instructor at Michigan, he first worked in bubble-chamber physics with DONALD A. GLASER. After the launch of the Russian satellite Sputnik galvanized complacent Americans into paying more attention to science, Perl and Lawrence W. Jones began a research program using "the now-forgotten luminescent chamber and then spark chambers."

"In eight wonderful and productive years at the University of Michigan," Perl wrote, "I learned the experimental techniques of research in elementary parti-

cle physics: scintillation counters, bubble chambers, trigger electronics, data analysis. With my research companions Lawrence Jones, Donald Meyer and later Michael Longo, we learned these techniques together, often adding our own new developments."

Perl concentrated on the physics of strong interactions—the physics of the nuclear force—using spark chambers to measure the elastic scattering of pions on protons. He was pleased with these experiments but "gradually became dissatisfied" with the theory needed to explain the measurements, he wrote. "I am a competent mathematician, but I dislike complex mathematical explanations and theories, and in the 1950s and 1960s the theory of strong interactions was a complex mess, going nowhere. I began to think about the electron and the muon, elementary particles which do not partake in the strong interaction." He wrestled with two classic puzzles about the connection between the two particles: why the muon is 207 times heavier than the electron even though their properties are the same with respect to particle interactions; and why the decay of the muon to an electron produces a neutrino and an antineutrino, contrary to what is expected. In trying to resolve these paradoxes, Perl sought to devise high-energy experiments on charged leptons, what he described as "an uncrowded area of physics."

In 1962 Perl had an opportunity to work on the electron-muon problem when Wolfgang K. H. Panofsky and Joseph Ballam offered him a position at the yet-to-be-built Stanford Linear Accelerator Center (SLAC). Although the linear accelerator would not be built until 1966, Perl and his colleagues began to design and build experimental equipment to test two hypotheses: that there might be unknown differences between the electron and the muon that might account for the differences in behavior; and that there might be some unknown charged leptons, similar to the electron and muon but heavier. Of these early speculations, he wrote: "My hope was that we would find a new x particle, perhaps a new charged lepton somehow related to the electron or muon. A vague hope by the standards of our knowledge of elementary particle physics today. We were certainly naive in the 1960s. We didn't find any new leptons or any new particles of any kind, and as we now know, there were no new particles to find in this experiment."

Perl and his colleagues next turned their attention to experiments to compare muon-proton scattering with electron-proton inelastic scattering, in the hope that a difference between the electron and the muon might be found other than the differences of mass and lepton type, "another naive hope when viewed by our present knowledge of particle physics." The researchers measured the scattering of muons on protons and then compared this scattering with the corresponding electron-muon scattering. They found no statistically significant differences between the two.

PERL

"Experimental science is a craft and an art," Perl wrote, "and part of the art is knowing when to end a fruitless experiment. There is a danger of becoming obsessed with an experiment even if it goes nowhere. I avoided obsession and gave up. That turned out to be a good decision, because modern experiments have shown that scattering experiments do not illuminate any differences between the electron and the muon beyond the mass difference."

While building the apparatus for the muon-proton scattering experiment, however, Perl kept thinking about his other idea: to look for a new charged lepton, a particle like the electron and muon but heavier and more massive. "There was no theoretical need for such a particle," he recalled, "but I thought if such a particle existed, it would help me solve the electron-muon problem." Perl carried on his lepton search by using the electron-positron collider, and by devising a model for the new lepton he hoped to find. After numerous funding delays, an SLAC group that included Perl and a Lawrence Berkeley Laboratory group began to build the SPEAR electron-positron collider at Berkeley. It became operational in 1973, and Perl soon began to find what he called "electron-muon events" with an electron, an opposite-sign muon, no other charged particles, and no visible photons.

"By early 1975, we had seen dozens of electron-muon events, but those of us who believed we had found a heavy lepton faced two problems: how to convince the rest of our collaboration and how to convince the physics world. The main focus of this early skepticism was the electron and muon identification systems: Had we underestimated hadron misidentification into leptons? Had we misunderstood particle misidentification so that the particles we called electrons were not electrons or the particles we called muons were not muons? Since our detection system only covered about half of all angles, what about undetected particles? What about inefficiencies and cracks in these systems?"

As the experiments continued, Perl became convinced "of the reality of the electron-muon events and the absence of a conventional explanation." In December 1975 he and his colleagues published a *Physical Review* letter entitled "Evidence for Anomalous Lepton Production in $e^+ - e^-$ Annihilation." The final paragraph of that paper stated: "We conclude that the signature e-μ events cannot be explained either by the production and decay of any presently known particles or as coming from any of the well-understood interactions which can conventionally lead to an e and a μ in the final state. A possible explanation for these events is the production and decay of a pair of new particles, each having a mass in the range of 1.6 to 2.0 GeV/c^2." Perl later wrote: "We were not yet prepared to claim that we had found a new charged lepton, but we were prepared to claim that we had found something new."

About a year later, Petros Rapidis, a graduate student who was working on the project, suggested the name "tau" because tau is the first letter of the Greek word "triton," meaning "third," and the tau is the third charged lepton in the sequence electron-muon-tau.

After these experiments, there followed three years of confusion and uncertainty about the validity and interpretation of these data. "There were several reasons for the uncertainties of that period," Perl wrote in 1995. "It was hard to believe that both a new quark—charm—and a new lepton—tau—would be found in the same narrow range of energies. And, while the existence of a fourth quark was required by theory, there was no such requirement for a third charged lepton. So there were claims that the other predicted decay modes of tau pairs could not be found. Indeed, finding such events was just at the limits of the particle identification capability of the detectors in the mid-1970s." Finally, other groups of physicists at SLAC and in Germany confirmed the existence of the tau lepton. "By the end of 1979," wrote Perl, "all confirmed measurements agreed with the hypothesis that the tau was a lepton which was produced by a known electromagnetic interaction and, at least in its main modes, decayed through the conventional weak interaction."

For this discovery and the discovery of the "third family" of elementary particles (tau, tau neutrino, top quark, and bottom quark), Perl was awarded the Wolf Prize in Physics in 1982. Since that time he has continued his experimental research in elementary particle physics, testing the hypothesis that perhaps there are a few isolated quarks left over from their creation at the beginning of the universe.

In 1995 Martin L. Perl and fellow American FREDERICK REINES shared the Nobel Prize for Physics for their separate work in subatomic physics, which resulted in the discovery of the tau and neutrino particles that—together with quarks—are part of the class of particles known as leptons. Perl's and Reines's work thus helped answer some of the most elusive and fundamental questions about the existence and properties of the tiniest particles making up matter and the universe. Perl's pioneering work with Stanford University's electron-positron collidor in the 1970s established the existence of the very unstable tau lepton. His investigation of leptons helped confirm the standard theoretical model used in elementary-particle physics by establishing conformity with fundamental principles of symmetry.

In addition to the Wolf and Nobel Prizes, Perl received an honorary doctorate in science from the University of Chicago and was a distinguished visiting professor at the University of Michigan. He is also a fellow of the American Physical Society.

Concluding his memoir, Perl wrote: "Looking back to my early years in Brooklyn, at the Polytechnic Institute, and at the General Electric Company, I am astonished to be writing a biographical note as a 1995 Nobel laureate in physics. I have tried to tell how it happened, yet I realize that I have left out the most crucial element: good fortune. It was good fortune to be a child during the Depression years and a youth during the war years. I lived in a country united by the belief that hard work and perseverance could get one through great difficulties. In the Second World War, I saw right triumph. The progression of my career coincided with the growth of universities and the tremendous expansion in federal support for basic research. Academic jobs were relatively easy to get and hold, research funds were relatively easy to get. All good fortune. Of course, my ultimate good fortune was that the tau existed.

"Life is much harder for the young women and men who are in science in present times. But they are smarter and better trained than I was at their age; they know more and have better equipment. I wish them good fortune."

SELECTED WORKS: High Energy Hadron Physics, 1974; Physics Careers, Employment and Education (ed.), 1977; The Search for New Elementary Particles (ed.), 1992; The Tau-Charm Factory (ed.), 1994; Reflections on Experimental Science, 1996.

THE PUGWASH CONFERENCES ON SCIENCE AND WORLD AFFAIRS
(founded 1957)
Nobel Prize for Peace, 1995 (shared with Joseph Rotblat)

With the detonation of the world's first atomic bombs over Hiroshima and Nagasaki in Japan in 1945, World War II ended and the nuclear age began. These detonations also signaled the emergence of Cold War tensions between the United States and its allies and the Soviet Union and its satellite nations. Warfare had entered a new phase; for the first time in history, mankind had the ability to end ideological and military conflicts with the simple and decisive ignition of a single nuclear device. With the continual buildup of nuclear devices on both sides, such warfare—and the destruction of humanity—seemed not only feasible to the thinkers of the 1940s and 1950s but likely. While most of the world considered the awesome destructive power of atomic and hydrogen bombs with a mixture of wonder and horror, a small group of scientists and thinkers began organizing a series of conferences in a small town in Nova Scotia, Canada. They used as their model the principles of peace set down in the Russell-Einstein Manifesto of 1955, which read in part: "In the tragic situation which confronts humanity, we feel that scientists should assemble in conference to appraise the perils that have arisen as a result of the development of weapons of mass destruction, and to discuss a resolution"

The Pugwash Conferences on Science and World Affairs were founded on the antiwar principles of the Russell-Einstein Manifesto of 1955. In that year the British philosopher BERTRAND RUSSELL had grown increasingly concerned with the nuclear arms race between the United States (and its allies) and the Soviet Union. Though the United States and the Soviet Union had made several proposals for nuclear disarmament since the end of World War II, they had had little success in applying them. In 1952 the United States detonated its first hydrogen device; in the next year the Soviet Union did the same. In the opinion of Russell, and of scientists and thinkers like him, the times they were living in were some of the most dangerous in the history of humanity.

Russell reached out to the scientific community for help. He spoke first to JOSEPH ROTBLAT, a physicist who had quit the Manhattan Project when he discovered that the Allies were planning to use the atomic bomb not against Germany but to keep the Soviet Union in check after the war. After the detonation of the atomic bombs over Japan, Rotblat spoke out around Great Britain, urging the public to demand that world governments stop nuclear testing. Rotblat had also gone on British television to speak against the testing of the hydrogen bomb.

According to The Bulletin of the Atomic Scientists, Russell next went to ALBERT EINSTEIN, with a suggestion that "a group of scientists be convened for the purpose of discussing nuclear disarmament and ways in which war could be abolished." Einstein agreed, and Russell drafted a statement that was eventually signed by MAX BORN, PERRY W. BRIDGMAN, Albert Einstein, Leopold Infeld, FREDERIC JOLIOT, HERMANN J. MULLER, LINUS N. PAULING, CECIL F. POWELL, Joseph Rotblat, Bertrand Russell, and HIDEKI YUKAWA.

On July 9, 1955, Rotblat and Russell held a press conference to publicize the manifesto. None of the men who signed the document knew how the press and the public would react to such an antiwar statement coming at the height of Cold War tensions. The scientists spoke not as representatives of any group or country but as individual human beings who feared for the future of mankind. The international press covered the conference and manifesto extensively.

The Russell-Einstein Manifesto called for a great many things. Not only did it request that the scientists of the world "assemble in conference to appraise the perils of weapons of mass destruction," it called on world leaders to stop war altogether. "No one knows how widely such lethal radioactive particles might be diffused, but the best authorities are unanimous in saying that a war with H-bombs might possibly put an end to the human race," the manifesto stated. "It is feared that if many H-bombs are used there will be universal death, sudden only for a minority, but for the majority a slow torture of disease and disintegration . . . Here, then, is the problem which we present to you, stark and dreadful and inescapable: Shall we put an end to the human race; or should mankind renounce war?"

The public response was enormous, and the group began to receive invitations to give lectures all over the world. According to the Canadian magazine *Maclean's*, Cyrus Eaton, a Canadian industrialist, offered to fund their international scientific meeting, so long as it would be held on his summer property in Pugwash, Nova Scotia. The first annual Pugwash Conference was conducted in July 1957; 22 people from 10 countries attended. According to Rotblat: "The participants included three Nobel laureates, the vice-president of the Soviet Academy of Sciences, a former director of the World Health Organization, as well as the editor of *The Bulletin of the Atomic Scientists*. These were scientists to whom the world leaders listened." The tone of the meeting was respectful; arguments were presented straightforwardly, with no flourishes of propaganda. This was especially surprising considering that the meeting was the first in which scientists from the East and West had come together to discuss problems that were both scientific and political in nature. Rotblat believed that it took a great deal of courage for the participants to attend, since anyone in the West who appeared at a meeting to talk peace with the Russians risked being considered a Communist sympathizer.

The first meeting concluded with the drafting of a brief statement, which in turn was delivered to President Eisenhower of the U.S., Premier Khrushchev of the U.S.S.R., Prime Minister Macmillan of the U.K., and Prime Minister Diefenbacker of Canada. The report detailed the hazards of radiation, including the probability that the tests could cause leukemia and bone cancer. It also made some recommendations about arms control and suggested the observance of several principles regarding the social responsibility of scientists who were involved with bomb construction. The first Pugwash report turned out to be successful; it was approved by everyone except Macmillan and was even endorsed by the Soviet Academy of Sciences.

The group decided to go ahead with more meetings and keep them as the first had been—quiet, informal, and with no one acting as an official representative of any nation. The participants came together as individuals who had influence on decision makers, and their conclusions went directly to world leaders. Since 1957 more than 200 Pugwash Conferences have been held, drawing more than 10,000 scientists, statesmen, and military personnel. These conferences have been prone to open, lively debate, partially because they are closed meetings in which the press is not allowed.

Pugwash has helped to spark a great deal of negotiation over the years. In 1961, the Pugwash Conferences in Vermont brought together Alexander Topchiev, who was then vice-president of the Soviet Academy of

Sciences, and President John Kennedy's science adviser, Jerome Wiesner. After the Pugwash Conference, Wiesner took Topchiev to see the president. This helped to lay the groundwork for the Partial Test Ban Treaty, signed in 1963. In 1967 Pugwash brought together for the first time Ho Chi Minh, the Communist leader of North Vietnam, and HENRY KISSINGER, who would be a chief negotiator for peace in Vietnam when he became national security adviser to President Richard Nixon. Pugwash also facilitated early talks on the Non-Proliferation Treaty of 1968. Finally, Pugwash took an early look at the antiballistic missile systems (ABMs). While the ABMs were to be used only as defensive weapons, the Pugwash conferees argued that if one side were to defend itself with ABMs, the other side would have to build better and stronger missiles in order to penetrate their defenses. After some negotiations, the U.S. and the U.S.S.R. signed the Antiballistic Missile Treaty of 1972.

Pugwash has also been influential in banning the use of biological and chemical weapons. In the 1980s the conferences helped to produce cuts in the intermediate range missile arsenals of the U.S. and the U.S.S.R. In the 1990s, since the end of the Cold War, Pugwash has led the fight to control and later shrink U.S. and Russian nuclear stockpiles and production. The goal has remained the same since 1957—a nuclear weapons–free world, a world without chemical or biological weapons, a world at peace.

Joseph Rotblat, the corecipient of the 1995 Nobel Prize for Peace, served for many years as the Pugwash Conferences' secretary-general, starting in 1957. In 1988, he became president of the conferences, a position he still held in 1996. In his Nobel lecture, Rotblat spoke about how, even in the aftermath of the Cold War, there are still Cold Warriors in Russia and in the United States who wish to hold onto their nuclear weapons for security, while denying nuclear capability to any other nations. Of the eight declared nuclear powers—the United States, the former Soviet Union, Great Britain, France, China, India, Pakistan, and Israel—both France and China have continued to conduct atmospheric tests of nuclear weapons. The nuclear powers are eight too many, according to Rotblat, who stated: "I do not believe that a permanent division between those who are allowed to have nuclear weapons and those who are not is a basis for stability in the world." In his lecture, he also urged the nations of the world to sign an accord banning nuclear weapons.

John P. Holdren, who accepted the Nobel Prize on behalf of the Pugwash Conferences, believes that peace is possible because even nations who wage war with one another must still share the same planet. As he explained in his Nobel address: "We live under one atmosphere, on the shores of one ocean, our countries linked by flows of people, money, goods, weapons, drugs, diseases, and ideas. Either we will achieve an environmentally sustainable prosperity for all, in a world where weapons of mass destruction have disappeared or become irrelevant, or we will all suffer from the chaos, conflict, and destruction resulting from the failure to achieve this."

ABOUT: Bulletin of the Atomic Scientists January/February 1996, March/April 1996; Maclean's October 23, 1995; New Statesman and Society October 27, 1995; Time October 23, 1995; USA Today February 16, 1996; U.S. News and World Report October 23, 1995.

RABIN, YITZHAK
(March 1, 1922–November 4, 1995)
Nobel Prize for Peace, 1994 (shared with Yasir Arafat and Shimon Peres)

The older of the two children of Nehemiah Rabin and Rosa (Cohen) Rabin, Yitzhak Rabin was born in Jerusalem, in what was then Palestine. (Four months later the League of Nations adopted the British mandate for Palestine, which affirmed Great Britain's commitment to supporting the establishment of a Jewish homeland in Palestine.) Rabin had a sister, Rahel. His father, who emigrated from his native Russia to the United States as a boy and who later settled in Palestine, was a worker, intellectual, and member of the Jewish Legion. His mother, also a Russia-born Jew who immigrated to Palestine, became well known in the Yishuv, the Jewish community in Palestine, because of her work as a leader in the Labor movement and as a member of the high command of the Hagana, the Jewish underground army. Both parents were nonreligious, Socialist Jews. Rosa Cohen, as she preferred to be called even after she got married, was the dominant figure in the family. Rabin has described her as "a very austere, extreme person, who stuck to what she believed in; there were no compromises with her."

Rabin began his education at the age of six, when he entered the Bet Hinuch, in Tel Aviv, where the family had moved several years before. The school had been established by Jewish settlers with the aim not only of educating students but also of providing them with the practical skills needed to settle what was then a largely undeveloped land. At the age of 13, Rabin entered Givat Hashlosha, an intermediate school organized by Rosa Cohen and modeled after Bet Hinuch. His mother's death in 1937 affected Rabin deeply. Following a period of mourning, he returned to Kadoorie Agricultural High School, which he had just entered, "with the feeling that [he] had crossed over the threshold of manhood," as he wrote in The Rabin Memoirs (1979). "Part of my home no longer existed," he continued, "and I had to strike out on my own path." Although on entering Kadoorie he had had no interest in pursuing a military career—"My purpose in life was

YITZHAK RABIN

to serve my country, and I believed that the best way to do it was to prepare myself to be a farmer," Rabin has said—that prospect became increasingly more likely as his years there passed.

After graduating from Kadoorie, with honors, in 1940, Rabin applied to the University of California to study hydraulic engineering. The idea appealed to him because an expertise in that field would serve the Yishuv well in the coming years, water being a scarce resource in the region. But the exigencies of World War II soon compelled him to abandon those plans. (Rabin's academic education thus ended when he left Kadoorie.) He instead joined the Hagana, the underground military arm of the Jewish Agency, and was assigned to the Palmach, the Hagana's secret commando force, soon after it was formed in May 1941. As part of the Palmach's campaign to prevent the Nazis from taking over the Middle East, in June of that year Rabin participated in sabotage operations conducted against the Vichy French government in Lebanon and Syria. He also attended a special military training course offered by the British, with whom the Hagana were allied.

Later in the war Rabin worked part-time on a kibbutz; all the while he remained in the Palmach, of which he was named platoon commander in 1943 and deputy battalion commander in 1944. According to Robert Slater, the author of the biography Rabin of Israel (1993), Rabin "acquired a reputation as one of the leading thinkers of the strike force. Other commanders, even his superiors, often sought his advice or opinion. He was not only a willing and persevering soldier, he had a special understanding of the unique role of the Palmach." With the conclusion of World War

II, Rabin considered reapplying to the University of California, but he decided to remain in Palestine to take part in the creation of a Jewish state.

Following World War II the already unstable alliance between Jewish settlers in Palestine and the British deteriorated further. (The settlers and the British had been united in their opposition to the Axis powers, but were deeply divided politically; in 1939 Great Britain greatly reduced its commitment to the establishment of a Jewish homeland, when the fate of European Jewry was at its most precarious.) A major point of contention was Britain's policy on Jewish immigration; Britain not only opposed the immigration of Holocaust survivors to Palestine but sought to return those immigrants who had entered Palestine "illegally." A confrontation occurred in the summer of 1945, when the Palmach, in an attempt to thwart Britain's plans to evict illegal Jewish immigrants who were being held at the Atlit detention camp, set out to rescue the detainees. Still with the Palmach, Rabin was a key participant in the daring raid on the camp. (The raid was fictionalized by Leon Uris in his novel *Exodus*; Rabin was said to be the basis for the character Ari Ben-Canaan.) As a result of that and similar exploits, Rabin became a wanted man, and in June 1946 he was among the many Jewish settlers who were arrested and imprisoned by the British.

Soon after Rabin's release from prison, in November 1946, the British decided to relinquish their responsibilities under the mandate. A year later the United Nations voted to partition Palestine into two states—one Palestinian, the other Jewish. Rabin joined in the general celebration in Tel Aviv, but, as he wrote in his memoirs, he "harbored few illusions." "The irony of it all was that the success of our political struggle left us more vulnerable than ever to destruction," he continued. "We would now have to protect our political gains by force of arms." Indeed, the partition plan was rejected by the neighboring Arab states, which invaded Israel as soon as it declared itself a sovereign state in May 1948.

During the Arab-Israeli War of 1948 (also known as the first Arab-Israeli War and the Israeli War of Independence), Rabin played an important role as commander of the Palmach's Harel Brigade. Early in the war he was given "the extremely difficult task," as Avishai Margalit described it in the *New York Review of Books*, of securing the route linking Jerusalem and Tel Aviv, but he was unable to do so. He was also placed in charge of carrying out Israeli prime minister David Ben-Gurion's controversial order to sink the *Altalena*, which was defying government orders by transporting arms to the Irgun, a militia whose politics were at odds with those of the government. In the final phase of the war, Rabin helped to push back Egyptian forces into the Negev desert, and he took part in the negotiations for the 1949 armistice.

In late 1948 David Ben-Gurion, feeling that the Palmach constituted a threat to his authority, had dissolved the organization and integrated it into the new Israel Defense Forces (IDF). Ben-Gurion was also distrustful of some of the former Palmach members and saw to it that they had no place in the IDF. Rabin's loyalty was thus divided between the Palmach veterans and the government, and when the ousted Palmach members held a gathering to demonstrate both their solidarity and their opposition to the government's action, Rabin attended it despite government orders not to do so. According to some observers, Ben-Gurion delayed promoting Rabin to a top leadership position because of the act of disloyalty. Some insiders have claimed that Rabin would have been promoted to chief of staff by 1953 but for that blemish on his record; as it turned out, he did not receive that promotion until 1964.

Following the war Rabin was named commander of the brigade that patrolled the Negev and was recruited to help in the overall organization of the Israeli military. Although he had grown comfortable with the methods employed by the Palmach, which has been likened to a guerrilla organization, he nevertheless successfully adapted his skills to the needs of the regular army. In 1954, after spending a year at the British Staff College in Camberley, England, which offered a nine-month course in military education, he was promoted to the rank of major general and was asked to head the training branch of the IDF.

Rabin was appointed commander in chief of the Northern Front, on Israel's border with Syria, in 1956; he thus played no direct part in the Sinai Campaign, waged that year. At one point he considered leaving the military to enter Harvard University's Graduate School of Business Administration, but he decided to remain with the service when changes in command made it clear that he could advance to a top leadership position. Rabin's most significant promotion—to chief of staff, in 1964—not only placed him in charge of the army but also brought him into a leadership role with respect to the government.

Following his promotion, Rabin flexed Israel's military muscle against the Syrians and ordered reprisals against terrorist operations encouraged by the formation of the Palestine Liberation Organization in the same year. According to some Israeli political leaders, including David Ben-Gurion, Rabin's aggressive stance contributed to the escalation of tensions between Israel and its Arab neighbors in the spring of 1967. Shaken by the view of Ben-Gurion and others that he was leading Israel to the brink of war, in May of that year Rabin experienced a nervous breakdown that rendered him unable to perform his duties for a 24-hour period. "There can be no doubt that I was suffering from a combination of tension, exhaustion, and the enormous amounts of cigarette smoke I had inhaled in recent days," he said, as quoted by Robert Slater. "But it was more than nicotine that brought me down. The heavy sense of guilt that had been dogging me of late became unbearably strong on 23 May . . . Perhaps I had failed in my duty as the prime minister's chief military adviser. Maybe that was why Israel now found itself in such difficult straits. Never before had even I come close to feeling so depressed."

The heightened tensions between Israel and its neighbors culminated in the outbreak of the Six-Day War, on June 5, 1967, with Israel launching preemptive strikes against Egypt, Jordan, Iraq, and Syria. Whatever his role in provoking Israel's neighbors, Rabin prosecuted the war with great efficiency, to the extent that Israel succeeded in taking control of the Sinai peninsula, the West Bank, the Gaza Strip, and the Golan Heights—and thus in growing to three and a half times its prewar size. While the international media, enamored of the charismatic Israeli defense minister Moshe Dayan, gave Dayan most of the credit for Israel's victory, among Israelis Rabin was the hero of the war. "No event shaped the image of Yitzhak Rabin in the pubic's mind as much as the Six-Day War . . . ," Robert Slater wrote. "When people asked themselves in later years whether Yitzhak Rabin would make a worthy prime minister or defense minister, his intimate involvement in the 1967 war was all the credentials he required. The Six-Day War . . . became Yitzhak Rabin's calling card for political leadership."

Before the war Rabin had lobbied to be appointed ambassador to the United States, which was proving to be Israel's most dependable ally, and in early 1968 he was posted to Washington, D.C. His assignment was to strengthen the relationship between the two countries, obtain economic and military aid, and gain support for Israel both within and outside government circles. Although he lacked the usual credentials of a diplomat, he made a highly creditable showing, and he succeeded in persuading the Americans to continue to supply Israel with arms and other forms of aid.

On his return to Israel in 1973, Rabin decided to run for a seat in the Knesset, Israel's parliament, as a member of the Labor Party. (Until 1971, when he joined Labor, he had not belonged to a political party.) The elections had been scheduled for October 31, 1973, but they were put on hold after Israel was attacked by Egypt and Syria on October 6, marking the beginning of the Yom Kippur War. While Israeli forces ultimately succeeded in driving back the enemy, the war was costly both in human and economic terms, and the government was blamed for having been poorly prepared to defend the country against attack. In the elections, held in December, Labor won a plurality of the vote, an outcome that enabled Prime Minister Golda Meir to form a government, but in April 1974 she resigned her post as a result of mounting public criticism of her government's lack of defense preparedness.

Rabin, who had won a seat in the Knesset in the elections, was a political beneficiary of those events. Thanks to his popularity among Israelis and his lingering reputation as the hero of the Six-Day War—and despite his lack of a solid political base within the Labor Party itself—he emerged as a candidate for prime minister. (The Labor Party's central committee was to choose the new prime minister, who would then form a new government.) His rival in the ensuing battle for the leadership of the party was SHIMON PERES, with whom Rabin had never been on the friendliest of terms. In winning the contest, Rabin became Israel's youngest prime minister and the first sabra, or native-born Israeli, to hold that post.

During his three years as prime minister, Rabin's challenges included contending with a new wave of immigration, reviving the economy, which was plagued by high inflation as a result of the 1973 war, and accommodating the heightened domestic concerns for security, also a result of the war. By most accounts, he had some success in the economic sphere, and he made rebuilding the IDF one of his top priorities. In 1976 Rabin won considerable praise for authorizing what turned out to be the successful military operation at Entebbe, Uganda, in which Israeli soldiers rescued 103 airline passengers who had been held hostage by the PLO. Another of his successes was the conclusion, through the mediation of United States secretary of state Henry Kissinger, of Sinai II, one of several Israeli-Egyptian disengagement agreements, in 1975.

In late 1976, hoping to receive a mandate to continue leading the country, Rabin resigned in favor of new elections. His reelection campaign was soon beset by a variety of problems, among them the revelation that his wife had an active bank account in Washington, D.C., which constituted a violation of Israel's unusually strict rules governing such matters. Although initially a minor issue, it eventually developed into a full-blown political scandal that, in May 1977, prompted Rabin to abandon the race for the prime ministership. His rival Shimon Peres took his place as the leader of the party. In the elections the right-wing Likud Party gained control of the Knesset, beginning what was to become its 15-year-long domination of Israeli politics.

For the first half of that period, Rabin, who remained a member of the Knesset, was relegated to the party's back benches. With the publication of his memoirs in 1979, Rabin's rivalry with Shimon Peres became a much-talked-about news item, for in it he accused Peres of "subversion" and of undermining Rabin's premiership. In spite of the criticism he received for airing his grievances, by 1980 Rabin's popularity among the electorate had rebounded, to the extent that he was again considered a leading candidate for prime minister. But as it turned out, Peres received the party's nomination, and the Likud was returned to power in the June 1981 vote.

The surprise resignation of Menachem Begin in 1984 was followed by a closely contested election in which Labor captured 44 seats in the Knesset, just three more than Likud. Neither party, however, could muster enough support from Israel's minor parties to form a government, with the unprecedented result that the two agreed to form a National Unity government, in which Shimon Peres and then Yitzhak Shamir would each serve a two-year term as prime minister. Also as part of this arrangement, Rabin was to serve as defense minister during the government's entire four-year term. The appointment reflected not only his return to a position of leadership within Israeli politics but also the confidence that both the left and the right had in his ability to head Israel's military establishment.

One of Rabin's major initiatives as defense minister was to withdraw Israeli forces from Lebanon, which it had invaded in 1982. Rabin had apparently supported the invasion initially but had later come to oppose it on the grounds that Israel's war aims, which included removing Syrian troops from Lebanon and trying to arrange the installation of a government friendly to Israel, were unattainable. The withdrawal was completed in 1985. Rabin was confronted with an even more serious problem when, in December 1987, impoverished and oppressed Palestinians living in the Gaza Strip and the West Bank launched a spontaneous revolt, which came to be known as the *intifada*. The revolt, which was characterized by mass demonstrations and random acts of violence, took Rabin, along with most Israeli and Arab leaders, by surprise, and he at first downplayed its significance. Viewing it as the work of a few extremists, he took a hard line against the rioters. Indeed, he is said to have commanded his soldiers not to shoot the demonstrators but to break their limbs—an order that many in the West found to be appalling. A. M. Rosenthal of the *New York Times*, for example, went so far as to call for his resignation.

Within several months, however, the failure of his policy convinced Rabin that the Palestinians could not be ignored indefinitely. "I've learned something in the past two and a half months—among other things that you can't rule by force over 1.5 million Palestinians," he said in early 1988, as quoted in *Time*. An alternative, he concluded, was to devise a political solution to the conflict. While he still opposed the creation of a Palestinian state, he came to believe that such a solution might involve ceding Israel's authority over territory inhabited by Palestinians to Jordan. He also expressed a willingness to negotiate with PLO officials, provided they adhered to certain conditions, including a recognition of Israel's right to exist. Rabin thus set himself apart from Yitzhak Shamir, who remained staunchly opposed to compromise of any kind.

Following the 1988 elections Labor and Likud again agreed to form a National Unity Government.

Rabin retained the post of defense minister until 1990, when Yitzhak Shamir formed a new, more conservative government. Although in his public utterances Shamir expressed an interest in working toward peace, he failed to advance the peace process substantively. As a result, he not only alienated Israel's closest ally, the United States, but also taxed the patience of both the Israeli public and Israeli political leaders—factors that contributed to the fall of the Likud-led government in January 1992.

Notwithstanding popular dissatisfaction with Shamir and Likud, a Labor victory was far from assured, for the Israeli electorate, while fed up with Shamir, could at least trust that he would not jeopardize Israel's security. Labor's electoral prospects were therefore enhanced after Rabin succeeded in wresting control of the party from Shimon Peres, in February, for while Rabin appeared to be more willing than Shamir to negotiate a peace settlement—he went so far as to say that he would be willing to trade land for peace—he was, unlike Peres, someone who could be trusted not to jeopardize the country's security. As predicted by the polls, Rabin led his party to victory in the June 23, 1992 elections.

Once in office, Rabin set out to make good on his promise to make significant progress in negotiating a peace settlement. A breakthrough occurred in August 1993, following secret talks between the Israeli government and the PLO in Norway, when the two parties concluded a preliminary accord on Palestinian self-rule in the occupied territories. In another dramatic development, in September Rabin wrote a sober note to YASIR ARAFAT that stated, "Israel has decided to recognize the PLO as the representative of the Palestinian people and commence negotiations with the PLO within the Middle East peace process." According to the agreement on Palestinian self-rule, an interim Palestinian government was to be established in the Gaza Strip, the West Bank town of Jericho, and, later on, in the rest of the West Bank. At the historic signing of the accord, on September 13, 1993, in Washington, D.C., Rabin shook hands, albeit somewhat tentatively, with his former enemy Yasir Arafat. The signing of the accord was followed by a torturous but ultimately fruitful series of negotiations with other of Israel's neighbors. A peace treaty between Israel and Jordan was signed on October 26, 1994; it was the second peace treaty Israel signed with an Arab country, coming 15 years after its accord with Egypt. At the historic signing ceremony, held at Arava Crossing, a desert outpost on the Israeli-Jordanian border, Rabin said: "For nearly two generations, desolation pervaded the heart of our two peoples. The time has now come not merely to dream of a better future but to realize it." Also in 1994, Rabin, Arafat, and Peres were awarded the Nobel Peace Prize by the Norwegian Nobel Committee, for their "efforts to create peace in the Middle East." By early 1995 Israel and Jordan had established full diplomatic relations and had also committed themselves to cooperate in such areas as agriculture, water, tourism, economic development, and environmental protection.

Eleven months after signing Israel's peace treaty with Jordan, Rabin put his pen to another historic document that expanded Palestinian self-rule in the West Bank and authorized the withdrawal of Israeli troops from cities where nearly half the West Bank population lives. The treaty with the Palestinians did not settle the final borders between Israel and the West Bank entity, which is not as yet—and may or may not become—a state. The pact with the PLO has aroused considerable controversy in Israel, where it is opposed by many in the Likud and other right-wing parties who see the West Bank as land to which Israel has a historical right. It has also generated opposition among radical elements of the Palestinians, who view peace with Israel as capitulation. Recognizing the fragility of the Israel-PLO accord, Rabin said at the signing ceremony, "If all the partners to the peace do not unite against the evil angels of death by terrorism, all that will remain of this ceremony are color snapshots, empty mementos."

Yitzhak Rabin was married to Leah Schlossberg, a German-born teacher he met in Tel Aviv, on August 28, 1948. They had a son, Yuval, and a daughter, Dalia. In addition to the Nobel Prize, he received many honors, including honorary doctorates from Jerusalem University, Brandeis University, and Yeshiva University, among other institutions. When he received the Nobel Prize, Rabin claimed it was "for the whole nation, for the citizens of the State of Israel, for the bereaved families and the disabled, for the hundreds of thousands who have fought in Israel's war." "Today," he said, "the Palestinians face the moment of truth. If they do not defeat the enemies of peace, the enemies of peace will defeat them."

Rabin, in his Nobel Prize lecture, spoke of his military career—of how he had been forced to live by arms, unwillingly as he described it. He then quoted the Israeli poet Yehudah Amichai: "God takes pity on kindergartners. / Less so on the schoolchildren, / And will no longer pity their elders, / Leaving them to their own, / And sometimes they will have to crawl on all fours, / Through the burning sand, / To reach the casualty station, / bleeding." "For decades, God has not taken pity on the kindergartners in the Middle East, or the schoolchildren, or their elders. There has been no pity in the Middle East for generations," Rabin added, concluding, "I stand here as the emissary today—if they will allow me—of our neighbors who were our enemies."

Yitzhak Rabin was assassinated on November 4, 1995, as he left a peace rally in Tel Aviv, by Yigal Amir, an Israeli right-wing extremist opposed to the Israeli government's self-rule agreement with the Palestine Liberation Organization.

ABOUT: International Who's Who, 1994-95; London Observer June 28, 1992; New York Review of Books June 11, 1992; New York Times November 5, 1995; Rabin, Yitzhak. The Rabin Memoirs, 1979; Slater, Robert. Rabin of Israel, 1993; Time January 3, 1994.

RAMOS-HORTA, JOSE

(December 26, 1949–   )
Nobel Prize for Peace 1996 (shared with Carlos Felipe Ximenes Belo)

Jose Ramos-Horta, the human rights activist and the chief spokesperson for East Timorese independence, was born in Dili, the capital of East Timor, during the long period of Portuguese colonization. There is little published information about his personal life, although what is known suggests that his personal history is greatly intertwined with the history of his homeland. Even in 1970, before the Indonesian invasion of East Timor, he was deported from the island by Portuguese authorities for his involvement with the independence movement. He would return to East Timor again before the Indonesian takeover in 1975.

Ramos-Horata's education took him around the world. He received a fellowship to study international relations at St. Anthony's College, Oxford University, and he went on to attain a master's degree in peace studies at Antioch College in the United States. He also attended the Hague Academy of International Law, in the Netherlands, and the International Institute of Human Rights, in Strasbourg.

East Timor has a population of approximately 750,000 people, most of whom are Roman Catholic, owing to Portuguese religious influences. The Portuguese and the Dutch settled Indonesia in the 16th and 17th centuries as they journeyed through the south seas looking for spices and other trading goods. In 1859 a treaty formalized the division of the island of Timor—the western half going to the Dutch, the eastern half to the Portuguese. This situation went unchanged for almost a century. After World War II the Netherlands granted independence to the western half of Timor, which became part of Indonesia. Portugal, however, kept control of their colony until 1974. In that year left-wing officials staged a coup in Lisbon in an attempt to take over the government and destroy the Portuguese empire. In August 1975 Portugal was forced to abandon its holdings in East Timor.

In September of the same year, the left-wing East Timorese independence group Fretilin occupied the seat of government in Dili. Jose Ramos-Horta, then a 25-year-old journalist, became the Fretilin government's foreign minister. There were four other political groups vying for power, each with a different political agenda for the future of East Timor. The leaders of these groups were executed by the Frelitin government during its brief hold on power. That regime came to an end, however, on December 7, as In-

JOSE RAMOS-HORTA

donesian paratroopers invaded East Timor and troops poured over the border from the western portion of the island. Ramos-Horta and other leaders fled the country so they could continue their struggle for East Timorese independence.

Though not normally considered an expansionist country, Indonesia, the world's largest Muslim nation, had two major reasons for invading East Timor. The first was the government's fear of a Communist infiltration into their own country. In 1965, just a decade before, the Indonesian government was nearly overthrown by Marxist insurgents. The Indonesian president Suharto feared another such uprising. Just as East Timor was gaining its long-sought independence in 1975, the last of the United States officials left the embassy in South Vietnam by helicopter; shortly afterwards, the government there fell to the Communists in North Vietnam. President Suharto, aware of the rising tide of Communist insurgency in Southeast Asia, and fearing that Indonesia's vulnerable neighbor— East Timor— would fall victim to it, wanted to preserve Indonesia from what he perceived as a growing threat of Communist takeover. The second reason for Indonesia's invasion was economic: an interest in the exploration of natural gas and oil deposits found in the Timor Sea.

In 1976 Indonesia annexed East Timor as its 27th province. Fretilin resistance groups still on the island retreated to the mountains and occasionally attacked Indonesian troops. As of 1996 the United Nations still did not officially recognize East Timor as a possession of Indonesia and maintained that the area was under the colonial control of Portugal. Portuguese authorities have also protested the annexation of East Timor, to

no avail. Starting in 1976, Ramos-Horta, as an official representative to the UN, began to protest Indonesia's actions. The UN called upon the Indonesian government to withdraw from East Timor. At approximately the same time—and while ignoring the UN's requests—the Indonesians began to violate international human rights laws. Over the next five years, between 100,000 and 200,000 East Timorese died at the hands of the Indonesian military, as reported by Amnesty International in 1985. Among those killed were Ramos-Horta's brother and sister. Another sister managed to escape and fled to join him in Australia.

During the 1980s the Roman Catholic Church took a stand against Indonesia and for East Timorese independence, first led by Bishop CARLOS FELIPE XIMENES BELO, the head of the Roman Catholic Church in East Timor. In October 1989 Bishop Belo was joined by Pope John Paul II, who protested against Indonesian occupation during a student-led demonstration in Dili. At the same time, Ramos-Horta traveled around the world seeking aid in his struggle for East Timor and speaking out at various important institutions, including the UN and the European Parliament.

In 1990, 150 independence demonstrators were arrested, jailed, and tortured, according to various human rights organizations. In the next year Indonesian troops opened fire on a crowd marching to the grave of a slain East Timorese activist. The Indonesian officials put the death toll at 50, while other groups claimed that up to 200 or more were killed. According to the *Washington Post*, "Portugal . . . summoned the ambassadors of all countries represented in Lisbon to issue a statement condemning what it called the massacre of defenseless citizens. . . . The statement called for an urgent international investigation and for the access of international humanitarian organizations to East Timor." The *Post* also reported that two American journalists, Amy Goodman of Pacifica Radio and Allan Nairn of the *New Yorker*, were beaten by Indonesian troops. According to a March 6, 1992 statement before the Senate Foreign Relations Committee by Kenneth M. Quinn, the deputy secretary for East Asian and Pacific Affairs, the U.S. government "publicly condemned the Dili incident" and suggested that "no provocation could have warranted such a wanton military reaction" to the demonstration. The U.S. government also scaled back its sales of light and heavy weaponry to the Indonesian government during that period, the only such reversal of policy towards Indonesia since the 1975 occupation of East Timor. In May 1994 Ramos-Horta and other East Timorese exiles were banned from an Asia Pacific Conference on East Timor in the Philippines. The Philippine government had bowed to pressure by Indonesia, fearing retaliation from the Indonesians, who have one of the fastest-growing economies in the South Asian area.

In October of 1994, the *New York Times* quoted

Ramos-Horta as saying that the make-up of East Timor was changing, due to the vast influx of non–East Timorese people coming into the territory, most of them coming from Indonesia. As he said in an interview, these foreigners "have taken over the best land, the best jobs, even the small shops on the streets." He also suggested that the trade in East Timor's resources, mostly marble, coffee, sandalwood, and oil, was dominated by people who are not natives.

Many people in the world were unaware of Ramos-Horta's protests until October 1996, when the Royal Swedish Academy awarded him and Bishop Carlos Felipe Ximenes Belo the Nobel Peace Prize, for their work in the struggle for East Timorese independence. According to *Time*, he displayed modesty upon receiving the award, suggesting that it should have gone to Jose Alexandre Gusmao, another Fretilin leader working for East Timor's independence, who was jailed in 1993. As of 1996 Ramos-Horta was living in Australia and was a member of the law faculty of the University of New South Wales. Upon hearing news of the award, he suggested that the independence struggle had reached a turning point and that he hoped that the award would be a signal to the Indonesian government that "the people of East Timor have suffered long enough."

The other awards Ramos-Horta has received in recognition of his work include the 1993 Professor Thorolf Rafto Human Rights Prize, the 1995 Gleitzman Foundation Award, and the 1996 UNPO award.

SELECTED WORKS: FUNU: The Unfinished Saga of East Timor, 1987; Timor: Amanha em Dili, 1994.

ABOUT: Economist October 15, 1994; Globe & Mail October 12, 1996; Newsday October 12, 1996; New Statesman & Society January 27, 1995; New York Times August 25, 1993, October 30, 1994, October 12, 1996; Time October 21, 1996; Washington Post November 13, 1991, December 27, 1991, May 22, 1994, October 12, 1996, October 29, 1996.

REINES, FREDERICK
(March 16, 1918–   )
Nobel Prize for Physics, 1995 (shared with Martin L. Perl)

The American physicist Frederick Reines was born in Patterson, New Jersey, the son of Israel and Gussie (Cohen) Reines. He was educated at Stevens Institute of Technology in Hoboken, New Jersey, where he received his M.E. degree in 1939 and his M.S. degree in 1941. Reines then went on to receive his Ph.D. in physics from New York University in 1944.

In that same year, Reines joined the staff of Los Alamos National Laboratory, in New Mexico. In 1945 he was promoted to group leader of the laboratory's theoretical division. This led to a year-long stint as director

FREDERICK REINES

of the Atomic Energy Commission's experiments on the Eniwetok Atoll in 1951. While working at Los Alamos, Reines teamed up with fellow physicist Clyde L. Cowan Jr. to provide concrete evidence of the existence of an elusive, subatomic particle known as the neutrino.

The origins of the neutrino theory can be traced back to 1930, when WOLFGANG PAULI proposed a hypothetical particle to explain some puzzling aspects of beta decay—the process by which atomic nuclei end their lives by emitting an electron. Beta decay seemed to defy all basic laws of physics, most notably the law of conservation of energy. In order to explain beta decay in terms of known physical laws, Pauli proposed what he described as a "desperate solution," suggesting that in addition to an electron, the nucleus also emits a massless, nonelectrically-charged particle called a neutrino. This neutrino takes some energy with it and then disappears. Though the proposed existence of the neutrino accounted for the more mysterious aspects of beta decay, Pauli thought that he had done a "frightful thing" by proposing a particle so elusive that it would never be discovered.

The combined talents of Reines and Cowan, however, would eventually lead to a discovery proving the existence of the neutrino and dispelling any doubts Pauli or the scientific community may have had. By the late 1940s, a string of failed searches by several scientists had led to some convolution of the methods and theories used to prove the existence of neutrinos. "The search for the neutrino turned to indirect methods. . . . Observations of conservation of energy and momentum, *assuming* the existence of a neutrino, became a popular argument *for* the tiny particle," Cowan stated in a 1964 article. "The concept of the neutrino had been developed to save the conservation laws. The fact that the concept then permitted their retention . . . was then taken as proof of the existence of the neutrino." Determined to prove scientifically the existence of the neutrino, Reines and Cowan began devising new search methods.

In 1951, after the dawn of the nuclear age had brought nuclear weapons and energy to the forefront of physics research, Reines and Cowan devised an experiment to use an atomic bomb to try to detect the neutrino. The plan was to suspend a detector in a specially built shaft near the detonation site. As the countdown reached zero, the detector would be released and fall freely through the tall shaft. While falling, the detector would record data that would, the scientists hoped, include a specific reaction that the pair believed would indicate the presence of neutrinos. "If the neutrino exists in the free state, this inversion of beta decay must occur," Reines said. "We chose to consider this reaction in particular because if we believe in detailed balancing and use the measured value of a neutron half-life, we know what the cross section must be—a nice clean result." The atomic explosion plan, however, was canceled after J. M. B. Kellogg, chairman of the physics division at Los Alamos, suggested that the pair study the possibility of using neutrinos from a fission reactor rather than those from a fission explosion.

After pondering this idea, Reines and Cowan proposed setting a tank of water salted with cadmium atoms and surrounded by light detectors next to a nuclear reactor. The pair theorized that when the neutrino hit a hydrogen nucleus, it would create two particles, a neutron and a positron. Falling through the water, the positron would be destroyed together with an electron. This destruction would produce two bursts of high-energy gamma radiation, detectable by the light sensors. The neutron would then be absorbed by a cadmium nucleus and emit more gamma radiation. Though only a microsecond or two, the time delay between the sets of gamma ray bursts would provide proof of neutrino capture. Unfortunately, the first experiment was thwarted by excessive amounts of background radiation at the testing site, in Hanford, Washington. "We felt that we had the neutrino by its coattails, but our evidence would not yet stand up in court."

Reines and Cowan then redesigned their detector, making it both more sensitive to beta decay and less likely to be affected by extraneous radiation. In 1955 the pair moved their experiment to the Savannah River facility in South Carolina. The facility offered a huge amount of power and a particularly well-suited location, 11 meters from the reactor's center and 12 meters below ground level. Reines and Cowan conducted their experiment in 100 days over approxi-

mately one year. By June 14, 1956, they were certain they had observed a neutrino. They immediately sent a telegram to Wolfgang Pauli, the man who had first proposed the neutrino's existence. "We are happy to inform you that we have definitely detected neutrinos from fission fragments by observing inverse beta decay of protons," they wrote. "Observed cross section agrees well with expected 6 x 10 to -44 square centimeters." Though Pauli drafted his reply that evening, it wasn't until 30 years later that Reines would receive a copy. The note read: "Thanks for the message. Everything comes to him who knows how to wait."

After the discovery, Reines resumed his work at Los Alamos. He remained there until 1959, when he became a professor of physics and head of the physics department at Case Institute of Technology, in Pittsburgh. His work at Case included extensive work in reactor neutrino physics. In 1966 Reines accepted a professorship at the University of California at Irvine. He soon became the university's first dean of physical sciences. In 1988, he retired and was granted professor emeritus status.

Reines was awarded the Nobel Prize for Physics in 1955. Sadly, the codiscoverer of the neutrino, Clyde Cowan, was unable to share in the prize, as he had died in 1974. The academy praised both Reines and Cowan, however, for achievements that "raised the status of the neutrino from its status as a figure of the imagination to an existence as a free particle." Reines shared his prize, along with the $1 million monetary award, with MARTIN L. PERL, discoverer of a subatomic particle called the tau. Members of the physics community applauded the academy's recognition of Reines. Dr. Henry Sobel of the University of California at Irvine termed Reines's work "a keystone to our understanding of elementary particle physics," adding, "All of us thought [Reines] would get the prize years ago."

Since 1940, Reines has been married to Sylvia (Samuels) Reines. They have two children.

In addition to the Nobel Prize, Reines has been the recipient of many other awards, including the J. Robert Oppenheimer Memorial Prize (1981), the National Medal of Science (1983), the Michelson Morley Award (1990), and the W. K. H. Panofsky Prize (1992). He has also been awarded fellowships by several organizations, including the American Physical Society and the Guggenheim Foundation. Reines has served as a member of such organizations as the American Association of Physics Teachers, the American Academy of Arts and Sciences, and the Russian Academy of Science, and he has lectured at universities around the world, among them the Israel Academy of Sciences and Humanities, Stanford University, and the University of Maryland.

SELECTED WORKS: Effects of Atomic Weapons

(contributing author), 1950; The Neutrino (with C. Cowan), Nature September 1956; Neutrino Physics (with C. Cowan), Physics Today August 1957.

ABOUT: New York Times October 12, 1995; Physics Today December 1995; Science October 20, 1995; Science News October 21, 1995; Who's Who in America, 1997.

RICHARDSON, ROBERT C.

(June 26, 1937–   )
Nobel Prize for Physics, 1996 (shared with David M. Lee and Douglas D. Osheroff)

The American physicist Robert C. Richardson was born in Washington, D.C. He was educated at the Virginia Polytechnic Institute, where he received his bachelor's degree in physics in 1958 and his master's degree in 1960. Richardson completed his doctoral studies at Duke University, in North Carolina, in 1966.

Upon graduating from Duke, Richardson became a research associate at Cornell University in Ithaca, New York. In 1967, he was promoted to assistant professor. By the early 1970s, Richardson, along with fellow Cornell faculty member DAVID M. LEE and Cornell graduate student DOUGLAS D. OSHEROFF, had begun an intensive study of a rare form of helium known as helium-3. The trio's experiments, which involved subjecting helium-3 to temperatures very close to absolute zero (0 degrees kelvin or -273.15 degrees centigrade), yielded unexpected results that would provide new insight into scientific arenas as diverse as the study of semiconductors and the big bang theory.

Helium, which, after hydrogen, is the most abundant element in the universe, was first identified in 1868 by Pierre Jules Cesar Janssen while he was observing a solar eclipse in India. Helium was subsequently found to be present in a variety of substances on Earth, in natural gas, and in the gas expelled when the mineral cleveite is heated. Helium is the first element in Group O, a band of elements with filled electronic shells, of the periodic table. It is an odorless, colorless, and tasteless gas that cannot be combined either with itself or with other elements. With the exception of hydrogen, helium is the least dense gas known. It is extremely unusual in that its light mass and relatively weak interatomic force combine to make it the only element on Earth that remains liquid when cooled to absolute zero. Additionally, helium has the lowest boiling point of any known substance. The most common isotope, or form, of helium is helium-4, whose two neutrons and two protons give it an atomic mass number of four.

In the last half of the 1930s, Russian physicist PYOTR KAPITZA discovered that liquid helium-4, when cooled to a temperature near absolute zero, exhibits a phenomenon known as superfluidity. In a superfluid state, ordinary helium appears to lose all viscosity and flows

ROBERT C. RICHARDSON

in frictionless streams. This frictionless motion is caused by helium atoms' lining up in such a way that they effectively behave as a single atom. Superfluid helium exhibits an array of characteristics not associated with a normal liquid, including the ability to climb up the inside of a laboratory beaker and then flow down the outside. Superfluid helium-4 has been utilized by physicists as, among other things, a coolant fluid for particle accelerators.

In 1939, around the same time that Kapitza was conducting his work on helium-4 superfluidity, a helium isotope with only one neutron and two protons, helium-3, was discovered by LUIS W. ALVAREZ and R. Cornog. Obtained from the radioactive decay of tritium, an isotope of hydrogen used in some nuclear fusion weapons, helium-3 constitutes only 10 to 15 percent of all helium on Earth. Though theorists predicted that helium-3, like helium-4, could exist in a superfluid state, until the 1970s all attempts to demonstrate this had ended in failure.

Then, in 1972, Richardson, Lee, and Osheroff proved that helium-3 superfluidity existed not only in the minds of theorists but in reality. The trio did not set out to discover superfluidity in helium-3; rather, their find was a byproduct of the scientists' work in attempting to discover an antiferromagnetic phase in solid helium-3. Using a specially built apparatus, the trio examined the behavior of helium-3 when it had been cooled to a temperature near absolute zero. A problem with their thermometer's readings led the scientists to monitor the internal pressure in the sample of helium-3 under external pressure that was increased over time. Osheroff, who noticed that the sample's internal pressure increased uniformly over time, knew that something was amiss. Further experiments proved that the trio were, indeed, observing superfluidity in helium-3. The substance exhibited certain unexpected magnetic properties. These properties were so different from those predicted by theorists that the trio's original paper reporting the discovery of helium-3 superfluidity was rejected by *Physical Review Letters*, a prominent physics journal. A subsequent reevaluation of the paper, however, resulted in its publication.

The study of superfluidity in both helium-3 and helium-4 is invaluable. Such substances, in that state, exhibit quantum traits normally associated with atoms, molecules, or subatomic particles. When rapidly stirred, superfluid helium tends to form swirls or waves that appear and disappear in rapid jumps, as if someone were controlling such motion with a switch, rather than in the gradual progression produced by stirring ordinary liquid. Such behavior of superfluid substances allow scientists to take a peek at the world of quantum mechanics, which relies on statistical laws that seem very odd to the uninitiated observer. Examination of some of the unusual properties of superfluid helium-3 may also one day lead to an increased knowledge of one of the most mysterious celestial anomalies, the neutron star.

Of great interest to physicists is the transition phase during which regular helium-3 is transformed into superfluid helium-3. It is hoped that the in-depth study of this transition may eventually lead to answers for a multitude of questions regarding the origin of the universe. Scientists speculate that the transition process that occurs as helium becomes superfluid is similar to the process that took place seconds after the big bang and led to the formation of galaxies.

Further, superfluidity is very similar to the more well-known phenomenon of superconductivity, a complete disappearance of electrical resistance that allows electric currents to flow endlessly without ever losing energy. Helium-3 superfluidity shares the intricate structure of a category of superconductors known as high-temperature superconductors. Scientists are hopeful that experimentation with helium-3 may lead to an increased understanding of high-temperature superconductors, which, in turn, could lead to a plethora of technological advances, including new varieties of extremely efficient engines and motors and an abundance of inexpensive electric power.

After the discovery of helium-3 superfluidity, Richardson continued to teach at Cornell. He was promoted to associate professor in 1972 and professor in 1975. In 1984, he worked briefly as a visiting scientist at Bell Laboratories in Murray Hill, New Jersey, before once again returning to Cornell.

In 1996, more than 20 years after the discovery of superfluid helium-3, Robert C. Richardson, the director of Cornell's Laboratory of Atomic and Solid State Physics since 1990, was awarded the Nobel Prize. He

shared the award, along with the $1.12 million monetary prize, with the codiscoverers of helium-3 superfluidity, Douglas D. Osheroff and David M. Lee. The academy applauded the trio for work that has made "a most valuable contribution to our current view of the manifestations of quantum effects in bulk matter." Colleagues praised the selection of Richardson, Lee, and Osheroff. "It's fundamental knowledge about how matter works," University of Oregon physicist Russell Donnelly told the Associated Press.

Richardson lives in Ithaca, New York, with Betty (McCarthy) Richardson, his wife since 1962. They have two daughters.

In addition to the Nobel Prize, Richardson has been the recipient of numerous other awards, including the British Physical Society's Eighth Simon Memorial Prize (with D. D. Osheroff and D. M. Lee, 1976) and the American Physical Society's Buckley Prize (with D. D. Osheroff and D. M. Lee, 1981). He has received multiple fellowships, from organizations including the Guggenheim Foundation (1975–1976 and 1982–1983), the American Physical Society (1983), and the American Association for the Advancement of Science (1981). Also, Richardson is a member of the National Academy of Sciences and the Finnish Academy of Science and Letters.

SELECTED WORKS: Low Temperature Science— What Remains for the Physicist?, Physics Today August 1981; Experimental Techniques in Condensed Matter Physics at Low Temperatures (with Eric N. Smith and 21 Cornell graduate students), 1988; The World at Absolute Zero (instructional video); Introductory Physics (series of instructional videos).

ABOUT: Colliers 1996 Encyclopedia CD-ROM; Los Angeles Times October 10, 1996; New York Times October 10, 1996; Newsday October 10, 1996; Royal Swedish Academy 1996 Nobel Prize Announcement.

ROBERTS, RICHARD J.
(September 6, 1943–   )
Nobel Prize for Physiology or Medicine, 1993 (shared with Phillip A. Sharp)

Richard J. Roberts submitted the following autobiography for inclusion in *Nobel Prize Winners*.

"I was born the only child of John and Edna (Allsop) Roberts in Derby, England. My father was a motor mechanic and my mother a homemaker. We moved to Bath when I was four, and so I consider myself a Bathonian. My elementary education was at Christ Church infant school and St. Stephen's junior school. At St. Stephen's I encountered my first real mentor, the headmaster Mr. Broakes. He must have spotted something unusual in me, for he spent lots of time encouraging my interest in mathematics. He would produce problems and puzzles for me to solve, and I still enjoy

RICHARD J. ROBERTS

the challenge of crossword and logical puzzles. Most importantly, I learned that logic and mathematics are fun! After passing the 'dreaded' 11 + exam, I moved on to the City of Bath Boys (now Beechen Cliff) School.

"At this time I wanted to be a detective, where it seemed they paid you to solve puzzles. This changed quickly when I received a chemistry set as a present. I soon exhausted the experiments that came with the set and started reading about less mundane ones. More interesting apparatus like Bunsen Burners, retorts, flasks, and beakers were purchased. My father, ever supportive of my endeavors, arranged for the construction of a large chemistry cabinet complete with a Formica top, drawers, cupboards, and shelves. This was to be my pride and joy for many years. Through my father, I met a local pharmacist who became a source of chemicals that were not in the toy stores. I soon discovered fireworks and other concoctions. Luckily I survived those years with no serious injuries or burns. I knew I had to be a chemist.

"I am a passionate reader, having been tutored very early by my mother. I avidly devoured all books on chemistry that I could find. Formal chemistry at school seemed boring by comparison, and my performance was routine. In contrast, I did spectacularly well in mathematics and sailed through classes and exams with ease. During these years at school I also discovered chess, which I loved, and billiards and snooker, which became a consuming passion. At age 15 I easily passed the O-level examinations and then began to specialize in the sciences, taking mathematics, physics, and chemistry. For exercise I discovered the sport of caving and would spend most weekends underground on the nearby Mendips.

"From age 16 on I found school boring and failed A-level physics at my first attempt. This was necessary for university entrance, and so I stayed an extra year to repeat it. This time I did splendidly and was admitted to Sheffield University, my first choice because of their excellent chemistry department. After chemistry, physics, and mathematics in the first year, I opted for biochemistry as a subsidiary subject in the second year. I loathed it. The lectures merely required rote learning, and the laboratory consisted of the most dull experiments imaginable. I was grateful when that year was over and I could concentrate wholly on chemistry. I graduated in 1965 with an upper-second-class honors degree.

" . . . David Ollis, the professor of organic chemistry, really caught my imagination. . . . Fortunately, he accepted me as his Ph.D. student, and I began to explore the neoflavonoids found in a piece of heartwood from a Brazilian tree. Two pieces of luck followed. My tree contained more than its fair share of interesting new compounds, and I was put in a lab with an exceptional postdoctoral fellow, Kazu Kurosawa, who proved a gifted teacher. Not only did he suggest the right experiments—he explained why they should be done. Within one year I had essentially enough for my thesis and an understanding of how to do research. I had the luxury of spending the next two years following my nose, reading, and experimenting.

"During this time I came across a book, by John Kendrew, that was to change the course of my research career. . . . It was my first exposure to molecular biology, and I became hooked. For postdoctoral studies, I looked for a laboratory doing biochemistry that might accept an organic chemist and provide a pathway into molecular biology. Luckily, Jack Strominger offered me a position, not in Wisconsin as I had thought, but at Harvard, where he had just been appointed professor of biochemistry and molecular biology. It was on January 1, 1969, that my family walked across the runway at Logan Airport with an outside temperature of 4 degrees Fahrenheit and a massive wind blowing, to start a new life.

"The next four years were wonderful. Mostly, I learned, although at first I was in a fog. Everyone spoke in acronyms: DNA, RNA, ATP, UDP, GlcNAc. . . . Tom Stewart patiently guided me into the world of tRNAs since it was his project that I was to pick up. I was assigned the job of sequencing a tRNA that was involved in bacterial cell wall biosynthesis. In 1969 only a handful of tRNAs had been sequenced previously, mostly by chemical techniques introduced by ROBERT W. HOLLY and his contemporaries. However, within a few months and much reading, I decided that a new method being pioneered in FREDERICK SANGER's lab in Cambridge was much better. In late 1970 I had succeeded in making enough pure tRNA^{Gly} to start sequencing and set off for a one-month sojourn in Cambridge to learn the techniques. . . .

"On my return to Harvard, my small sequencing operation was the first in the Boston area, and many researchers came to learn the techniques. My own sequencing was successful, and I managed two *Nature* papers during this postdoctoral period. When it came time to leave Harvard I wanted to return to the UK and applied for a job in Edinburgh. In the meantime, I was approached by Mark Ptashne, who told me that [JAMES D. WATSON] was looking for someone to sequence SV40. . . . I decided the offer was too good to turn down. In September, 1972, I moved to Cold Spring Harbor.

"Earlier in 1972, I attended a seminar at Harvard Medical School given by [DANIEL] NATHANS. He described an enzyme, Endonuclease R, that could cleave DNA into specific pieces. This was to shape much of my subsequent research career. Sanger had developed RNA sequencing because there were plenty of small RNA molecules to practice on, but no suitable DNA molecules. I realized that Nathans's restriction enzyme gave an immediate way to isolate small DNA molecules. Surely there must be more restriction enzymes with different specificities. DNA sequencing seemed within reach, and I was exhilarated.

"Upon moving to Cold Spring Harbor, I set out to make preparations of Endonuclease R and the few other restriction enzymes known at the time. We also began a systematic search for new ones. I also made some DNA, since I had never worked with it before!

"A key factor in our restriction enzyme success was a highly talented technician, Phyllis Myers, who joined me in 1973. She became the keeper of our enzyme collection and a valuable resource to scientists around the world. . . . Every meeting at Cold Spring Harbor brought a few people carrying tubes of DNA to see if we had an enzyme that would cut it. Three quarters of the world's first restriction enzymes were discovered, or characterized in my laboratory. I made a lot of friends in those days!

"Plans to sequence SV40 DNA were abandoned shortly after reaching Cold Spring Harbor. Instead we turned our attention to Adenovirus-2 DNA. . . . It seemed a good model system because it was similar in size to bacteriophage lambda, where many spectacular advances in prokaryotic molecular biology had taken place. We began to map the DNA. . . .

"In 1974 Richard Gelinas, whom I had first met at Harvard, joined my laboratory to characterize the initiation and termination signals for an Adenovirus-2 mRNA. The idea was to sequence the 5'-end of an mRNA, map its location on a restriction fragment, and then sequence the upstream region. This would be the promoter. Shortly after beginning the project, mRNA caps were discovered and we developed an assay for capped oligonucleotides. All seemed well until we came up with the startling finding that all late mRNAs seemed to begin with the same capped oligonucleo-

tide, which was not encoded on the DNA next to the main body of the mRNA. We had excellent biochemical evidence for this, but real proof was elusive.

"In March 1977 I hit on the right experiment to show that our proposed split structure for Adenovirus-2 mRNAs was correct. . . . We hoped to visualize the split structure by hybridizing an intact mRNA to its two different coding regions. Based on a guess about the location of the coding region for the 5'-end, we made appropriate DNA fragments. The reason for our guess turned out to be wrong, but luckily the fragment worked anyway! Finally, by direct visualization we could see the split genes in the electron microscope.

"Our own work turned to an analysis of the sequences involved in RNA splicing. Joe Sambrook and Walter Keller cloned the common leader sequence at the 5'-end of late Adenovirus-2 mRNAs, and Sayeeda Zain in my lab sequenced it. Later we undertook the complete sequence of Adenovirus-2 DNA. This required a lot of computer software development. . . . Eventually, I managed to get funding from NIH ([PHILLIP A. SHARP] was chairman of a site-visit team that reviewed this grant), and we are still active in this area. My most recent work has been in the area of DNA methylases. . . .

"In 1992 I moved to New England Biolabs, a small private company of 150 individuals making research reagents, most notably restriction enzymes, and carrying out basic research. . . . I am now joint research director with my good friend, Ira Schildkraut.

"The main theme of my work in biology has centered on the belief that we must know the structure of the molecules we work with if we are to understand how they function. This means knowing the sequence of macromolecules and cataloguing any modifications such as methylation. For proteins, three-dimensional structure and posttranslational modification are crucial. This latter area is a target for my future work. Throughout my life in science, I have been fortunate to have friends and family who will bring me back to Earth and remind me that there is much in life to be savored besides science. I enjoy music very much and love to collect and play games, especially video games. I am indebted to my wife, Jean, and my children, Alison, Andrew, Christopher, and Amanda, who have been a source of great joy and comfort."

The Nobel Committee, in announcing the award of the Nobel prize for Physiology or Medicine to Richard J. Roberts and Phillip A. Sharp, said that the discovery of split genes "has changed our view on how genes in higher organisms develop during evolution." The previously held view had been that genes were discrete, continuous segments in DNA. Proof of the existence of split genes "has been of fundamental importance for today's basic research in biology, as well as for more medically oriented research concerning the development of cancer and other diseases," the Nobel Committee said.

A new process—gene splicing—was predicted by the discovery of Roberts and Sharp. Split genes are the most common gene structure in higher organisms. "Everybody thought that genes were laid out in exactly the same way, and so it came as a tremendous surprise," according to Roberts, that they were different in higher organisms.

Roberts explained the split-gene discovery for *Nobel Prize Winners* by making an analogy to a movie. "What we usually see is a series of scenes that together make up a whole. We run the tape on which the movie has been recorded on a projector, and in a linear fashion we see the scenes one after another, until eventually we have the whole story. If we think of DNA as being the tape upon which the story has been recorded, then the whole tape, that is, the whole DNA, would contain a description of an organism. The individual scenes would correspond to the genes that encode the individual components of the organism.

"Now in the case of bacteria, by 1977 we had a very good idea of what the genes looked like and, in particular, how the information present in the gene was encoded. Essentially it was . . . like an individual scene in a movie. We would start at one point in the tape, read the information in a sequential fashion, and end up with the gene."

To the surprise of Roberts and his colleagues, genes from higher organisms differed radically from those of lower forms of life: In a higher organism "the story was not told in a simple linear fashion. Rather, as we moved along the DNA, we would find that first there was a small part of the story, but then there was a big break where there was no sensible information, and then we would come to the next part of the story and again, a big break with no sensible information. . . . It was as though the information in the DNA of higher organisms looked much more like the raw footage from which the movie was made.

"If you remember the way in which movies are made, bits and pieces of the movie are shot separately and then the tape is edited before we see it. The relevant bits of the story are joined together so that they make a coherent whole. So it is with the DNA in higher organisms. There is an editing process, which we call RNA splicing, that joins together the little bits of information from each gene before it is used by the cell."

The differing gene segments were named "introns" and "exons" by WALTER GILBERT of Harvard University. The exons are the main biochemical strands that contain the information to create a protein. "Interrupting the exons are introns: long, rambling biochemical stutters that do not contribute to the construction of a protein," Lawrence K. Altman explained in the *New York Times*. The introns are clipped out during the sequence of protein creation, and the exons are spliced together into the string of instructions that tell the cell how to create a protein.

Although the introns may not have a known function in the current life of a cell, scientists believe that they have "allowed the exons to be easily shuffled around over time to generate an almost infinite variety of molecules," according to Altman. Thus, the introns probably have a vital role in evolution. The Nobel Prize–winning discovery of split genes thus has many implications.

The discovery of split genes "does not give us cures, but the possibility to know how we are going to do therapy with genes in the future," Gusta Gahrton, a professor of medicine at the Karolinska Institute, said, according to the *New York Times*.

Roberts said after learning that he was to receive the award, "Everybody thought that all the interesting stuff had been discovered. . . . Several very prominent scientists . . . went on the record saying that the age of molecular biology was dead and there were no more interesting discoveries to make." Roberts continued to expand the boundaries of molecular biology, however. His efforts to deduce the DNA sequence of the Andeovirus-2 genome, obtaining a complete sequence of 35,937 nucleotides, required the extensive use of computer methods both for the assembly of the sequence and its subsequent analysis. His laboratory has continued the development of computer methods of protein and nucleic acid sequence analysis.

Lately, he has focused on studies of DNA methyltransferases, resulting in the determination of crystal structures for the Hhal methyltransferase, both alone and in complex with DNA. "The latter complex is quite remarkable as the protein causes the target cytosine base to flip completely out of the helix so that it is accessible for chemical reaction," Roberts said in a press release. "This extreme, but elegant, distortion of the double helix has not been seen previously," he added.

In addition to the Nobel Prize, other awards won by Roberts include a Guggenheim Fellowship for 1979–1980, honorary doctorates from the University of Uppsala in Sweden and Bath, Sheffield, and Derby Universities in England, a Golden Plate Award from the American Academy of Achievement, and election as a fellow of the Royal Society.

SELECTED WORKS: Virology, 1976, with others; CRC Critical Reviews in Biochemistry, 1976, with others; Recombinant Molecules: Impact on Science and Society (R. F. Beers, Jr. and E. G. Barrett, eds.), 1977; Methods in Enzymology (L. Grossman and K. Moldave, eds.), 1980; Nucleases (S. A. Linn and R. J. Roberts, Eds.), 1982; The Applications of Computers to Research on Nucleic Acids III (D. Soll and R. J. Roberts, eds.), 1986; Les Prix Nobel 1993, 1994

ABOUT: New York Times October 12, 1993.

RODBELL, MARTIN
(December 1, 1925–)
Nobel Prize for Medicine or Physiology, 1994
(shared with Alfred G. Gilman)

Martin Rodbell provided the following autobiography for use in *Nobel Prize Winners*:

"The American biochemist Martin Rodbell was born in Baltimore, Maryland, the first child of Milton Rodbell, also born in Baltimore, and Shirley (Abrams) Rodbell, who was born in London, England. He grew up in the Depression era, living over his father's grocery store in a suburban neighborhood where he developed a keen interest in societal relationships kindled by delivering groceries to a large multiethnic neighborhood. At age six he began playing the piano, inspired by his mother's ability to play without notes or previous training. Later his passion for music was buttressed by the musical talents of his daughter Suzanne, an accomplished violinist, and her two daughters, Sarah, a pianist, and Alexa, who enjoys playing the cello.

"Always interested in competitive sports, he enjoyed playing softball and touch football in the streets of his neighborhood and later learned tennis from his high school principal. An avid reader spurred by the extensive library of his father's brother Theodore, he benefited from the Enoch Pratt Library system in Baltimore, where nearly every area had a library within walking distance. His closest friends from boyhood through university were two mathematically gifted fellows who influenced his interest in math and chemistry, the latter because of the sharing of colorful and explosive chemistry sets.

"A good but not a brilliant student, he was selected along with his two friends to attend the accelerated curriculum at the Baltimore City College, the second-oldest high school in the United States, where the graduates effectively completed sufficient courses to enter the second year of a university. Inspired by the professors of language, particularly Latin and French, he seemed destined for a nonscientific career even though he declared in his graduating yearbook that he wished to be a chemical engineer. He entered Johns Hopkins University in its engineering school. Shortly afterwards he was drafted into the U.S. Navy, where he served in the South Pacific and China theaters during World War II as a radioman, first in the jungles of the Philippines and then on three ships plying the China seas.

"He reentered Johns Hopkins after the war, taking courses in French literature and as a pre-med student, but soon lost interest in the latter except for the biology courses. Under the tutelage and influence of the members of the biology department, he completed his university studies in both biology and chemistry. Thusly prepared he entered the biochemistry department at the University of Washington. His Ph.D. thesis, under the tutelage of Donald H. Hanahan, a noted lipid

MARTIN RODBELL

chemist, concerned the biosynthesis of lecithin, an essential membrane lipid, in rat liver. This was a prescient choice, since his ultimate scientific career mostly involved the structure and function of membranes.

"After serving for two years under Herbert E. Carter as a postdoctoral fellow at the University of Illinois, Rodbell entered the National Institutes of Health in the laboratory of CHRISTIAN B. ANFINSEN, where he investigated the structure and function of lipoproteins involved in the metabolism of chylomicrons, particles in blood and lymph that are the principal form of circulating fat. The lipoproteins coating these fat particles are essential for the breakdown and utilization of fat in a variety of tissues, especially adipose tissue. This tissue contains lipoprotein lipase, the enzyme that catalyses the breakdown of chylomicrons. Rodbell soon found that collagenase, a protease that breaks down the collagen matrix, disrupts adipose tissue into its constituent fat and blood vessel cells. With his simple technique for isolating fat cells, Rodbell established that fat cells are the principal source of lipoprotein lipase in adipose tissue. He subsequently demonstrated that fat cells are extraordinarily sensitive to the physiologically important action of insulin: promotion of glucose uptake. The isolated fat cell became one of the principal model systems for investigating the mechanism of action of insulin and other hormones. . . .

"In formulating his theory, [EARL W.] SUTHERLAND [JR.] invoked the idea that adenylyl cyclase contains an allosteric site for the regulatory actions of hormones; i.e. the receptor binding sites for hormones are linked to the same protein that catalyses the conversion of ATP to cyclic AMP. Since the hormone-regulated enzyme is attached to the surface or plasma membrane of cells, it appeared likely that the enzyme is asymmetrically structured, with the receptor binding site on the exterior, where it is exposed to incoming signals (or primary messengers) whereas the catalytic site is exposed to its substrate ATP at the cytosolic face of the membrane. Implicit in this model is the idea that separate adenylyl cyclases exist for each hormone or incoming signal and produce selectively to their actions the 'second messenger' cyclic AMP.

"Using isolated fat cells from the rat, Rodbell demonstrated that several different hormones act on the same cell to produce cyclic AMP with resultant increases in the breakdown of cellular fat to their constituent fatty acids, a major source of energy for the animal. These same hormones stimulated adenylyl cyclase activity in plasma membranes isolated from the cells.

"This preparation provided the means for testing Sutherland's theory that each hormone operates trough receptor sites on separate adenylyl cyclases. This model predicted that additions of various combinations of the hormones (at maximal stimulating concentrations) should give additive production of cyclic AMP. Instead, no combination of hormones yielded more activity than the most active hormone. Each hormone was shown to act through distinct receptor sites.

"The conclusion drawn from these studies was that the receptors are distinct molecules from adenylyl cyclase, but all receptors are capable of stimulating the same enzyme. Moreover, Rodbell and his colleague Lutz Birnbaumer discovered that the receptors stimulated the enzyme via a Mg^{2+} dependent process distinct from the MgATP-requiring catalyses of ATP to cyclic AMP.

"Out of these studies arose the concept that the informational transaction between receptor and enzyme is carried out through a process involving what Rodbell called transducers; thus arose the term 'signal transduction' that now generally defines transactions between all types of receptors and cellular regulatory processes.

"Rodbell and his colleagues subsequently investigated the binding and actions of glucagon through its receptor in isolated rat liver membranes. Employing radioactive glucagon to tag its receptor, they found that the hormone binds relatively slowly, compared to its rapid activation of adenylyl cyclase.

"Moreover, in a medium lacking MgATP as substrate, the hormone remained bound despite repeated washing of the membrane. Addition of substrate induced both rapid binding and release of the hormone from its receptor. When tested for the specificity of ATP, the apparent culprit, Rodbell discovered that GTP or GDP were far more effective in altering glucagon binding. Most importantly, when ATP devoid of contaminating GTP was added to the medium for ex-

amining the stimulating effects of glucagon on adenyl cyclase, no stimulation by the hormone was detected unless GTP was added at the same concentrations required for affecting glucagon binding to its receptor. The same requirement for GTP was required for the actions of several other hormones acting on various cellular systems. Furthermore, GTP was also required for the inhibition of adenylyl cyclase by hormones that inhibit rather than stimulate the enzyme system, as initially found in fat cells.

"From such findings Rodbell deduced that there are at least two types of transducers, one for stimulation and the other for inhibition of adenylyl cyclase, and that these transducers are separate proteins from receptors and enzyme. . . . Rodbell invoked a theory (Disaggregation Theory) to explain the concerted actions of hormones and GTP on receptors and the transducers (now termed G-proteins because of their preferential interaction with guanine nucleotides) and introduced the prescient notion that there are probably multiple types of G-proteins that transduce the actions of hundreds of signals on their receptors. The field of G-proteins as signal transducers touches on every area of biomedical research because of their coupling to numerous receptor types in all eukaryotic cells. Since 1980 Rodbell has concentrated his research on the multimeric or polymeric structures of G-proteins that play a prominent role in the coupling between receptors and a wide variety of effector systems such as ion transporters, phospholipases, and phosphodiesterases.

"Rodbell married Barbara Charlotte Ledermann in 1950; they have three sons, one daughter, and seven grandchildren. Rodbell has remained at the National Institutes of Health for his entire scientific career, serving as head of laboratories and as a scientific director until his retirement as scientist emeritus in 1994. He continues his research efforts at the National Institute of Environmental Health Sciences."

In 1994 Martin Rodbell was forced to step down as head of the laboratory of signal transduction at the National Institute of Environmental Health Sciences. The reason was lack of Federal funds for his research, according to the New York Times. Ironically, this occurred a few months before he won the Nobel Prize for discovering that cellular signal transmission requires a molecule called GTP and for continued work on the nature and mechanism of G protein action in cells and membranes.

Rodbell told the New York Times that the work he and Alfred G. Gilman had done on G proteins exploded into "one of the hottest fields of medicine and biology." The discovery of how signals are transmitted to the interior of cells—not only by an enzyme and a receptor, as previously thought, but by an intermediary transducer molecule—has implications for cancer research, where it has been discovered that some cancers are caused by mutated and overactive G proteins; for research in hereditary glandular disorders, including diabetes; and for studies of the mechanisms of such infectious diseases as cholera and diphtheria.

Using press attention surrounding the announcement of the prize to mount a bully pulpit, Rodbell criticized government shortsightedness. He observed that Congress and the White House have favored goal-oriented research over the kind of basic search for knowledge that drove his own work, according to the *New York Times.* "Underlying all of that is that they are not willing to take a chance on people like myself, exploring the unknown, really looking at things that we never considered."

Indeed, his research had brought him into conflict with other scientists, Rodbell said at a press conference. "People would challenge us at almost every meeting, saying 'Marty, you are crazy.'"

Rodbell has reacted strongly to what he considers the commercialization of science. He said, according to the *Boston Globe,* that "everything is targeted, everything is bottom line, how to make a buck." He added that "it is crucial to capture knowledge for its own sake and for humanity."

Honors bestowed on Rodbell besides the Nobel Prize include honorary degrees from Montpellier University in France in 1992, the University of Geneva in 1996, and Virginia Commonwealth University in 1996. He received the Gairdner International Award in 1984 and an Award of Scientific Merit from the National Institutes of Health in 1984.

SELECTED WORKS: The Role of Hormone Receptors and GTP-Regulatory Proteins in Membrane Transduction, Nature 1980; The Role of GTP-Binding Proteins in Signal Transduction: From the Sublimely Simple to the Conceptually Complex, Current Topics in Cellular Regulation 1992.

ABOUT: Boston Globe October 11, 1994; NIH Press Release October 18, 1994; New York Times October 11, 1994.

ROTBLAT, JOSEPH
(November 4, 1908–   )
Nobel Prize for Peace, 1995 (shared with the Pugwash Conferences on Science and World Affairs)

The English physicist Joseph Rotblat was born in Warsaw, Poland, the fifth of seven children in a Jewish family. His father, Zygmunt Rotblat, was in the paper-transporting business. The family was quite well-off, until the years immediately following World War I, when Zygmut Rotblat's business failed. Nearly starving, the family was forced to make and sell illegal vodka from their basement in order to survive. Rotblat recalled his youth to Susan Landau, in the *Bulletin of*

JOSEPH ROTBLAT

the Atomic Scientists: "It came to the stage of literally hunger, starvation . . . we distilled *somogonka*—illicit vodka—as a way of earning a living. One had to fight for one's survival." Forced to help his family make ends meet, young Rotblat found a job as an electrician running cables in the streets. The conditions he worked in were poor, and he was exposed to extreme cold while laying cables. From the experience, he became determined to educate himself, and to study to be a physicist.

He enrolled at the University of Warsaw, working all day and studying at night. While at a student summer camp in 1930, he met and fell in love with Tola Gryn, a fellow student who was studying Polish literature. They were married a few years later. In 1932, Rotblat received his master's degree in physics. While studying for his Ph.D., he began working at the Radiation Laboratory of Warsaw under Ludwik Werterstein, a physicist who had studied under MARIE CURIE. In 1938 he received his Ph.D., and in early 1939, he received two offers to do research abroad. One was to study in Paris with FRÉDÉRIC JOLIOT, the other to study at the University of Liverpool in England with JAMES CHADWICK. Rotblat chose the latter opportunity for reasons he later explained: "In Liverpool, they were building a cyclotron. It was my intention to build a cyclotron when I came back to Warsaw so that we could start a proper school of nuclear physics."

In March 1939 he left for Liverpool. For the first six months Rotblat was in England, he conducted experiments and wrote papers on his results for publication. He was one of the many physicists around the world who were attempting to discover if a self-sustaining chain reaction was possible. "He soon found that several surplus neutrons were released by the fissioning nuclei," according to the *Bulletin of the Atomic Scientists.* Rotblat published his results but was concerned about their ramifications, knowing that a chain reaction could proceed at a very fast rate and cause an explosion. If such explosive power could be harnessed, a bomb could be made of destructive power previously unimagined. He thought about the subject a great deal, but before deciding, as he later put it, "My job was to do the research, not to think about how it was to be applied." Regardless, the moral aspects of what he was doing haunted him.

James Chadwick was quite impressed with the young physicist and offered him a fellowship. Rotblat gladly accepted and returned to Poland to make arrangements for his wife, Tola, to join him. In late August 1939 he left Poland again, his wife intending to follow him shortly. On September 1, however, at the outset of World War II, the Germans invaded Poland, whose army was defeated quickly, and Tola was trapped there. The couple reestablished contact in early 1940 and attempted to make arrangements for Tola to depart for England through Belgium, which the Nazis invaded before she was able to leave. Rotblat then tried to get his wife out through Denmark, but that country too was conquered by the Nazis. He next attempted to get a visa to Italy for Tola, but Italy had joined the war on the German side. After that, Rotblat had no contact with his wife.

Rotblat decided to put aside his reservations about the atomic bomb as soon as he began to comprehend the power of the Nazis. He discussed the possible explosive capabilities of a chain reaction with Chadwick, who in turn told him to perform the necessary experiments. Rotblat took two young people on as assistants and was soon joined by Otto Frisch, one of the first men who found that fission released enormous amounts of energy. By 1941, this group established that the atomic bomb was, according to Rotblat, "theoretically possible."

As Chadwick and Rotblat's team attempted to make a working bomb, the scientists in the United States were still searching for the basis to build an atomic pile (a self-sustaining nuclear reaction). The U.S. project had been slowed by bureaucratic entanglements, but by the summer of 1941, a British scientific delegation informed the Americans about the progress of the British bomb effort. In June 1942 Prime Minister Winston Churchill and President Franklin D. Roosevelt agreed to have the United States and Great Britain combine their bomb programs. The research, codenamed the Manhattan Project, would be conducted in the United States, out of range of attack by German bombers. Still, the U.S. requested the highest security and the assurance of the British government that the physicists would be British subjects. Since many of the people working on the atomic program were émigrés from other countries in Europe, they had to become British subjects, literally overnight.

Rotblat, concerned about his missing wife and family, did not take British citizenship, believing that he was going to return to Poland after the war. As the first group left for Los Alamos, New Mexico, in late 1943, Rotblat was left behind, but his mentor Chadwick intervened on his behalf. He successfully urged General Leslie R. Groves, head of the Manhattan Project, to waive the citizenship clause for Rotblat. In early 1944 Rotblat traveled to the United States, just a few weeks behind his comrades.

In March Groves arrived at Los Alamos, where the group of scientists had already established a good rapport and conversed freely over dinner. According to Rotblat: "It was at this time that [Groves] mentioned that the real purpose in making the bomb was to subdue the Soviets. I was terribly shocked . . . when I came to Los Alamos and realized the magnitude of the project. I could see the enormous amount of resources that were needed. In 1944 the fortunes of the war were changing. Germany would not have the resources . . . Groves's comment was a shock. I felt that what I was doing was for no purpose."

In June 1944 the Allies had landed on the beach at Normandy in France. By August 25 they had reached Paris, a group of American scientists right behind them. They confirmed what Rotblat had suspected—the Germans had not even achieved a self-sustaining chain reaction and had no atomic bomb. A few days after receiving the intelligence report about the German bomb effort, Rotblat told Chadwick that he wanted to quit the project. Chadwick was disappointed but agreed to relay Rotblat's request to the Los Alamos authorities.

The authorities gave Rotblat a hard time about leaving and suspected him of being a spy. Their charges against him, however, proved to be unwarranted. In the end, they asked Rotblat not to speak to anyone about the bomb effort, and he complied. He told his fellow scientists that he was returning to Europe to be closer to his family. He had heard nothing from anyone in his family since the summer of 1940; he would later discover that his wife had been killed, though his parents and two brothers had survived the concentration camps. One of his brothers was in Soviet-held land after the war and was not seen by Rotblat or any of their family until after Stalin's death, in 1953.

When Rotblat returned to Britain, he became acting director of Chadwick's laboratory in Liverpool and kept his silence about the atomic bombs until after they were used on Japan. After 1945 he began giving lectures around Great Britain, trying to convince his fellow physicists of the dangers of nuclear weapons. He became fascinated with the medical applications of nuclear physics and in 1949 joined the staff at the University of London's Medical College of St. Bartholomew's Hospital, where he became an expert on the hazards of radiation and warned people about the possibility of developing cancer from undue exposure to such radiation, especially from nuclear testing. At around the same time, Poland was taken over by the Communists, and Rotblat chose to become a British subject.

While he was conducting his research he appeared on a British television program, *Panorama,* where he discussed the difference between the atomic and the hydrogen bombs. Rotblat, according to the *New York Times,* stated that the only difference between the bombs was the size of the blast. The hydrogen bomb, he said, was more powerful but did not give off any more radiation. As he studied more about the fallout from the bombs, however, he discovered that he had been wrong and that the bomb actually had three devices: an atom bomb, a hydrogen bomb, and a second, larger atom bomb, which would ignite successively. Such bombs created a great deal more fallout than he had previously deduced. Both Rotblat and the public in general became extremely worried about the possible health risks involved in testing the bombs.

In 1955 the United States Atomic Energy Commission issued a statement to the public suggesting that the dose of radiation people had received from the tests was no more than they would get from chest X rays. Rotblat was stunned by this statement, realizing that if the amount of radiation exposure for each person was the same as that from one X ray, then the radioactivity was descending through the atmosphere very quickly, even before it had time to decay.

When Rotblat published a paper setting forth these points, the British government, wanting to conduct more tests, criticized him. As it turned out, the statement made by the U.S. Atomic Energy Commission was inaccurate. In fact, it takes months or even years for the radiation from the mushroom cloud to come down through the stratosphere, and by that time it has decayed to some extent.

In 1955 BERTRAND RUSSELL and ALBERT EINSTEIN suggested that a group of scientists gather to discuss the possibility of nuclear and conventional disarmament. Eleven distinguished scientists, including Rotblat, drafted and signed a statement, which they called the Russell-Einstein Manifesto. In it, they urged nations with atomic capability to move toward the goal of peaceful coexistence. The manifesto became the basis of the Pugwash Conferences—annual meetings, begun in 1957, of scientists who urged control of nuclear weapons and an end to conventional warfare. The conferences derived their name from the little town in Nova Scotia where the first meeting was held on the property of Cyrus Eaton, a Canadian industrialist sympathetic to the scientists' cause. As Rotblat would later state, because of the anti-Communist temper of the times: "Anyone in the West who came to a meeting,

who talked peace with the Russians, was condemned as a Communist dupe."

Still, the meetings accomplished a great deal of good over the years. The first meeting outlined the hazards of nuclear testing, made recommendations on arms control, and criticized scientists for not being more socially responsible in their work. In 1961 Pugwash was the testing ground for a meeting between U.S. and Soviet representatives on the long-discussed nuclear test ban treaty, which was signed in 1963. In 1967 Pugwash established the first contact between Ho Chi Minh, the Communist leader of North Vietnam, and Henry Kissinger, (later national security adviser and then secretary of state under President Richard Nixon), and the chief negotiator of the peace treaty in Vietnam. In 1972 the United States and the Soviet Union signed a treaty banning the use of antiballistic missile systems, or ABMs. In that instance, Pugwash had conducted the first probe about the dangers of such defensive weapons.

Rotblat, while teaching physics and doing his research at the University of London, held the post of secretary-general of the Pugwash Conferences from 1957 to 1973. In 1988 he became president of the Pugwash conferences, a position he still held in 1996. In 1995 he shared the Nobel Peace Prize with the other participants of the Conferences. However, Rotblat remained modest about his accomplishments, stating in *Time:* "I see this honor not for me personally, but rather for the small group of scientists who have been working for 40 years to try and save the world, often against the world's wishes." Since the end of the Cold War, Rotblat and the Pugwash Conferences have been urging the world's nations to dismantle all the nuclear weapons they still maintain and to help establish a nuclear weapon–free world.

Joseph Rotblat has received various awards from around the world for his work. Among them are the Bertrand Russell Society Award in 1983, the Albert Einstein Peace Prize in 1992, and the Order of Merit from Poland in 1995.

SELECTED WORKS: Atomic Energy, a Survey, 1954; Atoms and the Universe, 1956; Science and World Affairs, 1962; Aspects of Medical Physics, 1966; Pugwash, 1967; Scientists on the Quest for Peace, 1972; Nuclear Reactors: To Breed or Not to Breed?, 1977; Nuclear Energy and Nuclear Weapon Proliferation, 1979; Nuclear Radiation in Warfare, 1981; Scientists, the Arms Race and Disarmament, 1982; The Arms Race at a Time of Decision, 1984; Nuclear Strategy and World Security, 1985; World Peace and the Developing Countries, 1986; Strategic Defense and the Future of the Arms Race, 1987; Coexistence, Cooperation and Common Security, 1988; Verification of Arms Reduction, 1989; Global Problems and Common Security, 1989; Nuclear Proliferation: Technical and Economic Aspects, 1990; Building Global Security through Co-operation, 1990; Towards a Secure World in the 21st Century, 1991; Striving for Peace, Security and Development in the World, 1992; A Nuclear Weapons Free World: Desirable? Feasible?, 1993; A World at the Crossroads, 1994.

ABOUT: Bulletin of the Atomic Scientists January/February 1996, March/April 1996; International Who's Who, 1996-97; Maclean's October 23, 1995; New York Times May 21, 1996; Time October 23, 1995; U.S. News & World Report October 23, 1995.

ROWLAND, F. SHERWOOD
(June 29, 1927–   )
Nobel Prize for Chemistry, 1995 (shared with Paul Crutzen and Mario J. Molina)

Frank Sherwood Rowland was born in Delaware, Ohio. He attended college in his native state, receiving his B.A. from Ohio Wesleyan University in 1948. In the same year he married Joan Lundberg, with whom he would later have two children. The couple soon moved to Illinois, so that Rowland could continue his education at the University of Chicago, where he received his M.S. in 1951 and his Ph.D. in 1952. While working on his doctoral degree, he was under the tutelage of WILLARD F. LIBBY. Rowland was soon offered a position as an instructor at Princeton University, and he moved to New Jersey.

Rowland taught at Princeton for just four years before he was offered a better position at the University of Kansas in 1956. Hired as an assistant professor, he soon moved up to associate professor, then full professor, before he left in 1964. In that year, he went to the University of California at Irvine. While Rowland was teaching chemistry at Irvine, the first steps in the study of the ozone layer—the very thin layer of atmosphere around the Earth that absorbs the sun's ultraviolet radiation and prevents it from reaching the planet's surface—were being undertaken by a meteorology student at Stockholm University. In the late 1960s, Paul Crutzen, looking at the ozone layer from a meteorological standpoint, tried to explain why the amounts of ozone he found in the atmosphere did not equal the amount that other scientists—who judged by the large quantity of photochemical reactions, involving only oxygen, that were occurring on Earth—had speculated to be there. Crutzen, according to a 1995 issue of Physics Today, "suspected there was another catalytic cycle, involving the nitrogen oxides." Crutzen soon learned of a chemical formula with which he would be able to detect the amount of nitrous oxide in the atmosphere. He published his results in a 1970 paper explaining the "discrepancy between observed and calculated ozone concentrations." In a 1971 paper, Crutzen explained how nitrous oxides get into the atmosphere. His theory suggests that nitrous dioxide from microbiological processes in the oceans of the world drifts into the biosphere in an inert form. When

F. SHERWOOD ROWLAND

brought into the stratosphere, it breaks down into nitrous oxide, in which form it can persist for decades. Ralph Cicerone of the University of California at Irvine stated in Physics Today: "Before Crutzen, no one had realized that reactive chemicals could be transported to the stratosphere in an inert form."

Also, independently of Crutzen, Harold Johnston of the University of California at Berkeley called attention to the "possible catalytic destruction of ozone by nitrogen oxide —especially those that would be created by the combustion in supersonic aircraft." In 1971, according to the Royal Swedish Academy, Johnston pointed out that plans for a fleet of supersonic jets would pose a great danger to the atmosphere because such planes would release nitrogen oxides directly into the ozone layer. Owing in part to Johnston's research, that fleet of supersonic jets was never created.

In 1974 Rowland and his future corecipient of the Nobel Prize, MARIO J. MOLINA, who was a postdoctoral assistant in Rowland's research lab in Irvine at the time, released their finding on chlorofluorocarbons (CFCs). During this period these chemicals were used as coolants in refrigerators and aerosol propellants, and when released into the atmosphere, they contributed to depletion of the ozone layer. Dr. Molina spoke about that phase of his work with an interviewer for the New York Times: "We both decided that we wanted to do more applied chemistry and learn about the atmosphere, and one way to do that was to try to solve a problem that forces you to learn the field."

Just a year before Rowland and Molina began their research, James Lovelock, a scientist who was living in Cornwall, England, had developed an instrument to measure the levels of CFCs. He found that "roughly all the CFCs produced up to that point were still around and had spread globally throughout the lower atmosphere." Molina and Rowland then calculated that CFCs would eventually be brought up into the stratosphere before any ultraviolet rays could break up the molecules. They estimated the mean atmospheric lifetime of CFCs to be 40–80 years for some compounds and 70–150 years for others. The pair also predicted that if the production of CFCs were to be continue at the same levels as in 1974, the ozone layer would be depleted by 7–13 percent. This prediction caused a big stir, because the potential increase in such production was large—and so were the potential economic costs of a ban on the products. The CFCs industry in 1974 had sales upwards of $2 billion, and perhaps not surprisingly, their scientists found Rowland's and Molina's work to be both hypothetical and ridiculous.

Regardless of the worries of industry, the United States government in 1976 felt it had enough evidence to ban the use of CFCs in aerosol sprays by 1978. As more data came in, the government's ban came to seem justified: balloons rigged with instruments found CFCs in the stratosphere and saw that they took a great deal of time to break down. However, CFCs were used in commercial goods other than aerosol sprays, and according to *Physics Today*, "The total commercial production remained constant worldwide from 1974 to 1990, at about 1 million tons annually."

In 1985, the urgency of protecting the ozone layer became apparent. An Englishman named Joseph Farman, along with his associates in the British Antarctic Survey had been tracking ozone levels at the South Pole for some years and had noticed that the levels of ozone in the atmosphere in 1984 had dropped to nearly half of what they had been at the beginning of the 1970s. They had also discovered and mapped a man-made hole in the ozone layer over Antarctica. This finding resulted almost immediately in a meeting for an international agreement on CFCs, the Montreal Protocol of 1987. In 1992 amendments to this meeting, industrialized countries all over the world agreed to phase out the production of CFCs from all aspects of industry by 1996. The *New York Times* reported that it was "Crutzen and his colleagues [Dr. Molina and Dr. Rowland] who identified the mechanisms as chemical reactions on the surface of cloud particles." The Montreal Protocol itself "was widely held up as a stellar example of international cooperation, including that of industry, on a global environmental problem." In October 1995 F. Sherwood Rowland, along with his colleagues, Paul Crutzen and Mario Molina, were awarded the Nobel Prize in Chemistry for their "pioneering contributions . . . explaining how ozone is formed and decomposes through chemical processes in the atmosphere." Most scientists believed that this was a vindication of their work and suggested the need for federal governments to help fund research in such

environmental areas. Still, the work of environmental researchers like Rowland continued to have its critics outside academic circles. In *Audubon*, Michael D. Lemonick reported that the then-House majority whip, Tom DeLay, "along with some fellow Republicans, has been trying to shove a bill through Congress that would force the United States to withdraw from the Montreal Protocol," arguing that "the phaseout is going to be costly to industry . . . and that the underlying science is 'debatable.'"

In November 1995 Rowland met with Congressional leaders to attempt to get more money for research on the ozone layer. Representative Dan Rohrabacher, a Republican from California, blasted the research of scientists such as Rowland and Molina as being nothing more than "liberal claptrap." After the meeting, Rowland downplayed Rohrabacher's rhetoric, telling *Science* that he wanted to avoid "an ideological shouting match which could have hardened up positions." In the end, Rowland was "surprised and grateful" for Congressional interest in the basic research, but he was very worried about the long-term budget prospects. Since that meeting, Rowland has continued his atmospheric research, looking at mid-latitude ozone concentrations by season to check for downward trends that would not register on annual reports.

F. Sherwood Rowland has chaired or been a member of numerous environmental groups and committees, including the ozone committee for the International Association of Meteorology and Atmospheric Physics (1980-1988). He was also a delegate for the International Council of Scientific Unions from 1993 to 1996. He has contributed numerous articles on his research to scientific journals and has been an outspoken advocate for the ban of CFCs globally. He has also received many awards and honors, including the John Wiley Jones Award from the Rochester Institute of Technology in 1975, the Tyler World Prize in Environmental Achievement in 1983, the Dickson Prize from Carnegie-Mellon University in 1991, and the Albert Einstein Prize of the World Cultural Council in 1994.

ABOUT: Audubon January/February 1996; New York Times October 12, 1995; Physics Today December 1995; Royal Swedish Academy of Sciences 1995 Nobel Prize Announcement; Science November 1995; Who's Who in America, 1996.

SELTEN, REINHARD
(October 5, 1930–   )
Nobel Memorial Prize in Economic Sciences, 1994 (shared with John F. Nash and John C. Harsanyi)

The German economist Reinhard Selten was born in Breslau to Adolf Selten, a bookseller, and Kathe Luther. In 1949, as a student, Selten read an article enti-

REINHARD SELTEN

tled "A Theory of Strategy," written by John McDonald for *Fortune*, and his fascination with game theory was born. "I remember how impressed I was by the existence of the theory, even without much knowledge of what it was," he has said. "It gave me interest in the subject and got me to the library to get the von Neumann-Morgenstern book [the original work on game theory]." His attraction to the topic was also due to game theory's impact on disciplines besides economics. "I was always interested in politics and psychology, learning beyond just the natural sciences," he once explained, "and this enabled me to expand economic thinking to include these areas."

Selten studied mathematics at the University of Frankfurt. During the late 1960s he spent two years as a visiting professor at the business school of the University of California at Berkeley. He was a professor at the Free University of Berlin in 1969, and he has also taught at the University of Bielefeld.

Before the work of game theorists such as Selten, economic theory held to the tenet that "perfect competition" existed among competitors in the marketplace—perfect in that the vast numbers of traders made it unnecessary for one buyer or seller to be concerned with the actions of others. Then, in 1944, two economists at Princeton University, John von Neumann and Oskar Morgenstern, published the book that so inspired Reinhard Selten five years later, *The Theory of Games and Economic Behavior*. The work examined the effectiveness of strategic moves by competitors who take into account the moves of others in the marketplace.

In 1955 JOHN F. NASH took this notion further by demonstrating in his doctoral thesis what came to be known as the "Nash equilibrium"—the point at which a player is no longer able to better his position by modifying his strategy, since another player would challenge it with a countervailing action. This situation, he theorized, occurs when the players involved are aware of the motives and resources of their competitors and are acting in ways that benefit only themselves. "At any time," Steven Pearlstein wrote in the *Washington Post*, "the economy is full of Nash equilibrium points—the $2.95 that both *Time* and *Newsweek* decide to use as the cover price for their weekly magazines or the 25 percent discount that fashion retailers know they can offer at sale time without cannibalizing their full-price business."

In the early 1960s JOHN C. HARSANYI expanded Nash's ideas by suggesting that players do not necessarily need to know the strategies of their competitors as long as they can foresee the likely results of the others' moves and countermoves. According to Harsanyi, it is sufficient to be able to predict the outcome of a situation based on probability. Then, in 1965, Reinhard Selten developed the Nash model still further, by theorizing upon how players determine whether the results of games are reasonable or unreasonable. By introducing the idea of "subgame perfection," Selten narrowed the notion of an equilibrium point to rule out unreasonable situations that might still qualify as Nash equilibria. For example, a monopoly that is held because one player threatens another with a price war is considered a Nash equilibrium. The threat might be a mirage, however, if the threatening player does not have the funds to wage such a price war. With his concept of "subgame perfection," Selten claimed that players will act rationally, even if the situations in which players find themselves have not evolved from rational actions. Peter Passell provided a further example of Selten's theory in the *New York Times*: "An outcome dependent on someone's taking an unreasonable threat seriously (as in 'buy my rug for $200, or I will kill your first-born child') may be discarded." Though the mathematics involved may be a bit daunting, Passell asserts, "the underlying ideas are intuitive." Selten was hailed for this expansion of the Nash equilibrium.

Game theory has a variety of practical applications. In the 1950s Pentagon officials used it in developing tactics for both avoiding and engaging in nuclear war. Game theorists acted as consultants for all major bidders during the auction of bands by the Federal Communications Commission for wireless communication. Game theory has also been used to influence interest rates set by the Federal Reserve, institute environmental regulations, reform insurance markets, and create ways for companies to provide their employees with incentive pay. As trends have turned economists toward scrutinizing market imperfections, game theory's popularity has been on the rise. Paul Krugman of Stanford University, who has used game theory to analyze world trade, says that it "opens up terrain for systematic thinking that was previously closed." Robert Frank, a Cornell University economist, summed up the influence that Nash, Harsanyi and Selten have had on their field. "In a sense," he said, "they made economics interactive."

Reinhard Selten's idea of subgame perfection has been used by evolutionary biologists to examine such questions as why animals abandon their mates and which decisions are crucial in raising children. Peter Hammerstein at the Max Planck Institute for Animal Behavior Research has said, "I spent a lot of time explaining to a group of biologists why Selten's idea of subgame perfection is important to them."

Selten and Hammerstein collaborated in applying game theory to the field of evolutionary biology. They looked at the fighting tendencies of animals, deeming the frays "asymmetric conflicts"—conflicts in which participants are up against different odds and are pursuing different goals.

In announcing Selten's receipt of the Nobel Prize, the Swedish Academy cited popular common games to demonstrate how game theory plays itself out in the world of economics. "Game theory emanates from the studies of games such as chess or poker," the Academy stated. "Everyone knows that in these games, players have to think ahead and devise a strategy based on expected countermoves from the other player. Such strategic interaction also characterizes many economic situations." In Selten's own words, game theory is "like playing chess. . . . (Y)ou have to think hard about what you think your opponent will do, and then you plan your whole strategy based on that. You may not always be right, but such thinking probably makes you play better and keeps you from making as many dumb moves."

Upon receiving the Nobel Prize, Selten, the first German to win the award in economics since it was first granted in 1969, was acclaimed a national hero. He nonetheless stated, "While I may be well known today—next week, they probably won't remember my name."

Selten, married to Elisabeth Langreiner since 1959, lives outside Bonn. Each Saturday he walks into the hills of the countryside for three to five hours. Hiking is the only sport in which Selten participates, if, in his words, "one can say that is a sport." His jaunts into the woods, he claims, are "very productive scientifically; I often get some very good ideas for my research while hiking." In addition to his native German, Selten speaks English, French, and Esperanto, an artificial language created during the 19th century with the hope that it would become a universal language. He says he is a member of the Esperanto movement and describes himself as an idealist.

Reinhard Selten has been a professor at the University of Bonn since 1984. He has been named a member of the Rheinisch-Westfalen Academy of Science, a fellow by the Econometric Society, and a foreign honorary member of the American Academy of Arts and Sciences. Among his numerous publications are *Models of Strategic Rationality* and, with John Harsanyi, *A General Theory of Equilibrium Selection in Games*, both published in 1988.

ABOUT: Fortune November 14, 1994; International Who's Who 1996-97, 1996; New York Times October 12, 1994; Science October 21, 1994; Wall Street Journal October 12, 1994; Washington Post October 12, 1994.

SHARP, PHILLIP A.

(June 6, 1944–   )
Nobel Prize for Physiology or Medicine, 1993
(shared with Richard J. Roberts)

Sections of the following biographical sketch appeared originally in Phillip A. Sharp's autobiography in *Les Prix Nobel*. Unless otherwise noted, all quoted material was taken directly from that source.

The American biologist Phillip Allen Sharp was born in Falmouth, Kentucky, the son of Joseph Walter and Kathrin (Colvin) Sharp (some sources say Katherin). Throughout his childhood, Sharp was surrounded by a strong "sense of place." The Sharp farm, located in a bend of the Licking River near McKinneysburg, was where his mother had been raised. Her family had been part of the community for many generations. As both of Sharp's parents came from extremely large families, he grew up surrounded by an extensive network of grandparents, uncles, aunts, and cousins in the local area.

Sharp was educated in the local public schools in and around Falmouth. In describing his early education, Sharp has stressed that, though he quickly became interested in certain academic subjects, he was never a child who let his studies eclipse the normal childhood pursuits of recreation and relaxation. "Even though my studies never interfered with sports or fun, I managed to gain an appreciation of math and science," he wrote. Throughout his childhood, Sharp's parents, neither of whom had a college degree, strongly encouraged their son to pursue higher education. To that end, they emphasized the importance of saving money for college and, perhaps more importantly, gave Sharp a small tobacco field to help him raise money. The proceeds from the crop, which eventually amounted to enough to pay for one and a half years of tuition, were put to use at Union College, a small liberal arts school in the foothills of eastern Kentucky. While there, Sharp met his future wife, Ann Holcombe, with whom he eventually had three daughters. In 1966 he graduated from Union College with bachelor's degrees in both chemistry and mathematics.

Sharp particularly enjoyed the subject of chemistry. Upon graduating from Union College, he was offered

PHILLIP A. SHARP

a fellowship by the University of Illinois to study physical chemistry under Victor Bloomfield. Bloomfield quickly became a mentor to Sharp, helping the budding young scientist expand both his scientific and cultural horizons. "He provided funds for my participation in national scientific meetings and broadened my perspective on society and culture by being a long-haired liberal, well-read and artistic friend," Sharp said. While at the University of Illinois, Sharp saw many of his compatriots drafted into the war in Vietnam, but he received a draft deferment that allowed him to finish graduate school. After completing a doctoral thesis that dealt with the "description of DNA as a polymer using statistical theories," he received his Ph.D. in 1969.

Sharp, who by this time had lost interest in the "complex 'hands on' manipulations" of such experimental science, soon sent a letter to Norman Davidson at the California Institute of Technology that resulted in an offer of a postdoctoral position in molecular biology. Surrounded by some of the top biologists in the world, Sharp began his "transition to experimental molecular biology by using the heteroduplex method and electron microscopy to study the structure of plasmids of the sex factors and drug-resistant factors of bacteria." Sharp eventually opted to extend his postdoctoral period at Caltech to study the structure and pathway of expression of genes in human cells. This work led to another year of postdoctoral work at Cold Spring Harbor Laboratory, in New York.

At Cold Spring Harbor, Sharp "used hybridization techniques to map sequences in the simian virus 40 genome that were expressed as stable RNAs in both infected cells and oncogenic cells transformed by the

virus." These experiments helped to move the laboratory's work toward the field of molecular and cell biology of tumors. This, in turn, led to a study of adenoviruses, which commonly cause respiratory infections in humans but can cause tumors in rodents. Sharp, working with fellow postdoctoral associate Ulf Peterson, generated the first restriction endonuclease maps of adenoviruses. Sharp then began a collaboration with Jane Flint in which they analyzed "the regions of the genome expressed as mRNAs in both productively infected cells and in adenovirus transformed cells." This work culminated in the discoveries "(a) that only one specific fragment of the genome, the E1 region, was responsible for oncogenic transformation; (b) that restriction endonuclease length polymorphism could be utilized to generate genetic maps; (c) the mapping of specific genes on the viral genome; and (d) generation of a viral map of sequences expressed as stable RNAs."

In 1974 Sharp accepted a position at the Massachusetts Institute of Technology's Center for Cancer Research and subsequently resumed his work on adenoviruses. Three years later his work led him to a discovery that would rock the medical community and eventually earn him the Nobel Prize. For decades it had been assumed that human genes, which are responsible for dominant and recessive patterns of inheritance, were arranged in linear order in chromosomes. Sharp, however, discovered that genes in humans, unlike the genes of simpler organisms, could be arranged in a discontinuous pattern on several DNA segments. Such genes are called "split genes."

The discovery of split genes has already led to knowledge of the genetic process of splicing. Further, split genes have allowed scientists to gain a better understanding of the development of certain cancers and hereditary diseases. The discovery of split genes "does not give us cures, but the possibility to know how we are going to do therapy with genes in the future," Gosta Gahrton, a professor of medicine at the Karolinska Institute, was quoted as saying by the New York Times.

Sharp became a professor of biology at MIT in 1979. In 1985 he became the director of MIT's Center for Cancer Research, a position he would hold until 1991. He was offered the presidency of the university in 1990; he accepted, then later declined, citing his commitment to science. "I don't consider it the brightest moment in my life," he later told the New York Times when recounting the incident, "meaning I should have been more decisive and known myself earlier in the process to say I was not ready for that position." He became the head of the MIT's biology department in 1991.

In 1996 Phillip Allen Sharp was awarded the Nobel Prize. He shared the award and the $842,000 prize with Englishman Richard J. Roberts for their separate discoveries of split genes. Upon hearing that he would receive the honor, Sharp was overwhelmed. "I was shaking," he said in an interview with the *New York Times*. "I said, 'Could you please repeat that?'" To celebrate the award, Sharp and his secretary, Margarita Siafaca, opened a bottle of champagne that they had kept refrigerated for more than 15 years awaiting the day Sharp would win the Nobel Prize.

In addition to the Nobel Prize, Sharp has received numerous awards from organizations, including the American Cancer Society, the New York Academy of Science, the Gairdner Foundation, and the University of Pittsburgh. He has been a member of the editorial board of the journal *Cell* and a member of multiple professional organizations including the National Academy of Sciences, the European Molecular Biology Association, and the American Academy of Arts and Sciences. Additionally, in 1978, Sharp cofounded and became a member of the board of directors of Biogen, a biotechnology company.

ABOUT: Les Prix Nobel, 1993; New York Times October 12, 1993; Who's Who in America, 1997.

CLIFFORD G. SHULL

SHULL, CLIFFORD G.
(September 23, 1915–   )
Nobel Prize for Physics, 1994 (shared with Bertram N. Brockhouse)

The American physicist Clifford G. Shull was born in Pittsburgh, Pennsylvania to David H. and Daisy I. (Bistline) Shull. He was educated at Pittsburgh's Carnegie Institute of Technology (now Carnegie Mellon University), where he received his bachelor's degree in 1937. He then went on to New York University, in New York City, where he received his Ph.D. in physics in 1941.

In that same year, Shull took a position as a research physicist with the Texas Company in Beacon, New York. He remained with the Texas Company until 1946, when he was offered a position as a research physicist at Oak Ridge National Laboratory in Tennessee. Shull was particularly attracted to the Oak Ridge facility, as it housed a nuclear reactor that had been used during the Manhattan Project to develop the atomic bomb. Also, he greatly admired many of the projects being undertaken at Oak Ridge. "Scientists at Oak Ridge were real eager to find real, honest-to-goodness uses for the technology they had developed," Shull said. Upon accepting the position at Oak Ridge, Shull ventured south to join Ernest O. Wollan in an attempt to study neutron scattering.

By 1946, physicists had established that neutrons, like X rays, produce waves that scatter when they interact with crystals, such as those composed of sodium chloride. Further, it was known that when diffracted by crystals, neutron waves of specific lengths produce specific patterns of scattered waves. The fact that neutrons are not electrically charged—and hence do not interact with electrons— had led many scientists to believe that neutrons should be able to probe deep within a solid object, as does an X ray. Whether or not this was true, however, remained to be discovered.

The early stages of Shull and Wollan's work involved studying factors that affected the neutron scattering patterns in a variety of nuclei in multiple environments. For this study, they cataloged more than 60 different nuclei and established that a given nucleus has the same neutron scattering pattern regardless of its environment. For example, a sodium nucleus has the same pattern whether it is in sodium hydride, sodium bromide, or sodium chloride. Through this work, they also discovered that hydrogen atoms, which are virtually invisible to X rays, have an identifiable neutron scattering pattern. Used in conjunction with X rays, this discovery led to improved understanding of the structure of biological and organic molecules.

Nuclear fission reactors, like the one at Oak Ridge used to produce the neutrons for the experiments of Shull and Wollan, generate a flow of neutrons of varying speeds. Shull and Wollan, however, knew that the waves that formed the neutron scattering patterns traveled in different directions depending on the speed of the incoming neutron. In order to produce an entirely accurate pattern on a regular basis, all neutrons penetrating an object would have to travel at the same speed. The pair soon set out to create a "monochromatic" beam of neutrons, all of which would have equal velocities.

To create this beam, Shull and Wollan put their own spin on an experiment used around the world to introduce youngsters to one of the basic properties of physics— shining light through a prism to show how the light is separated into different wavelengths, and, hence, different colors. In Shull and Wollan's more sophisticated effort, the pair passed beams of neutrons traveling at various speeds through several crystals made of different materials, such as sodium chloride. Upon passing through the crystals, neutrons of different speeds would be deflected in different directions. Shull and Wollan were then able to use the remaining beam of neutrons with equal velocities to probe solid objects and produce neutron diffraction patterns that revealed the atomic structure of the object.

This technique of neutron scattering quickly became invaluable to the scientific community. The technique has had "an influence on virtually every area of condensed matter physics," according to Thomas Greytak, a professor of physics at the Massachusetts Institute of Technology. "It's a technique that's used universally." Even today, scientists, particularly those involved in materials science, utilize the research conducted by Shull and Wollan in the 1950s. Plastic polymers, semiconductors, new magnetic materials, and high-temperature superconductors can all be traced to the work done by Shull and Wollan. "They had so much insight that the experiments they did in the first five years basically laid the groundwork for all the work since," Greytak told the *Boston Globe*. In many ways, neutron scattering is more useful than X rays. "Neutron beams are very penetrating," Robert Brigeneau, dean of science at MIT, said in an interview with the *Boston Globe*. "Unlike X-rays, which only probe the first 1/1000 of an inch, neutron beams can probe an inch deep."

After the discovery of the neutron scattering technique, Shull and Wollan continued their work at Oak Ridge. The ensuing years saw them delving into the possibilities of using their technique to probe magnetic atoms in sample objects. Their work yielded the first evidence of antiferromagnetism—a quality, displayed by some magnetic substances with two, oppositely directed electron spins, that causes the substance's magnetism to increase and then decrease when the substance is heated. In 1955, despite the fact that he had risen to the position of chief physicist, Shull left the Oak Ridge facility to become a professor of physics at the Massachusetts Institute of Technology. While teaching at MIT, Shull chaired numerous physics committees, including the Visiting Committee of the Solid State Division of Brookhaven National Laboratory (1961-62), the Visiting Committee of the Solid State Division of Oak Ridge National Laboratory (1974-75), and the Policy Committee of the National Small-Angle-Scattering Center (1978-81). In 1986, Shull retired and was granted professor emeritus status.

In 1994, more than 40 years after perfecting the technique of neutron scattering, Shull was awarded the Nobel Prize for Physics, becoming the 26th person affiliated with MIT to be so honored. Upon hearing that he had won the prize, he stated that he was "surprised" and "very excited to be honored in this fashion." Shull, however, expressed lament that his partner in the neutron scattering experiments, Ernest O. Wollan, who had died in 1984, was not able to share the prize. Instead, Shull shared the award, along with the $930,000 prize, with Bertram N. Brockhouse, honored for his work on neutron spectroscopy. As the academy stated, Shull "has helped to answer the question of where atoms are,'" and Brockhouse "the question of what atoms do.'" Colleagues applauded the selection of Shull. "I'm really happy they finally discovered his work," said JEROME I. FRIEDMAN of MIT. "With something as fundamental as this, it's easy to forget who discovered it."

Since 1941, Shull has been married to Martha-Nuel (Summer) Shull. They have three sons. Barring the excitement and hoopla surrounding his receipt of the Nobel Prize, Shull's post-MIT lifestyle has been decidedly laid-back. He described himself in an interview with the *Boston Globe* as "pretty much a home person."

In addition to the Nobel Prize, Shull has been the recipient of many awards, including the Alumni Association of Carnegie Mellon University's Distinguished Scientist Award (1968), Humboldt Senior U.S. Scientist Award (1979), the Governor of Tennessee's Distinguished Scientist Award (1986), the Gregori Aminoff Prize (1993), and the Ilja Frank Prize (1993). He has been awarded fellowships by a variety of organizations, among them the American Physical Society, the American Academy of Arts and Sciences, and the National Academy of Sciences. Additionally, Shull has been a member of the American Crystallographic Association and the Research Society of America.

ABOUT: Boston Globe October 13, 1994; New York Times October 13, 1994; Physics Today December 1994; Science October 21, 1994; Science News October 22, 1994; The Tech February 7, 1995; Who's Who in America, 1997.

SMALLEY, RICHARD E.

(June 6, 1943–   )

Nobel Prize for Chemistry, 1996 (shared with Robert F. Curl Jr. and Harold W. Kroto)

The American chemist Richard Errett Smalley was born in Akron, Ohio to Frank Dudley Smalley and Virginia (Rhoads) Smalley. For his first two years of undergraduate work, Smalley attended Hope College, in Holland, Michigan. He then went on to study at the University of Michigan in Ann Arbor, where he received his bachelor's degree in chemistry in 1965. For graduate studies, Smalley attended Princeton University. He received his master's degree in 1971 and his Ph.D. in 1973.

RICHARD E. SMALLEY

Upon graduation, Smalley worked as a postdoctoral research associate at the University of Chicago's James Frank Institute. In 1976 he became an assistant professor in the Department of Chemistry at Houston's Rice University, the institution where he would work for more than a quarter-century. Throughout the next several years, Smalley climbed the ranks of Rice's faculty. He was promoted to associate professor in 1980 and professor in 1981. In 1982, he was named Rice University's Gene and Norman Hackerman Professor of Chemistry.

Much of his work at Rice centered on the study of clusters. Aggregates of molecules or atoms, clusters exist in sizes somewhere between those of macroscopic and microscopic particles. Usually highly unstable, clusters normally exist for a very short time and only under specific circumstances. Using a special machine that he both designed and built, one which the 1996 Nobel Prize announcement describes as a "laser supersonic cluster beam apparatus," Smalley was able to make and study clusters. In this machine, an extremely powerful laser was blasted against a piece of metal or semiconductor. The atoms released then mixed with a stream of helium to form clusters. The resulting plume of gas then entered a vacuum chamber, where it was quickly chilled to a temperature only a few degrees above absolute zero (O degrees kelvin or -273.15 degrees centigrade). The clusters could then be analyzed with a mass spectrometer, an instrument that uses magnetic and electric fields to sort various particles according to their mass.

Throughout the early 1980s Smalley's cluster research included extensive work on semiconductors such as gallium arsenide, germanium, and silicon. A thorough understanding of the behavior of clusters of such materials, each of which can carry and store data, is vital to the development of further miniaturization of electronic circuitry. In 1984, however, Smalley received a request from HAROLD W. KROTO, a British chemist from the University of Sussex, that would soon lead to a partnership that would permanently alter the direction of Smalley's research. Through his acquaintance with ROBERT F. CURL JR., who often worked with Smalley, Kroto—the discoverer of cyanopolyynes, a kind of long-chained carbon and nitrogen molecule that exists in space—expressed his interest in using Smalley's machine to see if he could make these molecules on Earth. Smalley, however, wasn't particularly interested in Kroto's project. "We told him, 'That's fine, all this astrophysical stuff sounds very interesting,' but it, frankly, wasn't what we wanted to do in this laboratory," Smalley said on a 1995 installment of the PBS series *Nova*. "After all, we already knew everything there was to know about carbon, at least we assumed so. So we told Harry, 'Yes, fine, some other time, maybe this year, maybe next.'"

Another reason for Smalley's lack of interest in Kroto's project was that a similar experiment had already been conducted. Exxon, the oil company, had previously put graphite, a form of carbon, into a machine much like the one designed by Smalley. The Exxon experiment yielded an unusual mass spectrum that indicated the presence of unusual carbon chains and, even more puzzling, an abundance of carbon clusters of 60, and in some cases 70, atoms. Though Exxon published their findings, the issues were not pursued.

In mid-1985, about a year and a half after Kroto's initial request to conduct experiments with Smalley's machine, Curl phoned Kroto with the news that Smalley was now ready to begin the project. The experiments commenced on September 1, 1985, with a team that included not only Kroto, Smalley, and Curl, but also three Rice graduate students, James Heath, Yuan Liu, and Sean O'Brien. Though the team was quickly able to create the molecules Kroto had observed in space, within days another discovery led the research in quite a different direction.

Just as in the Exxon experiment, the mass spectrometer at Rice recorded numerous clusters of 60-carbon atoms. This time however, there was such an abundance that the clusters simply could not be ignored. Further research indicated that these clusters of 60 atoms were highly stable, something extremely unusual for clusters. The team had inadvertently stumbled upon what would come to be called C60, a third molecular form of carbon (added to the known forms of diamond and graphite). After using dozens of paper models to try to determine the clusters' shapes, the researchers finally reached the conclusion that the only way 60-carbon atoms could gather the stability to exist as a molecule and tie up any dangling bonds would be if the cluster formed a geodesic dome composed of 12 hexagonal surfaces and 12 pentagonal surfaces. This shape shares exactly the same structure as the geodesic dome designed by the American engineer and designer R. Buckminster Fuller for the 1967 Montreal World Exposition. The new carbon molecule, which also shares the same pattern as a soccer ball, was thus named the buckminsterfullerene or, more informally, "buckyball." Similarly, the scientists worked out a shape for C70, the molecules containing clusters of 70 carbon atoms. The team quickly drafted a paper detailing their findings, and on November 14, 1985, just 14 days after the start of their experiments, the article "C60: Buckminsterfullerene" was published in *Nature*.

The discovery of C60 was not without its problems. The team's equipment was not powerful enough to produce the magnitude of molecules needed to verify C60's existence and structure via chemical reactions or spectroscopy, and thus the existence of buckminsterfullerenes remained only a hypothesis. This led to the team's finding being challenged by a variety of organizations, most notably the Exxon corporation.

In the years immediately following the discovery of C60, Smalley, Kroto, and Curl continued their experimentation with buckminsterfullerenes. They succeeded in obtaining further evidence that indicated that the proposed structure of C60 was correct. They were even able to identify carbon clusters that enclosed metal atoms—but the ability to produce isolable amounts of C60 continued to elude them.

In 1990, however, Donald R. Huffman of the University of Arizona and Wolfgang Krätschmer of the Max Planck Institute for Nuclear Physics in Heidelberg, Germany, succeeded in making C60 in visible quantities for the first time. The scientists did this by running an electric current between two graphite rods placed in a vacuum chamber. Where the two rods touched, the electric current created a carbon vapor that collected on the inside surfaces of the vacuum chamber. When analyzed, this vapor proved to have measurable quantities of C60.

The easily reconstructible conditions of Huffman and Krätschmer's experiments led to a sudden boom in the production of C60 by scientists around the world. This in turn led to the invention of a burgeoning new branch of scientific study—fullerene chemistry. "The carbon-60 buckyball," Smalley told the *New York Times*, "was a kind of Rosetta Stone that opened a universe of possibilities, based on how nature likes to bond carbon atoms together."

Searches conducted by fullerene chemists have uncovered buckyballs in a variety of locations outside the laboratory, including interstellar clouds and ordinary candle flames. Buckminsterfullerenes have even been found in the layer of debris left by the meteor believed to have collided with the Earth more than 65 million years ago—the event that resulted in a worldwide climate change that some scientists believe eventually led to the extinction of dinosaurs. Inside the hollow center of each of those buckyballs is "a little bit of the last breath of dinosaurs," Smalley jokingly told the *Los Angeles Times*.

The future of fullerene chemistry has the potential to affect such diverse areas as synthetic chemistry, nanofibers and nanoparticles, astrophysics, and cluster beam studies. It is hoped that the study of fullerene chemistry will one day lead to a variety of technological advances, including new drug-delivery systems, incredibly strong yet light materials, improved solar cells, and new semiconductors for computers.

In 1996 Smalley—who, since 1990, had been working as a physics professor at Rice University—was awarded the Nobel Prize. He shared his award, along with the $1.12 million monetary prize, with the codiscoverers of buckyballs, Robert F. Curl and Harold W. Kroto. Numerous scientists applauded the academy's decision. "It's well deserved," said Stanford chemist Richard Zare in an interview with the *Los Angeles Times*. "It inspired chemists to study a whole new class of compounds."

Smalley, who has worked as the director of Rice University's Center for Nanoscale Science and Technology since mid-1997, lives in Houston with Mary Lynn (Chapieski) Smalley, his wife since 1980. He has one son, Chad R. Smalley, from a previous marriage.

In addition to the Nobel Prize, Smalley has been the recipient of numerous awards from a variety of organizations, including the American Physical Society (1991), the United States Department of Energy (1992), the American Chemical Society (1992), and the European Physical Society (1994). He has been awarded honorary doctorate degrees from the University of Liege (1991) in Liege, Belgium, and the University of Chicago (1995). Also, throughout his career, Smalley has been active in many professional organizations, among them the American Chemical Society, the American Physical Society, the National Academy of Sciences, and the Materials Research Society.

SELECTED WORKS: Probing C60 (with Robert F. Curl), Science November 18, 1988; Great Balls of Carbon: The Story of Buckminsterfullerene, The Sciences March/April 1991; Self Assembly of the Fullerenes, Accounts of Chemical Research 1992; Self-Assembly of Tubular Fullerenes (with T. Guo, P. Nikolaev, A. Rinzler, D. Tomanek, and D. Colbert), Journal of Physical Chemistry July 6, 1995.

ABOUT: Los Angeles Times October 10, 1996; New York Times October 10, 1996; Nova (PBS) December 19, 1995; Royal Swedish Academy of Sciences 1996 Nobel Prize Announcement; Technology Review January 1994; Who's Who in America, 1996.

SMITH, MICHAEL
(April 26, 1932–)
Nobel Prize for Chemistry, 1993 (shared with Kary B. Mullis)

The Canadian scientist Michael Smith was born in 1932 in Blackpool, England. Both of Smith's parents had to start working in their early teens; his father, Rowland Smith, worked in his family's market garden and his mother, Mary Agnes Armstead Smith, in a boarding house and as a bookkeeper. The couple struggled to get by and had little put aside for the education of their two sons. During this period in England, 11-year-old schoolchildren took an examination called the "Eleven-Plus," which would determine whether they would continue their schooling and go on to a university or learn a trade and finish school at age 16. Young Michael Smith did well on his exam and was offered a scholarship to a private school in Blackpool, but, according to Barry Shell's *Great Canadian Scientists*, "he didn't want to go because the students there were considered snobs, and he thought his friends would make fun of him." Regardless of the young boy's protests, his parents made him go.

Smith attended the Arnold School, where he worked hard but was unhappy because he had lost most of his old friends. Unlike them, he had homework to do every night. "He had few friends at the new school. His big front teeth stuck out so he was teased by his schoolmates." When he had his teeth corrected, a friendly dentist introduced him to the Boy Scouts, and he learned about camping and nature. Spending time in the outdoors would prove to be a life-long hobby for Smith.

In 1939, at the start of World War II, England went to war with Germany. In Blackpool, far in the north of England, the Smith family felt safe from the bombings that devastated other parts of the country—until Smith and his brother, Robin, were nearly hit by two German bombs that landed on either side of their house.

After the war, Smith attended Manchester University and worked in the honors chemistry program. He received his bachelor of science degree in 1953, and then, on scholarship again, got his Ph.D. in chemistry by 1956. He wanted to do his postdoctoral work in the United States, preferably on the West Coast, but all the universities he applied to rejected him. Then he heard of a young scientist in Canada, HAR GOBIND KHORANA, who had an opening for a postdoctoral student working on biologically vital molecules such as DNA. He went to Vancouver, and Khorana became his mentor in the work that would eventually earn him the Nobel Prize. Smith even moved with Khorana's research group to Wisconsin in 1960, but returned to Vancouver a year later. For the next several years he wrote scientific papers about crabs, mollusks, and salmon for

MICHAEL SMITH

the Fisheries Research Board of Canada Laboratory, in Vancouver. However, through outside grants, he still managed to continue doing research on the work he had started with Khorana on DNA (the molecular basis for heredity), trying to solve the mysteries of the genetic code.

In 1966 Smith was appointed an associate professor of biochemistry at the University of British Columbia (UBC). Four years later he became a full professor, a position he still held in 1993, when he received the Nobel Prize. While teaching at UBC, he also occupied various research positions at other universities, both in Canada and the United States, in which work on DNA was being conducted. From 1971 to 1972, he worked in England as a visiting researcher in the experimental laboratories at the University of Cambridge. While on a coffee break at Cambridge, he was struck with an idea that involved controlling and harnessing DNA coding errors. Scientists had long sought to use such coding errors, or natural mutations, to their advantage. *Science* suggested that before Smith's work, "researchers had no way to deliberately vary the DNA that encodes a protein's amino acids sequence. The best they could do was expose cells to chemical mutagen or radiation to induce random mutations in a gene, then forage among a crowd of mutated proteins for one that might shed light on the question at hand." Smith's work, however, created specific mutations in the DNA, allowing for customized proteins. According to *Science News*, Smith "saw a way to incorporate tailor-made DNA fragments into a host organism, where they would replicate." The method he developed is "site-directed mutagenesis," a process by which DNA molecule strands are manipulated and reprogrammed for changed proteins, whose actions differ from those of the original proteins and can be controlled.

However startling this ability might seem to the lay community—to be able to mutate at will the molecules that make up genetic coding—the scientific world wasn't, at first, impressed. In an interview for the Canadian magazine *Maclean's*, Smith recalled when he first submitted the paper detailing his work to the scientific journal *Cell*: "The editors sent it back— they said that technologically it was not of general interest." By 1996, thousands of researchers were using Smith's innovations in genetic engineering daily—for purposes that ranged from correcting hereditary diseases to developing strains of plant life that are more resistant to disease to creating therapies for cancer and other diseases. Smith himself is quite modest about his own accomplishment. As he told *Maclean's*: "We were just in a position to do it before people realized it might be done and was important."

Science described Smith's procedure: "The first step . . . is to splice a normal gene into the circular, single-stranded DNA of a virus. Next a researcher (now more likely a machine) chemically synthesizes a short segment of the DNA that is an exact complement of the normal gene sequence except at a single amino-acid coding site. The segment is allowed to bind to the normal gene, forming a short region of double-stranded DNA. A polymerase enzyme completes the second strand, and the double-stranded product is inserted into the genome of a bacterium. As the microbes grow, they use both the normal and the mutated versions of the gene as templates for synthesizing normal and mutated protein molecules, which can then be compared."

In 1981 Smith cofounded the Zymogenetics company in Seattle. The genetic engineering technology he had invented was applied commercially for the first time there. The company developed a strain of yeast that could be implanted in the human gene for insulin. By doing this, they, along with the drug company Novo-Nordisk, produced, according to Barry Shell, "a better process for the production of human insulin using yeast." In 1988 Smith sold his share of Zymogenetics and made a small fortune. Smith bought with his profits a cabin in a ski resort near Vancouver "for the use of his coworkers, staff, colleagues, friends, and children. A sign-up sheet hangs in his laboratory where people simply write in which weeks they'd like to use the cabin," Shell noted.

In 1993, Michael Smith was a corecipient of the Nobel Prize in Chemistry, sharing it with Kary B. Mullis, who, according to the *New York Times*, discovered a way to amplify DNA from a single molecule. This procedure, called the polymerase chain reaction (PMR), allows scientists to make multiple copies from vanishing amounts of DNA—everything from single molecules of DNA surviving in fossils to blood to hair

samples found at crime scenes. The Royal Swedish Academy announcement of the 1993 awards suggested that the methods Smith and Mullis pioneered "have greatly stimulated basic biochemical research and opened the way for new applications in medicine and biotechnology." Smith, normally a shy, reserved man, took a moment after the announcement to urge world governments to continue to give money to research and to place fewer restrictions on scientists. He also suggested that his winning such an award was an honor for Canada. According to *Maclean's*, he expressed the hope that young Canadian scientists could see that they could do "world-class research in this country," and noted, "I didn't have to be in Boston or Berkeley to do something that my colleagues around the world think is worthwhile."

Smith and Mullis split the $1 million prize money equally. According to Shell, Smith gave his half of the money to the researchers working on the genetics of schizophrenia, to Science World, and to the Society for Canadian Women in Science and Technology. When asked by reporters at his press conference what he was going to do with the money, Smith replied: "I guess I'll have to take my lab [staff] out for an expensive dinner." He went one better than that, taking 12 of his colleagues to Stockholm with him, all expenses paid, to have a part in the ceremony.

Smith has been the recipient of many other awards for his work in genetic engineering. In 1981, he became a fellow of the Royal Society of Canada. In 1984, he received the Gold Medal from the Science Council of British Columbia. Two years later he was awarded a fellowship by the Royal Society in the country of his birth, England. He was presented the Award of Excellence by the Genetics Society of Canada in 1988; he received his second honor from the Royal Society of Canada, the Flavelle Medal, in 1992; and was given the Manning Award and made a Laureate of the Canadian Medical Hall of Fame in 1995.

ABOUT: Shell, B. Great Canadian Scientists, 1996; Royal Swedish Academy of Sciences 1993 Nobel Prize Announcement; Maclean's October 25, 1993; New York Times October 14, 1993; Science October 22, 1993; Science News October 23, 1993.

SZYMBORSKA, WISŁAWA
(July 2, 1923–   )
Nobel Prize for Literature, 1996

The Polish poet Wisława Szymborska was born in Bnin in Western Poland. In 1931 she moved to Krakow. She studied Polish literature and sociology at the Jagiellonian University in Krakow from 1945 to 1949, and in 1953 she joined the Krakow literary weekly *Zycie literackie* as poetry editor and columnist.

Szymborska's volumes of poetry include: *Dlatego Zyjemy* (That's Why We Are Alive, 1952), *Pytania za-*

WISŁAWA SZYMBORSKA

dawane sobie (Questioning Oneself, 1954), *Wołanie do Yeti* (Calling Out to Yeti, 1957), *Sól* (Salt, 1962), *Sto pociech* (A Hundred Joys, 1967), *Wszelki wypadek* (Chance, 1972), *Wielka liczba* (A Great Number, 1976), *Poezje* (Poems, 1977), *Ludzie na moście* (People on a Bridge, 1986), and the collection translated into English in 1995 as *View with a Grain of Sand.* Two collections of her book reviews entitled *Lektury nadobowiazkowe* (Extra-Curricular Readings) appeared in 1973 and 1981. Szymborska's poetry has been translated into French, German, Russian, Czech, Hungarian, and Dutch as well as English.

Introducing Szymborska's collection *Poezje* in 1977, the critic Jerzy Kwiatkowski described her book as "one of the most important in contemporary Polish poetry. An amazing simplicity and communicability. The use of narrative and anecdote. A complete unpretentiousness. Yet at the same time—intellectually the most ambitious work, a poetic world with the most interesting mode of existence." This judgment has since been generously endorsed and confirmed by other critics as well as by the general public.

In spite of the warm critical reception of her work, Szymborska's road to preeminence and acclaim was slow. Her first two volumes reflected the political simplicities and evasions of the Stalinist era and are hard to distinguish formally, stylistically, or linguistically from the general mass of mediocre verse produced at the time. The 1957 volume signals her break with the naiveties of her youth, which are examined in her poem "Rehabilitation," in which she observed that Poles are engaged in an ongoing attempt to understand why so many able writers succumbed to the Communist government's call to participate in the creation of

a dreary and often dishonest social-realist literature for a decade beginning in about 1947.

Because of the strength of 19th-century Polish Romantic poetry and the fact that recent Polish history has favored confessional verse—emotionally, religiously, and patriotically committed—of a kind perfected by the Romantics, the classical tradition has at best played a supporting role in contemporary Polish poetry, as in the work of Zbigniew Herbert and CZESLAW MILOSZ. But the distinguishing features of Szymborska's mature work are those of the 18th-century Enlightenment: detachment; wit; erudition lightly employed; verbal brilliance centered not on elaborate metaphorical structures but on an exploitation of the punning possibilities of ordinary speech; and an ability to handle narrative and ideas in a fresh and arresting manner. At the same time, her poetry is permeated with a Nietzschean exuberance, a joyful drive and energy which banish any suspicions that she is shackled by conventions of classical decorum. The poet and critic Krzysztof Karasek has described as Mozartian her "joy arising from the play of intellect and imagination."

Like the detached, impersonal god of 18th-century Deism who was perceived as retreating into outer space, a watchmaker who had constructed a wondrously intricate clock which he left to its own devices after winding it up for eternity, Szymborska observes the earth, the creatures and objects found on it, as it were from outer space. Her training in scientific method doubtless accounts for Szymborska's clinical objectivity and voracious curiosity: "I read books on science, history, and anthropology. I read lexicons and guide books," she said in an interview, and the range of her book reviews—from cookery, tourism, gardening, and witchcraft to art history, T. S. ELIOT's cat poems, and Edward Lear's nonsense poems—bears this out. Szymborska imports all this bric-à-brac into her poetry. "There is no lack of subjects," she says, adding, "I would like each of my poems to be different," in contrast to those poets who "spend their lives effectively writing one long poem split into little bits." In this she most radically departs from her Enlightenment aesthetic, which claimed that it was proper for God to create everything but that the human artist had to confine himself to certain carefully defined topics. Szymborska writes, as a divine creator, of the joys of creation—of how her imagination, employing words rather than clay, can conjure objects and situations out of the air, as in the following verse translated by Sharon Olds: "Where is this written doe running through the written / forest / Does she want to drink from the written water / reflecting her mouth like carbon paper? / . . . In a drop of ink, quite a few hunters / wait, squinting, / to surround the doe, to shoot."

In "People on a Bridge" (the title of a print by the Japanese artist Hiroshige Utagawa), the poet used a

picture as a springboard for her metaphysical specula-
tion, exploiting the reader's amazement at the stillness
an artist can achieve in the midst of an inexorable flow
of time. Pictures, by their power to compel our attention, their immediacy, and their ability to subvert our
beliefs regarding what is seen and what exists, appeal
to Szymborska's puzzled curiosity about the world and
enable her to throw our daily reality into relief. Her
"Breughel's Two Monkeys" serves to confront humans
with the animal kingdom; "Pietà" employs the reference in the title to traditional representations of
Christ's passion to highlight a modern maternal trage-
dy; in "Byzantine Mosaic" the ascetically portrayed
characters are made to express their suitably ascetic
thoughts; and in "Landscape" the viewer literally steps
into a hallucinatorily depicted scene, of a kind perfected by the Dutch masters.

"Should someone classify my work as 'women's poetry' I would not be too upset, but I am not concerned
to make an issue of this fact," Szymborska declared.
But because in so many of her poems she has invented
a persona or enters the mind of a historical, legendary,
or imagined character, it is not surprising that portray-
als of women are often found in her work: those of
Lot's wife, Cassandra, Mary Stuart, and Queen Elizabeth, the women painted by Rubens. Among her poems there is "Portrait of a Woman" and "In Praise of
My Sister," and there are poems about childhood and
motherhood. Polish grammar can distinguish the
speaker's gender, and Szymborska's unattributed
monologues make it clear that a woman is speaking.
In "Homecoming," the grammar itself indicates a female perspective on the male as eternal child: "He was
back. / Said nothing. / But it was clear something had
upset him. / He lay down in his suit. / Hid his head
under the blanket. / Drew up his knees. / He's about
forty, but not at this moment. / He exists—but only as
much as in his mother's belly / behind seven skins, in
protective darkness. / Tomorrow he is lecturing on ho-
meostasis / in metagalactic space travel. / But now
he's curled up and fallen asleep."

Thus, however determinately Szymborska may
wish to strive for interstellar perspective, this last poem
especially illustrates her involvement with humanity.
She cannot in the end escape the somber truth that she
is part of the variety of situations she so coolly chronicles. This ambiguity of her situation (part divine, part
human) endows her work with tension and richness.

Echoing Rainer Maria Rilke's "Just once / everything, only for once. Once and no more. And we too
/ once. And never again," Szymborska asks "Why only
once as myself?" in a poem suitably entitled
"Wonderment," which in turn echoes Plato's observation that philosophy begins in wonder. As poets, Rilke
and Szymborska pose the question personally, just as
the philosopher Leibniz poses it in general terms
("Why is there something rather than nothing?").

Herein, in brief, lies the essential distinction between
the two modes of discourse. The danger for Szymborska emerges in her occasional failure to find a suitably
particularizing story for a concept—memory, the passing of time, the puzzles of perception—which she
wants to use as a core for a poem. As she has said, for
her the difficulty is not finding a subject for a poem—
there are plenty about—but "presenting [the subject]
as a problem." Here she admits to an intellectualist approach which has confined some of her poems to somewhat arid argument. The critic Piotr Concocts asks, «is
a poet a magus or only an interpreter?" and replies,
"Szymborska has failed to reach myth-creating forms.
There are only traces and echoes of what might have
been." Szymborska's aspirations are very high, and
where she succeeds the results are brilliant.

When Szymborska was awarded the Nobel Prize for
Literature in 1996, Piotr Sommer, her fellow Pole, said
about her in the *Times Literary Supplement*: "Giving
the Nobel Prize to her means giving it to a poet who,
being a major—and pleasantly old-fashioned—voice
in 20th-century European poetry, did not seek to be
put on any 'Polish pedestal.'" Sommer declared that
Szymborska could not have received the prize "for
anything else but being a discreetly reflective writer,
whose poetry only rarely reveals local color. The local
is written mostly into the language, its specific ways
and phraseology."

The Royal Swedish Academy cited Szymborska "for
poetry that with ironic precision allows the historical
and biological context to come to light in fragments of
human reality."

SELECTED WORKS IN ENGLISH TRANSLATION:
Sounds, Feelings, Thoughts: Seventy Poems by
Wisława Szymborska (tr. by Magnus J. Krynski and
Robert A. Maguire), 1981; People on a Bridge (tr. by
A. Czerniawski), 1990; View with a Grain of Sand (tr.
by S. Baranczak and C. Cavanagh), 1995.

ABOUT: New York Times October 4, 1996; New York
Times Magazine December 1, 1996; Royal Swedish
Academy of Sciences 1996 Nobel Prize Announce-
ment; Times Literary Supplement November 1, 1996.

TAYLOR, JOSEPH H., JR.
(March 29, 1941–   )
Nobel Prize for Physics, 1993 (shared with Rus-
sell A. Hulse)

The American physicist Joseph Hooton Taylor Jr.
was born in Philadelphia, Pennsylvania to Joseph Hooton and Sylvia Hathaway (Evans) Taylor. He attended
nearby Haverford College and received his degree in
physics in 1963. He then entered Harvard University
and worked under radioastronomer Alan Maxwell. According to *Physics Today*, his doctoral thesis research
involved "exploiting occultations by the moon to deter-

JOSEPH H. TAYLOR JR.

mine the directions of radio sources." This thesis would prove to be the basis for his life's work. He received his Ph.D. in astronomy in 1968 and then spent the next year lecturing at Harvard University.

In 1969 Taylor became a professor at the University of Massachusetts in Amherst, where he taught astronomy. He was also one of the organizers of the Five Colleges Radio Astronomy Observatory—a joint effort of the university and the four nearby colleges: Mount Holyoke, Smith, Hampshire, and Amherst. Taylor remembered: "The first instrument we built . . . was an array of small, low-frequency radiotelescopes designed explicitly to observe pulsars." Pulsars, or rotating neutron stars, are the source of pulsating radio waves characterized by an extemely short interval between each pulse. At the time of the group's work, pulsars were a recent discovery by Jocelyn Bell and ANTONY HEWISH, who had used an array of radio antennas at Cambridge University.

In December 1973 Taylor and his graduate assistant RUSSELL A. HULSE traveled to Arecibo, Puerto Rico, where the largest radio telescope in the world resides, to perform the most painstaking research ever done on pulsars. The telescope at Arecibo is over 300 meters in diameter, lying in a bowl-shaped depression in the mountains. Though the dish cannot move, the detector at the focus moves enough to let the telescope examine any source within 20 degrees of the zenith. Taylor and Hulse carried with them to Arecibo a homemade but powerful radio telescope made of discarded telephone poles and wire mesh ordered from the Sears catalogue. They later attached this to the telescope in Puerto Rico. They had a minicomputer with them, quite a luxury for those days before supercomputing.

At this time only about 100 pulsars were known. The *New York Times* described pulsars as "extremely dense stars made mostly of neutrons rather than whole atoms; their gravitation is so immense that a human being standing on the surface of one of these stars would weigh several hundred billion times his weight on Earth, and he would be crushed to a thin film. Pulsars are only about six miles wide but are as massive as the sun." Taylor and Hulse, along with the rest of the scientific community, had some idea as to how pulsars sent out radio frequency beams to Earth. Bertram Schwarzchild, writing in *Physics Today*, explained: "As the very compact neutron star spins with a period of seconds, or even milliseconds, the off-axis radio beams sweep out two celestial cones, like a cockeyed lighthouse." If aligned with Earth, the pulsars send very regular radio pulses, which can be picked up by radioastronomers. These pulses are some of the most accurate naturally occurring signals in the galaxy.

There are three key observational parameters by which to find a pulsar signal: period, pulse width, and frequency dispersion. Hulse explained to *Physics Today* the process he and Taylor had used to conduct their search for pulsars: "The problem is, you don't know these parameters when you're looking for new pulsars. So we had to search not only the sky but also this three-dimensional parameter space." The Arecibo telescope had to sweep across the entire Milky Way before the computer could scan all the collected data for a possible pulsar. When a possible pulsar was in evidence, the next test was to look in the same direction a few days or weeks later to see if the same signal was resonating. If it was still there, the next step in the process was to refine the measurements of the pulse period.

It took two weeks for Taylor and Hulse to decide if they had found a pulsar. They first detected one on July 2, 1974 and then reexamined it on August 25. It had a period of 59 milliseconds, the second fastest pulsar ever recorded. Hulse tried to refine the period, but something strange was occurring. "The computer analysis was alleging that the pulse periods at the beginning and end of the run differed by about 30 microseconds. Given the proverbial stability of pulsars, such an enormous variation was unheard of." Hulse attempted to solve this puzzling problem. Finally, as he explained to *Physics Today*, he "noticed that if he shifted the second day's curve forward by about 45 minutes it fell neatly onto the previous day's data." The next day's data then turned out to be 45 minutes behind the second day. Hulse deduced that he might have been looking at a binary pulsar, something Taylor had suggested the possibility of finding in his funding proposal to the National Science Foundation.

Hulse continued to observe the pulsar in order to gain the final proof needed to confirm its binary status: the period bottomed out and started climbing again as he and Taylor predicted it would. This occurred on September 16, and "after falling 70 microseconds in less than two hours, the pulse period started increasing." Hulse then telephoned Taylor, who had gone back to teach his classes in Massachusetts, and explained to him that this "59 millisecond pulsar was part of a binary system with an orbital period just 15 minutes shy of eight hours." As Taylor predicted and as Hulse observed, the possibility of a binary pulsar was now a reality. The binary, which they named PSR 1913+16, emits bursts of energy about 17 times per second, and its accuracy is comparable to that of the best atomic clocks.

Taylor soon realized that he and Hulse had more than an astronomical anomaly on their hands—they had an important tool by which they could test ALBERT EINSTEIN's general theory of relativity. As stated in Science's October 1993 announcement of the physics prize: "The powerful, shifting gravitational fields of the whirling neutron stars would magnify the subtle effects of relativity, and this enormous density would prevent exchanges of gas or tidal shifting from contaminating those effects." Within two years' time, Taylor and Hulse were able to show that their binary pulsar's system manifested several of the effects predicted by Einstein, including, according to Science, "the bending of the path of radio waves from the pulsar as it passes behind the other neutron star and a precession in the system's axis of rotation."

In 1976 Taylor married Marietta Bisson, with whom he has three children. In the following year he published the book *Pulsars*, on the subject of his research. In 1978 he and Hulse showed that the loss in time of the eight-hour orbiting period exactly matched what was expected if the system were emitting gravitational waves. Again, Einstein's theory was correct in predicting what would happen if such waves of gravity spilled into space from such massive oscillating bodies. Considering the work done by Taylor and Hulse, the Swedish Academy wrote in its announcement of the prize for physics: "So far, Einstein's theory has passed with flying colors."

Taylor left the University of Massachusetts in 1980 to teach physics at Princeton, becoming a James McDonnell Distinguished Professor of Physics in 1986. In 1993 Taylor and Hulse were jointly awarded the Nobel Prize for Physics for their work in binary pulsars. They shared the $825,000 prize equally. Taylor, when asked how the prize would affect his life, remarked: "I hope my life won't get so complicated that I won't be able to continue meeting with students every day."

Joseph H. Taylor Jr. has been the recipient of many other awards and citations, among them a MacArthur fellowship and a fellowship in the American Academy of Arts and Sciences. In 1991 he became an Einstein Prize laureate of the Albert Einstein Society. A year later he received the Wolf Prize in Physics from the Wolf Foundation.

SELECTED WORKS: Pulsars, 1977.

ABOUT: Boston Globe October 14, 1993; New York Times October 14, 1993; Physics Today December 1993; Science October 22, 1993; Science News October 23, 1993.

VICKREY, WILLIAM
(June 21, 1914–October 11, 1996)
Nobel Memorial Prize in Economic Sciences, 1996 (shared with James A. Mirrlees)

The American economist William Spencer Vickrey was born in Victoria, British Columbia, the eldest son of a Canadian mother and an American father. During the first year of his life, the family relocated to the United States, where Vickrey would eventually become a naturalized citizen. Vickrey was raised in and around New York City, where his father, Charles Vernon Vickrey, worked as the executive secretary of Near East Relief, a nonprofit organization devoted to helping the orphans of Armenia. His father's work affected Vickrey deeply. He would later say that during his youth he came to view any money otherwise used as money not spent to help the Armenian children.

Upon graduating from high school at the age of 16, Vickrey attended prep school for a year before enrolling in Yale University's mathematics program. He received his bachelor's degree (with high honors) from Yale in 1935. Vickrey then went on to Columbia University, where he received his master's degree in economics in 1937. He subsequently took a series of positions as an economist at organizations including the National Resources Committee and the Treasury Department's Division of Tax Research. The advent of World War II, however, forced Vickrey, a conscientious objector, into a three-year stint as a civilian public service assignee, beginning in 1943. During the final year of his public service, Vickrey's economic expertise led to an assignment involving the designing and instituting of a new inheritance tax for Puerto Rico.

Throughout much of his service, Vickrey continued to study economics at Columbia. In 1946, one year before he was awarded his Ph.D., Vickrey became a member of the university's faculty, on which he remained in one capacity or another for the the next half-century. By this time, many of the seeds for Vickrey's economic theories had already been sowed. Back in his days as an undergraduate at Yale, Vickrey first come up with the basics for his theory of "congestion pricing" while on a train trip from New Haven to his parents' home in Scarsdale, New York. Observing that many of the train's seats were empty, Vickrey thought that if the railroad dropped its prices during such off-peak hours, more of his fellow Yale students would travel. This would, of course, be mutually beneficial to both the railroad, which would be able to fill more seats, and to the students, who would

WILLIAM VICKREY

enjoy traveling at a reduced rate. Such practical applications for economics were to become the hallmark of Vickrey's work in a profession that he criticized for rarely coming up with solutions to everyday problems. "Too many economists," he said, "are basically astronomers, admiring our wonderful free-market system, or weathermen, predicting what the economy is going to do."

By 1959 Vickrey had expanded his theories about congestion pricing to include proposals to reduce traffic congestion in large cities. He proposed that traffic on crowded roads could be lessened if every car were equipped with a device that recorded when and how often the vehicle passed through a crowded area. The vehicle owner would then be charged a different fee for each trip based upon the time of day the trip occurred. Prices would be highest during rush hour and gradually decrease as off-peak hours approached. Vickrey went on to propose similar solutions to assuage the problems of overcrowding on city subways and buses and traffic congestion in tunnels and at tollbooths.

Despite the practicality of Vickrey's solutions, they were ill-received by officials. After testifying in 1959 before a congressional committee investigating problems in the Washington metropolitan area, Vickrey noted that his suggestion to install time-sensitive devices in vehicles was met with "a discreet silence." Vickrey did, however, receive some, albeit delayed, satisfaction many years later, when Singapore instituted a fare system similar to the one he had proposed. At home, however, his suggestions were still largely ignored.

Nonetheless, Vickrey continued to practice and pro-

mote his brand of reality-based economics. In the early 1960s he published two papers outlining a new kind of auction. In a standard sealed-bid auction, bidders regularly bid much less than they believe an item to be worth, but never offer more than they think it is worth. In a "Vickrey auction," bidders still make a sealed bid with the highest bidder winning. The difference, however, is that the winning bidder has to pay only the price of the second-highest bid. Such an auction forces bidders to offer the highest prices they can afford or risk losing to a bid far lower than the perceived value of the object. The practices involved in Vickrey auctions have influenced the work of countless economists studying the intricacies of modern auction theory. Despite this, the ever-humble Vickrey maintained that his auction work was nothing more than "one of my digressions into abstract economics. At best, it's of minor significance in terms of human welfare."

Perhaps a carryover from childhood days spent pondering the fate of Armenian orphans, finding ways to better the human condition was Vickrey's overriding concern. He was a great proponent of full employment, a situation in which unemployment would rise no higher than 1 or 2 percent and all people seeking employment would be able to find a job paying a suitable wage within 48 hours. "Full employment . . . would have salutary consequences for levels of production, would reduce budgetary drains for unemployment insurance benefits, welfare payments and the like, and would have a significant impact on levels of poverty, homelessness, drug addiction, and crime," Vickrey said in a 1993 address to the American Economic Association. "It would substantially ease tensions over such issues as defense cutbacks, race relations, free trade, and immigration as well as over many labor-management issues such as featherbedding, demarcation, seniority, and job tenure."

Vickrey was equally passionate about his work on taxation and tax reform. In the 1960s Vickrey outlined a plan for the "cumulative assessment of income taxes" designed to "keep progressivity and still throw away two-thirds of the tax forms." Much to the chagrin of the average taxpayer, Vickrey's plan was never enacted "because it would have put the Internal Revenue Service out of business." Despite the fact that his idea never came to fruition, Vickrey's work on taxation was highly respected and eventually earned him a position as a tax adviser to the United Nations during the mid 1970s.

In 1981 Vickrey retired from an illustrious career at Columbia that included chairing the economics department from 1964 to 1967, and he was granted professor emeritus status. His retirement was in name only, as Vickrey remained a familiar presence on the Columbia campus. He continued to publish books and papers and could often be spotted roller-skating to and from the tiny office that he once described as "the world's biggest mess." Additionally, Vickrey continued his career-long habit of attending university seminars and lectures on a multitude of subjects — usually with his eyes closed and his head tilted back in a sleeping position. Though by all appearances Vickrey was soundly napping, he would often suddenly bolt upright and provide "the most cogent comment or blockbuster question of the whole discussion," as the economist JAMES TOBIN noted while introducing Vickrey at a 1992 awards ceremony.

In 1996, after devoting nearly 60 years to the study of economics, William Spencer Vickrey was awarded the Nobel Memorial Prize in Economic Sciences. He was to share the award, along with the $1.12 million monetary prize, with Scotsman JAMES ALEXANDER MIRRLEES. The academy praised Vickrey for having "contributed to enhancing our knowledge about the efficient use of resources in the public sector." Upon hearing that he had won the Nobel Prize, Vickrey had a response typical of a man more concerned with the promotion and propagation of his ideas than with material wealth. "I don't need the money," he said, "but I sure need the platform."

Sadly, Vickrey was never able to utilize his newfound status or the platform it provided. On October 11, 1996, just three days after he was awarded the Nobel Prize, William Spencer Vickrey suffered cardiac arrest while driving to an academic conference in Boston. He was survived by Cecile Montez (Thompson) Vickrey, his wife since 1951. Vickrey's Nobel Prize was accepted by C. Lowell Harriss, professor emeritus of economics at Columbia University and Vickrey's longtime friend.

In addition to the Nobel Prize, Vickrey was the recipient of many fellowships from a variety of institutions that included the Institute for the Advanced Study of Behavioral Sciences (1967-68), the American Economic Association (1992), and the Econometric Society. Also, Vickrey was a member of a variety of organizations, among them the American Economic Association, the American Statistical Association, the Royal Economic Association, and the Eastern Economic Association.

SELECTED WORKS: Agenda for Progressive Taxation, 1947; Microstatics: Metastatics and Macroeconomics, 1964; Public Economies, 1994.

ABOUT: Boston Globe October 12, 1996; Challenge March/April 1993; New York Times January 4, 1992, October 9, 1996, October 12, 1996, October 25, 1996; Royal Swedish Academy of Sciences 1996 Nobel Prize Announcement; Who's Who in America, 1997.

WALCOTT, DEREK
(January 23, 1930–   )
Nobel Prize for Literature, 1992

DEREK WALCOTT

The West Indian poet and playwright Derek Alton Walcott was born in Castries on the West Indian island of St. Lucia, then a British dependency and now an independent nation. Both of Walcott's parents were schoolteachers. In addition, his father, Warwick Walcott, was a watercolor painter and his mother, Alix Walcott, "loved to act," as the poet has recalled. The father died when Derek was one, as Walcott told a New Yorker interviewer, and he and his brother and older sister "grew up with a terrific mother in a house full of books." He described St. Lucia to the interviewer as "a very green, misty island, which always has a low cloud hanging over the mountaintops," so that "when you come down by plane, you break through the mist, and it's as if you were entering some kind of prehistoric Eden." The strong visual element in Walcott's poetry was fostered in part by his boyhood practice of painting landscapes of a countryside where "the thick green hills boiled all day with their broad-leaved, volcanic vegetation." However, as he pointed out to James Atlas in an interview for the New York Times Magazine, he does not think that he has ever adequately "conveyed the elation" he felt "over the bounty, the beauty of being in a place like St. Lucia."

In school, Walcott told Atlas, "cultivated colonials of easy graces" presented poetry to him as "living speech," and he became "infatuated" with the style of the great poets in the English literary tradition. Like "every child all over the empire," he was raised to be "Civic Britannica." "When we sang Kipling's hymn in church on Sundays, that very hymn was being sung by people of all colors all over the world." He would later sum up the pros and cons of the colonial predicament in his patois line, "We was in chains, but chains made us unite."

159

In 1948, when he was 18, Walcott, with his mother's encouragement, began privately to publish slim books of poetry—three in all—conveying such experiences as "the fierce, barbarous, unchristened blaze of the tropical morning." After graduating from St. Mary's College in St. Lucia, Walcott went on scholarship to the University of the West Indies in Kingston, Jamaica, where he majored in French, Latin, and Spanish. While an undergraduate, he wrote his first play, *Henri Christophe: A Chronicle,* which was produced in St. Lucia in 1950, and his second, *Henri Dernier,* a play for radio.

After taking his B.A. degree in 1953, Walcott taught at St. Mary's College, his alma mater, at Boys Secondary School in Grenada, and at Kingston College in Jamaica. Meanwhile, he wrote art and literary criticism for the *Trinidad Guardian* and feature articles for the Jamaican publication *Public Opinion.* His plays *Ione* and *Sea at Dauphin* were produced in Trinidad in 1954. *Sea at Dauphin* is about an old fisherman who commits suicide when he is superannuated and about the crew that takes on a boy as his replacement. It depicts the sea as a "white man" God's "spit on Dauphin people" and the hard life of those who wrest a bare subsistence from it as an endless circle of despair. The government of Trinidad commissioned Walcott to write an epic pageant to mark the first convocation of the abortive West Indian Federal Parliament, and the result was *Drums and Colours,* produced in Trinidad in 1958. Also produced in Trinidad that year was Walcott's *Ti-Jean and His Brothers,* a metaphysical verse based on a Trinidad folk fable. In the play Lucifer sets out to capture the souls of three brothers, and he succeeds until he meets more than his match in the youngest of the three.

On a Rockefeller Foundation grant in New York in 1957 and 1958, Walcott attended José Quintero's directing classes and the rehearsals of the Phoenix Theater's repertory company. On returning to the West Indies, he founded his own company, the Trinidad Theater Workshop. The first play in the troupe's repertoire was Walcott's *Malcochon,* in which six characters speaking a blend of French Creole and West Indian English dialect exemplify six different views of God and justice and at the same time reveal their common frail humanity. First produced in St. Lucia in 1959, *Malcochon* was staged in London the following year under the title *Six in the Rain.* Finding little support for his theater workshop in the Caribbean, Walcott optioned his later plays to Joseph Papp, the director of the Public Theater in New York City.

The first collection of poetry in Walcott's definitive canon was *In a Green Night* (1962). Critics hailed it as a landmark in Caribbean literature in English, in which the previous notable achievements (aside from Edward Braithwaite's Creole dialect verse) were in prose. Reading it was, to use Walcott's own phrase,

"like entering a Renoir," a painting in verse described by P. N. Furbank in *The Listener* as "full of summery melancholy, fresh and stinging colors, luscious melody, and intense awareness of place." Reviewing Walcott's *Selected Poems* (1964) in the *New York Times Book Review,* Robert Mazzocco detected an "itch to be impressive" in many of the "orotund, mellifluously spun lines" that set the poet apart from his English-born contemporaries, "most of whom in the manner of the Movement write wry, inelegant miniatures, the new emblem of the Welfare State." Mazzocco went on to observe, "Walcott has special gifts . . . not much evident in younger poets, whether English or American: his textures are musical, he has a painter's eye, his craftmanship is adventurous, and his moral or imaginative responses aren't shabby . . . When these qualities triumph . . . then the full force of his personality, the personality of *place,* the troubled beauty of his Antillean land, comes strikingly to the surface."

Walcott continued to probe personal isolation and regional identity in surges of scenic delight balanced with descriptions of degradation in the poems of *The Castaway,* which won the Royal Society of Literature award. The title poem of *The Gulf* (1969) is a meditation on racial violence that seemed to Roy Fuller, writing in *London,* to be "entirely successful, a poem of vision and compassion, with just the right amount of concrete detail to make effective the rhetoric and imaginative use of vocabulary that have always been Walcott's strength." In the *American Poetry Review,* Valerie Trueblood described the verse in *The Gulf* as "lonely, fiery work" in which "the rage" that had been there all along for the looking in Walcott's poetry "is tougher now."

Among Walcott's plays, the best-received was *The Dream on Monkey Mountain,* first produced by the Eugene O'Neill Memorial Foundation in Waterford, Connecticut in 1969 and staged Off-Broadway the following year. The protagonist of that poetic drama is an old charcoal burner named Makak, who comes down from his hut on the mountain to sell his wares in town, gets drunk, and lands in jail, where he hallucinates about being the king of a united Africa. "Makak is an extreme representation of what colonialism can do to a man—he is reduced to an almost animal-like state of degradation," the playwright explained to the *New Yorker* interviewer. "When he dreams that he is king of united Africa, I am saying that some sort of spiritual return to Africa can be made, but it may not be necessary. The romanticized, pastoral vision of Africa that many black people hold can be an escape from the reality around us. In the West Indies, where all the races live and work together, we have the beginnings of a great and unique society. The problem is to recognize our African origins but not to romanticize them.... [Makak] thought he was going to an Africa where man could be primal and communal. Instead, it's back to original sin, with the tribes killing one another."

Walcott's play *In a Fine Castle*, produced in Los Angeles in 1972, is, in the author's words, "the story of a bourgeois French Creole family who live in one of Port of Spain's elaborate Victorian mansions" that "deals with the contrast between carnival and revolution." "Trinidad is a society where carnival is regarded as a serious matter and revolution as fun. It's the ambiguity of this view that makes life there so interesting." *The Charlatan*, a richly textured musical fantasy with a calypso beat, set in carnival time, dramatizes such matters as realistic social conscience, love, cultural mores, and contrasting unorthodoxies, personified, for example, in a white voodoo doctor and a black M.D. It was produced in Los Angeles in 1974. *Remembrance*, about a Port of Prince father and his two sons, one a martyred revolutionary and the other an impoverished artist, was produced in New York in 1979. *Pantomime*, set in a gazebo on a cliff in Tobago, was staged in Washington, D.C. in 1981. Among Walcott's other plays are *The Mulatto's Orgy* and *On the Right Hand of God the Father*.

In his autobiographical book-length poem *Another Life* (1973) Walcott looked back on his childhood and his magical rites of poetic passage as part of a Caribbean way of life that is sealed off "in a bell jar." Writing in the *New York Times Book Review*, George Lamming explained: "The increasing pressures of race and politics in Caribbean society always threaten to put such a writer on trial. Walcott is not popular among a later generation of cultural nationalists who, in his view, have sought to turn white mythology on its head by discovering in blackness a new aristocracy of skin. [His] turbulent meditation on the dilemma of his time . . . is a formidable achievement."

The emotional tenor of the 46 poems in *Sea Grapes* (1976), ranging from erudite and tender to desperate and bitter, is summed up in the concluding line of the title poem: "The classics can console. But not enough." That poem treats such important Walcott themes as the wanderer, home, "the ancient war between obsession and responsibility," and the elusiveness of peace. In one scene the poet contemplates London, where birds fly indiscriminately over the descendants of slaves and slave-holders alike and an "involuntary bell" of compassion tolls "for everything even in London / heart of our history, original sin." The moving narrative poems in *The Star-Apple Kingdom* (1980)— including one tracing the odyssey of a poor mulatto sailor, a fugitive from Trinidad—are mostly meditations on power relationships in the history of slavery and imperialism and in current developments between the industrialized countries and the Third World.

The long sequence titled, not entirely ironically, *The Fortunate Traveler* (1982) reflects the poet's international peregrinations—mostly between the West Indies and the United States—and expresses a linguistic as well as a geographical dislocation. In the poem "North and South" Walcott wrote: "I accept my function / as a provincial elegist at the end of an empire, / a single, circling satellite," and in the quatrains of "Sea Change" he juxtaposed images ("light rain and governments falling") to convey the picture of political trouble in a tourist's paradise. Reviewing *The Fortunate Traveler* in the *New York Review of Books*, Helen Vendler traced the poet's spiritual odyssey back to the early, often unhappy disjunction between his concern with the black colonial predicament and "his harmonious pentameters, his lyrical allusions, his stately rhymes, and his Yeatsian meditations." Now, she pointed out, he is "not only the colonial but also the exile and, in his returns to the West Indies, the prodigal son."

In 1988 Walcott published the poetry volume *The Arkansas Treatment*. His 1990 work *Omeros* (Greek for "Homer") has characters named for those in the *Iliad* and the *Odyssey* of Homer, but the book, according to Walcott, was meant to capture "the whole experience of the people of the Caribbean." Walcott's Helen, for example, is a woman looking for work and seen by the poet at a beachside hotel terrace: "I felt like standing in homage to a beauty / that left, like a ship, widening eyes in its wake . . . / As the carved lids of the unimaginable / ebony mask unwrapped from its cotton-wool cloud, / the waitress sneered, 'Helen.' And all the rest followed."

Cited by the Swedish Academy of Letters for "a poetic oeuvre of great luminosity," for his "historical vision, the outcome of a multicultural commitment," and for his "melodious and sensitive style," Walcott was awarded the Nobel Prize in Literature in 1992. Walcott published the book of poems *The Antilles* and the play *The Odyssey* in the following year.

Thrice married and divorced, Walcott has a son by his first wife and two daughters by his second. He lives in Boston. Among the institutions where he has taught or lectured are Harvard, Columbia, Yale, and Rutgers universities. He regularly gives readings on American college campuses, and he often flies to cities where his plays are being staged in order to supervise the productions, of which two were *Beef, No Chicken*, at the Yale Repertory Theater, and *The Isle Is Full of Noises*, in Hartford. Among the many other honors his poetry has drawn is the National Writers Prize of the Welsh Arts Council.

James Atlas in the *New York Times* (1992) described Walcott, whose 1997 work is *The Bounty*, as "a poet for whom exile—both geographic and personal—has been the informing fact of his life." He placed Walcott in the "evolving tradition" of T.S. Eliot: "In Derek Walcott we can discern the history of what is most enduring in our tradition, invigorated, as it has always been, by the voice of our most recent immigrants. Invigorated and made new."

SELECTED WORKS: In a Green Night, 1962; Selected Poems, 1964; The Castaway, 1969; Sea Grapes, 1976; Another Life, 1978; The Star-Apple Kingdom, 1980; The Fortunate Traveler, 1982; The Arkansas Testament, 1988; Omeros, 1990; The Antilles, 1993; Selected Poetry, 1993; The Odyssey, 1993; The Bounty, 1997.

ABOUT: Baer, W. Conversations with Derek Walcott, 1996; ContemporaryAuthors, 1980; Contemporary Poets, 1981; Derek Walcott (H. Bloom, ed.), 1988; New York Times October 9, 1992, October 10, 1992; New York Times Magazine May 23, 1982; New Yorker June 26, 1971; New York Review of Books November 10, 1983; World Authors 1950–1970, 1980.

WIESCHAUS, ERIC F.

(June 8, 1947–   )
Nobel Prize for Physiology or Medicine, 1995
(shared with Edward B. Lewis and Christiane
Nüsslein-Volhard)

ERIC F. WIESCHAUS

The American molecular biologist Eric F. Wieschaus was born in South Bend, Indiana. He lived there until 1953, when the Wieschaus family relocated to Birmingham, Alabama. For his undergraduate studies, however, Wieschaus returned to South Bend to attend the University of Notre Dame, where he received his bachelor's degree in 1969. He then went on to Yale University, obtaining his Ph.D. in biology there in 1974. During his studies at Yale, Wieschaus, under the tutelage of Walter Gehring, developed an interest in *Drosophila Melanogaster*, more commonly known as the fruit fly. His continued fascination with the species would eventually lead to pioneering studies in the field of developmental genetics, new insight into birth defects and miscarriages in humans, and a Nobel Prize.

Upon graduation from Yale, Wieschaus traveled to Switzerland to work as a postdoctoral fellow at the University of Zurich. While based in Zurich, he received a short-term fellowship at the Laboratoire de Genetique Moleculaire in Gif-sur-Yvette, France, in 1976. Additionally, he worked as a visiting researcher at the University of California Irvine's Center of Pathobiology in 1977. In 1978 Wieschaus left the University of Zurich to become a group leader at the European Molecular Biology Laboratory in the city of Heidelberg in what was then West Germany. While at EMBL, Wieschaus teamed up with the German biologist CHRISTIANE NÜSSLEIN-VOLHARD to expand upon the extensive research in the genetic mutations of fruit-flies conducted by American scientist EDWARD B. LEWIS.

Much of Lewis's work centered on a specific class of fruit-fly mutations: homeotic mutations, in which entire body parts, such as extra wings or antennas, sprout in abnormal locations. Through the introduction of gene alterations, Lewis discovered that genes were integral in the processes of forming an overall body plan and directing the development of specific body segments into organs and appendages. Further, he found that the arrangement of the genes on chromosomes is such that they are lined up according to the body segment that will eventually develop. For instance, the first genes controlled the development of the head region, the middle genes controlled the growth of the abdomen, and the final genes controlled the bottom or tail portion of the fruit fly. Lewis's research uncovered the fact that the various homeotic mutations resulted from genes that omitted an entire body section and duplicated another. As Lewis's work had been concentrated on the development of fruit-fly embryos after segmentation had occurred, it left many unanswered questions about genes' involvement in the start of the development process. Because of these remaining mysteries, the science community viewed his work with abundant skepticism.

In a quest to answer some of the questions prompted by Lewis's work, Wieschaus and Nüsslein-Volhard set out to identify the role of genes in the start of the development process. While they were nearly certain that genes were responsible for controlling all development, they were unsure of the number of genes involved in the process and of how to find that number. Faced with the possibility that the number of genes involved would simply be too great to classify, the young scientists nonetheless began the project that, in the case of failure, would almost surely be professional suicide.

To begin their study, the pair decided upon a systematic trial-and-error search to determine which of the fruit fly's genes played the most vital roles. They did this by breeding 40,000 fly families, most missing a single gene. Looking through a specially-equipped dual microscope, they observed the mutations resulting from the omission of each gene. "We would ask, do the embryos of a given stock look abnormal in the same way? Is there a mutant phenotype that did something constant during the development? Then we would try to classify the defects," Wieschaus said in an interview with *Science*. Many of the missing genes resulted in very minor defects. In an interview with the *New York Times*, Wieschaus explained that by looking at the various mutations resulting from different missing genes they "pieced together a picture of what was necessary." Upon sorting through the 20,000 genes of the fruit fly, Wieschaus and Nüsslein-Volhard discovered 5,000 genes that were important and 139 that were vital for growth and development. Mutations resulting from a lack of one of the genes classified as important or vital tended to be overt deformities, such as complete lack of muscles or skin totally covered with nerve cells.

Through further examination of the flies' mutations, Wieschaus and Nüsslein-Volhard were able to categorize the genes of the mutant flies into several distinct categories—gap, pair-rule, even-skipped, and segment polarity—all of which are involved in the process of subdividing a fly embryo into specific body segments. The gap genes, the first to be activated, are responsible for distinguishing a head-to-tail orientation. Pair-rule and even-skipped genes must then divide the embryo into sections. Finally, the segment-polarity genes tell each segment which end is the head and which is the tail.

The ramifications of the studies conducted by Wieschaus and Nüsslein-Volhard go far beyond the insect world. Because the genetic structure of the fruit fly is very close to that of a human, their research has yielded new insight into the development of human embryos. "We didn't know it at the time, but we found out everything in life is so similar, that the same genes that work in flies are the ones that work in humans," Wieschaus said. Many miscarriages and up to 40 percent of all human birth defects can be traced to genetic flaws that match those examined in the pair's fruit-fly study. The task at hand for scientists today, Wieschaus noted in an interview with the *New York Times*, is to extend the study and learn exactly how these genes "affect molecular processes in the human cell."

In 1995 Wieschaus, who had been teaching biology and molecular biology at Princeton University since ending his work with Nüsslein-Volhard at the European Molecular Biology Laboratory in 1981, was awarded the Nobel Prize. He shared the prize, along with a $1 million award, with Edward B. Lewis and Christiane Nüsslein-Volhard. The academy praised the three for achieving "a breakthrough that will help explain congenital malformations in man." When describing the early-morning phone call in which he was told he

had just won the Nobel Prize, Wieschaus said he was slightly dumbfounded. "We were asleep, there was this phone call. This man spoke to me in a Swedish accent. I thought he probably had the wrong number. Maybe he did, but they're not going to take it back."

In addition to the Nobel Prize, Wieschaus received a Merit Award from the National Institutes of Health (1989) and an award from the Genetics Society of America (1995). Also, he has been an American Academy of Arts and Sciences fellow and a member of the National Academy of Sciences.

SELECTED WORKS: Mutations Affecting Segment Number and Polarity in Drosophila (with C. Nüsslein-Volhard), Nature 287, 1980; Segmentierung Bei Drosophila, Ein Genetische Analyse (Segmentation in Drosophila, a Genetic Analysis, with C. Nüsslein-Volhard and G. Jurgens) Verh. Dtsch. Zool. Ges., 1982; Kruppel, a Gene Whose Activity is Required Early in the Zygotic Genome for Normal Segmentation (with C. Nsslein-Volhard and C. Kluding), Developmental Biology 104, 1984; Gene Activities and Segmental Patterning in Drosphila: Analysis of Odd-Skipped and Pair-Rule Double Mutants (with D.E. Coulter), Genes and Development 2, 1988; From Molecular Patterns to Morphogenesis: The Lessons From Drosophila, Les Prix Nobel, 1996.

ABOUT: Boston Globe October 10, 1995; New York Times October 10, 1995; Royal Swedish Academy of Sciences 1995 Nobel Prize Announcement; Science October 20, 1995; Science News October 14, 1995; USA Today October 10, 1995.

ZINKERNAGEL, ROLF M.
(January 6, 1944–)
Nobel Prize for Physiology or Medicine, 1996
(shared with Peter C. Doherty)

The Swiss immunologist Rolf M. Zinkernagel was born in Basel in 1944. He entered the University of Basel's Faculty of Medicine in 1962 and graduated in 1968, after having passed the Swiss National Board Examination. In 1969 he began doing research work as a postdoctoral fellow in the Laboratory for Electron Microscopy at the Institute for Anatomy. He finished his work at the laboratory and completed his M.D. thesis in 1970, then went on to his second postdoctoral fellowship, this time at the University of Lausanne, also in Switzerland. In Lausanne he spent the years 1971–1973 immersed in research at the Institute of Biochemistry.

In 1973, at the age of 29, Zinkernagel began the work for which he would eventually win the Nobel Prize. At that time he was a visiting fellow in the Department of Microbiology in the John Curtin School of Medical Research at the Australian National University, in Canberra, having just received a Swiss grant to do his research. The Curtin School was widely known

ROLF M. ZINKERNAGEL

as a research site with the proper resources for scientists to tackle difficult problems. Lacking sufficient research space of his own, Zinkernagel shared a small laboratory with PETER C. DOHERTY, a 34-year-old, newly graduated doctor of veterinary surgery. They were opposites in many ways. Doherty was described by friends as "quiet and sort of crotchety," while Zinkernagel was termed "flashier" and "more of an extrovert." Still, they had something in common besides their mutual interest in immunology: an "involvement" with opera. Doherty fondly recalled those days to an interviewer with the St. Jude Children's Research Hospital: "[Zinkernagel] sang grand opera, Mozart particularly. I was the only guy with sufficient musical taste to have him in the lab. The rest were all into rock-n-roll and country-and-western. He liked to sing Cherubino's song from 'The Marriage of Figaro.' Actually Cherubino is usually sung by a girl. He wasn't actually a Cherubino. He was tolerable, but loud."

Zinkernagel and Doherty's work concerned those aspects of the immune system made up of several kinds of white blood cells, including T and B lymphocytes (or T and B cells). These protect the organism, fighting off any invading microorganisms or any other alien invaders. When the pair began their immunology work in 1973, the scientific community knew more about B lymphocytes, which attack microorganisms like bacteria, than T cells, which attack foreign materials such as viruses. Specifically the Nobel Committee noted: "Far less was known about recognition mechanisms in the cellular immune system, for instance in conjunction with the killing of virus-infected cells by Tlymphocytes." One of the few things that was known

about T cells was that, after a transplant operation, they would attack foreign cells once they recognized the configuration of certain molecules in the transplant. These molecules were called major histocompatibility antigens.

According to the *New York Times*, Zinkernagel and Doherty "decided to investigate a particular viral infection of mice, one that provokes an immune response that is so strong that the immune system itself, not the virus, kills the animal." The infection was a viral strain that could cause meningitis, and the result was unexpected. The T cells would recognize the infected cells and kill them, but only if they came from the same strain of mice. If the cells came from a different strain of mice, the T cells would bypass the infected cells as if they didn't exist. Zinkernagel and Doherty agreed on a simple explanation—that the T lymphocytes were looking for two indicators: the protein called a major histocompatibility antigen that exists on the surface of every cell in the body and tells the immune system that the cell is part of the self, not foreign tissue; and a protein fragment from the infecting virus that signals the cell's infection.

With regard to transplanted organs, there was still one question for these scientists: What is the purpose of these naturally and universally occurring antigens that reject and attack transplanted organs as foreign, since transplants do not occur in nature? Zinkernagel's and Doherty's research answered this question. Such antigens are used by the T cells as part of a two-step recognition of infected cells.

Though the potential uses of such a discovery were clear, with researchers now having the ability to fight diseases in a new manner, it took Zinernagel and Doherty a decade to have their work fully recognized. Later, as more and more scientists began to gather data about molecular structures, it became clear that Zinkernagel and Doherty had been correct in their assumption that the mechanism by which the immune system recognizes infected or foreign cells is a two-pronged one. According to the Nobel Committee, their work has "fundamentally changed our understanding of the development and normal function of the immune system."

This work has broader applications than just recognition of cell structure. According to the *Los Angeles Times*, it has helped to develop new vaccines against viruses. It has been used in attempts to guide the immune system to kill any microscopic cancer cells that may have escaped from tumors. The scientists' work also has implications for preventing attacks by the body's immune system on good cell tissues, as happens in multiple sclerosis and diabetes. Finally, an article in *Newsday* suggested that such work "offers insight into how the body's white blood cells . . . struggle against the AIDS virus."

In 1975, after completing his work with Doherty,

Zinkernagel received his Ph.D. He moved to La Jolla, California and began teaching as an assistant professor in the Department of Immunopathology at the Research Institute of Scripps Clinic. He stayed at Scripps until 1977, when he moved to the Department of Pathology at the University of California in San Diego. In 1979 he returned to the Scripps Clinic as a full professor in the Department of Immunopathology.

Later in that same year, he returned to Switzerland, this time as an associate professor in the Department of Pathology at the University of Zurich's Hospital. He was made a full professor in 1988. By 1992, he was the head at the Institute of Experimental Immunology in Zurich, a position he still held as of 1996.

In 1996 Zinkernagel was awarded the Nobel Prize in Physiology or Medicine, worth $1.12 million, along with Doherty. The *Los Angeles Times* reported that William Weigle, a Scripps immunologist with whom Zinkernagel worked, remarked on hearing of the award: "The main thing I can say about him is he is a very perceptive person. He sees things way ahead of others." Zinkernagel himself was pleased and surprised at receiving science's most coveted prize, stating: "I believe that some things will change in my life now. But we know so little still that there is enough work to keep me busy for the coming years and decades."

For his work in immunology, Rolf Zinkernagel has been the recipient of numerous honors from around the world. In 1981 he was awarded the Cloetta Stiftung Award in Zurich; the next year he received the Jung Stiftung Award in Hamburg. He received the Paul Ehrlich Prize in Frankfurt in 1983, and the Mack-Forster Prize as well as the Gartner Foundation International Award in Toronto in 1985. He was granted fellowships by the Institute for Cancer Research in New York and the Louis Jeantet Foundation in Geneva, and in 1992 he went to Geneva to be presented with the Christoforo Colombo Award. In 1995 he received the Albert Lasker Medical Research Award, along with five other scientists including Peter Doherty, for their work on the immune system and bacterial ulcers.

SELECTED WORKS: Journal of Immunology April 1, 1996; Science January 12, 1996, May 31, 1996.

ABOUT: ANU Reporter October 16, 1996; Los Angeles Times September 26, 1995, October 8, 1996; Newsday October 8, 1996; New York Times October 8, 1996; Royal Swedish Academy of Sciences 1996 Nobel Prize Announcement.